WORLD 3.0

WORLD 3.0

GLOBAL PROSPERITY AND HOW TO ACHIEVE IT

Pankaj Ghemawat

HARVARD BUSINESS REVIEW PRESS

Boston, Massachusetts

Library of Congress Cataloging-in-Publication Data

Ghemawat, Pankaj.
 World 3.0 : global prosperity and how to achieve it / Pankaj Ghemawat.
  p. cm.
 Includes bibliographical references and index.
 ISBN 978-1-4221-3864-9 (alk. paper)
1. Globalization—Economic aspects. 2. International economic relations. 3. International trade.
4. Economic development—International cooperation. I. Title.
 HF1359.G486 2010
 337—dc22

                                                              2010044993

To Ananya
Who is already a rooted cosmopolitan

Contents

Preface

The Great Crisis of 2008 has forced many of us to reexamine our beliefs about markets and globalization. Do propositions about the gains from market integration survive the reality of market failures? Or might we be better off—as people are particularly prone to suggest in turbulent times—pulling back from rather than pushing forward with integration in order to deal with our problems on a smaller, more manageable scale?

Unfortunately, discussion of these and related questions seems to have broken down. Well-researched policy positions that inspire confidence among economists but stoke fear in large segments of the public aren't good enough. We need to reframe the debate in a way that addresses real concerns and builds broader, deeper, and more robust support for opening up further. This book aims to bring analysis to bear on those fundamental questions—in a way that advances the discussion among people who are interested in building a better world rather than tearing down the present one.

How do I propose to accomplish this? First, by exposing intuitions and fears to hard data. Do you know the extent to which goods and services, capital resources, information streams, and people actually cross national borders in the world we live in? Otherwise, it is hard to take a position on whether to expand or reduce integration that can be described as informed. Do you know how much GDP is estimated to grow if we open up more? How does the impact of globalization on labor markets compare to that of technological change? When you connect up volatile national markets, does that increase risk through contagion or reduce it via diversification? Does trade cause more or less environmental pollution? Sometimes the answers aren't black and white, but we *should* look at the best available data and analysis, which I have sought to compile here.

Second, by looking beyond economics to incorporate lessons from history, philosophy, and other disciplines, we can better understand the deeply held convictions of others—and perhaps even our own. Consider the calls for protectionism triggered by the crisis. For virtually all of human history, the best possible response to a threatening environment was to gather together those closest to us and build up barriers to keep the chaos at bay. And even today, trust and sympathy decline dramatically with distance. So, while economics teaches us that protectionism does more harm than good, people don't intuitively see it that way, especially when they're scared.

Third, I seek to improve policy and discourse by expanding the policy space itself. The crossfire over globalization is bound up with even more polarized wrangling over regulation. More globalization is widely believed to go hand-in-hand with deregulation, and vice versa. And, worse, globalization and regulation are both framed as take-it-or-leave-it propositions. Thus, the entire policy space collapses down to a single binary choice, which I will refer to in this book as the tug of war between World 1.0 and World 2.0. We have nowhere to aim but directly at each other's faces.

World 3.0's remapping of the terrain suggests a better path forward. Specifically, a more realistic appraisal of both globalization and regulation suggests a path to greater prosperity that involves more market integration as well as limited and targeted market regulation. While greater integration goes against the grain of the tendency to close ranks with neighbors in times of trouble, it does tap into and reinforce the trend through the millennia of increasing prosperity and safety by broadening circles of cooperation. It also has some specific implications for what it means to be cosmopolitan in such a context.

Disentangling integration and regulation as two separate, nonbinary domains of choices opens up countless potential paths toward greater prosperity and security. This is exciting, mainly because it hands us many more tools than most of us realize to improve the world. It also means that we don't have to aim all our arguments at people who believe the exact opposite of what we do. However, it does leave us with the challenge of choosing among a greatly expanded set of options. So, in addition to describing the range of possibilities, I articulate a set of propositions for managing the nexus of integration and regulation.

All of this draws heavily on the work of researchers in many areas, as opposed to being entirely my own creation. But there are disciplines and subdisciplines on which I lean particularly heavily. From economics, on which my doctoral studies were focused, I draw on industrial organization economics' analysis of market failures and their regulation and international economics' empirical studies of how differences and distances affect trade and other kinds of flows. A focus on business, which I have taught, researched, and written about for thirty years, adds realism in the sense that business firms, not markets, mediate most international exchanges. In addition, it underscores the importance of pragmatism and a focus on value. Looking at how businesses think about the gains from cross-border operation extends and enriches the discussion of social gains from opening up.

Ultimately, this book invites you to reexamine your own views about globalization. While you may not end up in the same place that I do, a willingness to revise your view of the world where it doesn't conform to the evidence *should* get you somewhere interesting. Smart policies can push us in the right direction, but if we change our mind-sets we can get farther. And a crisis can be the best time to get out of the groove of traditional thinking.

Acknowledgments

Behind this book is a journey that has stretched out over a long period of time—and that has drawn on the work of hundreds of people. While most of these debts are acknowledged in the endnotes, there are at least some that I should recognize here. Steven Altman, formerly my student at Harvard Business School and now a valued associate, provided invaluable help with the research and writing, particularly for chapters 6, 7 and 9. Jordi Olle was of great help with the research as well, and Seth Schulman, my editor, with the challenge of shaping a jumble of complex ideas into a book. Antonio Argandoña, Fariborz Ghadar, Thomas Hout, Sebastian Reiche, Willem Van der Geest, and three anonymous reviewers provided comments on or assistance with recent drafts of all or part of this book. Susana Minguell helped suggest the title and secure permissions and endorsements, and Marta Domenech supervised the preparation of the manuscript. I am also greatly indebted to Harvard Business Review Press for the job that it has done with this book, with particular thanks to Melinda Merino, and to my agent, Helen Rees, for leading me there. Finally, IESE Business School, under Dean Jordi Canals, has proven to be a wonderfully supportive environment for pursuing a project whose scope, broad to begin with, kept on expanding.

Part One

The Possibilities

Chapter One

Colliding Worldviews

T O SAY THAT these are challenging times is perhaps akin to starting a novel with "It was a dark and stormy night." But the challenges we face are real. Finance is in tumult, and while worries about a banking crisis may have ebbed, fears of a crisis in public finances are running high. Even without additional financial reversals, overall economic prospects look bleaker than just a few years ago. The global order also seems more uncertain. Prosperity and power are shifting to new places and peoples. Old political doctrines and divisions no longer seem viable. Technology and media are changing before our eyes. So, apparently, is the natural environment itself.

That's not all. The problem isn't just with our current situation, but with our responses to it. Simply repeating the mantra of free markets seems inadequate, yet some have clung to that dictum, with its insistence that markets are magical and government interventions in them inevitably mistaken. Others have lurched to the opposite extreme, proclaiming that markets are bad and governments good. Still others wish a pox on both houses and place their faith in mutualism or even anarchy. The trouble with all these "remedies" is that they hark back to the past, and to past ways of viewing the world. To quote Yogi Berra, we're left with déjà vu all over again. Not that this is a joking matter. We risk reverting to unhelpful and even dangerous views that, in the worst-case scenario, could lead to a catastrophic closing off of borders and global impoverishment rather than prosperity.

Today's challenges call for a new way of looking at the world. This book offers such a worldview—what I call World 3.0. As we'll see, World 3.0 has clear implications for governments, businesses, and individuals. It requires governments to treat market integration and market regulation as two different dimensions of choice that have to be coordinated, not a dichotomous, either-or choice. For businesses, it suggests a range of opportunities for adapting to, overcoming, and exploiting the differences between countries that I have described elsewhere as the "AAA strategies."[1] And for individuals, embracing World 3.0 involves developing a *rooted* cosmopolitanism that is distinct from notions of national or global citizenship.

Before describing World 3.0 in detail, we should first consider how we got to where we are today. Let's take a quick tour through the worldviews that preceded World 3.0 in historical time—what I call Worlds 0.0, 1.0, and 2.0. This review will help bring coherence to the huge mass of writings about globalization as well as suggest a new way forward.

In speaking of the three worldviews prior to World 3.0, I should acknowledge prior histories of the world that have organized human experience into three broad periods. For example, historian Wolf Schäfer has divided human history into a preglobal phase before AD 1500, a protoglobal phase spanning 1500 to 1950, and a global phase that extends to the present day.[2] And the Nobel Prize–winning economist Douglass North and colleagues distinguish between foraging, the natural state, and "open access orders . . . [in which] citizens interact over wide areas of social behavior with no need to be cognizant of the individual identity of their partners."[3]

With due respect to these earlier treatments, I prefer to give myself a bit more leeway by thinking of the three worlds preceding World 3.0 not as sharply defined time periods, but as more abstract archetypes or models of social organization that have become embedded in our present mind-sets and cultures, thanks to particular experiences in human history. Thus I am less concerned with offering a precise account of the past than with depicting Worlds 0.0 to 2.0 as distinct worldviews that underpin divergent positions about the way forward. And by introducing the notion of World 3.0, I try to expand and improve the set of possible intellectual positions rather than simply arguing for a choice among preexisting possibilities.

World 0.0

Think back as far as you can into human history. Back before all the dates and wars you learned about in school. If you see dinosaurs, you've gone much too far. Our general understanding is that modern humans came on the scene some two hundred thousand years ago[4] and lived in nomadic hunter-gatherer bands or tribes until the Neolithic revolution, five thousand to eleven thousand years ago.[5] During this time, humanity gradually adopted fixed settlements, basic agriculture, and more complex social arrangements. It's hard to imagine the thoughts of people so long ago, and it's especially hard to ascribe a worldview to them since they knew little beyond their immediate surroundings. But in hindsight, we can say that our ancestors did bequeath us a certain mind-set, one rooted in the long human experience of banding together in small groups to survive hostile conditions.

People lived at subsistence levels back then—and would continue to do so for millennia. As a result, economic inequality was minimal, but so, too, was growth.[6] Food was an obvious focus: the major occupational categories were foraging, hunting, and rudimentary farming. Security was critical as well. Among the hunter-gatherers of that era, the chances that one male would be killed by another are estimated to have ranged from 15 to 60 percent.[7] And when a murder or theft occurred, our ancestors didn't call the police and await prosecution in a court of law; those institutions didn't exist. They took matters into their own hands, with the help of whomever they could trust.

This was World 0.0, or Thomas Hobbes's "state of nature" in which life was "nasty, brutish, and short" in the absence of any government. It was a war zone, not a utopia of the sort conjured up by Jean-Jacques Rousseau's notion of the "noble savage" or Henry David Thoreau's romanticization of Walden. This was the wild world in which our species lived for nearly all of its existence.

In such an unforgiving environment, the question of whom to trust was always paramount. You couldn't survive alone—there was trade even back in World 0.0—but betrayal could mean losing your possessions, your freedom, or your life. People first trusted family—specifically, blood relatives with shared genes. Then they trusted relatives by marriage, or the clan. Then perhaps people in their band or tribe. But the circle of trust that defined the boundary between "us" and "them" did not extend far in such societies. Bands of hunter-gatherers usually numbered only twenty-five or thirty people, and agglomerations like tribes and chiefdoms seldom exceeded a thousand.[8] This is why one estimate holds that nearly a million independent political entities existed in 3000 BC, averaging only a few dozen people each.[9] Some argue these polities stayed so small because available technologies couldn't control violence in larger groups.[10]

Many scholars see low, personalized levels of trust as a key constraint holding back such societies and contributing to both security and economic problems. We do indeed find some validation for this idea in present-day societies with some of the same characteristics. Failed or failing states such as the Congo and Somalia are prone to high levels of political instability, civil wars, and declines in health, education, and welfare. Violent death rates in parts of the Congo even appear to have reached some of the levels reported for hunter-gatherers millennia ago.[11]

The point is not that all tribal societies fail, but that even stable ones seem to exhibit lower levels of generalized trust than modern, market-based societies. An ambitious economic experiment conducted across fifteen communities found that farmers and wageworkers in rural Missouri in the United States and wageworkers in Accra, Ghana, were significantly fairer to strangers than nomadic Hadza hunter-gatherers in the Serengeti savanna or Tsimane Indians in the Amazon.[12] Even more notable, the strongest correlate of fairness was market integration, measured by how much of its diet a community bought from outside.

Such cooperation with "them"—everybody outside a narrow, localized circle of personal relationships—was unheard of millennia ago. And although the distances over which cooperation takes place have expanded, the tribal loyalties of World 0.0 and associated fears of outsiders are still very much with us today. How much farther would *you* go to protect your family than your neighbor? How about your neighbor versus someone across town or across the country? Whom would *you* trust if your life depended on it?

World 1.0

Fast-forward several thousand years. You'll find that humanity—or at least most of it—did eventually emerge from the cycle of violence and economic stagnation of the wild world. Between 3000 BC and AD 2000, world population increased more than a hundredfold and gross world product more than a thousandfold in real terms. But by far the biggest change took place in the realm of social organization: the world consolidated into fewer than two hundred independent political entities, implying a several hundred thousandfold increase in their average size, measured in terms of number of people.[13] World 0.0's bands of several dozen people and its larger tribes and chiefdoms were largely succeeded by nation-states with millions of inhabitants, sovereignty over defined territories, and extensive state apparatus including armies, police forces, and bureaucrats.

We know of three waves of increases in polity size over time, taking place around 3000 BC, 600 BC, and AD 1600.[14] Even where large polities were quick to emerge, however, only limited strands of society (e.g., merchants and the military) engaged in interactions over any significant distance: the vast majority of people remained isolated at the local level in World 0.0.

Most political scientists focus on the period after AD 1600 as marking the real shift to a world defined primarily in terms of sovereign nation-states—as I call it, World 1.0.[15] The Treaty of Westphalia in 1648, although confined to European powers and frequently breached, is often treated as a key moment in the rise of the modern system of international relations. This system features sovereign nation-states that monopolize the use of force within their defined borders, but that are sworn not to interfere in the internal affairs of other states. In other words, *national borders became key in World 1.0, strictly separating the domestic and international realms*. The fuzzy "trust boundaries" of World 0.0 became national walls in World 1.0, enshrined in treaties that were enforced when necessary (but also sometimes violated) by military forces, usually fighting under national flags.

While nations did have some military interactions back then, they were otherwise largely self-contained; culture, society, and economics had a strongly national (as well as local) cast. Thus, international trade is estimated to have accounted for only one-tenth of one percent of world GDP in the sixteenth century—and even that was tightly controlled by national governments. The key shift embedded in the progression from World 0.0 to World 1.0 was, therefore, the scaling up of cooperative efforts from the local level to the national level.

In World 1.0, impersonal exchange and other forms of interdependence with strangers became more common. And in human terms, World 1.0 displaced some of the tribal loyalties of World 0.0, substituting broader loyalties to nation-states past, present, or prospective. Citizenship in a particular country became and to a large extent still is fundamental to most people's identity. Our hearts swell with pride when we hear "our" national anthem played in Olympic medal ceremonies. Even if we disagree with our government's foreign policies, we almost uniformly support our home country's troops in wars. And we must admit that we find it easier to be passive about misery in distant lands than within our own country's borders. For many purposes, "us" now refs to conationals and "them" to everybody else. Such nationalism is the handiwork of World 1.0.

Nationalism has had some terrible effects on our world—think of the last century's wars—and it continues to do so. That said, the national structure of World 1.0 did provide a framework for tremendous growth. As figure 1-1 indicates, the last five hundred years account for virtually *all* of the growth in population and in world product that our species has ever experienced! Also note the inflection point about two hundred years ago, around the first industrial revolution, after which growth *really* accelerated. World population swelled fivefold between 1820 and 2000 and gross world product fifty-five-fold—a much greater divergence between the two than ever before, reflecting unprecedented growth in average income.

FIGURE 1-1

Growth over the millennia

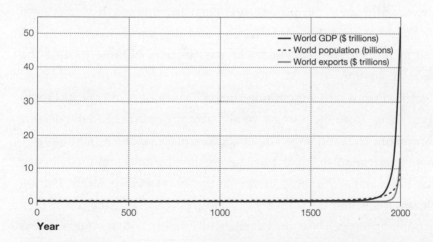

Sources: World population for AD 1–2000 based on Scott Manning, "Year-by-Year Population Estimates: 10,000 BC to 2007 AD," Appendix: World Population Estimate Sets, Digital Survivors, January 12, 2008, http://www. digitalsurvivors.com/archives/worldpopulation.php. World GDP is the result of the multiplication of World GDP per capita estimates and Manning population. For AD 1–2000, I use J. Bradford DeLong, "Estimating the World GDP: One Million BC–Present," http://econ161.berkeley.edu/TCEH/1998_Draft/World_GDP/Estimating_World_ GDP.html. World exports for 1500–1973 based on Maddison's *Monitoring the World Economy: 1820–1992* (Paris: OECD Development Center, 1995) and "Contours of the World Economy and the Art of Macromeasurement 1500–2001" (2004), http://www.ggdc.net/maddison/; 1973–2000 based on World Bank World Development Indicators (WDI).

World 2.0

Figure 1-1 also provides a glimpse of the widening cracks in the national walls of World 1.0 with its data on international exports. Small cracks had been evident from the outset; the Age of Discovery, in which Europeans sailed off to explore the world, *preceded* the Treaty of Westphalia, as did the formation of the Dutch and British East India companies, the forerunners of today's multinationals. But trade really took off more recently and even more sharply than GDP. By the middle of the nineteenth century, Karl Marx and Friedrich Engels were already able to assert that "the need of a constantly expanding market for its products chases the bourgeoisie over the whole surface of the globe. It must nestle everywhere, establish connections everywhere."[16] The export-to-GDP ratio of the world economy increased from around 1 percent in 1820 to more than 20 percent today.

Imperialistic consolidation continued to power significant increases in cross-border integration through the nineteenth century. But between the two world wars, this process was partially reversed. It wasn't until after World War II that globalization and the kinds of challenges it posed to the Westphalian model of nation-states became part of the broader discussion.

Globalization was first mentioned in a U.S. dictionary in 1951, although early writings from the postwar period actually emphasized the decline in internationalization levels that had taken place since the beginning of the twentieth century.[17] The buzz about the phenomenon really began in the 1980s and accelerated sharply in the 1990s and the 2000s. During the early 1990s, the U.S. Library of Congress catalog listed fewer than fifty publications per year on globalization; since 2000, the number has averaged more than a thousand per year.[18] Even more significantly, many social scientists—historians such as Paul Kennedy, sociologists such as Anthony Giddens, and political scientists such as Joseph Nye—now agree that we are living in a new age of globalization, one to which the national framework of World 1.0 may be ill-suited.[19] The pope and the Dalai Lama are in accord as well.[20]

Such discourse has been heavily channeled by its real-world backdrop, particularly the trend toward deregulation that has accompanied increasing integration in recent decades. As the conservatism of Ronald Reagan and Margaret Thatcher took hold in the 1980s, the role of government began to narrow, reinforcing the conviction that galloping globalization would flatten national, not to mention tribal, structures. Such a state of affairs that supposes competition over everything from everywhere is what I refer to as World 2.0.

World 2.0 worries antiglobalizers a lot but warms the hearts of most proglobalizers, regardless of their other political leanings. Thomas Friedman is generally a left-of-center journalist, at least relative to the U.S. center, but his books asserting the primacy of market forces over governments, *The World Is Flat* and *The Lexus and the Olive Tree*, place him in the company of the distinctly right-of-center Milton Friedman, the late Nobel Prize winner in Economics from the University of Chicago. The two Friedmans were driven by different reasoning: the former by his belief in the irresistible forces of globalization and the latter because he couldn't imagine government doing anything useful beyond regulating the money supply and protecting private property. But both converged on deregulated, integrated markets as the successors to World 1.0.

Even more oddly, agreement that World 2.0 is here bridges the great divide between those who think it good (e.g., the two Friedmans) and those who do not (e.g., social activist Naomi Klein). Supporters and opponents of globalization alike tend to agree that humanity has already created a largely if not totally integrated world. As we shall see in chapter 2, this is simply wrong. But for now, consider how proposed responses to the recent crisis relate to this precrisis worldview—and to the others that I have mentioned.

Retro Responses to Our Present Predicament

The global financial crisis has already inspired over a thousand books, not to mention myriad articles, blogs, and other commentary. Some are simply expressions of anger—primal screams in print. Others document the hole we find ourselves in or perform forensics on how we (nearly) buried ourselves alive. Fewer focus on what is to be done, and many of these either carry on with precrisis discussions of particular trends, are tactical, or are preoccupied by the short run. Discussions of the broader issues around the rediscovery of market failures and the implications for the cross-border integration of markets are rarer and, for the most part, can be related to the three worldviews I've already described.

Clinging to World 2.0

Some World 2.0 enthusiasts have refused to abandon their vision of deregulated, integrated markets in spite of the crisis. Media magnate Rupert Murdoch blamed government for the debacle, stating: "It's very easy to blame the free market but how did we get the housing bubble? We got it because of Congress pushing Fannie Mae and Freddie Mac into lending money to people who couldn't afford it and blowing up the price of housing; a Fed which was too loose with the money. It just led to this very naturally."[21] After a brief period of panic, Milton Friedman's acolytes at the University of Chicago mostly reached a similar conclusion. In their view, the trouble was that markets hadn't been free *enough* from governmental meddling. Less doctrinaire variants admit market failures but argue that governmental failures are generally worse and that we should therefore continue to plow the free market furrow.[22]

This degree of intellectual lock-in is perhaps predictable; as Karl Polanyi observed about the last big crisis of market capitalism in the 1930s, "Its apologists are repeating in endless variations . . . that not the competitive system and the self-regulating market, but interference with that system and interventions with that market are responsible for our ills."[23]

Predictability is not, however, the same as persuasiveness. The notion that market failures do not merit our attention seems unlikely to convince anybody who wasn't already in thrall to the magic of markets. That would seem to be a small minority postcrisis, even among elites.

Consider how a well-known journalist described the tone at the 2010 World Economic Forum in Davos, a forum long associated with globalization and deregulation: "The political and business leaders gathered here . . . take it as a given that the free market failed in the crash of 2008 and that the new system will be more regulated, more interventionist."[24]

World 1.0 Redux

Many people attracted to World 1.0 as a response to the crisis were drawn to it all along as protectionists and antiglobalizers. In addition to that core of support, World 1.0 also benefits from what sociologists call *cultural lag*. Many aspects of our nonmaterial culture have lagged behind the rapid economic changes that have led some to proclaim the arrival of World 2.0. At the level of institutions and identities, we are mostly still tuned nationally to World 1.0.

To see this, look at the responses to the economic crisis. While the unfolding debacle sparked many meetings involving many institutions, stimulus packages, bailouts, and other plans were mostly decided by national governments. In the process, they also greatly expanded their roles in their respective economies and fueled widespread discussions of state capitalism.[25] Meanwhile, individuals narrowed the circle of trust and cooperation back to the national or even local level—as often happens in times of crisis. Thus, in a poll by Pew Research in late 2009, more U.S. citizens (49 percent) agreed that the United States "should mind its own business internationally and let other countries get along the best they can on their own" than disagreed (44 percent)—for the first time in the four decades that such data have been gathered![26] Similar patterns are apparent in Europe with mounting concerns about immigration, and in Japan.

What might the policies associated with World 1.0 look like? Some variants on this worldview are frankly isolationist. And some focus on besting other countries. Thus, in the realm of international (political) relations, Henry Kissinger and others have championed *Realpolitik*, a World 1.0 doctrine that still wields enormous influence in foreign policy circles. Realpolitik treats nation-states as the primary actors, and supranational bodies like the UN and World Trade Organization (WTO), businesses, nongovernmental organizations (NGOs), and so on as of little consequence. The top priority of states is taken to be preservation of their sovereignty in the face of threats from other states. Long-term cooperation is deemphasized because each state is assumed always to pursue its own interests. Military and economic power are what count, and trying to apply morality to the international sphere supposedly makes the world a more dangerous place.

Such Realpolitik might seem somewhat plausible in conflict-ridden regions of the world (e.g., the Middle East today or the Europe of Metternich two centuries ago), but does it provide useful insights into contemporary relations among, say, members of the European Union? More importantly, does it sound like a recipe for a world that works? In the economic sphere, World 1.0 offers little that is new: it has been tried before, over several centuries. Even worse, if a reversion to World 1.0 were accompanied by general protectionism, a meltdown of the order of the Great Depression might result! Of course, such protectionism is exactly what the transplantation of Realpolitik's zero-sum logic of inter-state relations from the political to the economic sphere would seem likely to induce.

World 0.0 Redux

Although a reversion to World 1.0 would pose a number of major problems, its advocates generally have little to offer in the way of new solutions. Instead, the newer ideas that *have* emerged as responses to the crisis actually seem, with their common stress on communitarianism, to advocate a shift toward World 0.0! From the right, former theologian Phillip Blond, who has helped shape British prime minister David Cameron's advocacy of the "big society" as opposed to the "big state," inveighs against the state *and* markets, calling for relocalization of the economy and the "restoration and creation of human association."[27]

Joining him on the left is sociologist-activist Raj Patel (briefly declared the Messiah by a U.S. sect), who preaches grassroots movements, communal stewardship of common resources, and localization of food chains as substitutes for markets.[28]

The parts of this localizing agenda that involve rebuilding local social capital sound somewhat plausible—although it is worth imagining what it might be like to go to a meeting of the neighborhood council every Friday evening with the nosy neighbor in charge (not unlike arrangements in Cuba under Castro). When it comes to economics, though, much of the localizing agenda seems, on the basis of experiments in local procurement, to be simply preposterous. For example, Kelly Cobb, a textile designer in Philadelphia, set out to make a man's suit out of materials produced within 100 miles of her home. Two dozen artisans took more than 500 hours to make a very basic suit, unlikely to be confused with a cheap store-bought version—and even then, 8 percent of the materials had to be sourced from farther away.[29]

Cobb's own conclusion from this exercise is "that a small community could clothe itself . . . with reasonable expectations and a little ingenuity."[30] I'd be less sanguine based on a hundredfold escalation in (labor) costs, higher materials costs, and quality issues. And remember that suit manufacture is not subject to strong scale economies. Would there be any way to produce more scale-sensitive products like computers and airplanes locally? Maybe localizers have no need for the latter, but I'm sure they wouldn't like to give up the former.

Despite these obvious problems, localization is not just idle chatter. In Barcelona, where I live, the crisis prompted an ecological network focused on the Montseny National Park to launch the *ecoseny*, a "social currency" meant to promote local exchange and greening. Even if the concept were viable, the targeted region doesn't correspond to what economists call an "optimal currency area." Fewer than a million people live in the three districts targeted, and a large national park separates the three district headquarters. Meanwhile, another social currency encroaching from the south is exerting additional pressure. But suppose that the localizers *did* manage to overcome all these obstacles and implement their vision. We'd see a fragmentation of currency units—that is, ecosenys and other such currencies being promoted around Europe instead of the euro—as well as bias built into them to encourage localization. What's next, barter? Actually, the Montseny ecological network is already working on it.[31]

Even more than national protectionism, folding economic interactions back to the local level might precipitate an unprecedented economic collapse. (Please reread the earlier section on World 0.0 if necessary.) Even if you don't agree that this is the likely outcome, localizers certainly need to rule it out if they are to buttress their case. But they generally do not even acknowledge the potential for problems, let alone address them; they simply assume that localization will work. In other words, localizers are more than a tad reckless when they advocate large-scale social reengineering based on ideas that reverse the expanding circles of cooperation of the last few millennia, that remain to be fully worked out, and that seem prohibitively costly in economic terms. Reason enough for localizers to abandon the lofty claims they so often make to the moral high ground.

The Way Forward: World 3.0

I didn't set out to propose a new worldview or write a book with an audacious title like *World 3.0*. I have studied, taught, and written about business and economics for over thirty years, and focused on globalization-related issues for the last fifteen. By inclination, I tend to look for data to quantify important phenomena, so I started tracking how much particular activities or entities cross national borders.

As the flood of books proclaiming a new, globalized world (what I now call World 2.0) hit the shelves, I watched popular perceptions about the extent of globalization race well ahead of what I was seeing in my data on cross-border integration. It was obvious we were no longer in World 1.0, but it was also plain to me that World 2.0 was basically a chimera, dangerously exaggerating actual flows across borders. I introduced the term *semiglobalization* to characterize the true state of cross-border integration: borders still matter a great deal, but so do flows across them. This state of the world, elaborated on in chapter 2, spans the broad range of possibilities between the isolated countries of World 1.0 and the completely integrated globe of World 2.0.

Rejecting World 1.0 and 2.0 as inconsistent with actual levels of globalization was one thing; coming up with a full-fledged alternative was quite another. That had to wait until the global financial crisis reemphasized the importance of market failures. Like many people, I had associated globalization with deregulation, placing them at the same end of a continuum whose other end features regulation and strong national borders.[32] Intuitively, if markets have a tendency to fail, it seems to make sense to raise questions about connecting them across borders, since failures on a larger scale might be even more destructive.

The global financial crisis prompted me to take a closer look at this representation of our policy choices as a tug-of-war between World 1.0 and World 2.0. The food crisis that preceded the financial crisis—and that seems to be repeating itself as I write this—proved particularly illuminating. Between early 2007 and mid-2008, international rice prices tripled due to panic buying, triggering riots in more than a dozen importing countries and even toppling governments (in Haiti, for example). Preaching about free markets and prices does not constitute an adequate response in such situations because it leaves people free to starve; instead, governments do have to intervene to manage domestic prices. At the same time, since only about 5 percent of world rice production is traded internationally, deepening international rice markets would reduce the volatility that they have to deal with, as would the abandonment of export subsidies and tariffs.[33]

Rice provides, therefore, a clear example of markets prone to failure—and requiring some measure of regulation as a result—that could nonetheless benefit from increased cross-border integration. It helped me realize that the tension between World 1.0 and World 2.0 embodies not one fundamental trade-off but disagreements over two types of choices: choices concerning the regulation of markets and choices

FIGURE 1-2

Four worldviews

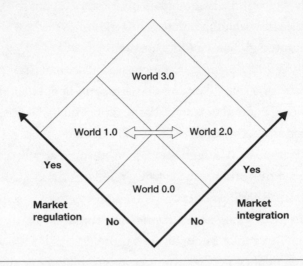

concerning cross-border integration. Distinguishing between these two dimensions of choice suggests a fourfold representation of the possibilities in which World 3.0 emerges as a distinct worldview (as does World 0.0): see figure 1-2. World 3.0 weaves together globalization and regulation, unlike the three other possibilities depicted in the figure, which opt for one or the other—or neither.

But why is World 3.0 *the* right box in the matrix to focus on, apart from the fact that it is the only one that hasn't already been discussed and found wanting?

World 3.0's first attraction is that it is more realistic. It not only recognizes actual levels of cross-border integration; it also accounts for how geographic and other forms of difference/distance typically affect cross-border flows, as described in chapter 3. World 3.0's empirically grounded, explicitly spatial structure, in which both borders and distance are important, is one of the key features that distinguish it from both World 1.0, in which only borders matter, and World 2.0, in which neither do.

World 3.0 is also more realistic about human nature. Transforming the world would be easy if we could—as Raj Patel proposes—motivate humans to curb their desires significantly. But how likely is that? World 3.0

strives for more realism about what drives us, but without sacrificing morality. It recognizes that self-interest is important, but also provides a basis, rooted in distance, for bringing awareness of, sympathy for, and altruism toward others into the picture, in order to consider how we might make *some* progress along those dimensions. By contrast, Worlds 0.0 and 1.0 embody an "us versus them" approach that ignores foreign welfare entirely. And World 2.0, where there is no us or them, weights foreign welfare the same as domestic welfare, which is frankly otherworldly.[34]

This emphasis here on realism may seem rather unreformed. After all, it was famously argued—by Milton Friedman, of course—that what matters about a model or, presumably, worldview is not the realism of its assumptions but the predictions that it permits one to make. Maybe, but if we aren't satisfied with existing models, dealing with key disconnects from reality seems like a good place to start reformulating them.

A rather different and, in some sense, more important attraction of World 3.0 is that it highlights the gains from opening up further. World 2.0 presumes that complete openness has been achieved or soon will be, so that while preventing losses due to backsliding is important, generating gains through further opening up is not. And World 1.0 (and to an even greater extent World 0.0) turns its back on gains through openness.

A final attraction of World 3.0 is that it provides a relatively specific, grounded framework for action. In addition to the clear delineation in figure 1-2, World 3.0 proceeds from different premises to prescriptions that differ substantially from the worldviews that preceded it. Some of these differences across Worlds 0.0–3.0 are summarized in table 1-1; they and others will, of course, be expanded on in the course of this book.

Especially given the possibility for terminological confusion, it is useful to contrast the specificity of World 3.0 with the "third way"—a political philosophy that, Tony Blair's memoir *Journey* reminds us, is now widely espoused if not actually practiced around the world. With its emphasis on integrating across left and right and refocusing on open versus closed, the third way has some obvious affinities with World 3.0 as opposed to the other worldviews depicted in figure 1-2.

TABLE 1-1

Worldviews: An initial characterization

Worldview	World 0.0: Wild world	World 1.0: Walled world	World 2.0: One world	World 3.0: A workable world
Period of emergence	Prehistoric	Age of Enlightenment	Late 20th century	The third millennium
Level of market integration	Subnational markets: local integration	National markets: national integration	Global markets: complete global integration	Semiglobal markets: partial global integration
Geographic structure	Local borders	National borders	None	Borders plus distance: spatiality
Governmental policies	Minimal	Regulator of market failures	Integrator (limited role)	Integrator plus regulator
Business strategies	Local	Domestic/ multidomestic	Global standardization	AAA strategies to adjust to, overcome, and harness differences
Individual mind-sets	Communitarianism	Nationalism	Cosmopolitanism	Rooted cosmopolitanism (cultural distance)

However, the third way has little if anything to say about the realities of semiglobalization and geography—even though it matters greatly for discussions of openness whether, for instance, we think of countries as billiard balls that may run up against each other but remain separate (World 1.0), as melting into each other (World 2.0), or as embedded in space, at varying distances from each other (World 3.0). And the third way also seems, especially given the recent surge in interest in state capitalism, to underplay the regulatory dimension with its too-quick dismissal of alternatives to market capitalism. In other words, one can raise questions about the third way's grasp of *both* of the axes in figure 1-2, which is why World 3.0 seems to me to be the better way forward in the third millennium.

The Rest of This Book

The rest of Part I explains in more detail why World 3.0 is a better basis for the pursuit of prosperity than the other worldviews considered. Part II addresses market failures and other fears that opponents of cross-border integration often invoke. Part III draws together the actionable implications of World 3.0 for governments, businesses, and individuals.

More specifically, chapter 2 argues that current and prospective levels of cross-border integration do not fit well with either World 1.0 or 2.0, and that overall, the globalization glass is more empty than full (i.e., the shortfall from levels predicted by World 2.0 is particularly large). Chapter 3 examines the cross-border differences and distances between countries that act as barriers to globalization. And chapter 4 explains why the potential gains from opening up are much larger than even proglobalizers tend to think.

That takes us through the rest of Part I. The first three chapters of Part II address how the rediscovery of conventional market failures—small numbers or concentration, externalities, and uncertainty/risk—should affect how we think about the potential for cross-border integration of markets under World 3.0. Chapter 8 takes on a new, still-controversial kind of failure, global imbalances, and the last three chapters in this section, chapters 9–11, examine the connections between globalization and deprivation of various sorts—economic, political, and cultural.

My broad conclusion is that while some failures and fears do need to be taken seriously, the truth is far less scary than it is made out to be. Globalization can alleviate the effects of some categories of market failures and fears; plus, even when it aggravates them, the negative effects are often overstated and generally subject to mitigation themselves. I nonetheless devote seven chapters to this broad topic because I really do want to convince the unconvinced, and this requires engaging with what worries them.

Part III of this book synthesizes Parts I and II into a discussion of what is to be done. The first chapter in Part III, chapter 12, presents some general propositions (apparent but not systematically presented in Part II) for thinking about market failures and market integration. I follow that chapter with three others that prescribe in more detail what countries, businesses, and individuals must do if they are to build toward—and maximize benefits from—World 3.0. But the basic prescriptions can, for now, be characterized as follows:

- Understand actual levels of integration, which are likely to be lower than intuited.

- Look for opportunities to increase integration, of which there are likely to be many.

- Regulate only to the extent necessary to manage market failures and fears—while remembering that integration actually helps rather than hurts with some failures and fears.

- Try to match the geographic scope of any regulatory responses to the geographic scope of the market failure.

Chapter Two

Semiglobalization Today and Tomorrow

IN MAKING THE CASE for World 3.0, I asserted that it captures the *real* levels of international integration much better than the negligible levels associated with World 1.0 and the (nearly) complete levels assumed by World 2.0. It is time to back up that assertion by reviewing some surprising facts about how global—or semiglobal—we actually are.

By most measures, the true state of the world today is that of semiglobalization—with "semi" as in partial rather than 50 percent. How partial? Try 10 to 25 percent. This is a far cry from the complete globalization envisaged by World 2.0. It is also significantly lower than the intuitions of the people I have polled. Such exaggerations about levels of cross-border integration reflect biased beliefs about globalization that can be dangerous in a variety of ways and are therefore worth exploding.

You'll notice that I'm focusing here on arguing for World 3.0's superiority over World 2.0. This is because of all the worldviews, World 2.0 is the one that has generated *by far* the most excitement. Proponents of World 2.0 have cited all sorts of globalization apocalypses that are supposed to pave the way for (nearly) complete integration, including the convergence of tastes, the end of the nation-state and of history, the death of distance, and probably the blockbuster of them all, the flattening of the earth, based on the vision of journalist Thomas Friedman: "The world got flat . . . [creating] a global, Web-enabled playing field that allows for multiple forms of collaboration on research and work in real time, without regard to geography, distance or, in the near future, even language."[1]

At the other end of the tug-of-war between World 1.0 and World 2.0 is the Indian novelist Arundhati Roy, one of globalization's most vocal and ardent critics, who seems no less certain about its apocalyptic impact when she proclaims, as she did in a 2002 speech, that "globalization is ripping through people's lives."[2] Other antiglobalizers critique globalization as "cancer stage capitalism," "casino capitalism," or, even worse, simply "McWorld." They call for resistance to the "international rule" of multinational corporations and their brands, advocating the disruption of G20 summits and other international meetings as a form of self-expression. Like Friedman, they seem sure that World 2.0 is here or well on the way. But they have a rather different, dystopic vision of the globalization apocalypse, associating it with such things as degradation of the environment, exploitation of the poor, the erosion of democratic values, and the death of cultural traditions—unless they can stop it dead in its tracks.

It is hard to overstate the rhetorical punch that such apocalyptics can pack. Friedman's view, while far from unique, has been particularly influential. By my reckoning, his globalization-related books, most notably *The World Is Flat*, may have sold about as many copies as all the globalization-related books written by his predecessors *combined*. And his World 2.0 arguments, including the language of flattening, have been taken up and championed by luminaries such as George Soros and Colin Powell. I remember being particularly nonplussed when I heard General Powell say that "if the world isn't flat today, it will be tomorrow." When I asked him whether he really thought borders would cease to matter, he gently suggested that I go read Tom Friedman.

Such rhetoric has left an imprint on people well beyond those who go to Davos or to "anti-Davos," the World Social Forum. Starting in 2007, I've polled several dozen audiences about their worldviews, asking them to choose which of three quotes about globalization—one apiece for Worlds 1.0 to 3.0, although without identifying them as such—they most agreed with. These audiences have mainly consisted of business executives and university students, although I have administered this Rorschach test to general audiences as well. The above quote from Friedman that I use as an authoritative stand-in for World 2.0 invariably commands the most support—usually a majority. World 3.0 tends to come in a fairly distant second, followed by World 1.0.[3] The basic rank ordering has stayed the same through the global financial crisis, although World 2.0 seems to have ceded a bit of its lead over World 3.0.

In fact, so far has the fascination with World 2.0 proceeded that it has even become the butt of comedy. Thus the U.S. fake-news Web site, *The Onion*, ran a video about parents shipping their children off to South Asia by FedEx to avoid the high cost of local nannies. "Sometimes I'm able to get [my son] into the box without even waking him up," one satisfied parent remarked. There was, however, the horror story of the little girl who had to eat her own fingers after getting lost in the mail.[4]

My point in taking on all these exaggerations is this—that despite significant increases in cross-border integration in recent decades, huge headroom remains. So let's look at some data because, as Daniel P. Moynihan once observed, "Everyone is entitled to his own opinions but not his own facts."

A Global Reality Check

While many methods exist for measuring globalization, the simplest, most intuitive one that I have found is to consider flows or activities that can take place either within or across national borders, and then to figure out the international component as a percentage of the total. Let's consider, therefore, such measures for cross-border flows of information, of people, of products and direct investment, and of other types of capital as a way of getting a handle on the cross-border integration of these different types of markets.[5]

An obvious place to start is with the cross-border component of mail and phone calls, since these ways of communicating gave rise to the first truly international organizations nearly 150 years ago—the Universal Postal Union and the International Telecommunications Union. What percentage of letters physically mailed in the world do you think cross national borders? The answer is *about 1 percent*. But of course, that's snail mail; the big improvements in communications in the last 150 years have been electronic. So what percentage of telephone calling minutes do you think involve international calls? Twenty percent? Thirty? The answer is *less than 2 percent*.[6] In our high-tech, *über*connected world, practically all of our calls are still restricted to people inside our own country.

Okay, but that is still plain old telephone service. Surely Internet traffic is mostly integrated across borders. Not exactly. You'll be surprised to learn that *an estimated 17 to 18 percent of all Internet traffic was routed across a national border between 2006 and 2008*.[7] Moreover, while cheap, high-bandwidth connectivity has led many firms to offshore IT services to India and elsewhere, the virtual counterpart of our comedic example, the volume still accounts for less than 20 percent of the addressable market—which might itself triple in size by 2020.[8]

Comprehensive data on the cross-border spread of content are (even) harder to come by. Thanks to Hollywood's dominance, it seems that foreign films account for about half of box office revenues worldwide (albeit a lower fraction of tickets sold), but this also seems to be an anomaly.[9] A look at magazines, for instance, reveals a very different situation. Even for an avowedly international newsweekly such as *Time*, only about 20 percent of its readership is outside its U.S. home base.

Somewhat more systematic data *are* available for news coverage. According to one study, 21 percent of U.S. news coverage was international, of which 11 percent dealt with U.S. foreign affairs (including topics such as U.S. involvement in international conflicts or diplomacy) and 10 percent with foreign affairs not involving the U.S.[10] In Europe, about 38 percent of news was international, but of this, almost half related to coverage of news stories involving other countries within Europe.[11] And what about foreign news sources? Calculations across thirty countries suggest that almost every country gets all but 5 percent of its news from domestic sources—prompting the person who undertook the research to propose that goods still travel much farther than ideas.[12]

Broadly similar patterns seem to apply to technological information. Of patents filed in rich OECD countries—which still account for about 95 percent of patents worldwide—foreign-owned patents represent only 15 percent of the total, and the percentage of patents actually involving international cooperation in research is only half that.

These are, of course, all indicators of informational flows. What about cross-border movements of people? To start with long-run movements, despite all the hubbub about immigration, *first-generation immigrants account for only 3 percent of the world's population*. For medium-run movements, we can look at university students, whom we might expect to be relatively mobile. Actually, *students studying overseas account for just 2 percent of all university students!* If one adds up all kinds of cross-border movements of people, it is estimated that *about 90 percent of the world's people will never leave the country in which they were born.*[13] World 2.0, indeed!

Okay, okay, you say, but where it really counts—the flows of goods and money—the world's economies must be much more integrated. After all, the broad debate about globalization hasn't been about coverage of foreign news or concentrations of foreign students; it's been about companies shutting down domestic factories and call centers and investing overseas or outsourcing those activities. Especially given trade's accelerating growth over the last two centuries, as described in chapter 1, product market integration *must* be close to complete. Or so a motley crew ranging from proglobalizers such as Thomas Friedman to rabid antiglobalizers have intuited.

Not quite. Trade intensity, measured by products and services exported from one country to another as a percentage of GDP, hit an all-time peak of 29 percent in 2008, before dropping to 23 percent in 2009 (a decline that is also a sign of its fragility). These are higher internationalization numbers than the ones cited earlier for informational and people flows, but they also inflate and distort the reality of trade. I should elaborate.

Consider Apple's iPod. Although it is labeled as made in China, China is just the final assembly platform for four hundred–plus components from East Asia and elsewhere, and adds only a few dollars of value, 1 to 2 percent of the retail selling price of $299.[14] Most of the value added—an estimated $163—goes to American companies and workers, with Apple alone pocketing almost half of that. Yet every such iPod sold in the United States is recorded as contributing about $150 to the U.S. trade deficit with China.[15] And since virtually all the components are shipped at least twice if not several times across national borders, the total trade officially recorded around that sale is a multiple of the $150 number!

Given such distortions and exaggerations, deflating official trade statistics to reflect value added rather than revenues is a key operational priority—not just according to me but according to the director-general of the World Trade Organization (WTO), Pascal Lamy. As Lamy recently explained to me, without such a correction, we are left with an illusory sense of surging trade when much of what is happening is that value chains have been getting sliced up ever more finely across national borders. And that exaggeration can, among other things, encourage protectionism—a concern of his that I share and will shortly return to, in a way that goes beyond the trade numbers.

The nonofficial academic estimates that we do have suggest that foreign content accounts for about 50 percent of the value of China's exports and 25 to 30 percent for world exports as a whole.[16] Sticking with these estimates—although Lamy thinks that they are too low, perhaps by 5 to 10 percent—and using them to deflate the numbers for nominal exports suggests that global exports account for only 20 percent of all the value produced in the world (GDP).[17] This is still a large number, but it's far below the roughly 90 percent export-to-GDP ratio we'd expect to see—without any double counting—if borders and distance didn't matter at all.[18]

If you remain skeptical, consider that trade economists—people who spend their professional lives focused on trying to understand trade flows—focus not on celebrating how much trade there is, but rather on trying to explain why *trade levels are much lower than simple models would lead us to expect*. We'll dig deeper into this mystery of the missing trade, as trade economists call it, in the next chapter.

When we move away from trade and consider the flow of investment around the world, the picture is strikingly similar. Economists define foreign direct investment (FDI) as a company from one country making a physical investment in building or buying operations in another country. FDI flowing across borders accounted for only 9 percent of all fixed investment (what economists call "gross fixed capital formation") in 2009. Of course, FDI flows also fluctuate a great deal, and peaked recently in 2007, at 16 percent of fixed investment. But they have averaged about 10 percent over the last few years, suggesting that about *90 percent of all fixed investment in the world is still domestic.*[19]

Other cross-border capital flows, based on cruder data, generally run somewhat higher but resonate with the same basic story. Only 15 to 20 percent of venture capital money is deployed outside the investing fund's home country.[20] Only about 20 percent of the stock market (equity) is owned by foreign investors.[21] And cross-border ownership of bank deposits and government debt remains closer to 25 percent and 35 percent, respectively.[22] Since this is precrisis data, capital was far from completely mobile internationally even at the height of global financial fever!

One notable and distressing exception to financial flows' comparatively greater internationalization involves noncommercial flows. The cross-border component of private charitable giving has been estimated at less than 10 and even 5 percent of the total, although billionaire philanthropists with global outlooks appear to be trying to change that.[23] Charity, even more than commerce or finance, begins at home.

Taking Stock of Semiglobalization

Figure 2-1 compiles the more systematic statistics among the ones cited above.[24] It is worth reminding ourselves at this point that these are global averages that mask huge amounts of cross-country variation, measure by measure. In other words, globalization is very uneven. Cross-country differences are the focus of the next chapter; for now, note that there is *some* useful information to be gleaned from the global averages.

The five purely financial measures of cross-border integration just discussed show average internationalization levels of 21 percent, and the other nine measures average 10 percent. Of the latter, the people-related measures both fall below 10 percent; the product market–related measures—FDI and adjusted exports—vary between 10 and 20 percent; and the informational measures are more dispersed, varying from zero to 20 percent. Overall, capital is more footloose across national borders than products, which in turn are more footloose than people. This ranking can be related to differences in the spreads of capital costs, product

FIGURE 2-1

Internationalization levels

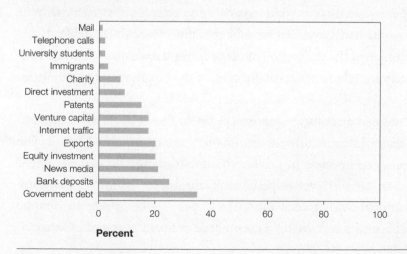

prices, and wages around the world. Although capital costs typically diverge by only a few percentage points or less in different countries, the prices for even a product as standardized as a Big Mac burger can easily vary 20 percent or more from one country to the next, and wages might be twenty times higher in an advanced Western country than in a country like India.[25]

But the biggest headline from this analysis relates not to differences across product, capital, people, and information flows, but to a commonality: *actual levels of internationalization across all these different types of markets fall very far short of the levels implied by World 2.0.*

Presentation of these data to the several dozen audiences mentioned earlier has also elicited two particularly common critiques that I need to address. First, people dismiss the data presented above as too narrow and, specifically, overly focused on economic flows. (This was Tom Friedman's critique of a subset of this data that I presented in a 2007 article in *Foreign Policy* titled "Why the World Isn't Flat"; I responded by pointing out that at least I had *some* data.)[26] Actually, rather than just picking a few random measures, I went through A. T. Kearney/Foreign Policy's 2007 Globalization Survey—the most recent available—and tried to figure out which of the broad dimensions of globalization it covered could be measured the way I wanted to (i.e., in terms of the cross-border component as a percentage of the total). The Globalization Survey's measures of political engagement were the ones that proved most resistant but, given their other attributes, their exclusion is not too much of a concern.[27] So I have deliberately tried to be broad— subject to the constraint of measurability—rather than narrow.

A second critique, worth considering at somewhat greater length, focuses on the fact that the data presented above provide a sense of *levels* of globalization but not of changes over time. So despite levels of cross-border integration that currently correspond to World 3.0, very rapid increases in those levels could conceivably make World 2.0 a better guide to the future. (This may have been the point that General Powell was trying to make.) Or very rapid decreases could achieve the same for World 1.0.

Long-run trends provide little support for the assertion of "World 2.0 tomorrow if not today." While measures of globalization discussed in this section have generally increased over the last few decades, they haven't all been setting new records. The percentage of the world's population composed of immigrants, for example, is the same now as it was in 1910. Also, some precrisis measures of cross-border capital flows/stocks were actually comparable to earlier peaks more than a hundred years ago—and thanks to the crisis, are now lower.

Second, the measures that *have* been setting new records, such as trade intensity, have a long way to go before approaching the levels associated with complete integration and World 2.0. Even if one were to simply extrapolate the faster growth rates experienced by trade than by GDP in recent decades, trade-to-GDP would still take decades to reach the point where one could say that national borders no longer affected international trade.

Third, the increases that have been achieved often exhibit clear geographic patterns that are inconsistent with World 2.0. Trade has become increasingly *regionalized* in recent decades, to the point that international trade within regions exceeds trade across regions. Based on rougher data, FDI also seems more regionalized than not. Even the Internet, it is generally agreed, exhibits increasing localization and regionalization for reasons ranging from increasing peer-to-peer traffic to the development of regional alternatives to the United States' earlier role of switching hub for the world. Strong distance dependence of this sort is inconsistent with World 2.0 but is an integral component of World 3.0, as the next chapter will stress.

Fourth, the precipitous declines in various cross-border flows in the aftermath of the crisis remind us of the limits of linear extrapolation. We shouldn't assume that cross-border integration will, along most dimensions, continue to progress. Evidently globalization *can* go into reverse—as it did between World War I and World War II.

In the wake of the financial crisis, this last point has led some to proclaim that instead of the imminent attainment of World 2.0, we're poised to revert all the way back to World 1.0. Once again, this claim can't survive contact with data. Consider in some detail a cross-border flow that has shown a particularly big percentage decline in the wake of the financial crisis, foreign direct investment. The United Nations Conference on Trade and Development, UNCTAD, estimates in its 2010 *World Investment Report* that FDI fell from nearly $2 trillion in 2007 to $1.7 trillion in 2008 and $1 trillion in 2009—or by nearly 50 percent. But before we get all apocalyptic, it is worth remembering that this is not an unprecedented decline. The 2000–2002 period supplies a more extreme example from within the same decade: while global GDP actually grew over that period, the stock market crashed in the wake of the Internet bubble—and FDI fell by *more than* 50 percent! Why? Because surges in FDI activity are typically driven by mergers and acquisitions activity, which tends to peak with stock market prices.

All of this suggests that the decline in FDI between 2007 and 2009 greatly overstates the true changes—so far—in the fundamentals facing the global economy. UNCTAD's own estimates suggest that FDI flows will recover—albeit not right away, to $1.2 trillion in 2010, $1.4 trillion in 2011, and $1.8 trillion in 2012. In other words, by 2012, FDI will surpass the 11 percent of gross fixed capital formation that it averaged between 2000 and 2009. But even if one discounts such a recovery by making the extreme assumption that FDI levels will maintain their (low) 2009 level of 9 percent of gross fixed capital formation, that still exceeds the averages of 6 percent for the 1990s, 3 percent for the 1980s, and 2 percent for the 1970s. So the argument that the aftermath of the crisis has somehow returned us to the world of a few decades ago—when World 1.0 did work better as a worldview—is greatly overstated. The caveat, elaborated in chapter 4 and later in this book, is that we may yet revert to World 1.0 if we succumb to protectionism.

Globaloney Analyzed

How surprised are you by the data thus far? If you overestimated actual levels of integration, you are not alone: the polls that I've conducted reveal overestimation as a widespread tendency rather than just a predictable bias of the prophets of World 2.0. Thus, in a survey of several hundred corporate managers conducted for me by *Harvard Business Review*, the respondents guessed an average level of internationalization of 30 percent for a subset of the measures in figure 2-1, versus an actual average of 10 percent! Interestingly, experience offered no substitute for actually looking at the data: very senior or internationally experienced executives were as likely to overestimate as much as all the rest. Such overestimation characterizes every group that I have surveyed so far, and the crisis seems to have only dented this tendency instead of dispelling it. The breadth and depth of this bias will cause me to refer to it frequently so, for the sake of compactness, I adopt Clare Booth Luce's useful tag of "globaloney."

Why are intelligent, informed, interested people so prone to globaloney? It is important to answer this question because globaloney is more than just a harmless way of calling more attention to the international domain. Globaloney, even if it stops short of the exaggerations of World 2.0, can be hazardous to global welfare by creating complacency among proglobalizers and provoking paranoia among antiglobalizers (cf. Lamy's point, cited earlier, about the effects of double counting in trade statistics).

The obvious reason for globaloney is that much of the debate about globalization takes place in a data-free zone. Compiling the numbers I've presented in this chapter wasn't easy. Broadcast media don't usually make the effort, and scholarly writings tend to be years if not decades out of date—as well as incomprehensible to nonspecialists. Without outside help, we have difficulty imagining, much less actually knowing, how others live, given how localized our own daily lives still are. It's simpler to assume that things are pretty much the same everywhere—which is consistent with a sense that total globalization is a *fait accompli*.

Having said that, the notion that data availability is *the* problem is itself problematic. Something other than data must account for the success of *The World Is Flat*, since its 450-plus pages contain not a single table, chart, or footnote to back up its pronouncements. I still find the comfort of Friedman's many fans with this data-free approach the most flabbergasting aspect of the flattening.

Psychology reminds us, of course, that beliefs aren't based just on data. The specter of apocalyptic occurrences (such as World 2.0) can mesmerize people; as the French writer of fables, Jean de la Fontaine, famously observed, "Everyone believes very easily whatever they fear or desire." This suggests some additional reasons why globaloney may be so popular: *fear*, as in the cases of those who worry about world domination by multinationals (including many Marxists), or who are simply concerned about losing their jobs to foreign competition; and *desire*, as in the cases of executives who like to see themselves as superheroes capable of solving business problems anywhere and, more broadly, all those who hope to gain personally from additional globalization.

Whether one actually believes in globaloney or not, professing to do so also carries social cachet. In many circles, you're "not with it" if you don't subscribe to Friedman's "world is flat" notion of globalization. I can testify to some personal experience in this regard: as a flat-world skeptic, I've often found myself treated as a relic, especially by reporters. I still remember the TV interview that began with the question, commingling disbelief and pity, "Professor Ghemawat, why do you *still* believe the world is round?" I am afraid I burst out laughing in response. It was in the aftermath that I decided to write my "Why the World Isn't Flat" article.

Technotrances

All these factors are important, but perhaps the most powerful reason most people buy into apocalyptic notions of globalization has to do with our almost religious worship of technology. I've already mentioned how empowering the Internet seems to many people. Since productivity growth and incomes really took off in the nineteenth century (see figure 1-1), people in the throes of industrial progress have been dazzled again and again by technology, enthralled with it, even locked into what I like to call a technotrance. (Younger readers will get the analogy with techno music and its effects on brain activity.)

As far back as the 1850s, the Scottish missionary and explorer David Livingstone remarked that "the extension and use of railroads, steamships, telegraphs, break down nationalities and bring peoples geographically remote into close connection commercially and politically. They make the world one, and capital, like water, tends to a common level."[28] U.S. philosopher John Dewey, writing in 1927, argued that steam, electricity, and the telephone were not only creating a new world by compressing space but might also challenge local forms of self-government.[29] In 1929, U.S. carmaker Henry Ford gushed that "the airplane and wireless know no boundary . . . they are binding the world together in a way no system can."[30] In 1933, English novelist and historian H. G. Wells, also an air enthusiast, imagined a world state based on air power that used the Basic English of aviators as its language and the air dollar as its currency—and had Basra, Iraq, as its capital.[31]

Such was the fascination with technology shrinking the world that it even prompted an early complaint by George Orwell, in 1944: "Reading recently a batch of rather shallowly optimistic 'progressive' books, I was struck by the automatic way people go on repeating certain phrases which were fashionable before 1914. Two great favourites are the 'abolition of distance' and the 'disappearance of frontiers.'"[32]

After World War II, German philosopher Martin Heidegger continued in this vein with his discussion in 1950 of the abolition of distance. He implied that "everything is equally far and equally near" and observed that "the peak of this abolition of every possibility of remoteness is reached by television, which will soon pervade and dominate the whole machinery of communication."[33] Canadian cultural critic Marshall McLuhan popularized this vision of television in the 1960s and extended it to other technologies: "Today, after more than a century of electric technology, we have extended our central nervous system in a global embrace, abolishing both space and time as far as our planet is concerned."[34] Since then, the focus has shifted from television to the Internet and information technology, as witness Friedman's contribution.

I should add that this emphasis on technology—especially, in the last few decades, communications technology—as *the* driver of World 2.0 seems, if anything, to have increased since the financial crisis, probably because the policy outlook appears less promising than it did precrisis. Back when Friedman wrote *The World Is Flat*, it was still possible to evoke (as he did) the 1989 fall of the Berlin Wall as capturing the spirit of the age. Not anymore. Other fences have, quite literally, gone up rather than come down: between the United States and Mexico, India and Bangladesh, and Israel and Palestine, for example. More broadly, the aftermath of the crisis has seen a collapse in public support for globalization, a surge in separatism, new challenges associated with multipolarity (particularly from a U.S. perspective), and uncertainty about the dollar's status as the world's reserve currency. Even the diehards straining to reassure believers that World 2.0 *can* be achieved recognize that recent changes in the policy climate do not help.[35]

Countering Technotrances

How can we answer the usual assertion that this time is different—that the technology *du jour* will lead, in fairly short order, to the nearly complete integration associated with World 2.0?[36] The simplest approach is to note from the preceding historical parade that the technologies previously supposed to be apocalyptic, while indubitably important, have clearly led to only limited cross-border integration so far. This suggests less than complete credulity in current predictions of the technological apocalypse. Historical comparisons also suggest more specific reasons for skepticism. Thus, the telegraph—the "Victorian Internet" cited by Livingstone as one of his three transformational technologies—arguably had a bigger impact on cross-border integration, at least in terms of commodity prices, than the Internet can because the telegraph cut previous barriers by well over one-half.[37]

We can also try to confront such apocalyptic assertions with real cases. Let's not just take any case; let's take a case where the idea of the

Internet abolishing borders and distance is relatively plausible. How about Google? If there were ever a business capable of using the Internet to project a powerful competitive advantage across national borders, Google should be it. In my last book, published in 2007, I noted Google's travails with Chinese censors, but focused primarily on its problems in Russia, where it trailed local market leaders Yandex and Rambler. I also highlighted cultural barriers, specifically linguistic complexities that affected Google's algorithms. (Russian nouns have three genders and up to six cases, verbs are very irregular, and the meaning of words can depend on their ending or on the context.) Four years and a global financial crisis later, is technology overpowering these and other barriers?

Given the company being studied, it is only natural that we google its globalization/internationalization since 2007 (although I did also talk to its CEO, Eric Schmidt). Doing so underlines how impressive Google's performance has been overall: it now offers its services in a dizzying array of languages, has grown non-U.S. revenues to more than half the total, and has established the kind of name recognition around the world that, according to one survey, makes it the world's first $100 billion brand.[38] But it is also clear that Google has encountered lots of national barriers along the way.

In Russia, Yandex has widened its lead.[39] And politics as well as culture is intruding: the Russian government has reacted to perceptions of increasingly close ties between Google and the U.S. government by announcing work on a "national search engine" to boost cybersecurity.[40]

Google's political/administrative situation in China has deteriorated even further. Although China was the only country in the world where Google was—after much internal debate—willing to offer a local site that complied with local censorship laws, cyberassaults prompted it to pull the plug in 2010. And Google has run into trouble in more than thirty countries for, among other things, violating local privacy laws while gathering data for its StreetView mapping service.

Of course, new apps such as Google Earth, Maps, StreetView, and Places emphasize rather than deemphasize geography, which is yet another inconsistency with World 2.0. Geography is also impinging on

Google's ambitious plans for cloud computing. As more governments worry about where "their country's" data will be housed, servers may have to be located locally: the Indian government is already pushing Google, along with BlackBerry, in this direction.

Finally, economic differences continue to matter as well. Thus, in India, where more people are offline than on, and where mobile devices greatly outnumber Internet connections, Google has tweaked its product line to include more offline and mobile offerings.[41] And to round out this coverage of big emerging BRIC (Brazil, Russia, India, and China) markets, perhaps the most unusual aspect of Google in Brazil is the success of its Orkut social network, which has a massive lead locally over Facebook. The last I heard, they were still scratching their heads at Google's Mountain View, California, headquarters about why Orkut should do better in Brazil than just about anywhere else.

Given this panoply of differences across countries, the fact that search is a worldwide need doesn't mean that Google can approach the world in a way that ignores national boundaries. Another strike against technology as the guarantor of World 2.0.

Finally, and more ambitiously, one could go beyond individual cases to look at the Internet itself and make the case that it does not correspond to the visions of World 2.0 either. While that goes beyond the scope of this chapter, I do have in front of me, as I write this, the most recent issue of the *Economist* bearing the title "The Web's New Walls" and the subtitle "How the Internet's Openness Is Under Threat." Let me quote an excerpt:

Fifteen years after its first manifestation as a global, unifying network, it [the internet] has entered its second phase: it appears to be balkanizing, torn apart by three separate, but related forces. First, governments are increasingly reasserting their sovereignty . . . Second, big IT companies are building their own digital territories, where they set the rules and control or limit connections to other parts of the internet. Third, network owners would like to treat different types of traffic differently, in effect creating faster and slower lanes on the internet. It is still too early to say that the internet has fragmented into "internets," but there is a danger that it may splinter along geographic and commercial boundaries.[42]

Another article in the same issue makes a parallel observation about the sociocultural fragmentation of the Internet—pointing out, among other things, that as Internet use in Brazil has risen, better-off Brazilians are leaving Google's locally dominant social network, Orkut, for Facebook and even have a new word—the equivalent of "orkutized"—for places undesirably full of strangers.[43]

The point of all this is not to deny the importance of the Internet or, more generally, technology. As I stressed in chapter 1, technological progress is probably the most exciting feature of the modern world. Cross-border communication in particular has experienced astonishing reductions in costs and expansion in capabilities. For example, the cost of a three-minute phone call from New York to London fell from $350 in 1930 to about 40 cents in 1999 and is now approaching zero with Internet telephony! But connectivity is not the same as convergence. Just because people in different parts of the world can talk to each other much more cheaply doesn't guarantee they will do so to any great extent (recall the 2 percent internationalization levels of phone calling minutes).

The broader point of this chapter has been to debunk exaggerations about unfettered globalization that persist on both sides of the globalization debate and across popular culture. If you feel drenched in data, that was the idea. It should now be clear that the world is only semiglobalized today—and still will be tomorrow.

This is more than just "college knowledge" of the sort that might come in handy at cocktail parties. Semiglobalization is exciting not primarily because it is realistic, but because it means that a lot of room still exists to increase cross-border integration. To understand whether and how to grasp these opportunities, though, we need to understand *why* integration still remains quite limited, even after decades of deliberate opening up. This is the task I take up in the next chapter.

Chapter Three

Borders, Differences, and the Law of Distance

THE LAST CHAPTER examined the cross-border integration of markets and concluded that the world economy is still only semiglobalized. This chapter digs into the barriers that underlie observed levels of cross-border integration—the borders, differences, and distances that still separate countries in our semiglobalized World 3.0. This chapter identifies the barriers that would have to be removed or reduced to increase integration—a possibility highlighted by the diagnosis of semiglobalization in chapter 2 and pursued further in chapter 4. It also indicates that instead of the Heideggerian vision of a world in which "everything is equally far and equally near," countries are better thought of as located in (and occupying) physical and virtual space at very different distances from one another.[1]

This more realistic vision suggests a distinctive geographic structure for World 3.0, in which both borders *and* distance are important. By contrast, World 1.0 presupposes that only borders matter; it buckets countries into "home" and "abroad" even when speaking of international relations. And in World 2.0, neither borders nor distance are supposed to matter. The geography I define for World 3.0, in which the intensity of interactions is affected not only by borders but also by distance—the "law" of distance, as I refer to it—will prove particularly helpful later in the book.

Note that this chapter's diagnosis is linked to the previous one's in the sense that semiglobalization is *necessary* for interesting variations in distance. With zero cross-border integration, all foreign countries would be prohibitively distant; with complete cross-border integration, all countries would be cheek by jowl. But semiglobalization isn't *sufficient* to establish that it is interesting to organize our thinking about the world out there in distance-dependent terms. That is the broader task at which this chapter makes a start.

We begin by looking at the case of a particular border, between the United States and Canada, that shouldn't, as national borders go, matter much. But it turns out to be a huge impediment to merchandise flows. To understand why, we go micro and look at a specific business, a small company named Ganong, that exports jelly beans from Canada to the United States. The cross-country differences flagged by this case and the earlier example of Google help introduce a research-based framework I've created for understanding distance. I call it the "CAGE" distance framework to refer to the cultural, administrative, geographic, and economic differences or distances between countries.

Studies using subsets of the CAGE factors do a good-to-great job of explaining patterns not just in trade and FDI flows, but in people, financial, and informational flows as well. Estimates drawn from such studies help us appreciate how much farther apart the typical country pair is on these dimensions than the United States and Canada, and how much that should be expected to matter. This chapter ends with a discussion of the broader significance of this distance-based geographic reconceptualization. Chapter 4 returns to the specifics about what to do about the CAGE-related barriers that continue to constrain cross-border integration.

The Mystery of the Missing Trade

The U.S.-Canadian border is the world's longest undefended border. Trade across it accounts for the world's largest bilateral trading relationship, still larger than that between the United States and China. Two-way trade between the United States and Canada amounted to nearly $750 billion in 2008 before falling to $600 billion in 2009, thanks largely to the decline in energy prices and weakness in the auto sector; in both areas, Canada is the United States' largest foreign supplier. So important is this trading relationship for Canada that the Canadian government regards several industries as more susceptible to U.S. economic conditions than to domestic ones.[2] Thus, Canada's $100 billion drop in exports to the United States between 2008 and 2009 was three times as large as the decline in Canada's GDP during that period.

All this suggests lots of trade, but we shouldn't just jump to the conclusion that the border doesn't matter. In fact, economists who've looked at U.S.-Canada trade in recent years haven't puzzled over why it is so large; rather, they've wondered *why it isn't nearly as large as one would expect if the border didn't matter*. There has been a spate of work on "the mystery of the missing trade," since the original finding that in 1988, when the United States and Canada signed a free trade agreement, merchandise trade between Canada's different provinces was *twenty-two times as intense* as their trade with the United States.

The 1988 free trade agreement did reduce the "home-bias multiple," as economists call it, by the mid-1990s, but only to twelve (and with the multiple remaining stuck at thirty to forty in the case of services).[3] It is currently estimated to be between five and ten—lower than before but still significantly greater than the level of one that would correspond to zero home bias.[4] Corroboration of significant border effects comes from the price differences between the United States and Canada. As so many border dwellers know, there's a reason to go on international shopping trips (although this type of "suitcase trade" amounts to only a small percentage of total trade, and is therefore insufficient to eliminate price differentials).[5]

How do other borders stack up to this one? It's hard to tell, since very few countries maintain data on within-country trade of the sort available for Canada. However, we can get a sense of merchandise trade across regions within a country by examining regional transportation flows.[6] One study that does so concludes that German länder, or states, traded four to six times as much with each other as with other EU countries in 2002, and that the corresponding home bias multiple for the French regions was about fifteen.[7] More than three decades after the EU eliminated all formal trade barriers, such as tariffs and quotas, between member states, the German and French borders still matter a great deal.

If borders still matter so much between neighbors, they cast an even bigger shadow on trade between countries farther away from each other. My analysis of Spanish regions' merchandise trade with other OECD countries over 1995–2005 found a home bias multiple ranging from fifteen with Portugal to *150* for Japan![8] As we know from other studies, Spain hasn't integrated with world markets as well as Germany or even France, and these numbers bear that out.[9] And the variation in the home bias multiple reminds us that a border effect is a "bilateral effect"—that is, it depends on which country pair one is talking about—rather than a "unilateral effect," which depends on the attributes of just one country.

For even more evidence that national borders impede trade, we can look to situations where new borders have arisen or old ones have gone away. In 1993, when the former Czechoslovakia broke into the Czech Republic and Slovakia, the two governments took significant measures to preserve open trading relations, including a customs union, a temporary payment mechanism to deal with delinked currencies, and an agreement stipulating free movement of labor. Yet, trade intensity between the two new countries fell from forty times the "normal" level of trade with other countries in 1991[10] to ten times by 1995.[11]

Meanwhile, Germany's experience illustrates the effects of removing national borders. In the five years that followed the reunification of the former East and West Germany in 1990, trade between the two shot up sixfold, and the share of intra-German trade in their overall trade grew fourfold.[12] These gains reflected large investments intended to facilitate integration, including spending on physical infrastructure like rail lines and highways, and the East's rapid development as a result.

Even more interesting than the rapid increase in trade, however, are estimates that it will take *decades* before effects of the former East-West border disappear.[13] Erection of a new border can cause trade to collapse almost overnight, as in the Czechoslovak example, but removing a border has a much slower economic impact. This makes sense when you think about the relationships that accrete over time between buyers and sellers, the investment in familiar brands, the knowledge that locals have about local markets, tastes, preferences, and, of course, connective infrastructure. Removal of a barrier doesn't put outsiders on equal footing with locals—not for decades, at least.

Of course, there are also studies focused on emerging markets. Although Brazil opened up to more international trade during the 1990s, Brazilian states still traded an estimated twenty-seven times more with each other than with foreign countries in 1999.[14] China's estimated home bias in the late 1990s was also in the twenties.[15] This figure would have been higher if Chinese provinces hadn't become significantly less integrated with each other: between 1987 and 1997, provincial border effects are estimated to have more than doubled.

The effects of borders *between* states or regions within the same country in limiting trade seem particularly large in the BRIC countries (Brazil, Russia, India, and China) because of their size, poor infrastructure (especially in the hinterlands), and administrative barriers to internal trade.[16] In general, though, the effects of internal borders are an order of magnitude smaller than those of international borders. Thus, in 1999, Brazilian states "traded" internally more than ten times as intensely as with other Brazilian states but *280* times as intensely as with foreign countries; for Chinese provinces in 1997, those multiples were estimated at twenty-seven and more than *400* times. The point is not that internal trade flows or barriers to them are unimportant: in large countries, in particular, internal trade is often significantly larger overall than international trade and therefore even relatively small impediments to it can matter a great deal.[17] Rather, the point is that if we want to "solve" the mystery of the missing trade, we ought to look at national borders, since that is where the really large drop-offs in trade are observed, not at state or regional borders. In other words, World 0.0, with its primary focus on the subnational level, turns out to be even less realistic a worldview than World 1.0.

From Canada with Candy

Let's dig deeper into the mystery of the missing trade by returning to the U.S.-Canadian border and focusing on a specific business trying to sell products across the border. Despite the general fascination with markets, businesses are, in many respects, the visible hand of trade. As international economist Edward Leamer observes (in the course of a critique of World 2.0):

> There are very few exchanges that are mediated by "markets" . . . Most exchanges take place within the context of long-term relationships that create the language needed for buyer and seller to communicate, that establish the trust needed to carry out the exchange, that allow ongoing servicing of implicit or explicit guarantees, that monitor the truthfulness of both parties, and that punish those who mislead. Many exchanges occur between colleagues who work for the same firm. Indeed, about 40% of US imports are carried out internal to multinational enterprises.[18]

In other words, 40 percent of U.S. imports have the same business firm at both ends of that cross-border exchange. It's pretty clear, then, that the majority of U.S. imports have *a* firm—not necessarily the same one—at both ends of such an exchange, and an even larger proportion have a business firm involved as either the importer or the exporter.

To explore what might lie behind border effects, let's look not just at a specific company, but at a smallish one; large companies often have a lot of infrastructure, capabilities, and experience that make it comparatively easy for them to cross national borders. (Note that the largest companies are much more globalized than markets in general: in 2008, the world's one hundred largest nonfinancial transnational companies had roughly 60 percent of their assets, employees, and sales *outside* their home markets, up 10 to 20 percentage points from 1990 levels.[19])

A company that fits the bill is Ganong Brothers, Canada's oldest candy maker and a firm roughly one-thousandth Google's size. While chocolates comprise its principal product line, what has really attracted attention are the company's attempts to sell jelly beans in the United States. Because of free trade agreements, there are no tariffs on jelly beans, and one might expect them to flow freely across the U.S.-Canadian border. And Ganong would seem well-positioned, literally, to serve the U.S. market: the state of Maine is just 1.8 kilometers away (1.1 miles for Americans) and visible from the offices of company president David Ganong. But it's not so simple.

Take labeling as an example. In Canada, nutritional labels read "5 mg," with a space between the number and the unit of measure. Yet Ganong's jelly beans can't get into America unless the nutritional label reads "5mg," without the space. Likewise, the two countries calculate daily nutritional values differently. His packages of jelly beans for American consumers need to state what percentage of an American's daily allotment of iron, say, the product provides, even if this percentage varies only slightly from that provided to a Canadian (e.g., 4 percent of the daily allotment of iron as opposed to 2 percent).[20]

Such bureaucratic differences may seem trivial, but their effects are not. To comply with U.S. labeling laws, Ganong has to produce jelly beans in separate runs for its American and Canadian markets; this means that production runs for each are smaller and less economical. Separate bags for the two countries elevate the costs of packaging, and the company needs to spend more money and devote more warehouse space to storing separate inventories of bagged jelly beans for the United States and Canada.[21]

Lest it seem that the United States is unilaterally unreasonable, it's worth adding that Canada ties up trade in red tape as well. According to the Canada Border Services Agency, commercial importers into the country must register their businesses by obtaining a fifteen-digit business number. They must also create an accounting package for their shipments consisting of two copies of a "cargo control document," two copies of an invoice, two copies of a Form B3 ("Canada Customs Coding Form"), any other required permits or forms, such as health certificates, and in many cases, a "Certificate of Origin" form. Once shipments are reported to the government, they are granted a unique fourteen-digit transaction number before they are released by customs and any duties or taxes are paid. To handle all this red tape, American exporters usually hire an export agent, who contracts with a shipper or carrier, who in turn deals with a clearing and forwarding agent in the destination country, who in turn deals with the buyer. Bank letters of credit are often required, as is insurance on the part of the exporter. Of course, none of this counts the documentation that is required on the American side to export goods.

Since September 11, 2001, the barriers to trade have increased further due to the application of new layers of security and more complex rules and regulations. Processing time to enter the United States from Canada by truck (the principal mode of transportation) now takes an estimated three times as long.[22] Delays have become such a problem that the Canadian government now has a Web site devoted to tracking them in real time.

These changes have directly affected Ganong Brothers: as David Ganong related, his firm had a candy shipment delayed for five weeks so that the American government could analyze whether the yellow food coloring used in the product had been FDA approved. For four weeks, the government wouldn't reveal why the shipment was being held, what they were checking into, and what it would take to get it released.[23] With Ganong's American customers expecting just-in-time delivery, surprise hold-ups such as this leave them looking elsewhere for more reliable sources.

Jelly beans aren't even the industry hit most by red tape; other sectors with more complex production chains fare far worse. Take cars, whose production chains crisscross the U.S.-Canadian border with parts and subassemblies being shipped back and forth.[24]

The red tape *has* prompted some efforts at reform. In 2005, the U.S., Canadian, and Mexican governments launched the Security and Prosperity Partnership (SPP) of North America to tackle issues such as regulatory harmonization—to supplement the nine hundred pages on the topic in the NAFTA treaty—as well as alleviate the impact of border controls.[25] But progress has been slow, partly because of domestic political resistance that taps into a rich vein of suspicion and resentment of the United States. Thus, as one Canadian think tank put it, "SPP regulatory harmonization is a policy straightjacket [sic] that tightens with each new agreement, narrowing Canadian regulatory policy flexibility as it conforms to the dominant US regime."[26]

David Ganong, of course, finds all this very frustrating. And Canadian prime minister Stephen Harper shares his exasperation: "Is the sovereignty of Canada going to fall apart if we standardize the jelly bean? I don't think so."[27]

As if administrative barriers weren't enough, Ganong faces other hurdles in selling to the United States. One is geographic. While the company is located right on the border, it does have to deal with distance *within* the United States. The U.S. state that it abuts from the north, Maine, is about the size of Portugal but has only 1.3 million people. It is more than 500 kilometers to Boston and nearly 900 kilometers to New York, over roads where the hazards include moose and snow. The dearth of nearby demand matters because sugar confectionery (given its relatively low value-to-weight ratio and limited scale economies) tends not to be shipped very far compared to, say, chocolate.

And then there is the economic constraint implied by currency exchange rates. Over the last few years, the U.S. dollar has hovered at around 1.1 Canadian dollars, compared to a level of around 1.5 in the late 1990s and early 2000s. From Ganong's perspective, this represents more than a 25 percent drop in the value of each U.S. dollar the company receives. Given that the profitability of the typical business in the United States or Canada is about 5 percent of sales, this kind of exchange rate realignment would be more than enough to wipe out export profits for the average company.[28] Unsurprisingly, Canadian sugar confectionery exports to the United States have stagnated in U.S. dollar terms since 2005, the last time the average exchange rate exceeded 1.2; in terms of Canadian dollars, they have declined.[29]

What has nonetheless kept Ganong and other Canadian sugar confectionery manufacturers interested in the U.S. market is the staggering amount of protection afforded the U.S. sugar industry. Since 1812, the U.S. government has used a maze of tariffs and quotas to set artificially high prices for domestically grown sugar and prevent the import of sugar grown elsewhere. While this is often rationalized as protecting the U.S. customer from the roller coaster of world sugar prices, this protection is achieved by setting domestic prices so high that the roller coaster never risks running into them.

As a result, U.S. domestic sugar prices are typically two to three times as high as world prices, and the multiple has ranged as high as seven! In this respect, the U.S. government actually seems kinder to foreigners than to its own. It subsidizes the export of products containing expensive U.S. sugar, effectively softening the effects of high U.S. sugar prices for foreign but not U.S. consumers. And it hurts U.S. sugar confectionery manufacturers by elevating their costs, but without affecting Canadian (and other) manufacturers' costs. But U.S. sugar growers make out like bandits and have been creative in finding ways of sharing some of the gains with the political establishment, which in turn looks set to carry the torch of U.S. protection of this sector into its third century.

The United States, by the way, is not alone; the European Union and Japan also keep domestic sugar prices very high. Canada is actually the only major developed country to allow free importation of sugar. This discussion as well as the earlier discussion of regulatory harmonization suggest that the potential gains from opening up merchandise trade are still very large—a theme pursued further in the next chapter.

Differences and Distances

The case study of Ganong suggests that differences between the United States and Canada, while subtle, have large effects on trade and can therefore help explain the Canadian home bias multiples of five to ten cited earlier. But think of how much more different two randomly selected countries are than Canada is from the United States. Or, equivalently, think of all the ways in which Canada and the United States are *atypically* similar.

Books can and have been written on this topic. Here, I'll simply summarize some of the "matches" between Canada and the United

States that directly affected Ganong, and the percentage of all the possible country pairs (roughly 13,000) in my CAGE dataset that also match on that dimension.

Culturally, Canada and the United States share the same dominant language (English), without which cross-border sales would have been even more challenging for Ganong. Communicating across a language barrier, even with a good (and hence expensive) interpreter, is still very hard—especially around subtleties like building trust, delivering constructive criticism, and motivating people. By way of comparison, the probability that a randomly selected country pair will exhibit a linguistic match is only 10 percent.[30]

Administratively, Canada and the United States are part of NAFTA (the North American Free Trade Agreement), which helped Ganong by eliminating formal trade barriers. Only 11 percent of all possible country pairs involve common membership in such a trading bloc. And Canada and the United States also (mostly) had a common colonizer, England, which has eased contracting and trade by fostering similarities in areas such as legal systems: both follow the traditions of English common law.[31] By contrast, 22 percent of all possible country pairs share a common colonizer, and 39 percent share a common legal origin.[32]

Geographically, Ottawa and Washington are only 738 kilometers from each other, almost exactly one-tenth the average distance between the capital cities of a pair of randomly selected countries (7,270 kilometers). And Canada and the United States also share a common land border—something that only 2 percent of all possible country pairs can claim. These geographic factors did more than all the others to induce Ganong's focus on the United States as its major export market, even though the company has recently been attempting to secure agents in other parts of the world.

We can summarize these data by excluding the continuous geographic distance measure and focusing on the five dimensions on which Canada and the United States matched. Multiplying the five percentages above (and assuming that they are independent) implies just a .002 percent probability that a randomly selected country pair would match on all five dimensions that Canada and the United States did! Dropping the independence assumption increases this probability but it seems pretty clear that Canada and the United States are about as close as two countries get in a world of about two hundred.

Beyond these factors that impinged specifically on Ganong's exports of jelly beans, all sorts of other commonalities between Canada and the United States have been cited as mattering for trade in general. More than one hundred thousand Americans and Canadians each live in the other country, a tie shared by only 1 percent of all possible country pairs. The two countries also share the same dominant religion, Christianity, although most Canadian Christians are Catholic, unlike their American coreligionists. The probability of matching coreligionists—past the usual 30 percent threshold—in a randomly selected country pair is 51 percent. Canada and the United States also align in a number of cultural groupings, ranging from Samuel Huntington's eight civilizations (the United States and Canada are both Western) to Geert Hofstede's six different cultural groupings (the United States and Canada are both Anglo-Saxon). Only one-quarter to one-fifth of country pairs match in such terms.[33]

Based on Hofstede's four dimensional schema for assessing national culture, the United States ranks second out of sixty-seven other countries/regions in terms of cultural proximity to Canada, behind Australia, and Canada is third closest to the United States, behind Australia and the United Kingdom.[34] This proximity is backed up by polling data. In one 2007 survey, 46 percent of Canadian respondents claimed that Canada's "values and goals" were "very similar" to those of Americans, higher than in Britain, Australia, and France.[35] U.S. citizens tend to agree and, in many surveys, they rank Canada as their favorite foreign nation.[36] Even U.S. politician Sarah Palin, no xenophile, has cited Canada as one of two trustworthy foreign countries (the other is Kuwait). But that said, the United States focuses far less on Canada than Canada does on it—which is unsurprising given their relative sizes.

The Canadian focus *does* contain an undercurrent of suspicion that sometimes boils over into overt U.S.-baiting. In a recent election campaign, former prime minister Paul Martin accused his opponent, then prime minister Stephen Harper, of being "an extremist with ties to the United States."[37] Sounds a lot like how American politicians describe terrorists! Harper denied the charges, was reelected, and continued on with his pro-integration agenda.

In addition, economic integration generates international tensions of its own. Of the forty-eight disputes before the World Trade Organization in which Canada is listed as complainant or respondent, the United States figures in twenty—less than its share of Canadian trade but not indicative of complete amity either. Still, the *absence* of such disputes is more worrying, for lack of integration tends to go hand in hand with the militarization of problems, as we will see in the next chapter.

But despite ongoing trade disputes and occasional political grandstanding, the U.S.-Canadian political relationship remains basically friendly. By comparison, take India and Pakistan. Since the Indian subcontinent was partitioned at the time of independence, in 1947, this relationship has been marked by overt and covert conflict as well as open hostility. As a result, Indo-Pakistani trade is just a fraction of what might be expected based on the patterns across other countries—only 2 to 4 percent, according to one study from 2004.[38] Emotions about other countries still matter.

Our discussion of Canada and the United States has so far focused on international distance, and pointed out that Canada and the United States are far closer than most country pairs. To complete the picture, one should look at internal as well as external distance. Thus, treating Canada, the world's second largest country, as a point mass is clearly inappropriate; as William Mackenzie King, who served as Canadian prime minister over much of the interwar years complained, "We have too much geography." The effects have been alleviated by the fact that 90 percent of all Canadians live within 250 kilometers of the U.S. border. Nonetheless, ignoring residual internal distance within Canada to the border with the United States leads to overestimation of the latter's effects.[39]

More subjective internal factors have also been shown to affect trade. A good example is the extent to which a country's culture is insular.

Marshall McLuhan (a Canadian) once asserted that "Canada is the only country in the world that knows how to live without an identity." Although this statement and its cruder cousin—the jibe about Canada being the fifty-first (U.S.) state—are obvious exaggerations, Canada does, as a nation of immigrants, seem much more open to outside influences in general than, say, much of western Europe, not to mention East Asia. Toronto and Vancouver, to name two of my personal favorites, are particularly vibrant, multicultural cities.

To organize thinking about how distance along multiple dimensions affects the relationships between *any* two countries, I have assembled these and other dimensions of difference flagged by research into the CAGE framework depicted in table 3-1. The columns group dimensions of difference into these four CAGE categories (cultural, administrative, geographic, and economic) and the rows track the distinction between external and internal distance cited earlier.

Perhaps most fundamentally, table 3-1 recasts differences—the focus of most of the prior discussion—into distances. This reflects the fact that it isn't enough just to register differences: leaving it at that would bog us down in the details of more than ten thousand country pairs. Rather, we need to appreciate *degrees of difference or distance* in order to distinguish what is near from what is far. This is a more complicated but ultimately more fruitful notion of distance than either World 1.0 (which sees foreign countries as equally far) and World 2.0 (which sees them as equally close). As we'll see in the next section, the multidimensional CAGE distance construct does such a good job of explaining bilateral trade patterns and other important cross-border flows that it even suggests a "law" (or, more modestly, a heuristic) of distance. This broadens geographer Waldo Tobler's First Law of Geography, "everything is related to everything else, but near things are more related than distant things" to also include cultural, administrative, and economic distance.[40]

Second, it is worth acknowledging that the columns do tend to blur into each other in some respects. Linguistic linkages from the cultural column are clearly correlated with colonial-era ties from the

TABLE 3-1

The CAGE distance framework

	Cultural distance	Administrative distance	Geographic distance	Economic distance

External distance (bilateral/plurilateral/multilateral attributes)	• Different languages
	• Different ethnicities/lack of connective ethnic or social networks
	• Different religions
	• Differences in national work systems
	• Different values, norms, and dispositions
		• Lack of colonial ties
		• Lack of shared regional trading bloc
		• Lack of common currency
		• Different legal system
		• Political hostility
			• Physical distance
			• Lack of land border
			• Differences in climates (and disease environments)
			• Differences in time zones
				• Differences in consumer incomes
				• Differences in availability of:
				  • Human resources
				  • Financial resources
				  • Natural resources
				  • Intermediate inputs
				  • Infrastructure
				  • Supplier/distribution structure
				  • Complements
				  • Organizational capabilities

Internal distance (unilateral attributes)	• Traditionalism • Insularity • Spiritualism • Inscrutability	• Nonmarket/closed economy (home bias versus foreign bias) • Lack of membership in international organizations • Weak legal institutions/corruption • Lack of government checks and balances • Societal conflict • Political/expropriation risk	• Landlockedness • Geographic size • Geographic remoteness	• Economic size • Low per capita income • Low level of monetization • Limited resources, inputs, infrastructure, complements, capabilities

Source: Adapted from Pankaj Ghemawat, "Distance Still Matters: The Hard Reality of Global Expansion," *Harvard Business Review* 79, no. 8 (2001): 137–147.

administrative column. And there is some ambiguity about whether to slot the availability/unavailability of transport and communications infrastructure into the geographic column or the economic one. The simple summary point that I would make is that the bullet points in table 3-1 remain relevant no matter which columns we place them in; the arrangement here represents just one possibility.

Third, the last column in the list, concerning economic distances, deserves special comment both because discussion of it so far has been relatively limited and because it presents some particular complexities. The earlier discussions did suggest—and the results of the studies summarized in the next section confirm—that cultural, administrative, and geographic distances between countries tend to depress the interactions between them substantially.[41] The same pattern holds up for the internal economic factors listed under economic distance in the figure: large countries with low levels of per capita GDP and monetization tend to trade proportionately less than others. But predictions around external economic distance are more mixed: thus, one kind of model suggests that trade should increase as a result of differences in per capita income, while another kind implies that it should decrease.[42] I find it efficient to simply look and see.

The most obvious use of the CAGE framework is to force broad-based consideration of the many possible differences between countries instead of simply passing them over, as so often happens. I've seen first-hand that even large international companies are prone to miss out on cultural and administrative differences, in particular. Economists, too, probably share such biases. People gripped by technotrances are likely to overlook geographic differences. And so on.

The rows of the matrix provide a second kind of reminder: they call attention to the internal as well as external dimensions of distance, broadly defined. Faced with the same external realities, countries, companies, or individuals differ greatly in how well they engage with them. Internal distance is relevant at each of these levels—although it takes different forms—and will prove a particularly helpful construct in Part III of this book.

The "Law" of Distance

I have mentioned the research base of the CAGE framework several times now. It consists for the most part of empirical studies—probably more than one thousand have been executed by now—that use "gravity models" to study bilateral interactions. Such models resemble Newton's law of gravitation in linking interactions between countries to the product of their sizes (usually their gross domestic products) divided by some composite measure of distance that incorporates some of the factors listed in table 3-1. I tend to think of them as *distance models* because what is most interesting about them resides in the denominator term: which types of distance really matter, and how much? Either way, such models explain not only why the U.S.-Canadian trading relationship is so large, but also *one-half to two-thirds of all variation in bilateral trade flows between all possible pairs of countries*. As a result, they have been described as providing "some of the clearest and most robust empirical findings in economics."[43]

To present an example that is based on some of the same information that is relied on elsewhere in this chapter, let me describe the results of a study I undertook. After controlling for economic size, I estimated the sensitivity of trade between all country pairs for which data were available to various types of distance, both at the (cross-industry) country level and at the level of individual industries. I report here the results at the country level.[44]

To start with geographic or physical distance, a useful stylized fact is that a 1 percent increase in the geographic distance between two locations leads to about a 1 percent decrease in trade between them. Put another way, the distance sensitivity is −1.[45] This particular value simplifies the calculations: it implies that trade intensity is inversely related to geographic distance. Applying this coefficient to the U.S.-Canada example, for instance, recall that Ottawa and Washington are only one-tenth as far from each other as the capitals of a randomly selected country pair. So, with a distance coefficient of −1, trade between Canada and the United States should be expected to be ten times as intense for that reason compared to the typical country pair. To say the same thing from a different perspective, U.S. trade with Chile *is only 6 percent of what it would be* if Chile were as close to the United States as Canada.

Then there are the other dimensions of distance/proximity. I found that two countries with a common language trade 42 percent more on average than a similar pair of countries that lack that link. Countries sharing membership in a trade bloc (e.g., NAFTA) trade 47 percent more than otherwise similar countries that lack such shared membership. A common currency (like the euro) increases trade by 114 percent. And if a country has ever colonized the other, the two countries trade 188 percent more on average (even though many colonial ties were dissolved decades or even centuries ago). Differences in levels of corruption and political stability tend to depress trade volumes. Countries like the United States and Canada that share a common land border typically see 125 percent more trade than two nonadjoining countries—above and beyond the geographic proximity effect discussed earlier. And the baseline estimates indicate that differences in per capita income generally have a positive effect on trade intensities, although that gets reversed in other specifications.[46]

Interested readers can go to my Web site (www.ghemawat.org) and play around with implications of these and other estimates. One way of summarizing them is, once again, to exclude the continuous geographic distance measure and focus on the five dichotomous ones for which coefficients are reported above. Based on those coefficients, a country pair that matches perfectly across all five should trade twenty-nine times as intensely as a country pair that differs across all five.[47] So the difference between near and far matters a great deal as far as trade is concerned—especially when one reckons with the direct effects of physical distance, which were excluded from the calculation.

Scholars have fitted similar gravity/distance models to other flows, including foreign direct investment, cross-border equity trading, sovereign lending, patent citations, phone calls, and migration patterns (not to mention remittances, e-commerce, international air traffic, and even the incidence of wars). None of these flows has been studied nearly as intensively as trade, the traditional focus of international economics, and in some cases, all we have is a study or two to rely on. That said, there *are* some broad headlines here that I group under the law of distance.

First, geographic distance matters across the board. It was probably obvious—except to World 2.0 extremists—that geographic distance would affect trade (although probably less obvious that the effect would be so large). But it isn't obvious that weightless *financial and informational flows* should decay as distance increases: one might expect FDI, at least, to increase with geographic distance as it substitutes for trade. Yet decay they generally do.

The estimated sensitivity of financial flows to geographic distance varies between –0.5 and –1.0,[48] with FDI and bank lending typically falling off faster with distance than portfolio investment.[49] In fact, some studies estimate FDI to be *more* distance-sensitive than the usual benchmark of –1 for trade. Perhaps even more surprisingly, phone traffic's distance sensitivity also seems comparable to or a bit greater than trade's![50] The distance sensitivity of immigration does turn out to be lower in absolute terms, about –0.25 in one study,[51] presumably because of the large interregional flows from East Asia, Latin America, and the Middle East and North Africa to OECD countries (other flows tend to be more intraregional).[52] The distance sensitivity of knowledge flows, variously measured, may be slightly lower yet.[53] The implications of these variations for how much intensity drops as physical distances increase are quite large.[54]

The second headline is that other dimensions of distance discussed earlier in the specific context of the trade, particularly cultural and administrative distance, typically reduce FDI, knowledge, and other cross-border flows as well. Thus, one study found that a common language led to 43 percent more bilateral FDI, colonial links to 118 percent more, and common legal origins to 94 percent more.[55] In fact, when FDI does take place in spite of significant cultural and administrative distance, it often involves not a solo venture but a joint venture with a local. The discussion of Google in the last chapter, which involved FDI rather than trade, points in the same direction: we saw it wrestling with cultural and administrative differences in particular. Another illustration of sensitivity: if you look at all U.S. companies that operate in just one foreign country, that country is Canada 60 percent of the time (and 10 percent of the time, the United Kingdom).[56] This suggests that cultural and administrative commonalities loom even larger for FDI than they do for trade.

A New View of Economic Geography?

Given the broad law of distance, remapping or reimagining the world along those lines seems important—and certainly more important than it would be if just trade were involved, or if flows didn't mostly tend to decay over different types of distance. Of course, a call for a remapping is strong stuff. Yet Paul Krugman, whose seminal work on economic geography won him the Nobel Prize, has argued for just such a shift.

About twenty years ago, Krugman relates, views of the world split harshly between those seeing countries as "discrete economic points, whose location in space is irrelevant"; those who thought "location in space is all and borders are irrelevant"; and those who believed in "the vision of a spaceless, borderless world in which distance had been abolished—not a world that yet exists, but possibly one just over the horizon." Krugman's conclusion, based on empirical research:

> Distance matters a lot, though possibly less than it did before telecommunications. Borders also matter a lot, though possibly less than they did before free trade agreements. The spaceless, borderless world is still a Platonic ideal, a long way from coming into existence. The compromise view isn't as radical as some would like. But it's a significant change from the way most of us viewed the world economy not too long ago.[57]

I generally agree with this: World 3.0 involves taking an integrative perspective in which both borders and distance matter. More specifically, World 3.0 treats flows as typically declining with distance—and also being subject to discontinuous drop-offs at borders of various

FIGURE 3-1

Distance sensitivity and border effects

Distance

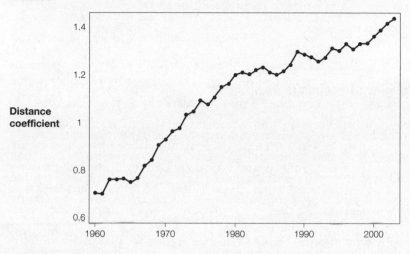

National borders

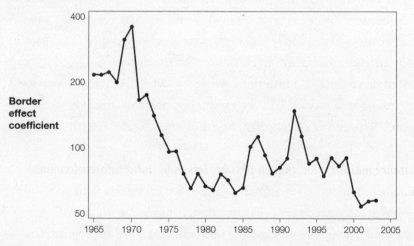

Source: Thierry Mayer, "Market Potential and Development," Centre d'Etudes Prospectives et d'Informations Internationales (CEPII) working paper no. 2009-24 (October), 13.

sorts. I would, however, place a bit more of an emphasis than Krugman does on distance effects, and not just for their novelty (to traditional trade theory). Figure 3-1 summarizes just one of several studies show-ing that border effects have decreased substantially over the last few decades, whereas geographic distance sensitivity actually seems to have increased! Shorter average shipping distances for exports point in the same direction.[58] In fact, a meta-analysis over a longer time frame suggests that geographic distance effects may actually have gone up relative to a hundred years ago![59] Distance seems to be in robust good health rather than dead.

Krugman suggests that this represents a changed view of economic geography if not a new one. World 3.0 certainly distinguishes itself in this regard from World 1.0 and World 2.0, neither of which takes geography seriously: World 1.0 emphasizes national borders while giving short shrift to distance effects and World 2.0 ignores both with its focus on a borderless, spaceless world. But it is useful to remind ourselves that the distinction extends beyond geography to encompass the other dimensions of the CAGE framework as well. And while differences along these dimensions are often (weakly) correlated with geographic distance, there is little to be gained and much to be lost by collapsing them all down to just geography.

Chapter Four

ADDING Value by Opening Up

THE LAST TWO chapters explained why the world isn't as globalized as many people think and analyzed how sensitive actual levels of cross-border integration are to the cultural, administrative, geographic, and economic differences between countries. This chapter explores the case for further integration given such headroom. It looks at how much we might gain by reducing the barriers between countries and further opening up.

Of course, thinking about gains from more openness only makes sense within the context of World 3.0. Believers in World 1.0 tend to either ignore cross-border interactions or focus on restricting/reversing them. And those still true to World 2.0 presumably see integration as having proceeded so far that relatively little is to be gained through more openness.

Adopting a World 3.0 perspective, then, let's begin by considering previous estimates of the gains from liberalizing trade. Standard estimates of the gains from the proposals on the table in the stalled Doha round of world trade talks tend to fall in the $50–100 billion range, and gains from complete liberalization of merchandise trade range from less than $100 billion up to $300 billion.[1] While those are a lot of billions, even that last estimate appears modest when we recall that in the wake of the financial crisis, banks such as Citigroup and Royal Bank of Scotland *individually* transferred larger amounts of "toxic" assets into "bad banks," and trillions were spent on stimulus programs.

More precisely, the estimated gains from the Doha proposals represent roughly 0.1 percent of a $60 trillion world economy, or about $10 for every person on the planet, and even the estimates for complete liberalization amount to only 0.5 percent of world GDP or about $50 per capita. Note that these are also much smaller than estimates based on similar models suggesting that the United States, for instance, could add 8 to 10 percent to its GDP by reforming its tax code.[2] Finally, the estimated gains from liberalizing merchandise trade have shrunk since the early 1990s because of rapid tariff reductions in general and growth in relatively open East Asian economies in particular.

In light of these estimates, think of an elected politician, possessed of some desire to be of service to constituents, but certainly not indifferent to personal political survival. Offer such a politician a 0.5 percent boost in GDP in return for a complete scrapping of controls on merchandise trade, and see how many takers you get. There probably wouldn't be many in normal times and perhaps none during periods of high unemployment.

That's the bad news. The good news is that the standard estimates of potential gains from globalization focus on just the tip of the iceberg. In fact, these estimates fail to capture the full potential of opening up for half a dozen broad reasons. First, we possess a more extensive set of policy instruments and levers than the models underlying these estimates presuppose. Second, while it is traditional to focus on volume and cost effects, cross-border interactions actually yield a broader array of economic benefits, as elaborated in this chapter in the specific context of merchandise trade. Third, looking beyond the usual focus on merchandise trade and including trade in services, as well as cross-border flows other than trade—flows of capital, people, and information— amplifies the economic gains from opening up. Fourth, not just economic value but also the cultural and political value of opening up must be considered. Fifth, complementarities across different channels of cross-border integration—such as between trade and migration, as described later—imply that channel-by-channel analysis will underestimate total gains. And finally, there is the *commitment* to cutting barriers to trade over time that has been built up over several decades of global trade negotiations. Conclusion of the Doha round would lock in some of the past gains as well as maintaining psychological momentum.

Reviewing all these omissions and assigning very rough magnitudes to some of them (drawing on studies cited later in this chapter, among others), I reckon the potential gains from opening up to be several times as large as the estimates of $100 to $300 billion cited earlier: several hundred if not as much as a thousand dollars for everyone on the planet, *every year*. Beyond these or other numbers, though, the more basic point is that the models used to generate them conceive of the potential gains from opening up far too narrowly. In making this argument, it is useful to begin with a brief description of the mathematical models that underlie standard estimates of the gains from trade liberalization.

CGE Models and CAGE Barriers

The estimates of the gains from freeing up trade cited above are based on computational general equilibrium (CGE) models that use computers to calculate the behavior of supply, demand, and prices in the whole economy—or, in the context of trade liberalization, across multiple economies. This is a challenging task that has elicited very complex modeling efforts. Thus, the World Bank's LINKAGE model incorporates eighty-seven countries/regions, fifty-seven sectors, multiple labor skills and capital vintages, and on the order of fifty thousand mathematical equations.[3]

That said, the real world is much, much more complex and so CGE models have to simplify reality a great deal.[4] At the macroeconomic level, most such models assume full (or fixed) employment and zero governmental and trade deficits. The few real-world distortions that they do recognize mostly reflect state intervention. In the context of trade liberalization, these distortions include tariffs on imports and exports (or "tariff equivalents" in the form of exchange controls, quotas, etc.) and production subsidies, all of which are typically tacked onto transportation costs. The question that CGE models address is, How much would welfare rise if such distortions were removed? The models answer it by reshuffling a fixed amount of resources across industries (but within countries) to maximize cost efficiency as distortions are reduced or removed.[5] The total gains from trade are the increased output observed as countries proceed to specialize in line with the principle of comparative advantage.[6]

Juxtaposing the kinds of administrative changes contemplated in CGE models against the administrative barriers discussed in the previous chapter, it becomes clear that the former tackle only a subset of the latter. For instance, standard CGE models generally don't consider harmonization of regulations of the sort necessary to simplify the packaging problems confronting the Canadian jelly bean manufacturer who would like to export to the United States—although some work on this has begun. Trade facilitation measures also tend to be omitted despite estimates (in nonstandard modeling) that they might yield gains worth 1 percent of global GDP—more than the sorts of liberalization that are the usual focus of such analysis.[7]

We can expand this list of administrative barriers that might be targeted to include many areas of gross administrative inefficiency within or across countries. Examples include countries in which it takes three months or more to obtain trade documents and regional trade agreements that are so complex that they have never actually been invoked. Such inefficiencies clearly dampen cross-border economic interactions by increasing internal distance but again, aren't part of the standard set-up.

As we look beyond administrative barriers to the other broad categories of impediments highlighted in the previous chapter, cultural barriers stand out as another obvious target. Without suggesting that cultures can or should be homogenized, we can clearly engage in "cultural facilitation" to ease at least some cultural barriers—examples include insularity, hubris, and distrust of foreigners—that impede cross-border economic activity. Possible policy initiatives include broadening and ensuring more balanced coverage of foreign news, limiting nationalistic chest thumping, insisting on education, promoting second and third languages (particularly English as a language of wider communication), encouraging more cross-border trips and longer stays including immigration, and so on. Chapters 11 and 15 will deal at greater length with cultural barriers and what to do about them; the point here is that they fall outside the compass of CGE models.

Unlike administrative and cultural barriers, the geographic barriers highlighted by the CAGE framework might seem immutable, but even here, there is room for remediation. Consider Africa, whose trade performance, interregional as well as intraregional, has lagged that of other regions. Part of the problem is that Africa is very far away from major world markets, so that when one divides foreign market sizes by geographic distance (i.e., assumes a distance sensitivity of −1) and adds them up, sub-Saharan African countries can access one-third the foreign demand that European countries can. We can't do anything about this geographic reality. Yet distance to markets isn't the only factor underlying very poor African trade performance.

African exports to the United States illustrate the interregional problems: these exports experience transport costs three times as high as those from developed countries. Some of that higher cost reflects the incidence of landlocked countries, but much also seems related to ports that are among the slowest and costliest in the world—about which something could presumably be done.[8]

Africa's intraregional trade is also low, and reveals even more clearly the influence of very bad infrastructure. By one estimate, if all the interstate roads in West Africa were paved, that might as much as triple trade within the (sub)region![9] And that estimate does not include the effects of, for instance, reducing the checkpoints on roads that *are* paved. More than a dozen of these checkpoints typically crop up between one capital city and the next, adding to corruption as well as transportation costs and times.[10] Landlocked countries in sub-Saharan

Africa are hit particularly hard by such problems: they incur inland transport costs that are more than four times as high on average as those experienced by coastal countries in the region.[11]

Note that this discussion of geographic barriers has circled back toward administrative barriers, reminding us that the categories of barriers discussed in the previous chapter have a tendency to intertwine.[12] Instead of focusing further on different types of barriers, then, I will simply point to the existence of a broad array of policy instruments and institutions that represent levers for increasing openness.

These levers aren't fully accounted for in CGE modeling, and their effects are often viewed too narrowly. The usefulness of the CAGE framework in this context, as Supachai Panitchpakdi, secretary-general of UNCTAD, put it to me, is that it helps expand what he calls the policy space. And according to him, the need for more policy space to implement appropriate development strategies has only gone up since the crisis.

ADDING Value Through Merchandise Trade

My own perspective on models of the gains from trade reflects my graduate training in economics—micro rather than macro—at Harvard, followed by twenty-five years on the faculty at the Harvard Business School, and now at IESE Business School in Barcelona, studying business and global strategy. I've come to think that business is fertile in insights about the derivation and distribution of value from globalization for society generally (although, obviously, such insights have to be adapted to focus on the public interest or total welfare rather than just private interests or profits). This is because of the business world's general emphasis on value creation and capture (my own textbook on business strategy is organized around these themes[13]) as well as its extensive experience with internationalization. As discussed in chapter 2, businesses, especially large ones, exhibit greater levels of cross-border activity than markets in general and are key intermediaries in trade as well as in other types of cross-border flows.

Figure 4-1 presents a simple scorecard that I developed to help businesses assess the *private* economic value created or destroyed by cross-border operations. I use it here to understand the *social* value of increased openness. The scorecard parses value creation into six components—volume, cost, willingness to pay, intensity of competition, risk, and knowledge dynamics—that, with a bit of wordsmithing, lend themselves to the acronym of ADDING value. Pascal Lamy, director-general of the World Trade Organization, was a discussant when I presented the ADDING value scorecard at the World Export Development Forum 2010 in Chongqing, China, and provided a powerful summary of the action implications: *Focus on value, not on volume.* He also pointed out that while businesses had figured out this value proposition decades earlier, trade professionals had yet to fully take it on board.

I contend that standard estimates of the gains from opening up focus on the first two components of the scorecard, adding volume and decreasing costs (the shaded ones in the figure), but miss out on the other four. Let me elaborate.

FIGURE 4-1

The ADDING value scorecard

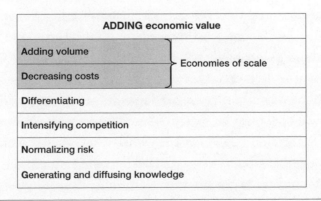

The first component of the scorecard, *Adding volume* or *growth*, is the one that is most evident in discussions of trade liberalization. Thus, in their introductory economics text, Paul Samuelson and William Nordhaus observe that to arrive at the total gains from trade, you need to add up all the consumer surplus and producer profits generated by the increased trade, or more roughly, all the increased output you see from specialization and production.[14] When you hear people say, "Trade liberalization will expand GDP by 0.5 percent," that's the logic they're following.

This added volume does, in a sense, depend on the second component of the scorecard, *Decreasing costs*; more cost-efficient allocations of resources underlie the expansion of output in CGE models. But the typical treatment of cost effects in such models is narrow. They don't consider investments in cost reduction, such as improving the infrastructure that seems the real bottleneck in sub-Saharan African trade. And since economies of scale—broadly speaking, negative relationships between volume and costs—can't easily be squeezed into general equilibrium models (they are a distinct potential source of market failure that I will revisit in chapter 5), they tend to be ignored as well.

This is a big mistake. Economies of scale, while perhaps not as pervasive as businesspeople often assume, are more important than economists, particularly international economists, have allowed. But even the latter are starting to shift perspectives. Thus, a recent study covering several dozen countries over two decades found that a third of the manufacturing and natural resources industries studied showed increasing returns to scale, one-third showed constant returns, and one-third did not exhibit a clear pattern.[15] The industries most highly affected by economies of scale experienced a 10 to 20 percent cost reduction with each doubling of output. These are large numbers compared with the numbers we've looked at so far. If increased openness does unlock greater scale economies in industries where they matter, then that's an added benefit that is left out of standard modeling efforts.

The third way trade can add value is through its role in *Differentiating* the products or services available to buyers, thereby improving their willingness to pay. CGE models do allow goods to be differentiated in a very particular way, by country of origin; otherwise, however, they focus, like most economic models, on costs as opposed to other product attributes. But as my thesis adviser, Nobel Prize winner Michael Spence, used to tell us in graduate school, differentiation is 90 percent of what business competition is about. In this context, trade can help expand variety, improve available quality, or promote upgrading over time.[16] And particularly for small countries, the very availability of a scale-sensitive product may hinge on integration with world markets. The cost of trade restrictions that lead to products being unavailable can be an order of magnitude larger than those associated with tariffs, that is, products being available at a higher cost.[17]

A fourth way more openness can add value is by *Intensifying competition.*[18] CGE models generally assume that competition within an industry is perfect: that it features many small businesses individually incapable of influencing market outcomes. Or occasionally, they allow for *monopolistic competition*: a slightly less perfect form of competition that involves some fixed costs, and, as a result, a large but finite number of differentiated producers, each with a limited amount of market power.[19] Models of monopolistic competition have been particularly helpful in understanding intraindustry trade in variety, with different varieties produced in a few (different) locations due to fixed set-up costs but then traded internationally to satisfy within-country preferences for diversity.[20] But they do not allow for concentrated industry structures featuring just a few competitors. The study of scale economies cited earlier and a lot of other research, not to mention common sense (think Toyota or Google), suggest that this is a bad idea: while not all parts of the economy are concentrated, some surely are.

With concentrated structures, there are very few competitors, in effect, and competition may become sluggish and market performance suffer due to high prices and—this is probably even more important—greater technical inefficiency. The question here is how greater openness affects this small-numbers problem. Both economic logic and empirical evidence suggest that openness generally helps allay the problem, as discussed at greater length in chapter 5. So does practical experience. Thus, at a WTO workshop in Geneva where I presented the ADDING value scorecard, my fellow panelist, Eduardo Pérez Motta, the head of the Competition Commission of Mexico and previously its envoy to the WTO, stressed the intensification of competition as perhaps *the* biggest benefit of trade liberalization, especially in a country rife with cozy domestic oligopolies.[21]

These arguments all focus on industry-level competition. Openness can also provide a tonic to competitive vitality in a broader sense. In closed economies, businesses and industries tend to lobby—and spend money on—securing purely pecuniary (and private) advantages from trade restrictions. Such "rent-seeking" uses up real resources but doesn't actually produce anything, and as such, represents a huge hidden cost of protectionism—and a huge benefit of openness. The classic example is Anne Krueger's estimate in the early 1970s that such pursuits may have swallowed up as much as 40 percent of Turkish GDP![22]

A fifth way openness can add value is by helping *Normalize risks.* Most models used to estimate the gains from opening up presuppose a risk-free world: economic agents are fully informed about future events, have access to a complete set of contingent markets, and can compute benefits and optimize across all courses of action. But to discuss issues of social welfare without taking risks into account seems, especially in the aftermath of a crisis, more than a bit limiting.

What my scorecard emphasizes is normalizing or balancing risks instead of simply trying to minimize them. This reflects a basic trade-off. In a world where markets are semiglobalized, diversification across national markets still washes out "unsystematic" risk, but connecting them up does create the risk of contagion. Minimizing one type of risk and ignoring the other usually doesn't make sense—even though there is a natural tendency to (over)emphasize contagion risk in the wake of a global economic crisis. I elaborate on these points and on the management of global risks in chapter 7. In addition to capital risks, chapter 7 focuses, within merchandise, on the risk-sensitive category of food grains—where market integration affords significant risk diversification benefits whereas moves to close off markets through measures such as export bans raise riskiness.

The sixth way trade can add economic value is by helping *Generate and diffuse knowledge* faster. Economists have been interested in technological progress, in particular, since Nobel Prize-winner Robert Solow's landmark finding more than half a century ago that productivity gains explain more than 80 percent of U.S. economic growth.[23] Standard estimates of the gains from trade liberalization have little to say about this engine of economic growth because they describe the differences between two "steady states" but don't really address changes over time.[24] Conceptually, though, openness should increase incentives to innovate by expanding the market and permit quicker diffusion of innovations. In addition, given cross-country diversity, openness might add to the creativity of the innovation process, as discussed later in this chapter. And finally, there is the argument about extra competitive pressure cited earlier.

It has long been known that imports of capital goods—machinery, equipment, and so forth—boost productivity by facilitating adoption of new technologies. More recent evidence suggests that imports—and inbound FDI—may facilitate innovation as well as imitation.[25] Exports (and outbound FDI) are correlated with rapid productivity growth as well, and the more recent evidence, in particular, suggests that this is partly because foreign markets serve as learning labs.[26] In addition, openness also seems to increase the rate at which more efficient firms replace less efficient ones. Since such turnover, especially among small firms, accounts for more productivity growth in countries such as the United States than upgrading by establishments that continue operating, this is no small matter.[27]

To fully appreciate the possibilities associated with a faster productivity growth rate over time, consider two initially identical countries, one of which liberalizes and one that does not. If liberalization yields a one-off gain of, say, 0.5 percent of GDP, then the country that liberalized will be 0.5 percent larger than the one that didn't—forever. But if liberalization yields 0.5 percent faster productivity growth, the country that liberalized will be 5 percent larger than the other in ten years, and more than 25 percent larger in fifty!

To conclude this section, recall that standard estimates of the economic gains from merchandise trade—for example, the 0.5 percent of global GDP cited earlier—focus on the first two components of the ADDING value scorecard, adding volume and decreasing costs, and omit the others. Including the other components (as well as exploiting the expanded set of policy levers identified in the previous section) should, to my mind, push the estimate well past 1 percent of global GDP, to 2–3 percent or more.

More speculatively, the expanded conception of value might afford a better handle on how openness could benefit developing countries in particular. As Pascal Lamy explained to me, most of the action in standard models of the gains from trade involves price reductions, effectively locking in the biggest benefits for those who spend the most—that is, rich countries. Greater emphasis on scale economies, differentiation, the intensity of competition, risks, and knowledge development, he felt, might increase not only assessments of the potential gains from trade but also affect the fraction estimated to accrue to developing countries.[28]

Not by Merchandise Trade Alone

The ADDING value scorecard can be applied not only to merchandise trade, but also to other types of cross-border flows. Services are the most obvious extension: they account for roughly two-thirds of global GDP but only one-fifth of global trade, leaving trade in services only about an eighth as intense as trade in merchandise. While some services are intrinsically untradable—think of the market for haircuts—services' overall level of trade intensity appears to be much lower than it could be. Policy restrictions are particularly pronounced in transportation and professional services.[29]

Service liberalization commitments require a sophisticated system of rules and regulation whose effects are hard to quantify. The few academic studies that have nonetheless attempted to calibrate their effects using CGE models tend to conclude that a given percentage cut in services barriers would produce greater gains than those from a comparable cut in merchandise trade barriers.[30] In addition, these studies, like the ones cited in the previous section, focus on a subset of the economic gains identified by the ADDING value scorecard and therefore presumably understate total economic gains. And finally, because of improvements in cross-border service delivery enabled by information technology, it is possible to argue that the potential gains from liberalizing trade in services are increasing over time—unlike the decreasing estimates for gains from merchandise trade liberalization cited at the beginning of this chapter.

Beyond trade in products and services, there are also cross-border flows of capital, people, and knowledge. Let's start with capital. It might seem strange to talk right now about the benefits of cross-border capital flows. But it is important to distinguish among different types of capital flows. Foreign direct investment (FDI)—foreign companies buying, setting up, or reinvesting in businesses in a country—represents a long-term commitment even if the rate at which such commitments are entered into varies greatly from year to year. FDI helps transfer knowledge and information as well as capital, and functions, like trade, as a channel for product market integration with the prospect of ADDING value just as broadly.[31]

Other cross-border capital flows offer a narrower set of gains focused on exploiting international differences in the cost and marginal productivity of capital as well as diversifying risk. Such flows are also capable, however, of increasing volatility, because they don't simply vary from year to year: they can and often do go into reverse. So such capital flows do have to be managed, although it is rarely optimal to manage them to zero. These points are discussed further in chapters 7 and 8. For now, I offer two conclusions. First, some degree of cross-border capital mobility makes fundamental sense despite contagion risk; managed properly, such capital flows add to rather than detract from the gains from globalization. And second, even if there was a move to staunch such flows or associated speculative activity, that would not eliminate the need exposed by the crisis for better cross-border coordination of financial markets. Such coordination would represent further finance-related globalization, albeit of another sort.

Turning next to cross-border labor flows, prior work suggests that the potential for gains is simply *enormous*. CGE-style estimates of the benefits to eliminating *all* restrictions on cross-border labor mobility are on the order of 100 percent of global GDP or more, rather than 1 percent![32] This will seem less surprising if we remember that productivity in rich countries is several dozen times as high as in poor ones. Migrants from poor countries to rich ones close a substantial part of that gap when they move and can take advantage of rich countries' superior capital, technology, and institutions—and contribute to those countries' general labor supply, specific skill/occupational categories, the diversity of goods and services available there, and levels of entrepreneurial activity.

Of course, some readers may object that complete liberalization simply isn't in the cards. Yes, but the real point is that even moderate relaxation of current restrictions on labor mobility might yield economic gains substantially larger than the other dimensions of opening up discussed so far. Estimates that assume more reasonable (i.e., restricted) liberalization of cross-border labor flows still predict gains of several percentage points of GDP.

That said, the readiness with which we can agree that complete labor liberalization is unlikely attests to the continued importance of barriers. These must be managed, but in a way that emphasizes integration—using some of the mechanisms for reducing cultural barriers discussed earlier—rather than interdiction. In other words, management isn't always code for moderation. Some developed countries, in particular, seem to have no real choice but to liberalize. Thus, the European Union is haunted by 50:50:50: the prediction that by 2050, 50 percent of its population will be fifty years old or older. Japan's demographics are even worse. The OECD has estimated that without large-scale immigration, U.S. living standards could drop by 10 percent, the EU's by 18 percent, and Japan's by 23 percent.[33] Again, these are very large numbers! The challenge of balancing labor supply and demand is discussed at greater length in chapter 8.

Finally, there is the matter of cross-border flows of knowledge. The flows already discussed can carry knowledge from nation to nation (whether embedded in traded products, transferred as a result of FDI, or vested in people), but knowledge can also move across borders in other ways (e.g., licensing, consulting, piracy). Also note that knowledge flows embody strong increasing returns to scale: unlike many other commodities, using knowledge in one place doesn't reduce the ability to use it elsewhere. (This is an example of a positive externality; negative externalities are tackled in chapter 6, with a focus on global warming.)

On the one hand, cross-border knowledge flows are clearly already significant: most countries are estimated to rely on foreign sources of technology for 90 percent or more of their productivity growth.[34] For small, poor countries, this percentage approaches 100 percent. And based on R&D expenditures, only one country, the United States, can plausibly be argued to depend more on domestic than on foreign technology development.[35]

On the other hand, knowledge is still quite localized. Thus, patents with inventors in different countries cite each other only 50 to 75 percent as much as patents with inventors in the same country.[36] And a study of G7 countries estimates that a dollar of foreign R&D is worth 74 cents of domestic R&D at distances under 2,000 kilometers (within North America or Europe), 37 cents at distances between 2,000 and 7,500 kilometers (between North America and Europe), and 5 cents at even larger distances (between Japan and the other parts of the "Triad").[37]

Attempts have also been made to unpack this distance effect. The G7 study concludes that trade, FDI, and language skills all serve as channels for international technology spillovers. A study of OECD countries emphasizes that the ease of doing business in a particular country and the quality of its tertiary education system raise both the productivity of its own R&D and international R&D spillovers.[38] And then there are issues of mind-set. Businesses, even within the same country, are notoriously prone to the "not invented here" syndrome—which is probably aggravated internationally by lack of familiarity and other cultural barriers discussed earlier. But the key point is that all these determinants of cross-border knowledge spillovers are amenable to policy influence.

To understand the magnitude of the potential gains, consider a stylized calculation that ignores the distance-related effects just discussed and buckets R&D into "domestic" and "foreign." An increase in cross-border spillovers by ten percentage points would overshadow domestic R&D efforts for all but the three top spenders on R&D—the United States, Japan, and China. Even for the United States, which accounts for over one-third of global R&D, the boost would come close to 20 percent of domestic spending. And of course, spillovers are even more vital for countries that are behind or are very small.

In summary, the potential economic gains from liberalizing cross-border labor flows are very large and those from boosting services trade and knowledge flows also seem significant. Added to the economic gains from liberalizing merchandise, they probably push the potential gains from opening up past 5 percent of global GDP. The additional cultural and political benefits discussed in the next section supply a further boost.

Beyond Economic Value

To assess the cultural gains from openness, one must take cultural differences—and preferences for cultural diversity—seriously. This clashes with economists' aversion to "unnecessary" differences. Thus, even Jagdish Bhagwati, the distinguished trade economist, has suggested that "if everyone's alike, of course you're better off economically."[39] Whatever the intent, the effect is to get people freaked out about cultural homogenization.

Such fears are unnecessary: as the last chapter indicated, cultural differences are alive and well in World 3.0, even between the United States and Canada. Chapter 11 elaborates on this point and on the potential for culture-related gains rather than just losses from increased interactions across cultural boundaries. One benefit is suggested by work in cognitive science on the advantages of different perspectives, frameworks, and the like—cognitive diversity—in prob-lem solving.[40] Given the international differences discussed in the previous chapter, national cultural diversity is likely to generate *lots* of cognitive diversity.

But that is still an economic benefit. Openness can also add to cul-tural variety through *inspiration* (e.g., African inspiration of New World music and, recently, reverse flows), *mixture* (e.g., creole languages), *transplantation plus adaptation* (e.g., Balti curries from Birmingham), or *transnationalization* (e.g., the culture joining the global scientific com-munity). Even more important, it can expand the variety available to individuals. As cultural economist Tyler Cowen notes, "Trade, even when it supports choice and diverse achievement, homogenizes culture in the following sense: it gives individuals, regardless of their country, a similarly rich set of consumption opportunities. It makes countries or societies 'commonly diverse' as opposed to making them different from each other."[41]

That sounds rather good from an individual perspective! In fact, a similar argument about the political benefits of openness—that it goes hand in hand with democracy and enriched political opportunities—has been made by people as diverse as Immanuel Kant, the philosopher; Joseph Schumpeter, the economist; and Seymour Martin Lipset, the political scientist. (Note that this has occurred without much fretting about the spread of democracy being unduly homogenizing.)

The possible connections between openness and democracy rely par-ticularly heavily on informational flows and include the freer exchange of ideas and increased political competition that result from openness, and the discouragement of autocracy by the transparency required to keep capital markets happy. While the actual connections aren't as clear as one would like, the weight of the evidence does suggest a positive relationship between trade and democracy.[42]

That last conclusion is subject to a particular caveat: democratizing a country afflicted by a high degree of inequality may lead to a backlash against globalization (e.g., Bolivia in recent times). For this reason and others, chapter 9 explores at length the connections between economic inequality and openness. Particularly worth stressing here is the suggestion that domestic entrenchment of the sort that a closed economy is more likely to spawn than an open one significantly impairs overall economic performance. Thus, one study found that country growth varied positively with the wealth of self-made billionaires but negatively with heir-controlled wealth.[43] In fact, high levels of the latter, typically found in countries with restrictions on inbound foreign direct investment, reduced growth by as much *two percentage points a year*! This is a huge effect, but its magnitude is less surprising if one recalls the earlier discussion of rent-seeking and its social costs.

In addition to its domestic political ramifications, cross-border integration also seems linked to international political harmony. Specifically, the parts of the world that are isolated economically have also experienced far more military interventions by outsiders. The simplest way to see this is to look at the map in figure 4-2. The shading captures the number of disputes that countries are involved in at the WTO, with the darkest indicating more than a hundred. And the dashed line is drawn around the locations of 95 percent of all U.S.

FIGURE 4-2

Trade frictions versus military frictions

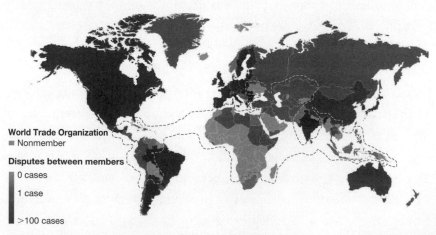

Source: Map shaded according to WTO disputes is from WTO website, http://www.wto.org/english/tratop_e/dispu_e/dispu_maps_e.htm; dashed line based on U.S. military interventions is from Thomas P. M. Barnett, *The Pentagon's New Map: War and Peace in the Twenty-First Century*, (New York: G.P. Putnam's Sons, 2004).

military interventions between 1990 and 2002.[44] The map suggests that economic engagement and military trouble tend to be substitutes: if you don't get the one, you get the other.

Thomas Barnett, a U.S. military strategist who originally drew the dashed line, moved to the U.S. Defense Department in the wake of September 11, 2001, where he devised a set of rules for the "Functioning Core," the relatively secure countries outside that line, to deal with the "Nonintegrating Gap," the more troubled countries within it:

> *First, we need to improve our immune-system response to 9/11-like shocks to the system that I like to call System Perturbations . . . Second, we need to firewall the Core off from the Gap's worst exports, like drugs, pandemics, terror . . . Third and most important tenet: the Core's big powers must come together to shrink the Gap progressively by tackling bad actors and security "sinkholes."* [45]

This security-first approach did supply a geopolitical justification for the Iraq war, but partly as a result, there seems to be little appetite for further investments in "exporting security" to the Gap. That leaves open the option of stressing economic integration instead—the approach advocated in this book. Such integration may not work everywhere in the Gap but it *can* be pursued selectively: there is a world of difference between, say, Somalia, which is stuck in World 0.0, and Senegal. Progress might help reduce annual global military spending of $1.6 billion, or 2.7 percent of global GDP. Not to mention risks to life and limb. These and other political benefits of openness will be elaborated—and political fears dispelled—in chapter 10.

In conclusion, recall that cultural and political suspicions about globalization—as well as about markets and other economic institutions—tend to vary inversely with how well people think they are doing economically. So tapping some of the potential gains from globalization that World 3.0 flags and that this chapter has tried to characterize more fully may be the best softener, in the long run, for general attitudes toward globalization.

All Together Now

Figure 4-3 summarizes the discussion so far as well as two additional considerations that favor further opening up. Let's examine these considerations in turn. First, pursuing more integration along one particular dimension can make it advantageous to push farther along other dimensions as well. While several such *complementarities* have already been mentioned in passing, it might help to look at a particular example in more detail. Take the link between trade and migration. One study suggests that doubling the number of immigrants from a particular country is associated with 9 percent higher imports from that nation.[46] This is a substantial effect given the typically small shares of migrants in the total population. It implies that labor liberalization, in addition to producing large direct gains, would also generate substantial indirect ones by boosting trade. Yet the latter don't figure in the estimated gains from labor liberalization cited earlier in this chapter.

FIGURE 4-3

ADDING value by opening up

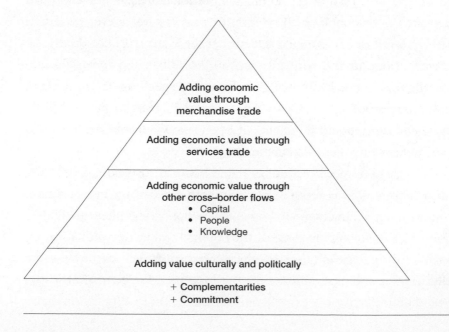

Adding economic
value through
merchandise trade

Adding economic value through
services trade

Adding economic value through
other cross-border flows
- Capital
- People
- Knowledge

Adding value culturally and politically

+ Complementarities
+ Commitment

More broadly, the existence of complementarities means that piece-meal evaluations of gains miss out on valuable cross-effects. To the extent that complementarities are important, the estimates discussed so far in this chapter are likely to understate the true potential associated with opening up further.

A second broad consideration that favors opening up further also involves links across choices—in this case, over time—in the form of a psychologically powerful *commitment* to reducing trade barriers. The nations of the world have sustained this commitment through several decades of global trade negotiations, a fact that in itself paves the way for future negotiations. A major setback, such as a failure to reach even a scaled-back agreement in the Doha trade talks, could signal a shift of momentum, making future gains harder to achieve. Policy expectations are important because trade doesn't just reflect day-to-day decisions based on spot market prices and tariffs. Rather, today's expectations drive long term commitments such as where factories are built, what relationships are cultivated, and even what children learn in school (and not just foreign languages) that shape the conditions of future cross-border engagement.[47]

In fact, given high unemployment and other macroeconomic pressures, the alternative to conclusion of the Doha round or, more broadly, continuing to move to increase cross-border integration might not be stagnation but reversion toward World 1.0. Illustrating the potential ramifications is a recent study that found that the costs of intensified protectionism might be "almost five times greater than the gains realized from trade creation resulting from the DDA [Doha]."[48] Because of large past reductions in tariffs, losses from rolling them back loom much larger than gains from further tariff reductions (although as noted earlier, many, many sources of gains other than tariff reductions exist).

Summing up, I reckon that the considerations covered in this chapter increase estimates of the potential for globalization-related gains from 0.5 percent of global GDP to more than ten times that. But the precise numbers one ends up with are highly subjective. More robustly, I hope I have established that the usual economic models miss many of the ways freer trade can create economic benefits, and they barely begin to account for the ways that freer flows of capital, people, and knowledge would increase world prosperity. It's also important to remember that the gains aren't all about economics: more cross-border exchange also offers cultural and political benefits. And complementarities and commitment are other factors to consider.

Particularly at a time when the general economic outlook remains weak, this creates a strong temptation to simply push the pedal to the metal. But not so fast. The discussion in this chapter has focused, as mentioned at the outset, on the potential gains from globalization, particularly those left out of CGE models. We also need to consider the omitted factors whose inclusion might tilt things the other way if we want to assess *net* gains rather than just upside potential.

One type of generalization emerges when we recall that CGE models assume perfect markets. They do not offer much of a basis, therefore, for addressing the fundamental question with which this book began: should the rediscovery of market failures—factors that can lead unregulated markets to inefficient outcomes—affect how we view the cross-border integration of markets?

The first few chapters of Part II of this book start to answer this question by analyzing how globalization affects standard types of market failures. Specifically, chapter 5 focuses on how globalization affects concentration problems; chapter 6 studies global externalities; chapter 7 delves into informational imperfections and their risk implications. Then chapter 8 looks at a nonstandard type of failure, global imbalances, in line with concerns that the financial crisis stirred about the self-stabilization properties of markets.

A second type of generalization involves market outcomes that, while unrelated to standard market failures, spark widespread concerns or, frankly, fears about globalization. As an empirical matter, these fears mostly seem to focus on deprivation of various sorts: economic, political, and cultural. Instead of simply shrugging off such fears, I consider them at some length. Chapter 9 focuses on globalization and economic inequality; chapter 10 on political fears about globalization that all involve political disenfranchisement or dependence in some sense; and chapter 11 on cultural fears, particularly fears of homogenization.

The tack taken in all the chapters in Part II is frankly empirical. While there *are* trade-theoretic models relevant to the issues discussed, they tend to suffer from the same basic problem as the CGE models discussed earlier: their emphasis on embedding market interactions within a general equilibrium framework limits their ability to treat market failures and fears. Thus, models that don't allow for concentrated market structures can't shed much light on whether openness might exacerbate producer concentration. Models of pure exchange with no money or capital offer no visibility into issues of capital contagion. Models in which trade always ends up being balanced do not lend themselves to exploration of the risks, if any, associated with imbalances. Models featuring full or at least fixed employment cannot credibly address concerns that openness will lead to domestic job losses. And so on, although work *is* under way on each of these problems.

Recognizing these limitations, I haven't attempted in this book to cite or test deductions from trade theory. Rather I've worked *inductively* through specific cases of market failures and fears, examining how they affect or are affected by a range of cross-border flows, including trade. In other words, I have used the case method developed at Harvard Business School, but with "cases" focused on specific issues that instantiate broader failures and fears—for instance, global warming as an example of the worst kind of externality or food price spikes as a particularly worrying example of the risk of global contagion. The point is not just to come up with specific policy recommendations grounded in reality for the issues considered, but to uncover broader patterns in the nexus between cross-border flows and market failures.

Of course, I'm not an expert on all the issues covered in chapters 5–11; in fact, the issue of global concentration that is addressed in chapter 5 is the only one on which I am recognized as an authority of any kind. Why read the other chapters? They offer concise, and I hope evenhanded treatments of some of the key issues of our times—anchored in and illuminated by the worldviews discussed in chapter 1. They therefore constitute a train of argumentation that readers who disagree or want to go farther can follow at least part of the way. And as noted above, they are an essential complement to the argument in this chapter that trade experts tend to think of the potential benefits from globalization too narrowly. Since trade models typically ignore market failures, it is plausible that they underestimate the potential costs of globalization as well as the benefits, leaving a bias of indeterminate direction—unless we actually try to size up the issues discussed in Part II.

To provide a brief preview of the conclusions: the bottom line from Part II is that the market failures and fears commonly cited as reasons to curb cross-border integration are overblown—and that where real dangers exist, so do preventive and corrective measures that typically do *not* involve closing off borders.

Part Two

Seven Possible Problems

Chapter Five

Global Concentration

Source: Terry Mosher/Aislin Inc.

HOW SHOULD the rediscovery of *market failures*—factors that can lead unregulated markets to inefficient or undesirable outcomes—affect how we think about markets' cross-border integration? This chapter focuses on one market failure that has come in for particular discussion in the context of globalization: small numbers of competitors, or high concentration. Both pro- and antiglobalizers associate globalization with what the late William Safire called "the norm of enormity": they believe that most industries are coming to be dominated by a small number of competitors as markets become more integrated.

This kind of concentration argument is not new. More than a hundred years ago, Karl Marx wrote, "One capitalist always kills many . . . [leading to] a constantly diminishing number of the magnates of capital, who usurp and monopolize all advantages."[1] Numerous antiglobalizers have rallied to this point of view. So, more oddly, have some proglobalization business types who should know better. During the 1970s, Boston Consulting Group founder Bruce Henderson promulgated his Rule of Three: "A stable competitive market never has more than three significant competitors."[2] In the early 1980s, Jack Welch seemed to reduce the magic number further with his widely remarked insistence that General Electric be either first or second in its various fields of business. And in the late 1990s, Mercer Management Consulting went to the winner-take-all extreme by popularizing the "plight of the silver medalist": You're either number one, or you're nowhere.[3] Obviously, the next level of hype is the Rule of Zero, in which no one, not even a monopolist, makes money (the eventuality Marx seems to have had in mind).

Many professional managers still buy into such notions. In an online survey I conducted before the global financial crisis, 58 percent of the several hundred managers who responded agreed that "globalization tends to make industries become more concentrated." In addition, 64 percent believed that "the truly global company should aim to compete everywhere." These results are yet another manifestation of the tendency toward globaloney and belief in World 2.0 that was discussed in chapter 2. If you feel that cross-country differences don't matter much, you probably find it much easier to think of multinational companies (MNCs) as a few colossi carrying the world on their broad shoulders—or in the case of antiglobalizers, as a few great vampire squid with their tentacles increasingly tightly wrapped around the face of humanity. Either way, a World 2.0 perspective goes hand in hand with a focus on global concentration levels and, as the surveys indicate, an expectation that those levels are increasing over time.

Much of the rhetoric about globalization leading to global monopolies or oligopolies is, as we shall see, overheated. Still, it is useful to start out by understanding why the possibility of concentration is worrisome. In perfectly competitive markets with many equally efficient firms, sellers can't raise prices above costs. As a result, products and services are available to consumers at the lowest possible prices that make production worthwhile for sellers. This is Adam Smith's famous invisible hand. By contrast, (some) economists worry that the few players in concentrated markets may possess *market power*, that is, be able to raise prices and profits at customers' expense and hurt social welfare. High, stable levels of concentration can also dampen entrepreneurial zeal: why try to start a new firm if the big guys rule? And then there are also concerns about how business concentration might affect political processes—concerns that are addressed in chapter 10.

This chapter focuses on how globalization affects the incidence of this kind of market failure rather than on its consequences. It shows that even if we focus on the global concentration measures preferred by World 2.0 enthusiasts (we'll critique these later in the chapter), there is no clear evidence that globalization leads to increasing industry concentration. In fact, in most situations, globalization appears to promote more competition, not more concentration. Furthermore, a focus on global concentration can miss out on the real market power problems, identification of which requires attention to distance sensitivity in defining the scope of markets. And when a concentration problem *is* diagnosed, domestic regulation is generally the recommended public policy response, rather than restrictions on cross-border competition. But we also need to be wary of too much government intervention: many restraints on competition are in fact due to governmental action rather than to its absence. It is useful to start out with a detailed case study that illustrates some of these points before developing them more generally.

Auto Delusions

The auto industry is a heavyweight sector that for many people epito-mizes big global companies. Five of the world's top twenty MNCs are automakers, more than any other sector except big oil.[4] And industry executives themselves have looked to global concentration as the wave of the future since at least the 1980s, when Fiat's chairman, Giovanni Agnelli, envisioned the industry as affording room for no more than six major players worldwide.

The top firms have yet to drive such changes through, however: as figure 5-1 shows, the share of the industry output that they control has, if anything, declined since 1970. Over longer time frames, the decline is even more pronounced. In 2010, the top six companies accounted for 50 percent of global auto production. Back in the 1970s, five companies did; in the 1950s, two; and in the 1920s, just one, Ford. Hardly a chroni-cle of concentration. And for those who worry about country rather than company concentration, the high point of hegemony was again back in the 1920s, when the United States accounted for 95 percent of world auto production![5] Overall, cross-border integration seems to have intensified competition in the auto industry rather than reduced it; that is, it has improved the *I* in the ADDING value scorecard. And in addi-tion to reducing bloated margins in formerly cozy oligopolies (e.g., in North America), it seems to have wrought real improvements in cost efficiencies, quality, and design.

If you find these concentration data surprising, you're not alone. When I've presented them to auto executives, disbelief has been the most common reaction. While the CGE modelers discussed in chapter 4 were prone to ignore economies of scale, business executives typically overestimate them. The standard example from the auto industry is the assertion that you can't make less than several million small cars and still be profitable. Yet I have trouble squaring this with the performance of an Indian automaker I know, Maruti Suzuki, which made a million cars

FIGURE 5-1

Global concentration levels in the auto industry

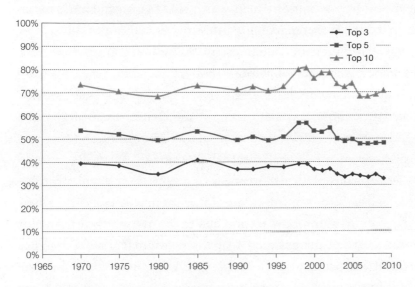

Source: 1970–1999 based on Center for Global Business Studies; 2000–2009 based on Organisation Internationale des Constructeurs d'Automobiles (OICA), http://oica.net/category/production-statistics/.

for the first time in 2009. Comparing Maruti with a sample of ten top automakers indicates that the former's profitability has exceeded its larger competitors' every year since 2004: its operating margin averaged 11 percent over 2004–2009, versus 6 percent for Honda and Toyota, the most profitable of the ten top competitors, and an average of 3 percent for the ten as a whole. At the same time, Maruti managed to expand unit production at a 13 percent annual clip, versus stagnant production for the top ten as a whole. Back in 2004, Maruti made and sold only *half* a million vehicles.[6]

How did Maruti outpace its larger rivals? Partly through the help with small-car technology that it receives from its Japanese parent, Suzuki. But Suzuki itself accounts for the production of only 2 million cars a year, which made it the world's tenth-largest automaker in the world in 2009. So while the Maruti Suzuki link might narrow the scale-based disadvantage that Maruti faces versus larger players, it shouldn't, by itself, lead to superior performance.

The most obvious part of the answer is that Maruti still holds nearly 50 percent of the Indian market for automobiles, although that number is coming under pressure as interest in that market intensifies. Local scale/share clearly counts for more than global scale when it comes to localized production, distribution, marketing, and postsales service. The more general point is that except in the extreme case of zero distance and border effects (World 2.0), local market position and structure still matter—even in a "global" industry like autos.

The less obvious part of the answer has to do with how Maruti has managed its early mover advantage in applying, in the early 1980s, up-to-date foreign automotive technology to the Indian market. A highly politicized joint venture between a Japanese automaker and the Indian government was not necessarily fated to succeed. Ever since I met him nearly twenty years ago, I have been struck by the ability of Maruti Suzuki's long-time managing director and chairman, R. C. Bhargava, to negotiate a minefield of competing interests while overseeing a gradual but inevitable migration of capabilities and decision making from the Japanese parent to the Indian jewel in its crown. The game isn't just about scale or other structural factors: management matters, even and perhaps especially in the "public" sector.

Global Concentration Increases That Weren't

Looking beyond the auto industry, how globally concentrated have industries generally become over the last few decades? While there are no comprehensive data on this topic, I have for more than a decade now (mostly in collaboration with Georgetown University's Fariborz Ghadar) been tracking global concentration levels for selected industries and writing about the patterns in those data. This chapter will summarize some of this earlier work as well as check whether the conclusions from it continue to hold up.

In 2000, Ghadar and I published an article in *Harvard Business Review* presenting detailed concentration data on three industries: auto production, oil production, and aluminum smelting. We argued that despite feverish merger and acquisition activity in these industries, the hype about global consolidation seemed overblown. While all three had experienced some increases in concentration between the late 1980s and the late 1990s, that trend seemed modest compared to the large *decreases* in concentration experienced by these industries since the early 1970s—and the even larger ones since World War II.[7]

In a 2006 article, Ghadar and I followed up by adding eight other industries to the three we had discussed previously.[8] These eight were selected because global concentration data were available in volume terms (as opposed to revenue terms) for ten to fifteen years over the 1980s and 1990s.[9] Of them, four showed increases in the five-firm concentration ratio: carbonated soft drinks, cement, steel, and paper and board. And four showed decreases: cargo airlines, copper, iron ore, and passenger airlines. Overall, average global concentration in the eleven-industry sample increased slightly between the 1980s and the late 1990s, from 35 percent to 38 percent. But as in the case of autos, changes since the 1980s were greatly overshadowed by the decreases reported since 1950 by the seven industries out of the eleven for which data were available. We concluded that rising hype about global consolidation was not matched by actual changes in global concentration levels—and that over longer time frames, global concentration appeared to have declined steeply![10]

Updating the analysis to include changes in concentration levels between the late 1990s and the late 2000s, I find that the average five-firm concentration ratio for the eleven industry sample has *fallen*, from 38 percent to 35 percent. In other words, the increase in average concentration between the 1980s and the late 1990s has been exactly reversed. Figure 5-2 combines these two time periods to depict industry-by-industry changes.

Note from the figure that carbonated soft drinks, which had a relatively high global concentration level to begin with, reported the

FIGURE 5-2

Changes in five-firm global concentration ratios (C5) since the 1980s

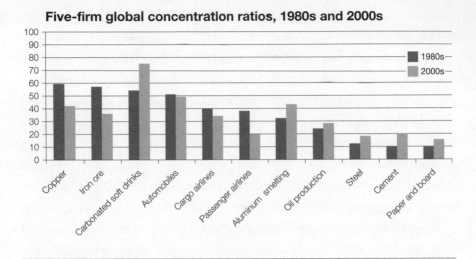

Five-firm global concentration ratios, 1980s and 2000s

greatest increase in global concentration. Otherwise, however, all industries with initial concentration levels above the median reported concentration decreases, and all industries with initial concentration levels below the median reported concentration increases. This suggests that even if the average remains the same, outliers tend to regress back toward it over time. This presents, once again, a more vibrant picture of competition than if the average stayed the same but industries that were already relatively concentrated became even more so.

The soft drink industry, the one exception to that rule, does raise the concern that the preceding conclusions may have been swayed by the sample's bias toward commodities rather than differentiated industries—especially because economists think that differentiated industries offer more room for large companies to dominate small ones by ramping up marketing outlays, and for concentrated industry structures to emerge as a result.[11]

To address this concern, I went beyond the eleven industries mentioned above and assembled Euromonitor data for thirty-seven (other) consumer goods industries. I found that the average five-firm concentration ratio did increase slightly—from 32 percent in the early 2000s to 35 percent toward the end of the decade. But this exactly matches the increase experienced by the eleven-industry sample between the 1980s and the 1990s—and since reversed.[12] In addition, a recent study of market share changes in more than a hundred categories of food products found that the three-firm concentration ratio was as likely to decrease as to increase.[13] Besides, the basic mechanism of concern to economists—increases in advertising outlays squeezing out the smaller players—seems unlikely to apply at a global level given cross-country differences and the consequent dearth of global advertising campaigns in consumer products. None of this creates a strong sense of globalization leading to large increases in concentration in consumer goods industries.

The technology sector comprises another important area of the economy unrepresented in my original sample of eleven. Here the escalated investment in, say, R&D that might increase concentration does have plausibly global effects for many products (unlike escalated advertising spending). The classic if extreme example is the color film revolution in photography. Opportunities to improve black-and-white film had largely been tapped out by the 1960s as the technology matured. But the increasing consumer preference for color film, which requires physical and chemical interactions of a dozen or more layers of emulsions, triggered an intense R&D race. Kodak, the industry leader, won the race by outspending its competitors. Until the next big technological shift, to digital photography, Kodak and Fuji remained the top two global competitors at the cutting edge of photo technology. Note that while global seller concentration rose, so did global consumer surplus from better picture quality.[14]

Of course, what digital photography has since done to film photography is a reminder that the high-tech sector tends to be particularly subject to creative destruction, in which innovations drive economic growth by creating value at the same time that they destroy the value of the sources of market power possessed by established firms (and their workers). In 2005, Kodak still sold $15 billion in film; 2010 sales of film to consumers were projected to be less than $200 million, which would mean nearly a 99 percent drop-off in five years.[15] Note that competition of a new kind is what ultimately destroyed Kodak's market power, not competition in kind.

Competition of new kinds shifts and blurs industry boundaries, complicating attempts to compile meaningful concentration data over time. Still, computations by the *Economist* indicate that between 1988 and 1998, the top five high-tech companies' combined share of global revenues in each of three broad information industries—long-distance telephony, computer software, and computer hardware—declined by fifteen to thirty percentage points! Since then, based on my work in and knowledge of this sector, long-distance telephony has gotten less concentrated, as have software services, although specific software products and offerings *may* have become more concentrated. And computer hardware has been transformed beyond recognition by, among other things, integration with communications products, but there is no current counterpart to the way IBM dominated hardware in the era of computer mainframes.

Of course, we can all think of "exceptions": high-tech companies that *have* accumulated significant market shares and, presumably, market power, in specific lines of business in recent years. Dominant positions in information industries are often built on network externalities, which imply that individual willingness to pay for a product or service increases with the number of other people using it (e.g., Google in search or Facebook in social networking).

Such information monopolies raise real policy issues—as do all "natural monopolies" or situations disposed to winner-take-all outcomes—that will be addressed later in this chapter, when we look at policy responses. But in assessing how concerned to be about such industries, one has to remember to give the process of creative destruction its due. As Joseph Schumpeter put it, "Competition from the new commodity, the new technology, the new type of organization . . . is as much more effective than the other [competition of the same kind] as a bombardment is in comparison with forcing a door."[16]

In 1998, when the *Economist's* tech concentration data ends, Microsoft was seen as the big bad wolf, with no major competitor in view. Google wasn't at all visible then since it was literally incorporated in a garage that year. Since then, however, it has replaced Microsoft as the company that makes many nervous. Without being able to predict future disruptions, it's a safe bet that there will be some, especially in the technology-driven part of the economy. These represent competition of a different kind rather than competition in kind—a source of competitive pressure that slips through the nets of concentration measures.

Beyond Changes in Global Concentration

The last section should have laid to rest the concern that fewer and fewer competitors are fated to control global markets as a result of global integration. If I wanted simply to debunk World 2.0, we could stop right here. But my objective is more ambitious: to point the way ahead. That means also explaining why we need to move beyond a focus on global concentration levels, and how the World 3.0 notions of cross-country differences and distance sensitivity can help in this regard.

To understand the limitations of global concentration levels, take another look at figure 5-2, and in particular, at an industry reporting a big decrease, iron ore.[17] Despite that, more ink seems to have been spilled about concentration in iron ore than any of the ten other industries in the sample—including carbonated soft drinks, which registered the biggest *increase* in concentration. Why the asymmetry?

High and increasing global concentration levels haven't prompted much concern in carbonated soft drinks because, as former Coca-Cola CEO Douglas Daft put it, "No one drinks globally. Local people get thirsty and go to their retailer and buy a locally made Coke."[18] Competition occurs market by market and even if concentration becomes an issue, it does so at the national or regional level, not the global level.

Iron ore, by contrast, is less sensitive to culture and geography. Indeed, when it comes to sensitivity to language differences and physical distance, iron ore ranks in the bottom quintile of all industries. The top three producers, Vale, BHP Billiton, and Rio Tinto, control 35 percent of world production in 2009 and, more significantly, 61 percent of seaborne trade.[19] As a result, this triopoly possesses substantial market power in the globally traded segment, where it has been very aggressive in raising prices. And regulators are the main reason there isn't even more concentration: opposition by the European Commission, among others, helped derail both a hostile takeover bid for Rio Tinto by BHP, and a plan to pool their west Australian assets to save on infrastructure and overhead that might also have made it easier for them to coordinate on higher prices.

To summarize, global concentration may be high in soft drinks, but concern about it is mitigated by the fact that distance sensitivity tends to be high as well, separating global markets into local markets. Global concentration levels are lower in iron ore (albeit still high in absolute terms), yet spark more concern because distance sensitivity is limited. So instead of looking just at changes in concentration levels, we must look at concentration levels *and* distance, since the problematic situations are the ones where the global concentration level is high *and* distance effects are low.

These and other examples also underline the need to take multiple dimensions of distance into account in deciding whether to calculate concentration at the global, regional, or national levels. (World 2.0 always assumes the first of these possibilities, and World 1.0 the last one.) This, effectively, is what some of the governmental agencies charged with preserving competition—and, particularly, ruling on mergers— have figured out. Thus, the European Commission has historically looked at not just one factor but at several "sources of globalization" and "revealed measures of globalization"[20] to define market boundaries. While these are usually presented as a mishmash, table 5-1 regroups them to highlight the correspondence with some of the dimensions of distance presented in the CAGE distance framework in table 3-1.

TABLE 5-1

Factors assessed by the European Commission in defining the relevant geographic market

Cultural distance	Administrative distance	Geographic distance	Economic distance
• Consumer preferences/brand loyalty	• Local specification requirements	• Transport costs	• Potential competition
• Language, culure, lifestyle	• Regulatory barriers to market inter-penetration	• Cross-border import, distribution and marketing infrastructure	• Price differences
			• Large market share differences

Source: Leo Sleuwaegen, Isabelle De Voldere, and Enrico Pennings, "The Implications of Globalization for the Definition of the Relevant Geographic Market in Competition and Competitiveness Analysis," final report, January 2001.

U.S. competition policy has historically been even less structured in this regard: a 1996 report by the U.S. Federal Trade Commission concluded that "geographic markets should be defined to include foreign supply response as appropriate, giving due regard both to actual barriers to trade and to the increasing trend towards the globalization of trade and services."[21] While it is hard to argue with the invocation of barriers and levels of cross-border integration, it leaves even more room for discretion—and arbitrariness—in this regard than the European Commission's guidelines.

What are more interesting are the revised merger guidelines issued in 2010 by the U.S. authorities, which downplay the traditional focus on market definition and concentration levels in favor of evaluation of the likely anticompetitive effects, if any, of proposed transactions on price levels and innovation rates.[22] From a globalization-related perspective, these revisions dictate a shift from thinking about how opening up affects industry concentration (the focus of the cartoon with which this chapter began) to how it affects competitive intensity and market outcomes. This is important because competitive intensity can go up at the same time as concentration, rather than being inversely related. An example is provided by the major home appliance industry, in which the five-firm concentration ratio has increased from 30 to 32 percent since 2000. But the relationship between size and performance is even more negative in this sector than in autos, with the two largest players (and consolidators), Whirlpool and Electrolux, lagging most of the other players in the top ten in terms of growth as well as profitability, and depressing overall profitability as well.

These problems reflect the consolidators' mistaken belief that consumers everywhere will want the same thing—which somehow obscured the reality of still having to offer them thousands of varieties (more than fifteen thousand at one point for Electrolux). Some of the variety reflects significant domestic differences in preference over color, material, size, energy efficiency, noisiness, other aspects of environmental friendliness, basic layout, controls, and so on. But consolidators like Whirlpool and Electrolux face the additional challenges of dealing with the cross-border differences that are summarized in table 5-2.

Most of these categories are obvious, but the cultural differences, in particular, are worth elaborating. Most obviously, differences in national cuisines significantly impact demand in a number of appliance categories. For example, compared to U.S. refrigerator buyers, Germans want more space for meat, Italians prefer special compartments for vegetables, and Indian families, with a mix of vegetarians and nonvegetarians, require internal seals to stop food smells from mingling. To hold Christmas turkeys, ovens are larger in England than in Germany, where geese are cooked. Germans also don't need self-cleaning ovens since they cook at lower temperatures than the French do. And Indian households tend not to need ovens at all.

Then there are cultural differences that, while hard to explain, are undeniable, such as the preferences for top-loading washers in some countries and front-loading washers in others. Furthermore, preferences concerning older categories of home appliances are

TABLE 5-2

Cross-border differences that drive variety in major home appliances

Cultural differences	Administrative differences	Geographic differences	Economic differences
• Taste variations	• Electrical standards: plugs, voltages, cycles	• Climate: temperature, sunshine	• Income levels
• Mostly mature products	• Environmental and other regulations	• Bulk or low value-to-weight ratios	• Rate of new household formation
• No cross-border demonstration effects	• Protectionism (e.g., 20% tariffs into U.S)		• Price/availability of substitutes or complements (space, electricity, etc.)

relatively well formed. As one marketing expert put it, "The home is the most culture-bound part of one's life. Consumers in Paris don't care what kind of refrigerator they are using in New York."[23] And note that this discussion has focused on just the cultural differences that affect demand for variety across countries—not all the ones that make cross-border management in this industry challenging (e.g., the linguistic differences underlying the infamous "Nothing sucks like an Electrolux" advertising campaign for vacuum cleaners in the United States).

Given all these differences, markets are still national or regional for most major home appliances—as they still are for many manufactured products and most services, as discussed in chapters 2 and 3. In such situations, concerns about global concentration are unwarranted, whether it is going up or not. But governments have intervened in home appliances to impede not only imports but also takeover attempts by foreign producers, when they should have focused on how opening up influences prices and productivity growth. More appropriate governmental policies are the focus of the next section.

Toward a More Competitive World

The chapter began by focusing on global concentration measures of the sort that many proglobalizers as well as antiglobalizers believe are going up as markets become more integrated. The available evidence, while partial, indicates no general tendency of this sort: while some industries exhibit increases in global concentration, others exhibit decreases, leaving average concentration levels (for the sample of industries for which I have data) more or less unchanged since the 1980s. And looking even farther back in time at the industries for which data are available suggests very steep declines in global concentration since 1950.[24] In addition, the fact that executives in autos (and a number of other industries) seem unaware of how concentration has evolved over time *within their own industries* underlines the point made earlier about data-free discussions of globalization and its effects. Clearly, even partial data are better than none.

Thinking through how concentration affects market power further narrows the scope of the concentration-related problems that could be caused by opening up. A focus on global concentration fits with a perfectly integrated World 2.0—but not with a semiglobalized World 3.0. Given the general diagnosis of semiglobalization, choosing whether to measure concentration at the global, regional, or national level requires assessing how sensitive a specific industry is to distance of various sorts. Concentration at the global level, as opposed to lower levels of aggregation, is the appropriate focus only when distance sensitivity is low.

Additionally, even if concentration measured appropriately is high or increasing, that *need not* indicate an absence of competition. In some situations, even two competitors can be a large number. Think, for instance, about the "airliner wars" between Boeing and Airbus. The high fixed costs associated with developing new aircraft now run into tens of billions of dollars, creating a very large wedge between full costs and marginal costs—and a lot of room for prices to fall. These tendencies are amplified by the cyclicality of the industry and the price sensitivity of the airline customers who, as a group, fail to cover their full costs in most years. In addition, the noncommercial objectives of the two players (and the governments that subsidize them) and the high corporate stakes, given that both are focused on aerospace and can't easily get out of each other's way, put further pressure on pricing. And finally, there is the simple fact that the two players have a high degree of antagonism toward each other. For all these reasons, one expects tough rather than soft competition between the two.

The more general point is that instead of focusing on concentration, one needs to look more broadly at industry structure—and if there is a small number of competitors, at their profiles as well. Industrial organization (IO) economists have long emphasized the importance of structural analysis that goes beyond a focus on the number and size distribution of competitors. And business economists, most prominently Michael Porter, have extended IO's list of structural determinants of rivalry—and added an emphasis on behavioral determinants as well. I should add that these aren't just academic niceties. Such frameworks for industry and competitive analysis are what many business school students get taught—and what many businesses actually employ to analyze their competitive environment.[25]

From a globalization-related perspective, then, the key public policy issue is how opening up is likely to affect overall competitive intensity rather than just concentration. As discussed in the previous chapter, cross-border integration almost invariably intensifies competition, that is, improves the *I* in the ADDING value scorecard. And the example of autos discussed in this chapter indicates that in addition to reducing bloated margins in formerly cozy oligopolies (e.g., in North America), cross-border integration seems to have wrought real improvements in cost efficiencies, quality, and design over time—which can be thought of as improving some of the other components of the ADDING value scorecard as well.

None of this is meant to suggest that there aren't some hard cases— some situations, typically characterized by high concentration and low distance sensitivity, where opening up does not, by itself, adequately address structural problems or barriers to competition. Thus in the airliner industry, Airbus is a direct result of investments by European governments aimed at creating some competition for Boeing. In the case of iron ore, big steelmakers and steelmaking countries have responded by looking for new sources of supply around the world, effectively increasing cross-border integration rather than closing off borders. While this solution will take some time to work, an influential United Nations study sees a surge in global iron ore supplies from 2012 onward, and a drop in prices.[26]

To take another example that has generated many headlines, rare earths are a set of seventeen natural elements that are required in small quantities in electronics displays and a variety of green technologies. China accounts for 37 percent of the world's proven reserves but 95 percent of world output.[27] This dominance dates back to heavy Chinese investments in rare earth production in the 1980s that flooded world markets, depressing prices and inducing mines in the United States and elsewhere, already under pressure because of their environmental impact, to shut down. Perhaps this was just what Deng Xiaoping had in mind when he said, "Arabia has oil, China has rare earth."[28]

But what initially looked like a bargain for the rest of the world—import cheap materials and let China deal with the pollution—has turned increasingly sour as China has begun exercising its market power. China began cutting exports in 2006 and reduced its export quota by 40 percent in July 2010, causing prices outside China to soar.[29] The Chinese justify these moves on the basis of environmental protection, but foreign critics allege their real aim has been to pressure manufacturers of products containing rare earths to move production to China. In late 2010, tensions rose sharply as a territorial dispute with Japan led to shipments there and, later, to the West, to be held up in Chinese ports.[30]

The race is on now to rebuild a supply chain not controlled by the Chinese, but that may take a decade or longer and require some cross-border restrictions (e.g., on acquisitions of U.S. mines by Chinese competitors). But the point, as in iron ore, is not to turn one's back on globalization. Thus, Japan, which had already started an aggressive rare earth recycling program, agreed in late 2010 to partner with Vietnam on developing production there.[31] More broadly, trade in rare earths will continue to be important in the long run because of the uneven distribution of reserves and the efficiency and environmental benefits of concentrating production at larger, more sophisticated mines.

But in most problematic cases, especially ones where distance sensitivity isn't as low, one doesn't need to set up new competitors to address structural problems: more standard policy instruments such as antitrust policy and price regulation should suffice. And remember that the total incidence of problematic cases is far fewer than globaloney-based intuitions would suggest.

Having pointed out the potential benefits—in a few cases—of governmental intervention aimed at containing or reducing market power, it is important to add that national governments actually do much to *compound* market power. In iron ore, Australia and Brazil are interested in keeping prices high, at the expense of (mostly foreign) customers and global welfare, because that fattens governmental tax revenues as well as mining companies' profits. In rare earths, the problem is not company concentration but country concentration and governmental muscle flexing. In a number of other natural resource sectors, governments actually rely on formal export cartels: OPEC provides a multilateral example and the American Natural Soda Ash Corporation a unilateral one.

In agriculture, one finds not only export cartels (which can be rationalized at least in terms of national self-interest), but also protection of a sort that hurts national as well as global welfare by restricting competition. Think back to the restrictions on sugar imports discussed in chapter 3, which help U.S. sugar producers but impose much larger costs on the rest of the U.S. economy. Protectionism based on tariffs and quotas is less visible in manufacturing and services but administrative barriers such as differences in standards, red tape, and processing delays loom large, particularly in services, where commitments to liberalization are intrinsically complex to set up and enforce.[32] In addition, foreign ownership is often restricted in "sensitive" sectors such as defense and media.

An ironic footnote: some of the most explicit restraints on cross-border competition are to be encountered in services that are vital to globalization such as air travel (where entry is often restricted by bilateral aviation treaties) and ocean shipping (where pricing is cartelized).

More controversially, intellectual property (IP) laws can also be seen as governmentally enforced restrictions on competition. The justification for such laws is clear—to ensure incentives for the development of IP. Still, economists are very clear that this is not a first-best solution: once knowledge has been developed, its use by one person or entity doesn't affect others' ability to use it as well, so unrestricted use is what would maximize social welfare. In fact, this is why Thomas Jefferson, the first overseer of U.S. patent policy, originally opposed the granting of any patent protection at all—before settling on protections much more limited than those currently in place. And when one sees phenomena such as thirty-nine pharmaceutical companies suing the South African government for violating their patents on exorbitantly priced anti-HIV retrovirals, or companies trying to patent traditional knowledge of the curative properties of Amazonian plants or patent trolls trying to hold up or even wreck collaborative efforts like Linux, one starts to realize that treating IP rights as absolute for the (limited) duration may not even be a second-best solution.

Also keep in mind that many governmental entities (e.g., public enterprises) and processes (e.g., public procurement) are largely if not entirely exempt from the bracing effects of competition. Layer on top of that the possibilities of inert, incompetent, or venal bureaucrats—a possibility particularly emphasized by the Chicago school given its faith in the irreducible selfishness and, frankly, amorality of human nature—and you are handed a reminder of the limits to regulation. Market failures have to be balanced against governmental failures.

All this suggests that while a government may need to intervene in market processes to preserve competition, it must be very careful that it doesn't end up becoming the principal restraint on competition. And despite the paranoia on display in the cartoon at the beginning of this chapter, openness isn't part of the problem but a key part of the solution. It generally increases the effective number of competitors, and therefore enables competition instead of inhibiting it.

Thus, openness often reduces the need for regulation. Any remaining problems with concentration or, to be more exact, the intensity of competition can, in highly distance-sensitive industries, generally be addressed within the domestic sphere. Low distance sensitivity, in contrast, while relatively rare, may require regulation at the border, or across borders. But in both cases, the possibility of governmental failures suggests a highly focused approach to trying to regulate small-numbers problems. In particular, when dealing with natural monopolies or oligopolies—situations in which small numbers reflect real efficiencies— cures that impair efficiency may be worse than the conditions they are trying to alleviate. For example, instead of breaking up a natural monopoly, it is usually better to subject it to price regulation.[33]

This emphasis on openness distinguishes World 3.0 from World 1.0, and the emphasis on regulation distinguishes it from World 2.0: note the broad principle that government has dual functions in World 3.0. The specific prescriptions presented here prefigure some of the more general ones that will emerge as we look in the next few chapters at other market failures and fears. But for now, we can check off at least one argument in the antiglobalizer's tool box as more of a molehill (if that) than a mountain. Far from being harmful, globalization is generally a huge help in dealing with small-number problems—in the limited number of situations where they *are* a real concern.

Chapter Six

Global Externalities

Source: Arcadio

THIS CHAPTER considers a second form of market failure that globalization is charged with exacerbating: externalities—specifically, environmental externalities. The cartoon deftly captures the antiglobalization screed that globalization is causing an ecological catastrophe, and adds the twist that that benefits business.

The underlying idea is that market transactions fail to price in harms ranging from air and water pollution to depletion of natural resource stocks to global warming. And as a result of this *externalization* of ecological harms, we see too much of them.

Environmentalists have devised rather varied responses to this ecological meltdown. Many deploy a World 2.0 mind-set, at least in terms of their focus on cross-border phenomena (they don't like the unregulated markets of World 2.0): they call for global accords while often railing against multinational companies and multilateral institutions such as the World Trade Organization (WTO) and treating international summits as important venues for protest. There is also a "dark green" fringe that seems inclined to return to World 0.0's local self-sufficiency and to end cross-border trade, especially in food products. Appeals for national standards and national enforcement, à la World 1.0, are also common, but these tend to have less novelty value.

The sound and fury of dramatic protests—amplified by our emotional connection to "mother" nature—have cast significant haze (or shall I say smog) over environmental issues. The globalization bogeyman, in particular, is overdrawn. Most ecological problems still reside within countries or their immediate neighbors, making them amenable to regulation via the usual World 1.0 structures. And globalization's effects on the environment itself are mixed. For some pollutants and in some places, trade and cross-border integration probably make the environment cleaner, while in other cases they make the environment dirtier.

The toughest cases to deal with from a policy perspective, irrespective of their causes, are the ones in which the environmental effects are highly negative *and* externalized, as in insensitive to distance. The potential for global warming as a result of greenhouse gas emissions is *the* example. But addressing such problems requires *more* cross-border coordination of policies, not less—albeit in more varied, imaginative ways than the World 2.0–inspired approach attempted at the Copenhagen Climate Change Summit of assembling 190 countries and expecting them to reach a legally binding agreement with bite. And it is worth adding that green innovation—with businesses presumably playing an important part and globalization providing high-powered incentives—is likely to be a central component of any feasible solution. Otherwise, preserving the environment would require a significant proportion of the world's population to take a permanent vow of poverty.

The World 3.0 approach to the environment starts with market failures due to environmental externalities, superimposes on them an understanding of the geography of pollution (using, among other things, the notion of distance sensitivity), and seeks to identify and improve globalization's environmental effects, positive and negative. It does so, in part, by suggesting how countries can work together to address environmental harms in ways that more fully account for large differences in their positions and interests on key issues—and also reflect different possible ways of structuring their interactions.

Bad Externalities

Externalities arise when the price paid for something doesn't account for all the costs and benefits for all the people actually affected by the transaction. Positive or good externalities involve important uninternalized benefits, such as the knowledge spillovers discussed in chapter 4. And negative or bad externalities involve important uninternalized costs, of which pollution and other environmental harms are leading examples.

Let me start with a very simple example of a negative externality. Say I run a homemade peanut butter–making business in my apartment. In my homestyle manufacturing process, I manually deshell all the peanuts and throw the shells out my window before grinding up the peanuts and making peanut butter. In the absence of any regulation, I can throw the shells out the window for free, so the price at which I'm willing to sell peanut butter doesn't have to account for the cost of cleaning up the mess I leave on my downstairs neighbor's balcony and on the street below. I offer you a good price and you enjoy my delicious peanut butter. Considering all of the costs and benefits "internal" to the transaction, we are both satisfied. But the "external" effects on my neighbors (not parties to our transaction) make them decidedly unhappy. Our little transaction has a negative "externality."

When externalities crop up, there are two basic ways of solving the problem. One option is changing ownership of the resources involved so as to internalize the externality—in this example, by making me buy the whole apartment complex and the street below, so I myself bear the cost of the mess I make. Alas, that's not feasible in this case, because I can't afford to buy up the whole area, and I certainly won't be given it for free. The other approach is to create a regulation that changes my incentives, like a tax that pays for the cost of cleaning up my mess or a rule that says nobody is allowed to throw garbage out the window. Either way, some regulatory authority must set and enforce a policy ensuring that I bear the full costs of my polluting production process. If I have to bear the full costs, I will have to increase my price, reducing my sales and shell volume, or change my production process. If the penalty is stiff enough, I will be forced to clean up or shut down.

In this homely example, some authority, ranging from my apartment association to the government, might be expected to act to restrict my behavior if it generates enough outrage. But what if I live on a national border and my peanut shells fall into another country? Or what if I power my peanut grinder by cutting down tropical rainforests and burning the trees, so my production process contributes to global warming? In those cases, my government is unlikely to solve the problem alone. In fact, my government might actually be *happy* for me to pollute some other country if it helps our national economy. Worse still, what if my country prohibits me from creating a mess at home but the country across the street lets me go ahead and pollute there for free, so that I move my little factory there and export the peanut butter back home? And what if somebody like the WTO forces my home country to accept the peanut butter I import from across the street even when my fellow citizens and our government already made it clear they don't want to contribute to such environmental destruction?

There are many variations on this problem but the same fundamental market failure underlies all of them: if I can harm someone else without bearing the costs, I'm likely to keep doing so until some authority steps in to fix the problem. And when these kinds of harms cross borders, governments have to coordinate their responses to address them effectively. The more governments that need to be involved and the more diverse their interests, the harder it is to achieve effective regulation. This phenomenon creates the *potential* for globalization to harm the environment. Whether that actually happens or not is the question to which I turn next.

The Direct Effects of Globalization

Globalization's most obvious direct environmental impact involves pollution caused by transporting goods and people between countries. Transportation accounted for 23 percent of energy-related CO_2 emissions in 2004,[1] or more broadly, 13 percent of all human-caused greenhouse gas emissions in the same year.[2] Yet most of those emissions reflected *domestic* transportation. A full 74 percent of transport-related emissions were caused by ground transportation,[3] mainly from trips within the borders of a given country. International aviation and marine transportation accounted for 6 and 9 percent of transport-related CO_2 emissions respectively in 2007.[4] Multiplying all this out, international air and sea transport emissions, those most directly traceable to globalization, were 1.4 and 2.1 percent of total energy-related CO_2 emissions respectively (and an even smaller proportion of human-caused greenhouse gas emissions).

Given all the concern about the environmental impact of moving products and people over long distances, let's dig a little bit deeper into international shipping and air transport, starting with international shipping of products, which embodies the most direct environmental impact of merchandise trade. According to the WTO, "90 percent of global merchandise trade by volume is transported by sea, and the bulk of CO_2 emissions in the transport sector comes from road transport, [so] international trade does not seem to play a major role in the generation of emissions from the transport sector."[5] Other sources put maritime transport's impact at a level similar to the one cited above. The International Maritime Organization estimates that international shipping produced 2.7 percent of world CO_2 emissions in 2007 (and maritime shipping 3.3 percent overall).[6] On a per-ton-kilometer basis, a cargo ship emits only 15–21 grams of CO_2, compared to a heavy truck and trailer's 50 grams and a jumbo jet's 550 grams on a 1,200-kilometer flight.[7] Environmental damage therefore varies greatly based on mode of transportation, not just the distance over which goods are transported. Something carried a very long distance across the ocean may actually cause less harm than something transported a shorter distance over land.

Given marine transport's importance to globalization, it's also worth noting other environmental harms stemming from shipping cargo around the world. One particular focus in the shipping industry has been oil spills, whose incidence has come down significantly since the 1970s. Regulations have also been put in place to limit releases of other pollutants and to address the unintended transport of marine organisms into nonnative environments in ships' ballast water.[8] Thus, while marine transport does create environmental harms, in relative terms this is a very energy efficient and clean mode of transport.

Aviation, both passenger and cargo, is the other form of transportation particularly associated with long-distance international flows. According to a group representing the air transport industry, "Aviation's overall contribution to human climate change is currently thought to be about 3.5 percent. This share can be expected to grow to 5 percent in 2050 due to the high level of demand for aviation services."[9] The same source indicates that 80 percent of aviation greenhouse gas emissions come from flights of 1,500 kilometers or longer, so we can assume that a large portion of aviation emissions *are* due to international flights.[10]

Proportionally, though, long-distance flights cause less noise and air pollution near airports than short flights.

In sum, the two modes of transport that are most critical to cross-border flows of products and people do indeed contribute to global warming and other environmental harms, but in a modest way compared to domestic causes. You could have predicted this based on chapter 2. Since most kinds of human activity are mostly domestic, it shouldn't surprise us that domestic transportation is a much bigger polluter than international transportation. Of course, that isn't to say that that should let shipping and airline industries off the hook internationally or domestically for the damage that they do.

Another environmental harm that arises directly from globalization is the introduction, intentional or otherwise, of alien species (and diseases) into local environments, which in some cases wreaks havoc on local ecosystems. Examples of the former include the introduction of rabbits into Australia and kudzu and Asian carp into the United States, and of the latter, the Mediterranean fruit fly (in infested imported fruit) and the Asian longhorn beetle (in wooden packing material). A review of this literature cites a report from the Office of Technology Assessment (OTA) estimating the direct monetary costs of such phenomena in the United States at $5 billion annually.[11]

We could go farther and analyze the spread of infectious disease—most often, through international travel—in similar terms. This does, however, raise a practical issue. Even the sub–1 percent globalization of the Middle Ages was enough for the Black Death, transmitted by rats from Asia, to ravage Europe—and reshuffle the ranks of trading cities. Unless what is being contemplated is an extreme World 0.0/1.0 clampdown on cross-border interactions, some of the risks of global pandemics are going to be with us no matter how we choose among the globalization-related choices that we face. So while pandemics and other risks do need to be managed—the next chapter discusses the principles of risk management in World 3.0—they are, to a first approximation, neutral with respect to the choices that we must make.

The Indirect Effects of Globalization

We saw in the preceding section that cross-border flows' direct environmental effects are nonnegligible but much smaller than other sources of environmental harm, like domestic land transport, domestic industry, and deforestation. But does globalization cause more problems *indirectly*, through changes it induces in the broader volume and pattern of economic output? Environmental economists have distinguished among three types of indirect environmental effects. First, there are *scale effects*: globalization expands output and therefore pollution. More broadly, while economic growth is good, it does have this environmental downside that must be accounted for. Second, there are *technique effects* related to the degree of cleanliness or dirtiness of the production and disposal techniques used. Despite fears of a "race to the bottom," globalization is generally viewed as having a positive influence on the environment through this channel by promoting the adoption of better techniques. And third, there are *composition effects* that derive from shifts in the mix of output across countries. These can have either positive or negative effects, and one particular concern is that dirty industries might migrate to poor countries with laxer environmental standards or enforcement, leading to the creation of "pollution havens" even if aggregate world pollution does not increase.[12]

All three effects seem to be real, so globalization's indirect environmental impact depends on their relative strengths. If the negative effects exceed the positive ones on balance, we can expect globalization to lead to economic growth but a dirtier environment. If this were the case, we would have to address some really hard trade-offs and distributional questions, particularly in less developed countries. We certainly don't want our rallying cry to be, "protecting the planet through poverty." On the other hand, if the positive effects are greater, we arrive at the surprising but hopeful conclusion that globalization and economic development can help make the environment *cleaner*.

Research suggests that it is impossible to conclude that globalization (or economic growth) is always bad (or good) for the environment;

there are simply too many different types of pollutants and country situations. For sulfur dioxide, to take one example, the evidence generally indicates a positive effect. Multiple studies have linked openness to international trade and lower sulfur dioxide concentrations, with one finding that "a 1-percent increase in the scale of economic activity raises pollution concentrations by 0.25 to 0.5 percent for an average country in our sample, but the accompanying increase in income drives concentrations down by 1.25–1.5 percent via a technique effect."[13] While the evidence isn't quite as clear for nitrogen dioxide and particulate matter, it seems that openness is associated with lower concentrations of these pollutants as well.[14]

The idea that trade may not increase many types of air pollution and may even help decrease some of them is consistent with broader research on the ecological impacts of economic growth. For most pollutants (particularly those with localized impacts), economic growth in relatively poor countries leads to more pollution: the scale effect dominates. But as countries get richer, more output leads to *less* pollution; governments and polluters come under pressure to improve the environment and they have the wherewithal to do so, so they clean things up (the technique effect). Also, dirty industries generally form a smaller proportion of economic output as countries shift from primary production to more sophisticated manufacturing and eventually to services (the composition effect). This pattern has been observed for a broad range of pollutants, including sulfur dioxide, particulates, nitrous oxide, automotive lead emissions, and arsenic.[15]

Trade and foreign investment can also enhance positive technique and composition effects. To maintain consistency across their plants and avoid negative publicity, foreign companies bring in new technologies and sometimes apply higher environmental standards than local firms. A related positive effect, particularly in agriculture, can come from leveraging cross-country geographic differences pertaining to climate and natural resources. Sometimes it is beneficial to produce products where their environmental impact is *lowest* (e.g., agricultural products where the climate is most favorable and industrial products closest to required natural resource inputs) and then ship them across borders for additional processing or final sale.

Still, there *are* exceptions to this pattern and to the generally good-to-neutral tone of the news about trade, the most important one being carbon dioxide. Most research indicates that CO_2 emissions have not fallen as countries get richer. Instead they have kept on growing, although as I write this, there are some tentative indications that this might be starting to change, perhaps due to the Kyoto Protocol and continuing multilateral efforts to regulate these emissions. But trade still seems to exacerbate CO_2.[16] So clearly CO_2 is more vexing than other pollutants. The next section looks at some of its distinctive properties, and the problem of climate change is considered in a bit more detail in the section after that.

But let's first address two other, related concerns about globalization's general environmental impact, the potential for a "race to the bottom" in environmental standards and for "pollution havens" to develop in poor countries. The race to the bottom simply doesn't seem to have happened. We already saw some evidence of this in the positive relationship between openness to trade and some kinds of environmental quality, the opposite of what would be predicted if there were such a race. Furthermore, developed countries have consistently raised—not lowered—environmental standards over the past thirty to forty years, and developing countries have followed suit.

Germany is a prime example. Nearly a third of its GDP comes from exports, so it's exactly the kind of country that would be expected, in a race to the bottom, to experience pressure to lower its environmental standards. Instead, the opposite happened. In the 1970s and 1980s, Germany was reportedly considered one of Europe's "environmental laggards," according to *Newsweek*, and its "river Rhine was a stinking cesspool, poisoned by heavy industry." But by 2008, "Germany may be the world's greenest country—and not just because salmon once again return to spawn in the Rhine."[17] Germany now is cleaner on a host of environmental metrics.

Tighter German standards have also, in an instance of positive rather than negative externalities, spilled over to other countries, including developing ones. Thus, some Chinese companies have matched German requirements even for their own domestic products, standardizing output in support of exports to Europe. Transfer of clean production processes via foreign direct investment, exports of clean technology products, and environmental provisions in trade agreements have also supported environmental protection in developing countries. And governments and firms in developing as well as developed countries are excited about global markets for green products and the jobs they might generate.

What about evidence for pollution havens in poor countries? If globalization isn't leading to more pollution overall, is it saddling the poor with more pollution while allowing rich countries to dispatch their polluting industries far away? Here, the evidence is mixed. A recent study found that in low-income countries, more trade is associated with higher per capita energy consumption—and more emissions—while the opposite holds true in high-income countries.[18] This seems to fit with findings that imports into rich countries are more pollution-intensive than rich countries' exports.[19] On the other hand, for SO_2 emissions, "trade apparently leads to a reallocation of pollution from the poor country to the rich country, rather than the other way around."[20] It turns out that industries that cause a lot of SO_2 emissions also tend to have high capital-to-labor ratios. Since capital costs are normally lower and labor costs higher in wealthier countries, this consideration can offset higher environmental compliance costs.

Those, of course, are the most broad-brush of characterizations. More detailed studies of other aspects of the pollution haven hypothesis—for example, the links with foreign direct investment rather than trade—yield more equivocal results. Part of the difficulty of making sense of the results seems to me to be intrinsic to the pollution haven hypothesis, in terms of what it assumes and what it leaves out. It assumes that all redeployment of dirty industries from countries with tough environmental standards to countries with looser ones is potentially problematic. But surely, some responsiveness to differences in standards is to be expected: the question is whether it reaches problematic levels. And it glosses over the fact that environmental impact depends on the standards actually applied to the production transferred and how they develop over time. While India has severe environmental problems, when a company with high standards such as Bharat Forge shuts an antiquated foundry in Europe and transfers production to India, I'm not very concerned about the environmental impact. And while China became a haven for dirty rare earth extraction in the 1980s and 1990s, by the late 2000s, China began sending police to shut down illegal mines and blowtorch their equipment,[21] indicating that such problems can also be self-correcting.

More broadly, a focus on pollution havens implies looking at pollution based on its putative source. But since there are many sources of pollution and globalization's contribution to the total is generally limited, a focus on whether globalization has or hasn't led to the emergence of pollution havens may miss out on the very real problems of areas that are—for whatever reason—pollution hotspots. So for purposes of thinking about how to regulate environmental problems, we shift to looking at overall patterns of pollution and what to do about them instead of trying to refine estimates of how much pollution to attribute to globalization.

Pollution and Distance

To figure out what to do about environmental externalities, it is useful to begin by looking at their actual incidence, that is, their actual geographic scope. Focusing on pollution as a singularly important case is helpful because most forms of pollution are subject to the law of distance: the greater the geographic distance between polluter and pollutee, the lower the pollutant concentrations experienced by the pollutee.

A general sense of the distance sensitivity of pollutants is conveyed by maps such as the one in figure 6-1, which depicts air quality in the United States at the county level. As you can see from the map, air quality exhibits significant regional variation, broadly reflecting patterns of human habitation and industrial production. And variation is also apparent at smaller scales. At the metropolitan level, maps of the intensity of many air pollutants are mostly tracings of a city's major traffic arteries.

As subnational differences in air quality imply, environmental harms still have a significant local dimension. Thus, Jeffrey Frankel concludes in his excellent review of the literature that for "most kinds of air and water pollution, the latter a particularly great health hazard in the third world . . . *most of the damage is felt within the country in question.*"[22] Nobel Prize winner Joseph Stiglitz takes a similar perspective, noting that "the quality of ground water, lakes, or air usually affects only those nearby."[23]

Those average effects do, however, mask significant variation across pollutants, especially air pollutants. Figure 6-2 summarizes the "effective distances" that various air pollutants travel and indicates a significant difference between short-lived air pollutants with very localized effects, moderately long-lived pollutants with national/regional effects, and really long-lived pollutants with potentially global effects. These distance effects are measured a bit differently than the ones discussed previously, but for SO_2 (sulfur dioxide), to take one example, the distance sensitivity, calculated as in chapter 3, is about -1, implying a regional footprint, as corroborated by other sources. For some of the really short-lived air pollutants in the figure, the distance effects might be as much as -3 or -4. CO_2 (carbon dioxide), in contrast, is literally off the charts: its distance sensitivity is close to 0 in the sense that a ton of CO_2 will make the same contribution to global warming irrespective of where it is emitted.

As in the previous chapter, the concept of distance sensitivity helps scope the problem. For highly distance-sensitive pollutants, pollution is likely to happen within a single country (or province or city). In such situations, people expect the relevant governmental authority to take care of the matter. It might take some pressure from environmental activists,

FIGURE 6-1

United States air quality

■ A ■ B ■ C ■ D ■ F

A = Best/cleanest in the U.S.; F = Worst/dirtiest in the U.S.

Source: Creative Methods.

but in countries with democratic governance and sufficient resources to tackle the problem, such matters tend to get addressed.[24] Special safeguards may be required, however, to prevent countries without much money or representative democracy from turning themselves into trash dumps to the world. And if such pollution happens close to national borders, cross-border agreements may also be necessary, as in the acrimonious case of the paper mill in Fray Bentos, Uruguay, just across the border from Argentina. But apart from such complexities, these are the simplest kinds of externalities to deal with given their limited geographic scope.

Other pollution problems have a regional footprint. Acid rain (or more technically, "acid deposition") results from interactions of emissions containing sulfur and nitrogen with water molecules in the atmosphere, rather than the direct effects of the same pollutants breathed locally. Thus it quite naturally affects a larger area. Downstream effects of pollution released into rivers also tend to have a regional impact.

FIGURE 6-2

Distance sensitivity of air pollutants

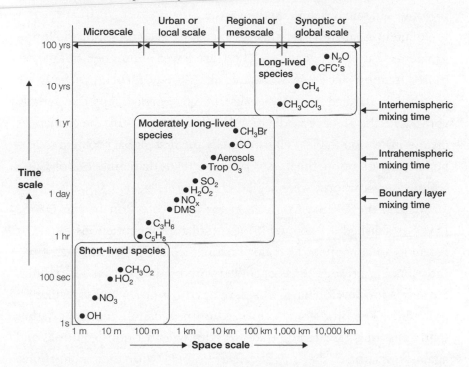

Source: National Research Council, *The Atmospheric Sciences Entering the Twenty-First Century* (Washington, DC: National Academy Press, 1998).

Regulation of regional pollutants does require cross-border cooperation, but that's not a hopeless requirement. Consider how North America has addressed its regional acid rain problem. Title IV of the 1990 U.S. Clean Air Act established a cap-and-trade program, initially targeted at reducing sulfur dioxide emissions, and later expanded to cover nitrous oxides. In 1991, the U.S.-Canada Air Quality Agreement was set up to address cross-border air pollution problems, again initially focused on the causes of acid rain. With cooperation aligned to the scale of the problem, North American initiatives against acid rain have reduced it by 65 percent since 1976, according to the Pacific Research Institute.[25] Many other examples exist of neighboring countries working together to address cross-border pollution problems. That said, we shouldn't fool ourselves into thinking that this makes regional pollution a problem of the past. In other parts of the world, especially developing regions, acid rain remains a serious issue.

Pollutants that aren't very distance sensitive account for the pollution problems that are truly global. These are fewer in number, but garner more attention since they impact us all. Moreover, such problems are particularly hard to address because of governance gaps that greatly complicate the global coordination that is required. Still, the challenges are not insurmountable, as illustrated by the first global problem to garner serious attention: the discovery in the 1970s that emissions of CFCs (chlorofluorocarbons) were depleting the ozone layer.

In 1985, the Vienna Convention for the Protection of the Ozone Layer established a framework for multilateral negotiations aimed at reaching an agreement to control ozone-depleting pollution. In 1987, the Montreal Protocol was concluded with binding targets set at different levels for developing versus developed countries and for different pollutants. The protocol also focused on production and trade rather than emissions, threatening trade sanctions against nonsignatories and against signatories that might fail to comply with their obligations. Nearly the whole world eventually signed on, trade sanctions never were levied, and "95% of the production of ozone-depleting substances has been phased out."[26] Global regulation with real teeth to it and sensitivity to cross-country differences effectively tackled a global externality. Former UN secretary general Kofi Annan hailed the Montreal Protocol as "perhaps the most successful international agreement to date."[27]

The Case of Climate Change

Today, we face an even harder global environmental challenge: the impact of emissions of CO_2 and other greenhouse gases. There is now general agreement that such emissions are causing dangerous climate change with potential for significant global warming. Thus, according to the 2010 iteration of Shell's energy scenarios, "stabilising GHG [green-house gas] levels in the atmosphere at or below 450 ppm of CO_2-equivalent—a level scientific evidence suggests is necessary to significantly reduce the risks of climate change—remains a significant challenge . . . [but would] limit temperature rises to no more than 2°C above pre-industrial levels"[28] And this is Shell's aggressively optimistic scenario! In its pessimistic scenario, "concentration is on a path to a long-term level well above 550 ppm"—which would likely create a climate catastrophe.[29]

I take this perspective as a point of departure to start to illustrate some of the principles for global cooperation that apply to World 3.0—in the context of a really difficult problem. Note that global warming would be hard to address even if it occurred within a single country (without any cross-border externalities), because dealing with it involves making significant sacrifices today to avert a future catastrophe. Deferring gratification even on the individual or local level isn't easy, but to get the whole world to do so on a concerted basis is about as hard a challenge as you can find. On top of that, climate change is a global externality: what Sir Nicholas Stern, the author of the *Stern Review on the Economics of Climate Change* for the British government, called "the greatest market failure the world has seen."[30] That means the sacrifice of some will come to naught if others simply free-ride on their efforts. We need a solid agreement in place, and if we take a World 3.0 approach, we can improve our chances of reaching it.

While scientific research started earlier, formal multilateral efforts to address climate change date to the Rio Earth Summit in 1992, when the United Nations Framework Convention on Climate Change (UNFCCC) treaty was negotiated. Much good work has been done under the auspices of the UNFCCC, but we still have a long way to go. As I write this, a great deal of disappointment lingers over the failure of the December 2009 Copenhagen Conference of the Parties to reach a binding accord with specific targets for reduction of greenhouse gases.

Given the economics of global externalities, the UNFCCC's emphasis on binding targets is rightly placed. And the mechanisms that it envisions, such as trading in emissions permits, technology transfer, and financial assistance to developing countries, generally make sense—although there is reason to think that a carbon tax would be superior to a scheme of tradable permits since the latter often degenerates into handouts of valuable permits to heavy polluters. The principle of "common but differentiated responsibilities" (different requirements for developed versus developing countries) is also appropriate since a one-size-fits-all approach is unlikely to work.

How might the odds of reaching an agreement along these lines be improved? One prescription that fits with World 3.0's focus on cross-country differences would be to go *even farther* to deal with such differences between countries. For example, while the UN process distinguishes between developed and developing countries, the latter grouping includes large developing countries on track to emit the majority of the world's greenhouse gas emissions (China has already overtaken the United States as the world's largest source), "small island developing states" that face existential threats from global warming, and very poor countries that have yet to see rapid growth and development.

Two other kinds of cross-country differences that, inevitably, must be accounted for relate to variations in countries' bargaining power and, in negotiations jargon, their best alternatives to a negotiated agreement. Thus, while China and India have significant bargaining power, they also stand to be hit particularly hard—or so most projections imply—by the consequences of global warming. (In contrast, the CIA estimates that Canada and Russia might do relatively well—although they too would experience massive disruptions.)

Recognizing these national differences and accounting for them as countries focused on their own welfare interact with each other is very different from the usual (World 2.0-inspired) focus in academic exercises of simply optimizing global welfare (with the implicit and improbable assumption that each country will do what makes sense for the world as a whole). Anthoff and Tol illustrate the very large differences this can make in the context of global warming in terms of the carbon taxes that different countries are willing to impose.[31] Their calculations also suggest that global warming would be easier to deal with if we placed more weight on the harms inflicted on others. Relatively high weights could even get us to carbon prices high enough to interest industry in general in carbon capture and storage. The broader point, expanded on in chapter 15, is that caring for others is one way of internalizing the kinds of externalities that we have been worrying about.

A corollary of the points made above is that the emphasis on *consensus* in decision making at the UN's large climate change meetings, while admirable, is probably misplaced. One specific alternative involves a two-track approach, with all countries being consulted as well as informed, but with negotiations concentrated among a core group of countries—what Dr. Supachai Panitchpakdi, secretary-general of UNCTAD, described to me in another context as a "G20-plus" approach that might be reasonably inclusive without becoming unwieldy. The core countries in this context, of course, consist of the largest current and future polluters.

Beyond that, World 3.0 is about multiple parallel efforts and diversity, not single-track uniformity. Although the UN should probably remain the primary venue for fighting climate change, World 3.0's emphasis on cross-country differences also offers lessons about how to make progress outside of the UN process.

Thus, in addressing global problems, domestic activism and politics still have big roles to play. Probably at least as much effort and money should be expended on convincing governments (and voting publics in democratic countries) at a national level to act, as on international agitation. The most important spur to Chinese efforts to control global warming and pollution more generally seems to me to likely be the deterioration of China's natural environment, and the air quality in its larger cities in particular (thanks to local pollutants). International efforts of less than fully global scale (such as regional efforts like those undertaken by the EU and bilateral negotiations that have taken place between the United States and China) can also prove constructive. Additionally, progress doesn't always have to be channeled by governments; nongovernmental organizations (NGOs) and businesses can also have a large impact, especially now that we see some collaboration across that divide. Businesses and NGOs are, for instance, leading the REDD (Reduced Emissions from Deforestation and Forest Degradation) projects to save rainforests instead of simply sitting around waiting for governments to strike a comprehensive global climate deal.

The role of business is worthy of additional description, especially because of the rude characterization in the cartoon with which this chapter began. Certainly, business emissions are like all other emissions, candidates for regulation. But the fundamental challenge that we face in relation to a natural environment of limited natural resources and absorptive capacity is that of burgeoning demand. With a 50 percent increase in world population projected for 2050 and a severalfold increase in average per capita income, we're talking not of continuing to generate as much gross world product as today without causing further environmental harm, but about squeezing out maybe five times as much world product by 2050. Because of this massive projected increase in scale, taxation, quotas, and nudges to conserve, while important in reducing the coefficient of the scale effect, are likely to fall far short in reconciling limited supply with burgeoning demand.

Given this arithmetic, innovation will be needed. It will presumably involve business firms in prominent roles, although maybe as parts of public-private partnerships (the Chinese, in particular, are pursuing more of a state capitalist approach). And businesses' appetite for developing and bringing the necessary innovations to market will depend to an important extent on the world being open rather than closed to trade and investment. That may yet turn out to be the most important link between globalization and the environment.

Toward a More Sustainable World 3.0

Environmentalists have long called for us to "think global" and "act local." With increasing focus on global problems such as ozone depletion and global warming, we shouldn't lose sight of the local and national dimensions of caring for our planet. We need to approach ecological problems with responses scaled appropriately to their causes and impacts. In most cases, this still means focusing on problems that lie within our own countries or regions.

Globalization's environmental impact has been mixed—not entirely positive (especially with respect to CO_2 emissions), but not the cause of most of the world's ecological problems. On balance, globalization has probably done more good than bad for the planet, especially if you don't advocate protecting the environment through poverty in developing countries. If all countries maintained their current standards of living without any cross-border trade and investment, the environment clearly would suffer far more. How could we grow all the food we enjoy today without the benefit of trade across climate zones? What about trying to produce fuel cells without the precious metal catalysts that come almost exclusively from South Africa, Russia, and Canada (or hybrid or electric car batteries without those pesky Chinese rare earths)?

If you still find this hard to believe, please review the ADDING value framework again with an eye to its implications for the environment. You'll find that a lot of globalization's benefits don't get much play in the media, if only because they are a bit more complicated or esoteric. Scale benefits make production more efficient. Trade can reduce costs and improve the product variety—as true for products required to protect the environment as much as for any other products. Industry structures with multinational corporations make it easier for NGOs to go after large targets to clean up messes across many countries—a lot simpler than hunting down small producers around the world.

Additionally, with *some* climate change seeming unavoidable, the ability to normalize risk across countries (especially with respect to food production) is especially useful. Last, and perhaps most important, globalization is crucial to the development and dissemination of green technologies. By one estimate, "75 percent of all international technology transfers stem from trade."[32] If every country had to try to figure out how to produce a high standard of living and protect the planet on its own, solutions would be much more difficult and time-consuming to achieve.

Global warming's seriousness also suggests that what we need is *more* cross-border cooperation among governments and regulatory authorities, not less. I can't think of a single environmental problem that crosses borders where the right response is to close off interactions with other countries. We do need to remain vigilant against potential harms that globalization could cause, like pollution havens, but the answer isn't to close borders in the name of protecting the environment. We need to work together to preserve the planet for future generations, remaining sensitive to cross-country differences. The mind-set I advocate as part of the shift to World 3.0 can strengthen globalization's positive contributions to sustainability while giving us tools to address environmental harms, regardless of their causes. More on that is coming in the third part of this book.

Chapter Seven

Global Risks

Source: Mike Luckovich

THE LAST FEW YEARS have provided a startling reminder that we still live in a world full of risks. We've seen recession, stock market gyrations, and unemployment streak between countries like an epidemic. Homes and retirement portfolios have been lost, and those starting off with less have fared far worse. An estimated 100 million *more* people went hungry in 2009 than in 2008.[1] Globalization has been blamed for increasing volatility, and for spreading problems that would otherwise have remained localized.

Consider how a recent report by Lloyd's, the famed specialist insurance market, put it: "Businesses have reaped unprecedented benefits from global trade. However, at the same time, globalization has introduced new forms of risk, notably systemic risk. Due to the increasing interdependence of global systems, risks now transmit much farther and more quickly than before, jumping from one industry or country into several countries or sectors."[2] The general view that globalization increases systemic risk but is still worth it is basically the World 2.0 position today; few are still willing to spell out the real implication of a flat world—that additional integration poses no risk because everything is already effectively harmonized. Risk-related objections to globalization inspired by World 1.0 take the opposite view of that trade-off between systemic risk and the gains from globalization although, after the global financial crisis, they are usually framed more simply as "I told you so." And they find a receptive audience because of a generalized mistrust of foreigners that is fueled by economic difficulties, as discussed later in chapter 11.

Both strands of discourse, however, underplay the benefits of diversification to reduce risk. Between 1875 and 1919, some 15 to 30 million people died in localized famines in India. What marked the end of this pattern? The extension of railroads throughout the country. When communities were isolated, local weather patterns were a matter of life and death, but as districts got linked up to the railroad, "the ability of rainfall shortages to cause famine disappeared almost completely."[3]

Or take a more modern example. In the 1980s, a U.S. investor holding only domestic stocks would have experienced 30 percent more volatility than an investor with an optimally diversified international stock portfolio (holding returns constant) or accepted 30 percent lower annual returns (holding volatility constant).[4] Of course, ex post optimality in this sense requires foreknowledge of stock market correlations. But more recent studies that dispense with this assumption generally suggest that international diversification still yields significant benefits—although they *have* diminished in recent years.[5] Also note that the estimated benefits from international diversification are generally greater for investors from other countries given the relatively high correlation of U.S. and world market indexes. Thus, according to one study, the U.S. ranks in the bottom quintile of more than 50 countries in terms of the risk-adjusted returns to domestic investors from international diversification: gains in the median country, South Korea, are twice as high.[6]

Add in the fact that most people are highly dependent on income from their home country's labor market and investors' low levels of international diversification (home bias, as discussed in chapter 2), seems even more troubling.[7] Yet World 2.0 overlooks diversification opportunities because it misses cross-country differences, and World 1.0 doesn't even look to other countries as a source of safety, seeing integration only as a source of danger. In that sense, World 3.0 *does* explicitly identify risk-related (potential) gains from globalization that prior worldviews do not.

In order to think even more broadly about integration and risk, it is useful to focus explicitly on interdependence. To start at a personal level, getting connected to the right people in the right way makes our lives richer and safer, but bad entanglements produce enough grief to keep screenwriters and novelists employed in perpetuity. Human progress since World 0.0 has been marked by increasing interdependence, supported by a host of institutions that make reliance on others less risky: cultural norms, courts of law, insurance markets, welfare protections, and so on. The task of this chapter is to shed some light on the risk implications of international economic interdependence so that we can shape integration to make World 3.0 not only more prosperous but also safer.

Managing interdependence, as in figuring out whom we should depend on for what as well as the commitments we can prudently make to others would be much simpler if we could accurately predict the future, or at least always understand the present correctly. The lack of crystal balls in the real world is a source of market failure that complicates the question of whether or not to link up volatile markets. So this chapter starts with background on informational imperfections and how they relate to market volatility. It goes on to look at how macroeconomic volatility has evolved as levels of integration have increased and the related worry of macroeconomic contagion—importing a recession or depression. It then examines the risk implications of cross-border flows of different types of capital and of food grain staples—two specific but challenging market arenas in the context of risk. The chapter concludes by returning to the broad relationship between integration and risk and offering recommendations for how to make globalization safer.

Informational Imperfections

The fact that we can't know the future for certain doesn't necessarily make markets fail. Chicago School economists, most notably Robert Lucas, espoused the "rational expectations hypothesis," which says that everybody essentially optimizes their choices based on forecasts incorporating all available information. If that hypothesis were true and we all operated like little supercomputers, instantly processing humanity's cumulative knowledge, then in the absence of any other sources of market failure (like concentration and externalities, which we explored in the last two chapters), we could trust that prices would always transmit the right information to producers and consumers to guide them toward efficient deployment of society's resources. But as we'll see, reality often differs markedly from that utopian hypothesis, causing prices to diverge from fundamentals, boosting volatility and wasting scarce resources.

Consider the experience of deciding how to invest your retirement savings. Suppose you own a particular stock. The firm's CEO knows much more than you about the firm's strengths and weaknesses—what economists call an "information asymmetry." In fact, you might decide to sell shares if you learn that the CEO just sold some of hers. If others do the same, the stock price tumbles, even if the CEO's share sale reflected nothing about the firm at all (maybe she just wanted cash to buy a new home). Conversely, if the firm buys back some of its own shares, this might send a positive signal. In both cases, the firm's stock price may swing sharply without any real change in its "fundamental" value.

Information asymmetries are just one information problem among many. Another factor contributing to volatility is the difficulty investors have figuring out what to do with all the information they do have. Few can conduct even rudimentary financial analyses, leading economists to peg them as possessing only "bounded rationality." If you think you can get around this by hiring a financial advisor, then you have to wonder whether he or she is operating in your best interest or not, a "principal-agent problem." And any serious effort at figuring out what to do takes time and money, a "transaction cost" comprised, in part, of "search costs." The salience of the latter was highlighted by the selection of three of the leading thinkers in search theory for the 2010 Nobel Prize in Economics.

Keynes likened financial markets to a beauty contest where the way to win is to predict the other judges' opinions rather than to assess the contestants' beauty yourself.[8] Even professional investment managers can gain by following the crowd against their own better judgment. As Jeremy Stein explained, "The underlying idea is that if you do something dumb, but everybody else is doing the same dumb thing at the same time, people won't think of you as stupid, and it won't be harmful to your reputation."[9] Think about your own financial decisions. Do you really make independent choices? According to Robert Shiller, "investing in speculative assets is a social activity" where "attitudes or fashions" can shift around much like they do "in many other popular topics of conversation, such as food, clothing, health, or politics."[10]

Distance, furthermore, can exacerbate informational problems. We've already seen how foreign news provides a very limited diet of information to the general public. Worse, professional investors get tripped up even by within-country internal distance. A recent study found that "the average [mutual] fund manager generates an additional return of 2.67 percent per year from her local investments (defined as holdings within 100 kilometers of the fund headquarters) relative to her nonlocal holdings."[11]

There are also indications that speculative activity might be making such problems worse. In volatile markets, the ability to hedge risk via the use of derivative contracts is very useful, but speculation can also increase volatility. It's hard to specify the balance, but the fact that the notional value of the world's derivative contracts (some $615 trillion in over-the-counter markets alone) far exceeds its total financial assets gives some sense that derivatives are being used for a lot more than hedging real risk exposure.[12] And the rapid growth of high-frequency trading, now accounting for some 60 percent of U.S. and 40 percent of European stock market volume, is another worry.[13] Computerized trading algorithms that buy and sell their positions multiple times per day have been pinned as a likely contributor to the twenty-minute "flash crash" of May 6, 2010, that temporarily erased $1 trillion of market value.[14] Economist Joseph Stiglitz, who won the Nobel Prize for his work on information asymmetry, commented, "I think a number of us are coming to the view that this high-frequency trading has negative social value, and that it's not information discovery."[15]

Thus, informational imperfections *can* contribute to herding, bubbles, and of course volatility. But such problems don't plague all markets equally, nor do imperfections in all markets pose similar levels of danger to the general public. Consider the market for euros versus the market for this book. Both currency traders and my publisher operate under conditions of uncertain demand. But the euro, traded on liquid markets, supplied according to European Central Bank policy, and valued from an individual holder's perspective almost entirely based on other traders' expectations, is a much more attractive target for speculation. Even if after reading this book, you think it's going to be a runaway best seller, I can't in good conscience advise you to start hoarding copies to profit from a speculative bubble. You'll have a hard time offloading them, and soon enough the publisher will be on the scene with another printing. Publishers adjust supply to maximize profits; central banks don't. To my regret, this book will never be something readers really can't do without if it temporarily goes out of stock. And if this book is mispriced, the effects won't spread beyond the submarket of related books. Not so for the euro.

This is just one way of illustrating that most product markets are not subject to the full extent of the informational problems and volatility on which this chapter focuses. So, as we turn to the potential dangers of connecting markets across countries, with a particular focus on capital and food markets, there should be some comfort in remembering that you *don't* have to worry about similar problems affecting most of what you buy on a daily basis. The cases focused on here are particularly hard ones.

Present Tense, Past Perfect?

As of this writing, most of us are still pretty dazed by the last few years of macroeconomic instability, but it's important to avoid what psychologists call the "recency bias" and put present conditions into longer-term perspective. The broader trend is that as cross-border integration increased in the latter part of the twentieth century and early twenty-first century, volatility generally declined, to the extent that this period has been termed the "Great Moderation." Thus, the volatility of U.S. aggregate income from 1984 to 2004 was roughly one-half the average for the period from 1960 to 1983.[16] More broadly, macroeconomic volatility has declined in most major industrial economies since the mid-1980s and "output volatility seems to have been on a declining trend in emerging markets and developing countries as well."[17] This should provide some reassurance that globalization doesn't inevitably lead to macroeconomic instability.

What about stock market returns? It can be scary to watch how what happens in U.S. markets impacts Asian markets, whose trends carry over to Europe, and so on, around the clock. Returns *have* become more correlated across countries since the 1970s,[18] but several offsets are worth citing. Taking the long view, correlations have fluctuated widely over the past 150 years instead of increasing monotonically. In fact, stock markets were more closely correlated during the great depression than in the late twentieth century, as shown in figure 7-1.[19] In the 2000s, correlations did increase with global financial flows in the run-up to the global financial crisis (with the worst of the crisis obviously marking a period of very high correlation), but they remain far from perfect and may yet decrease with the financial slowdown if the decades-long declines after prior peaks are any guide. And stock market correlations also continue to reflect distance effects.[20] So while higher levels of correlation imply less risk reduction potential from international diversification, there still does seem to be significant potential.

How can we square this seemingly benign pattern with our worries that connecting volatile markets increases systemic risk? A good starting point is to note that while contagion really can happen, it is usually moderated by the law of distance. Thus, when Greece got into a full-blown

FIGURE 7-1

Average correlation of capital appreciation returns for all available markets, 1860–2000

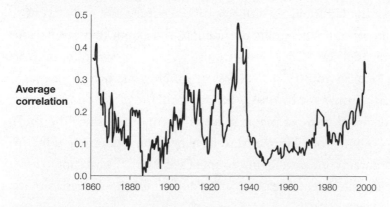

Correlations based on rolling window of 60 months. Number of countries covered rises over time from 4 in 1860 to roughly 50 by 2000, reflecting the development of stock markets in more countries and improvements in data availability.

Source: William N. Goetzmann, Lingfeng Li, and K. Geert Rouwenhorst, "Long-Term Global Market Correlations," DNB Staff Reports, no. 09/2003.

crisis around the state of its public finances, it was a problem more for the Eurozone than for the whole world. And within the Eurozone, financial markets focused on whether "Aegean contagion" would spread to other southern European countries judged to be relatively similar to Greece along the CAGE dimensions. As the very term contagion implies, distance still matters, and contiguous or near-contiguous countries are usually at greater risk. Figure 7-2 makes the same point in the context of real rather than financial contagion.

Numerous other historical examples also highlight the relationship between geographic distance and contagion. The "tequila effect" spread Mexico's 1994 crisis to Brazil and beyond. The 1997 Asian crisis spread from Thailand to Indonesia and then later to much of Asia before hitting Russia in 1998. And in terms of economic distance, note that individual countries' GDP growth has become *less* tightly tied to global trends and more tightly tied to patterns in other countries at similar levels of development, generating discussion of "decoupling" or growing distance between developing and developed countries.[21]

FIGURE 7-2

Sensitivity of GDP growth trends to distance: Estimated impact of a 1% decline in U.S. GDP growth on other countries and regions

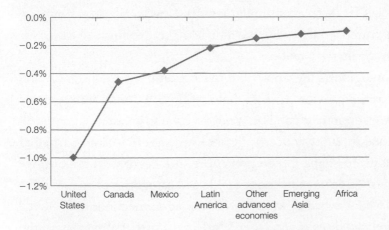

Sources: Based on figure 4.5 of Thomas Helbling, Peter Berezin, Ayhan Kose, Michael Kumhof, Doug Laxton, and Nikola Spatafora, "Decoupling the Train? Spillovers and Cycles in the Global Economy," chapter 4, in IMF, *World Economic Outlook*, 2007.

To summarize, we see evidence that macroeconomic trends—regional or global, coupled or decoupled—do cross national borders to an extent that can usefully be parametrized in terms of distance sensitivity. But if we want to reverse cross-border integration enough to stop the transmission of financial shocks, in particular, across countries, we'd have to go back at least to World 1.0, and probably to a pretty extreme variety of it (close to autarky). Such shocks (and their real correlates) have been transmitted around the world through major financial centers for at least two hundred years now, so tinkering with globalization around the edges seems unlikely to stop contagion.[22] In part, that's because real flows aren't the only ones that spread crises; fear and confidence play a role, and tariffs or capital controls can't stop them from leaping borders.

Furthermore, any World 1.0-inspired attempt to curtail integration enough to eradicate contagion would also mean forgoing outside sources of stabilization and growth. Quarantine might seem appealing, but don't forget that the "growth bug" is also contagious. What would Greece's prospects for recovery be without foreign capital and tourists? What about bailout-weary Germany without the third of its GDP generated by exports? Not that World 2.0 is any better. False perceptions of complete integration contribute to the contagion problem. Fear flies across borders far faster than fundamentals. If we really stop to understand cross-country differences, we'll be less likely to mistake Korea for Thailand, or Spain for Greece.

Some contagion is inevitable, but it's conditioned by distance, and long-term trends provide comfort that integration does not necessarily cause macroeconomic instability. We don't have to abandon integration wholesale due to safety concerns. Rather, we should look to particular kinds of flows to shape integration more intelligently. Therefore, we turn next to specific worries about two broad categories of markets, for capital and for food grains, whose cross-border connections have stirred many risk-related discussions. Does World 3.0, with its emphasis on the differences between countries and the law of distance offer any help in thinking through these issues?

Capital Gains or Capital Punishment?

Capital, like food and oxygen for living bodies, is the lifeblood of a market economy. When capital markets are functioning well, they may seem as invisible as the air we breathe, but as we have been painfully reminded, when they seize up, even the healthiest among us start to choke. And as the section on informational imperfections described, capital markets are prone to extreme bouts of volatility. Thus, some careful analysis and reflection is called for before deciding whether or not we want to connect them across countries.

Advocates of opening up financial markets started off with the simple argument that with liberalization, capital would flow from rich to poor countries (where capital is scarcer), accelerating economic development in poor countries and providing high returns for investors. Such flows, however, turned out to be much smaller than models would predict—the "Lucas paradox"[23]—and recently we have seen large flows of capital "uphill" from poor to rich countries.[24] Economists have since provided a variety of explanations for this phenomenon, ranging from "increasing returns to human capital" and "institutional failures" to "recurrent defaults and financial crises."[25]

Another argument in favor of opening up capital markets relates to reducing consumption volatility. When ordinary people worry about economic risk, they're most concerned about sustaining consumption levels. Access to funds from foreign sources in times of trouble should help countries to smooth consumption while domestic output fluctuates. In fact, there is evidence that developed countries do share risk in this way, that emerging markets have largely been unable to do so, and that there is potential for more international risk sharing among countries at all development levels.[26] More recent arguments in favor of capital market liberalization emphasize indirect or "catalytic" benefits, such as spurring domestic financial maturity, strengthening institutions, and improving macroeconomic policies.[27]

On the other side of the debate, we find, in addition to incredulity, lots of counterarguments. Some detractors of open capital markets go so far as to accuse institutions like the IMF of pushing hard for liberalization not because it is good for developing countries, but because it benefits rich-country investors. Others emphasize how open capital markets can cause or worsen economic crises. An extensive literature has detailed the macroeconomic damage wrought when foreign capital surges into a country and then rushes out or slows. Capital flows to emerging markets overreact much as stock prices do. A country gets "hot" and money flows in. The longer the "bonanza," the greater the chances of its ending in a "sudden stop"—a sharp decline or, even worse, reversal in capital inflows.[28] To recall the adage about automobile accidents, it is the sudden deceleration that kills, not the speed.

Fallout from large shifts in capital flows can prove staggering. Countries often experience current account reversals, unless they can stave them off or soften them by spending down foreign currency reserves. Currency and banking crises follow, as do extended periods of slower growth. Even beyond the most violent cycles of bonanzas and sudden stops, volatile capital flows correlate with slower growth. However, these calamities shouldn't be blamed on capital flows alone; in most crises, they have formed part of a toxic mix of high foreign debt levels (often denominated in foreign currencies), inflexible exchange rates, domestic financial market imperfections, and so on, which is why one large literature review concluded that "there is little formal empirical evidence to support the oft-cited claims that financial globalization in and of itself is responsible for the spate of financial crises that the world has seen over the last three decades."[29]

Thus, the debate on the overall impact of capital account liberalization rages on. But from the World 3.0 perspective, what's more interesting is the evidence on the benefits and risks involved with specific types of international capital flows. Foreign direct investment (FDI)—foreign companies buying, setting up, or reinvesting in businesses in a country—tends to represent a long-term commitment since such decisions are typically driven by long-term strategic considerations.[30] As a result, while the amount of new FDI can fluctuate quite a bit—especially around waves of mergers and acquisitions—investments are seldom withdrawn quickly and, from the host country's perspective, have the advantage of not requiring regular interest payments. If host markets do falter, such firms tend to be relatively well positioned to reorient production to exports rather than pulling out. And more broadly, FDI helps transfer knowledge and information as well as capital, and functions, like trade, as a channel for product market integration with the prospect of ADDING value in ways that go beyond the ones listed here.

Opening up to international stock market investment (portfolio equity flows) has also been shown to have positive effects. Equity market liberalization has been linked to faster growth.[31] And increasing financial integration, as measured based on the convergence of equity risk premia, has also been associated with less volatile growth.[32]

International portfolio debt and bank loans, however, are substantially more problematic. When host country conditions deteriorate, such "procyclical and highly volatile" flows don't simply shrink: they are susceptible to reversing course and making a mad dash for the exits precisely when a country needs them most.[33] Thus, "there is a systematic empirical link between exposure to short-term debt and the likelihood (and severity) of financial crises."[34] And heavy reliance on portfolio debt has been identified as a likely contributor to developing countries' inability to smooth consumption via international risk sharing.

To summarize, opening up to international capital flows is a mixed bag. Thus, the conventional wisdom today is that "countries should liberalize trade in goods before trade in financial assets."[35] When countries do open up their capital markets, they can still favor some flows (FDI, equity) over others (debt), and retain the policy flexibility to manage extreme bouts of volatility. As Paul Krugman put it, "just as the right to free speech does not necessarily include the right to shout 'Fire' in a crowded theater, the principle of free markets does not necessarily mean that investors must be allowed to trample each other in a stampede."[36] If capital is like air to a market economy, its supply can't be left entirely in the hands of financial markets that, because of informational and other imperfections, have a history of "manias, panics, and crashes."[37] The wake of a global financial crisis should be an easy time to secure agreement—except from hardcore "free-marketeers"—on that basic proposition.

Food Fights

Losing money is scary, but the prospect of not having enough to eat is far scarier. Roughly 1 billion people were undernourished in 2009, one-sixth of humanity, a number that, disturbingly, has risen since the mid-1990s after declining steadily for decades.[38] Globalization often takes heat for this, in large part by allegedly contributing to food price volatility. What the evidence actually indicates, though, is that *impediments* to food trade cause much of the trade-induced volatility, not exposure to free international markets. Only 18 percent of wheat, 7 percent of rice, and 10 percent of coarse grains (including corn) were traded across borders in 2008,[39] and these three staples account for 60 percent of the world's caloric intake.[40] Overall, agricultural trade constituted only 8.5 percent of total merchandise trade (down from 12.2 percent in 1990).[41]

One reason is protectionism. Developed countries in particular maintain tariffs, subsidies, quotas, production "set-asides," and so on. Many readers have heard the alarming statistic that farmers in the EU received a $913 subsidy in 2000 for each dairy cow they raised, while Japanese farmers got $2,700.[42] Billions of people live on fewer dollars per day.

To see how limited trade contributes to food price volatility, consider rice markets. The proportion of rice traded across borders rose from 4 percent in the 1980s to 7 percent in the early 2000s—a deepening of trade accompanied by falling price levels and declining price volatility.[43] Rice trade remained thin and unstable, though. From early 2007 to mid-2008, international rice prices tripled. Why? Following a run-up in wheat prices and a poor wheat harvest in India, India and Vietnam (which together with Thailand account for 60 percent of rice exports) placed restrictions on rice exports (see figure 7-3). This triggered a cycle of panic buying, hoarding (speculation), and more export restrictions until prices overshot what fundamentals could possibly justify. Then, after some reassurance

FIGURE 7-3

Rice price trend and major trade-related events during the financial crisis

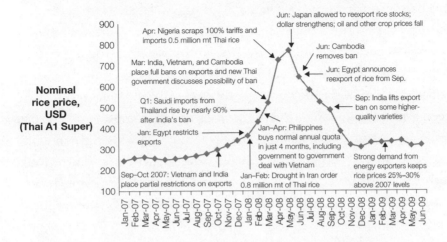

Source: Derek D. Headley, "Rethinking the Global Food Crisis: The Role of Trade Shocks," International Food Policy Research Institute discussion paper 0958, March 2010.

from Japan, prices fell almost as fast as they had risen.[44] Sound familiar? A similar cycle appeared to be under way in 2010.

The impact of export restrictions in the rice market spike suggests that open markets would have led to *more* stable prices, improving food security. Other research supports this view. An analysis of wheat prices in Zambia indicates that in a bad year, with harvests 30 percent below normal, prices might increase 30–40 percent if imports (from within the region) were allowed, but more than 150 percent if they weren't![45]

Despite such evidence, some continue to worry that foreign pressure on food prices will be exacerbated by population growth and global warming. However, there are actually good historical and scientific reasons to be optimistic that our planet can sustainably feed the 9 billion population projected by the mid-twenty-first century. According to Matt Ridley, from 1968 to 2005 alone, the amount of cereal grains produced from the same amount of land doubled, and "since 1900 the world has increased its population by 400 percent; its cropland area by 30 percent; its average yields by 400 percent and its total crop harvest by 600 percent."

In Ridley's view, the natural limit is about 100 square meters of cultivated land to feed one person. Based on the yields of the most important food crops, he estimates that we now use about 1,250 square meters to feed one person, down from 4,000 in the 1950s, and still far enough above 100 to imply there's still a huge scope for improvement.[46] Furthermore, he believes—I am not so sure of this—that global warming would probably improve agricultural yields and food supplies.[47]

So trade can *reduce* food price levels and volatility. While pressure to keep a lid on domestic prices sometimes creates incentives to restrict trade, basics such as enhancing market transparency, hedging, maintaining buffer stocks, and so on are usually better policies to promote food security. And macro trends like population growth and climate change certainly *don't* imply we'd be better off with isolated national food markets.

Risking Integration

Now that we've looked broadly at how macroeconomic volatility has trended as integration has increased, and drilled down on capital and food markets, let's come back to the fundamental relationship between integration and risk. In the complex real world, we can't slam down the gavel and say definitively that integration always makes life more dangerous, or that it always makes us safer. I deliberately juxtaposed capital and food flows to make the point that reducing risk sometimes means curtailing flows (e.g., short-term debt) but in other cases calls for freeing them up (e.g., food). Contrasting these two examples more explicitly calls attention to factors that are generally useful to consider in analyzing the broad relationship between integration and risk.

Begin by making sure that your policy objectives are clear. Food is critical to sustaining life, and shortages and price spikes cause hunger. Sudden capital flow reversals are also life-threatening to an economy, but foreign capital inflows are seldom essential, particularly when one considers that developing countries typically invest just over 20 percent of national income and are rarely able to borrow more than around 5 percent of national income.[48] Thus, availability and price stability are most critical for food, while avoiding sudden outflows is most important for capital.

Then, think about the nature of volatility in these markets and how it relates to informational imperfections. Food production fluctuates due to natural phenomena such as weather. Weather is a "risk" in the terminology introduced by Chicago economist Frank Knight in his famous 1921 book, *Risk, Uncertainty and Profit*, meaning that its outcome is unknown but it does conform to known probability distributions. Food export restrictions embody more of what Knight calls "uncertainty" in the sense that outcomes *aren't* based on a known probability distribution. Informational problems associated with uncertain trade barriers are likely to cause food prices to veer away from fundamentals to a greater extent than those rooted in more easily quantified production risks. The volatility of short-term capital flows is likely to be even more problematic since it is rooted in sentiments rather than in a specific natural production risk at all, and will tend toward the hot and cold pattern of overshooting that is common to financial markets.

Furthermore, compare the likely benefits of diversification in these two markets. Diversifying food sources across locations with different weather patterns yields obvious benefits. In capital markets, there are also diversification benefits associated with bridging economic distance, but "herding" reduces the benefit of diversification for borrowers, as we saw in the cases of sudden stops.

Based on this analysis, it should be fairly clear why ensuring open markets for food grains reduces risk while freeing up short-term debt flows can raise it. Furthermore, even when a flow does appear to offer big benefits, it's important to think about risks rooted in the relationships between the specific countries involved. A short digression beyond capital and food to energy—another essential commodity that requires management of cross-border risks—illustrates the point. Denmark exports wind energy to Norway when the wind is blowing, enabling Norway to cut the flow across its hydroelectric plants and store energy for later. When winds are light, the flow reverses, and Denmark imports hydroelectric power from Norway. In this case, relations between the countries involved are such that little risk of unexpected electricity cutoffs exists. On the other hand, the proposed natural gas pipeline from Iran to India across Pakistan seems to raise lots of issues in this respect. Similarly, if there are public concerns about a flow, that should be a signal to proceed cautiously, if at all: when the going gets tough, institutions come under pressure and rules may be broken.

Toward a Safer World

The last section provided examples of the potential for risk reduction through international diversification that is effectively ignored in World 1.0 and World 2.0. World 1.0 is integration-averse and seeks safety behind closed borders. World 2.0, at the other extreme, also fails to emphasize the potential benefits of risk-pooling because it ignores cross-country differences; in addition, it suggests no protections against the real risks described in this chapter. By tuning us in to differences and market failures, World 3.0 flags both the potential to reduce risk through integration and the challenges of combating the risks that integration and interdependency can themselves generate. It is time to discuss how to deal with those challenges.

As a starting point, pursue diversification. Any investor knows it's too dangerous to hold only one stock. But World 1.0 tells us it's better to depend on just one country—home—than to diversify. That's awfully risky. I don't suggest going to the World 2.0 extreme and trying to spread a country's exposure evenly across all other countries. Watch out, for example, for exposure to countries with which your home country has hostile relations. But all else equal, insurance through risk pooling does have some value.

That said, diversification is far from sufficient to manage risks in a semiglobalized world with informational imperfections. As highlighted in the previous section, certain kinds of cross-border flows can amplify systemic risk—which diversification *doesn't* alleviate—or create new dangers. And since waiting to deal with such problems until they become pressing is typically less effective and more expensive, we need to think of prudential measures to take to counter cross-border risks, particularly capital risks, rather than simply reacting on an ad hoc basis as problems come up. I summarize some of the possibilities under the rubric of the ABCs: *alarms*, *breakers*, and *cushions*. Alarms are early warning systems, breakers curb contagion, and cushions soften the blows, particularly for the most vulnerable.

Setting effective alarms often begins with bolstering information flows: to manage risks, you have to know your exposure. The fact that initial estimates of Swiss banks' exposure to Greece were off by 95 percent—a matter of some $60 billion—due to a classification error is staggering.[49] What makes it worse is that we are talking about the *Swiss* banking authorities! Discovery of the error reduced (non-Greek) European banks' estimated exposure to Greece by nearly one-quarter.

To use alarms effectively, define specific exposure metrics and threat levels. Alarms may simply be advisory but can also, especially when the degree of threat is acute, trigger specific responses, as in the case of U.S. Homeland Security's terror alert level. For capital flows, an obvious focus given the discussion in this chapter and the next is on the absolute value of countries' current account balances. Based on the historical data summarized in figure 7-4, start paying attention when they reach 3 percent of GDP and start getting worried when they exceed 4 percent. Other possible metrics include foreign debt as a proportion of GDP, and the measures of cross-border capital mobility calibrated in chapter 2. And threat levels often need to be tuned to country characteristics.

One specific action that serious threats can trigger is the activation of various kinds of breakers to curb market excesses. Joseph Stiglitz provides the following analogy in a paper subtitled "Why Full Financial Integration May Be Undesirable," which also reminds us that some of the same ideas about managing systemic risk should also apply to energy, transportation, and information infrastructure, among other areas:

> With an integrated electric grid the total capacity required to limit the probability of a blackout to a particular level can be reduced. But a failure in one part of the system can lead to system-wide failure; in the absence

FIGURE 7-4

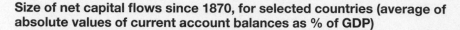

Size of net capital flows since 1870, for selected countries (average of absolute values of current account balances as % of GDP)

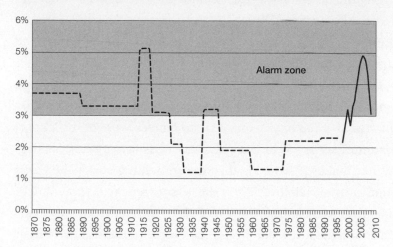

Countries covered: Argentina, Australia, Canada, Denmark, France, Germany, Italy, Japan, Norway, Sweden, United Kingdom, and United States.

Sources: Maurice Obstfeld and Alan Taylor, "The Great Depression as a Watershed: International Capital Mobility Over the Long Run," NBER Working Paper 5960, March 1997 (data before 1997), World Bank, World Development Indicators (data after 1997).

of integration, the failure would have been geographically constrained. Well-designed networks have circuit breakers, to prevent the "contagion" of the failure of one part of the system to others.[50]

In a general capital market context, limits on daily movements in prices of individual stocks or broad market aggregates and suspension of trading when those limits are reached provide an example of circuit breakers. In a specifically cross-border context, capital controls may have to be considered as a moderating influence, especially by small economies, although they do have undesirable side effects. More broadly, figure out which of the dominos (as in the cartoon at the beginning of this chapter) should be kept farther apart or be reinforced or be removable in times of crisis to keep negative chain reactions from running amok and causing systemwide as opposed to isolated damage.

When safety mechanisms fail and trouble does develop, cushions can help soften the blow. Maintain strategic reserves. Put appropriate hedging and insurance arrangements in place. Prepare policy responses ahead of time to a range of macroeconomic contingencies. Remember the special role of the government: when disaster strikes, it's still national governments that get the call, and so they need to be in a position to meet basic requirements such as food security. And perhaps most importantly, build redundancy into critical systems. Thus Nassim Taleb, the author of *The Black Swan*, chides economists for failing to respect nature's preference for redundancy and the robustness that it implies: "An economist would find it inefficient to maintain two lungs and two kidneys."[51]

More controversially, these ABC's might be augmented with a D in the form of dampeners. Breakers are designed to be applied only in the event of trouble, but there are some indications that with widespread speculation and high frequency trading, it might be necessary to "throw some sand in the wheels" of market operations on an ongoing basis to make them function better. This was the idea behind Nobel laureate James Tobin's proposal for a small tax on all international currency transactions, intended to curb waves of speculative capital flowing in and out of countries while leaving healthier longer-term flows basically unaffected.

Given all this discussion of the regulation of risks, I should conclude with the reminder that it is not meant to supersede the emphasis on integration earlier in this chapter and in the rest of this book. Some degree of cross-border integration usually makes sense for the purposes of reducing risk through diversification as well as ADDING value in other ways. But trouble *can* develop, and prudence provides a better basis for dealing with that possibility than panic. Hence the idea of keeping alarms activated, breakers on standby, and cushions ready just in case in order to manage the risks associated with cross-border capital flows in particular. And the example of food is a reminder that risk management doesn't always mean restricting flows—sometimes it means opening them up. The key is to evaluate particular flows on their merit and shape globalization to maximize the gains while managing the risks—rather than to seek an illusory safety behind closed borders or effectively ignore the risks altogether.

Chapter Eight

Global Imbalances

Source: John Coe

THE LAST THREE CHAPTERS focused on economists' standard trilogy of market failures: small numbers, externalities, and informational problems. This chapter deals with a different kind of phenomenon—one subject to a spirited debate about whether leave-it-to-the-market policies really are prone to create problems (as they do in the presence of the standard sorts of market failures) or not.

The phenomenon concerns cross-border imbalances. These are illustrated by the cartoon, which depicts the imbalance that has resulted from the chronic U.S. trade deficit and accumulation of debt obligations vis-à-vis China. Dividing out the world's biggest sovereign debt obligation across the respective populations, the average American owes some $3,300 to China, which amounts to $800 lent to the United States per Chinese citizen. Pretty striking, considering that at the prevailing exchange rate, the United States' per capita income is about twelve times higher than China's. When was the last time you came across someone who had already lent more than 20 percent of his or her annual income to someone twelve times richer, and continued to lend more?[1]

There has been a broad increase in trade and capital imbalances in recent years (and not just between the United States and China), to the point where, by late 2010, they were making headlines—and setting the global policy agenda. Thus, the meeting of the G20 leaders in Seoul in late 2010 was mostly focused on limiting such imbalances, and they basically managed to agree that these imbalances needed to be managed.

If that doesn't sound like much, remember that there is still fundamental disagreement about whether such imbalances really require (additional) policy intervention. Fans of World 2.0 tend to think not, asserting that markets do a better job of balancing supply and demand than the alternatives. The Chinese concur, although they employ a somewhat different argument. Meanwhile, countries that run large trade deficits, most notably the United States, are more receptive to World 1.0 arguments for protectionism or mercantilism as ways of reducing external borrowing requirements.

The first half of this chapter focuses on capital imbalances, helping round out the previous chapter's discussion of capital risks. It summarizes evidence on cumulating imbalances before looking in more detail at the imbalance between the United States and China. The specifics of this case inform a simple model of growth in which market processes *can* lead to problematic outcomes, suggesting a need for intervention—ideally on a multilateral basis.

The second half of this chapter focuses on another important imbalance, involving labor instead of capital. Populations are shrinking in Japan and parts of Europe but swelling in some of the poorest areas in Africa and South Asia. And it's not only population growth rates that vary widely: age distributions are diverging as well. We will see that imbalances within and across countries could be alleviated through more cross-border migration. In other words, more active management of imbalances isn't always code for restricting openness; depending on the context, it can involve more of an emphasis on integration than on regulation.

Capital Imbalances

Before looking at evidence on capital imbalances over time, it is useful to review how they are related to trade imbalances. In a closed economy, there are no imbalances of either kind: trade is zero, and savings equal investment. Trade has the potential to drive a wedge between savings and investment: if a country runs a trade surplus, domestic savings exceeds domestic investment, and if it runs a trade deficit, the reverse is true. With no other cross-border capital flows, domestic savings minus domestic investment is equal to the *trade balance*: exports minus imports. And adding in other kinds of capital flows, savings minus investment becomes equal to the *current account balance*: the trade balance plus net factor income from abroad (earnings/losses on foreign investments) and net transfer payments (e.g., foreign aid received).

Figure 7-4 in the previous chapter tracked the evolution of current account balances for twelve countries over more than a hundred years and underlined a recent surge in the sum of their absolute values, from 2 percent of GDP in 1990 to nearly 5 percent in 2007. Data for a broader sample of countries indicates a precrisis peak of nearly 6 percent—and shows that two-thirds of the increase since 1990 in current account (im)balances was due to increased trade (im)balances.

FIGURE 8-1

Historical and estimated world current account balances, 1990–2015

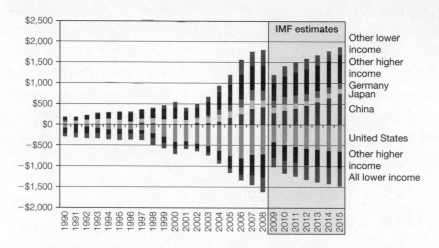

Notes: This chart reflects summation of positive and negative current account balances by year. Country income categories are based on World Bank classifications. 2009 figures reflect actual data for 66 countries and estimates for 105 countries. All data in current-year USD (not adjusted for inflation).

Source: IMF, World Economic Outlook, April 2010.

What figure 7-4 did not highlight was the persistent nature of the imbalances in recent years. This is clearer in figure 8-1, which also provides data on overall magnitudes: certain countries, most notably the United States, have run and are forecast to continue to run current account deficits that they import capital to fund, whereas others, such as Germany, Japan, and China, have typically run current account surpluses, that is, had capital left over to export.

Chronic surpluses or deficits at the country level matter because they imply that imbalances will tend to cumulate—as opposed to canceling out from one year to the next. These effects show up in the form of sustained changes in countries' net international investment positions (NIIPs, or the stock of foreign assets owned by citizens of a particular country minus the stock of that country's assets owned by foreigners), as depicted in figure 8-2.

Of course, current account balances are just one influence—albeit an important one—on NIIPs. Thus, despite the massive current account deficits that the United States ran from 2003 to 2007, figure 8-2 indicates

FIGURE 8-2

Historical world net international investment positions, 1990–2007

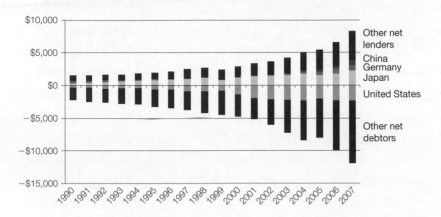

Note: No distinction is made here between Net Foreign Assets and Net International Investment Position.

Source: Based on Net Foreign Assets series from Philip R. Lane and Gian Maria Milesi-Ferretti, "The External Wealth of Nations Mark II," *Journal of International Economics* 73 (November 2007; August 2009 update): 223–250.

its NIIP declined only moderately, and revised estimates indicate it even improved over this period.[2] How could that be? The U.S. dollar fell over this period and the United States invested in higher-yielding foreign assets (portfolio equity and FDI) while foreign investors in the United States mainly held lower-yielding government bonds. But the United States' negative NIIP almost doubled in 2008 as the dollar rose and equity values fell, so Americans shouldn't take too much comfort from that aspect of the chart. Also, keep in mind that these are net figures that balance out larger *gross* stocks. At the end of 2009, the United States owned $18.4 trillion of foreign assets and foreign owners held $21.1 trillion of U.S. assets, leaving the United States with a NIIP of negative $2.7 trillion, or about 19 percent of GDP.[3]

Returning to current account (im)balances, many explanations have been offered as to why they have widened in recent years. Some invoke fundamental factors, such as demographics, which are discussed in the second half of this chapter. Note for now that the connection between age and propensity to save is quite intuitive: young people can't save much and many borrow to pay for education; adults save in their working years but then dissave in retirement. One recent study defines people aged thirty-five to sixty-nine as "prime savers" and finds a correlation between the proportion of a country's population in this range and its current account balance.[4] This suggests, among other things, that since prime savers' share of the population will peak in developed markets well before emerging ones, the imbalances—with developed markets increasingly running current account deficits and emerging markets surpluses—will widen through 2025.

Demographics, however, don't fully explain today's current account imbalances. China's surplus and the United States' deficit in 2009 were more than four and two times, respectively, what one would expect based on the calibration of demographics and growth trends in the study cited above. Let's look at those two countries' imbalances, and their relationship with each other, in more detail.

Chimerica Continued

In recent years (2007–2009), China's merchandise trade surplus with the United States has accounted for about two-thirds of China's total current account surplus, and more than one-third to one-half (in 2009) of the United States' total current account deficit. China's trade surplus adds to its foreign currency reserves, as do its purchases of foreign currency coming into the country that are aimed at holding down the renminbi. These reserves are used to underwrite further borrowing by the U.S. government—China is the largest holder of U.S. treasuries in the world—and help prop up the U.S. dollar. This, in turn, fuels U.S. consumption and trade deficits, perpetuating imbalances. It is this complementarity that Niall Ferguson and Moritz Schularick had in mind when they coined the term "Chimerica"—in happier, precrisis times—to describe the two countries' relationship.[5]

To dig deeper into how a relatively poor country such as China has been able to finance a good part of the large current account deficit posted by the United States, it is useful to analyze both countries' current accounts on the basis laid out in the previous section. Note that imbalances can be caused both internally (by a savings-investment gap) and externally (through trade deficits and currency disparities). Tables 8-1 and 8-2 break down the internal imbalances for China and the United States, respectively, by the sources of savings (households, corporations, and government) and investment before listing external contributors.

As table 8-1 illustrates, China's current account surplus reflects a complex mix of factors, many of which the Chinese government has long recognized as problematic. Back in March 2007, Premier Wen Jiabao stated that "the biggest problem with China's economy is that the growth is unstable, unbalanced, uncoordinated, and unsustainable."[6] Since then, there *have* been some dramatic shifts. Thus, health insurance coverage has expanded from 15 percent of the population in 2003 to 85 percent in 2008.[7] And boomtowns in China's interior such as Chongqing are visible manifestations of the attention now being paid to boosting domestic demand. Overall, however, China's government is judged unlikely to significantly change its overall policy framework very quickly, given its dependence on continuing growth for its legitimacy and the interlocking character of its various market interventions. That's why the IMF's current account projections through 2015 in figure 8-1 forecast a swelling rather than shrinking Chinese current account surplus—as do other sources.[8]

Table 8-2 presents a parallel analysis for the United States. While the reasons for the U.S. deficits are not quite as complex as China's, figure 8-1 indicates that they have persisted over an even longer period. And although 2009 saw a rise in the risibly low U.S. household savings rate and a narrowing of the U.S. trade deficit, decisive policy shifts aren't expected there either, leading to forecasts that U.S. current account deficits will start to widen again (e.g., in figure 8-1).

Such predictions that imbalances would, after a correction in 2008–2009, continue to widen in the short to medium run precipitated global acrimony over exchange rates and trade imbalances in fall 2010. The global nature of the problem is highlighted by the fact that it was Brazil's finance minister rather than a U.S. or Chinese official who termed

TABLE 8-1

China's current account decomposition and potential causes

Decomposition		Potential causes
Gross savings: 54% of GDP	Household savings: 23% of GDP	• *Preventive savings:* Social safety nets (such as health insurance) were dismantled during reforms and are only gradually being redeveloped. • *Underdeveloped credit markets:* With limited access to credit, families must save more for expensive big-ticket items like housing. • *Catch-up and culture:* Families are building wealth after near-zero savings rates under planned economy; culture supports saving. • *Bride competition:* Gender imbalance (20% more boys at birth) may spur parents to save to boost sons' marriage prospects.*
	Corporate savings: 19% of GDP	• *Low cost of capital and dividends:* State-owned firms access low-cost bank credit; until recently did not have to pay out dividends for use of state assets; encouraged to reinvest profits. • *Corporate governance:* Insiders may save to keep control of funds. • *Underdeveloped capital markets:* Uncertain access to funds later.
	Government savings: 12% of GDP	• *Rising government revenues:* Dividends from state-owned firms, land sales, tax collection. • *Investment over consumption:* Government traditionally prefers to spend on investment (e.g., infrastructure) versus consumption.
Gross capital formation (investment): 43% of GDP		• [China's level of investment is already very high; raising investment would reduce the current account deficit but risk allocating funds to wasteful uses.]
Current account balance: 11% of GDP		• *Undervalued currency and employment:* Cheap currency enhances export competitiveness, supporting employment and contributing to domestic political stability. • *Accumulation of reserves:* Asian countries after the 1997 crisis prioritized building up foreign currency reserves to improve macroeconomic stability; holding large amounts of reserves also increases China's foreign policy leverage.

Note: Potential causes shown in [brackets] in tables 8-1 and 8-2 reduce the size of current account imbalances or otherwise make them less problematic.

Source: The percentage of GDP figures are 2007 data from World Bank, World Development Indicators, with savings distributed among sources based on the ratios (but not the exact amounts) shown in "China's Savings Rate and Its Long-Term Outlook," Goldman Sachs Global Economics Paper 191, October 16, 2009. Potential causes are drawn from a variety of sources; for China, the same Goldman Sachs report was particularly useful.
* Sex ratio is from 2005. Broader argument is elaborated in Shang-JinWei and Xiaobo Zhang, "The Competitive Saving Motive: Evidence from Rising Sex Ratios and Savings Rates in China," NBER Working Paper 15093, June 2009.

TABLE 8-2

U.S. current account decomposition and potential causes

Decomposition		Potential causes
Gross savings: 14% of GDP	Household savings: 3%	• *Asset price gains (wealth effects):* Rising stock market and housing values led households to perceive less need to save. • *Credit availability:* Access to credit reduces need to save up for major purchases and to engage in preventive saving. • *Stagnant wages among the less skilled:* Borrowing to maintain and/or raise living standards without accustomed wage gains.
	Corporate savings: 10%	[Generally, corporate savings have been high across OECD economies in recent years. This partially offsets low household and government savings rates in the U.S.]
	Government savings: 1%	• *Fiscal deficits:* Since the brief period of budget balance under the Clinton administration, G. W. Bush tax cuts, wartime military spending, and, more recently, stimulus measures have all led to large fiscal deficits.
Gross capital formation (investment): 18% of GDP		[Optimists point to profitable investment opportunities in the U.S. in excess of savings as a positive rationale for the current account deficit, but this is countered by the high proportion invested in treasuries.]
Current account balance: –5% of GDP		• *Trade competitiveness:* Competition versus countries with lower labor costs and other cost savings such as lower health care costs (and trade deficit with China elevated by its undervalued currency). • *Developed capital markets:* Attraction of U.S. capital markets (until recently perceived as most advanced, secure, well regulated). • *Reserve currency:* U.S. dollar status as reserve currency attracts capital inflows.

Note: Potential causes shown in [brackets] in tables 8-1 and 8-2 reduce the size of current account imbalances or otherwise make them less problematic.

Source: The percentage of GDP figures are 2007 data from World Bank, World Development Indicators, with savings distributed among sources based on the ratios (but not the exact amounts) shown in Goldman Sachs Global Economics Paper 191, "China's Savings Rate and Its Long-Term Outlook," October 16, 2009. Potential causes drawn from a variety of sources.

---

the situation a "currency war"—and effectively forced the G20 to rush to defuse such talk. But before discussing the policy interventions that are being proposed to deal with such imbalances, it seems useful to ask whether there really is a problem here that market forces cannot sort out. Some think not. Thus, according to Larry Lindsey, the first director of the National Economic Council under President George W. Bush,

America, however, benefits from this arrangement. The Chinese clearly undervalue their exchange rate. This means American consumers are able to buy goods at an artificially low price, making them winners.

In order to maintain this arrangement, the People's Bank of China must buy excess dollars, and has accumulated nearly $1 trillion of reserves. Since it has no domestic use for them, it turns around and lends them back to America in our Treasury, corporate and housing loan markets. This means that both Treasury borrowing costs and mortgage interest rates are lower than they otherwise would be. American home-owners and taxpayers are winners as a result.

There are losers, of course, most notably American producers of goods that are now made in China. Yet the losses to these producers are out-weighed by the benefits from Chinese subsidies of our imports of consumer goods and the reductions in our borrowing costs from generous Chinese lending.[9]

According to Lindsey, then, there is no market failure or fear to worry about here, and nothing to be gained economically, from G20 get-togethers. This emphasis on integration-without-intervention clearly aligns with World 2.0. The question here is whether that worldview provides a good perspective on imbalances.

Models and Messages

Since imbalances do not show up on the standard list of market failures, the case that market-based processes can lead to problems in this regard needs to be made. This section does so by considering a suite of simple theoretical models of growth that exclude all the standard sorts of market failures to make the point that it is nonetheless possible for market processes to lead to problematic imbalances. Note that this approach of using a theoretical model to illustrate a possibility that has been denied is very different from—and logically much more defensible than—the usual approach of using incomplete models to make predictions about what will actually happen in the real world (which is what chapter 4 critiqued).

So there are no small numbers, externalities, or informational imperfections in the suite of models considered here, nor any currency problems. Instead, attention is reserved for the effects of two kinds of differences between two countries: in terms of initial capital stocks per capita, or how rich the two countries are, and in terms of time rates of preference, or how patient they are.[10] In line with the discussion of Chimerica, the poorer country, denoted as C, is assumed to be more patient than the richer country, A, as elaborated below. But apart from these cross-country differences, the rest of the context is simplified (e.g., technological progress is ignored) so as to minimize the number of moving parts extraneous to the dynamic mechanism highlighted by the models.

Begin by considering, as a simplifying baseline, a model in which A and C have different capital stocks per capita—A's are higher—but are otherwise identical, including in terms of access to technology and, for now, time rates of preference. Also assume provisionally that they operate side-by-side but in isolation from each other. In other words, this baseline allows for one of the two kinds of cross-country differences that we ultimately want to consider (the second kind will be considered next).

Convergence in the long run is guaranteed under these assumptions because if you run time far enough out, initial conditions don't affect projected outcomes. Convergence in the long run implies that C is going to have higher rates of capital accumulation and growth than A in the short to medium run. The asymmetry in growth rates—in favor of C—will be higher the greater is the initial asymmetry in capital stocks (wealth endowments). And extending this basic model to include governmental investment and consumption suggests that C will also have a proportionately bigger public sector than A in terms of productive investments—but not in terms of consumption (e.g., environmental public goods). So this very simple setup suffices to generate some of the differences evident in tables 8-1 and 8-2.

Now, add to this baseline setup an asymmetry in terms of discount rates, with C also being more patient or long-term-oriented than A— but continue, for now, to keep the two economies isolated from each other. This assumption of different discount rates is motivated by several aspects of Chimerica: the long decline in U.S. savings rates that began in the mid-1950s and accelerated in the 1980s, the much higher savings and investment rates in China, the Chinese government's emphasis on maximizing growth rather than welfare,[11] and suggestions by culture gurus that the disparity in short-term versus long-term orientation is perhaps the key cultural difference between the two countries.[12] While economists may not be convinced, especially by the cultural evidence, note that there is nothing in economic theory to rule out the possibility of different time rates of preference across countries. So this is a possibility that must be accounted for by those who assert that no need can arise for governments to intervene to fix imbalances.

Allowing for different discount rates has such extreme implications in terms of tilting long-run outcomes in favor of C that the impacts of different discount rates usually go unanalyzed in most theoretical treatments. But one textbook provides a summary (for the case of multiple countries):

> *If all countries have different discount rates, the country with the lowest discount rate determines up to which point capital is accumulated in the world economy. The country with the lowest discount rate provides capital until its discount rate and the real interest rate are equal. Then its consumption stays constant. For the other countries, consumption decreases in the course of time.*[13]

The country with the lower discount rate, C, eventually also becomes richer than A under this scenario (unlike the baseline scenario, which implied convergence in their incomes). One could imagine this outcome being at least mildly disturbing from the perspective of A's citizenry.

Even more disturbing, though, is what happens when one connects two countries with different rates of time preference: the divergence implied is much more dramatic. The spendthrift economy, A, falls behind even more quickly as it borrows from C to finance current consumption. Exactly how this happens depends on the channels that connect A and C. Start by allowing capital mobility while continuing to disallow trade in output. With different discount rates, the less patient country, A, will import capital from a more patient country, C, in the short run and incur some level of ongoing debt service payments in the long run that effectively reduce its long-run consumption levels.

But at least the physical capital formation that corresponds to this process of capital-based connection is expected to occur in A (although it is financed by C). With trade as a channel of connection as well, there need not be physical capital investment in A at all: trade opens up the possibility of C running a trade surplus based on productive capacity at home and accumulating IOUs from A rather than investing in productive capacity in A! If we focused on just the trade part of the relationship, we might characterize it as benignly as Lindsey: since trade embodies a voluntary exchange, it supposedly can't be bad. Yet the possibility of cross-border connections (further) shifting consumption from the future toward the present, in the spendthrift economy to the point of putting pressure on living standards over time, is surely very disturbing.

To those potential problems with opening up, one can add currency issues—which were simplified away from the suite of models presented above, even though they occupied center stage in the G20 leaders' discussions in late 2010 of imbalances. Imagine that A issues IOUs to C in A's own currency, which it can print as much of as it likes. Obviously A has a huge incentive to devalue its currency over time. And C could anticipate this, taking us out of the reach of the "nonstrategic" models that we have looked at.[14] But even without modeling, currency issues clearly create additional challenges for those of us intent on preserving the benefits of international exchange while managing the side effects—that is, avoiding reversion to World 1.0 just because World 2.0 doesn't work.

The broad message from the suite of models discussed in this section is that World 3.0 clearly requires some management of imbalances of the sort exemplified by Chimerica. While the precise approach that will be undertaken remains to be determined, the models do provide grounding for discussions of the proposals in the air in late 2010, as this issue moved to center stage. First, the G20 leaders' vague agreement to move toward more market-based determination of exchange rates might be a step in the right direction (if there were any specific follow-up) since the renminbi does seem to me, as it does to many others, to be significantly undervalued. But to leave matters there would be to peel off once again into the "markets know best" camp, problematic both because of the character of foreign exchange markets (they are considered very inefficient compared to other categories of financial markets and, relatedly, have a very high speculative component) and because there are reasons for imbalances that have nothing to do with exchange rate misalignments (for a recap, consult tables 8-1 and 8-2).

Second, the idea of moving toward some kind of cap on imbalances seems attractive in light of the discussion in the last chapter, particularly around figure 7-4. So, at first blush, does the initial U.S. proposal in 2010 of specific limits on current account balances as a percentage of GDP that, once reached, trigger remediation. However, the proposal was rejected in summary fashion by countries whose current account balances have recently exceeded the proposed limits (e.g., China). Looking beyond Chimerica, there is also an issue of fairness in imposing the same percentage caps on large economies and small ones when they translate into very different contributions in absolute terms to global imbalances. The broader implication, encountered before (in chapter 6), is that one might want to have differentiated targets to account for vast differences across countries.

Third, despite the differences across countries, this is a situation that illustrates how multilateral approaches are, in at least some situations, to be preferred to narrower ones. There is no presumption that, in a world without trade barriers and currency manipulation, trade would balance out between country pairs; rather, the presumption is that of a rough balance in a country's trade with the rest of the world. As a result, it is natural to think of capping imbalances in those terms—but that requires multilateral agreement rather than unilateral action.

The final thought worth adding in regard to Chimerica is that while currency and trade adjustments have a role to play in reducing the problem of imbalances, the United States also needs to address the domestic factors that underlie its savings-investment gap (if not the overall low levels of both). At the first academic conference on international competition that I ever attended, in 1985, similar concerns were in the air in the United States about Japan. A young Larry Summers pointed out that while forcing adjustments on the Japanese might help alleviate the chronic U.S. current account deficit in the short to medium run, action was required on the domestic front if the problem was to be solved in the long run. Looking at recent numbers, I suspect the same idea can be applied to the United States and China in 2010. Which illustrates another broader World 3.0 theme: don't focus on the international to the exclusion of the domestic since many—or most—effects are still highly localized.

Human Imbalances

Demographers Wolfgang Lutz and Warren C. Sanderson pegged the dawn of the twenty-first century as the shift from the "century of population growth" to the "century of aging."[15] After rapid growth dating back to the advent of World 1.0, world population is expected to level off at some 9 billion-plus by the middle of the twenty-first century. The "demographic transition" that generates this pattern—rising life expectancies followed by falling birth rates—is well along in rich countries but at different stages and progressing at different rates across the developing world, creating widening demographic disparities.

Consider the world's oldest and youngest large countries, Japan and Niger. In Japan, the median age is already forty-four years and by 2050 is expected to reach fifty-five! And from 2010 to 2050, Japan's population is projected to *shrink* by 20 percent to only 100 million. There's so much concern about how Japan's declining working-age population can support an unprecedented number of elderly that they're racing to develop robots to help them out. Much of Europe faces similar conditions, and the challenge is particularly difficult in eastern European countries with a fraction of Japan's per-capita income. The OECD has estimated that without large-scale immigration, Japan's living standards could drop by 23 percent, the EU's by 18 percent, and the United States' by 10 percent.[16]

In Niger, in contrast, the median age is only fifteen and a full 68 percent of the population is under twenty-five years old. While it seems everyone in Japan is sprouting gray hairs, in Niger it's hard to find an adult, much less a senior citizen (Niger is also one of the world's least densely populated countries). And Niger's population is projected to more than triple over the next forty years. Figure 8-3 puts these examples in broader context. In the chart on the left, South Asia and Africa are shifted to the top to emphasize that most of the population growth through 2050 will take place in those regions.

Thinking about the link between demographics and economics has come a long way since the old Malthusian caricatures of people as mouths to feed. More recently, the "neutralist" perspective has gained favor as research has indicated no clear positive or negative effect of population growth on per capita income.[17] Age distributions, however, do seem to have a significant impact, with countries enjoying favorable "windows of opportunity" when a high proportion of their populations are of working age. A bulge of children like Niger's or a high proportion of retirees like in Japan both mean that each worker has to support more dependents (a high dependency ratio), which makes it harder to accumulate wealth. As figure 8-4 shows, the proportion of working-age people in East Asia (including Japan), Europe, and the United States will be declining while it rises in South Asia and Africa.

More migration is an obvious remedy for demographic imbalances but it stirs up many fears. This section summarizes patterns of migration and the potential global gains from enhancing such cross-border

FIGURE 8-3

Long-term population growth and age distribution trends

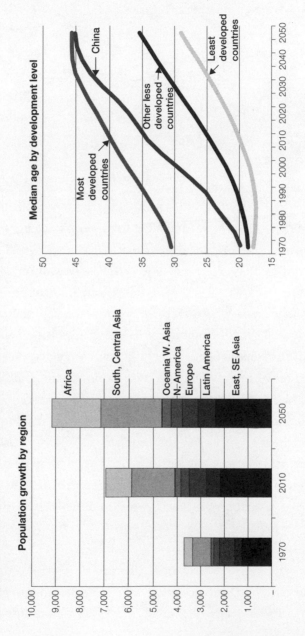

Population growth by region

Median age by development level

Source: United Nations, World Population Prospects, 2008.

FIGURE 8-4

Ratio of working-age to dependent population, 1950–2050

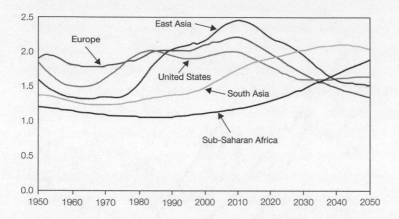

Source: David E. Bloom and David Canning, "Global Demographic Change: Dimensions and Economic Significance," NBER Working Paper 10817, September 2004.

flows of people, and the sections that follow look at migration's impact in sending and receiving countries.

As we saw in chapter 2, human flows across borders are much smaller than product or capital flows, with only about 3 percent of people living outside the country where they were born, roughly the same proportion as fifty years ago.[18] And today's levels of migration pale in comparison to the late 1800s, when "total emigrants over a decade accounted for 14 percent of the Irish population, 1 in 10 Norwegians, and 7 percent of the populations of both Sweden and the United Kingdom."[19] With stark wage disparities, falling transportation costs, and the addition of more national borders, why hasn't the number of migrants surged upward like other kinds of cross-border flows?

The simple answer is that while the benefits of migration net of the costs *have* gone up, barriers have been raised to block its growth. As Ng and Whalley explain:

> *Prior to 1913, visas were not required for transit between most countries, and work permits were also not required for employment of foreigners. Passports were largely used as proof of identity and/or citizenship once*

inside national borders in case help were needed, typically from an embassy or ambassador abroad. Border formalities focused on revenue collection via tariffs from those crossing borders with goods in transit, not on documentary proof of identity.[20]

In fact, up to 1924, visas weren't required to settle in the United States and "in 1905 only 1 percent of the one million people who made the transatlantic journey to Ellis Island were denied entry into the country."[21] Migration was even subsidized in many cases by both sending and receiving countries to address labor market imbalances.

In today's "borderless" world, visas and work permits are almost always required, and the processing of these documents alone has been estimated to cost $88 billion globally, or about 0.3 percent of world GDP.[22] In one in ten countries a passport itself costs more than 10 percent of the country's per capita income. In the Democratic Republic of the Congo, a passport costs 125 percent of the per capita income—and does not, of course, guarantee visas to travel![23] Furthermore, there's no organization like the WTO dedicated to removing barriers to migration.

Because of the fears I will address below, policies in most countries are aimed more at restricting than facilitating migration. And yet, with such strong incentives for movement, enforcement is highly uneven. Some 50 million people live and work abroad without proper authorization, and many endure unspeakable horrors trying to cross borders illegally, with thousands dying each year.

With figures like that, one might assume that most migration is from developing countries to developed countries, but actually that is not the case. Sixty percent of migration from developing countries is to other developing countries—although almost always *relatively* more developed ones. Thirty-seven percent is from developing countries to developed countries, and the balance (3 percent) is from developed countries to developing countries. And we can see the usual distance effects here, too. Nearly half of migrants stay within their home regions, 60 percent stay in a country with the same major religion, 40 percent move to a place with the same major language, and so on.[24]

Readers from developed countries might have a hard time believing that the stock of immigrants hasn't gone up in recent years. Intuitions about rising immigration in developed countries are, in fact, correct, but reflect a shift in the composition of migratory flows, with a higher proportion of migrants now going to developed countries, rather than larger aggregate flows. This change, combined with different population growth rates, has led the proportion of immigrants in the populations of developed countries to rise from 4.6 percent in 1960 to 12.1 percent in 2010. It's also true that a much larger proportion of new immigrants into developed countries come from developing countries. In the United States, this proportion rose from about half in the 1960s to about 90 percent in the 1990s and early 2000s.[25]

Despite increasing developed-to-developing country migration, further increases in such flows account for by far the largest part of the estimated gains from liberalizing cross-border movements of people. And the estimated gains are themselves very large: as noted in chapter 4, the gains from completely opening up immigration have been estimated to be so large as to exceed current world GDP; and even more conservative estimates of partial moves to increase immigration imply gains that dwarf those from liberalization of trade and capital flows.[26] Workers, particularly those who move freely from a poor country to a rich one with proper documents, gain tremendously. Most of us are excited about a salary raise of a few percentage points. Compare that to a World Bank estimate that the real income of workers moving from developing to developed countries triples![27] Immigrants and their children often enjoy other benefits such as improved education and health care. And migrants from the world's poorest countries benefit even more, on average enjoying "a 15-fold increase in income, a doubling in education enrollment rate, and a 16-fold reduction in child mortality." Yet, despite these gains, the poorest are also the least mobile. The "median emigration rate in countries with low levels of human development is only about one third the rate out of countries with high levels of human development."[28]

While the discussion of immigration in chapter 4 mostly focused on economic benefits, the cultural, administrative, and geographic advantages of migration are also worth mentioning. Cultural benefits, such as access to diverse cuisines, are plain. Administratively, migrants themselves often enjoy political benefits such as greater freedom and more effective governance in their destination countries. And to cite a geographic example, newcomers from a country such as Bangladesh (with a population density of 1,125 people per square kilometer) appreciate the amount of space available in countries like Australia and Canada (with 3 people per square kilometer).

To summarize this section, the wide gaps in living standards between rich countries and poor ones and the low levels of migration relative to other kinds of cross-border flows make large potential gains from migration plausible. The more controversial question relates to negative impacts and whether they are sufficient to justify giving up the gains. We turn next to fears about migration in receiving countries and then finally to fears in sending countries.

Resistance Among Receivers

The most prevalent fears about inflows of migrants relate to their impacts on labor markets. Natives fear that an influx of foreigners will mean more competition for jobs, lower wages, and potentially more unemployment. If all workers were identical and the demand for labor were fixed, such fears would make more sense, for then an influx of immigrants would indeed increase the supply of labor, reducing natives' wages or employment. Instead, the reality is that immigrants' labor *substitutes* for some natives' labor, potentially harming them, but at the same time it *complements* other natives' labor, helping to improve their employment and wage prospects. One notable complementarity is how immigrant child care workers help native women in developed countries stay in the workforce. And immigrants also demand goods and services in the economies they move to, creating additional work for natives. Weighing these factors, economists have largely concluded that the aggregate impact of immigration for developed countries is positive.

One study estimates that destination countries "would capture about one-fifth of the gains from a 5 percent increase in the number of migrants in developed countries."[29]

It is also worth addressing the concern about migration's impact on unskilled or low-skilled native workers in developed countries, since a large proportion of immigrants from developing countries—especially the undocumented—have only limited education. Two-thirds of illegal immigrants entering the United States since 1980 never completed high school.[30] Most solid research, however, indicates that the impact of immigration on low-skilled native workers is quite small. One study that stirred up a lot of fear was George Borjas's 2003 simulation that estimated that immigration into the United States depressed average wages by 3.2 percent and wages of high school dropouts by 8.9 percent.[31] However, that study assumed that native workers and immigrants were perfect substitutes and that capital stocks don't adjust to changes in the labor supply.[32] Allowing for capital stocks to adjust, more recent research by Borjas and Lawrence Katz indicates that illegal immigration had a negligible or even positive impact on Americans' average wages and that the wages of high school dropouts were reduced by only 3.6 percent.[33] Even more recent research by Gianmarco Ottaviano and Giovanni Peri concludes that "immigration (1990–2006) had small negative effects in the short run on native workers with no high school degree (−0.7%) and on average wages (−0.4%) while it had small positive effects on native workers with no high school degree (+0.3%) and on average native wages (+0.6%) in the long run."[34]

Research on the impact of immigration on natives' employment levels showed a similar pattern: "One European study found that a 10 percent increase in the share of migrants in total employment would lower the employment of residents by between 0.2 and 0.7%," but research also indicated that "the massive inflows associated with European Union accession led neither to displacement of local workers nor to unemployment in Ireland and the U.K."[35]

If big econometric studies don't convince you that immigration doesn't decimate natives' employment and wage prospects, consider a concrete historical example. Look at what happened when Britain opened up to migration from eastern Europe: "Growth soared. Unemployment fell. Wages continued to rise. Newcomers paid much more in taxes than they took out in benefits and public services. After the global financial crisis plunged the economy into recession, many Poles went home rather than remain unemployed in Britain."[36]

Freer immigration is necessary, too, from the point of view of labor quality. At present, developing countries have twice the number of university-educated professionals as developed countries. And immigrants tend to be big contributors to entrepreneurship. According to Legrain, "Nearly half of Silicon Valley's venture capital-funded startups were cofounded by immigrants," who are "30 percent more likely than native-born Americans to start their own business."[37]

Immigration can also help address demographic imbalances, staving off shrinking populations and workforce sizes in developed countries.[38] But before we get too excited (or fearful) about youths from Niger heading en masse to Japan to staff factories and care for the elderly, we should apply some foresight and recognize that migrants too eventually grow old, tempering the impact of migration on dependency ratios. Thus, we get calculations like the UN's estimate that Japan would have to take on 550 million migrants (more than five times its present population) to match its 1995 dependency ratio in 2050.[39] Migration indeed can help address the problem of old-age dependency, but it's not a silver bullet. Temporary migration is particularly helpful in this context, but also raises difficult questions about how to manage transitions and enforce return requirements, while respecting the rights and interests of all parties involved.[40] So, immigration should be part of a policy mix that also involves boosting productivity, increasing labor force participation, and in many cases facilitating higher fertility and raising retirement ages.

Let's turn briefly to cultural and administrative fears about migration into developed countries. From a cultural standpoint, it's true that some natives prefer to avoid inward migration in order to preserve the historic cultural and ethnic flavor of their communities. That's a legitimate interest that should be weighed against the benefits of immigration. It's important, however, not to let small numbers of impassioned opponents spoil the debate. Many communities value diversity and welcome the cultural richness that immigrants can contribute.

Regarding administrative fears, there are concerns that immigration leads to higher levels of crime. Data on incarceration rates in the United States should provide some comfort. According to a UN report, "On average, among men aged 18 to 39 (who comprise the vast majority of the prison population), the incarceration rate of the locally born was 3.5 percent, five times higher than the 0.7 percent rate of the foreign-born." European data *do* show higher incarceration rates for migrants in many countries and serve as one reminder of multidimensional integration challenges.[41]

Another "administrative" fear about immigrants is that they will use up proportionately more welfare and other benefits than natives and therefore represent a net drain on receiving countries. But despite its administrative accents, this is really an argument about one of the cost elements that cost-benefit analyses of immigration of the sort undertaken by economists and cited in the second half of this chapter do try to account for.

Persistence with such arguments reflects the zero-sum conviction that there is a fixed amount of prosperity to go around and if immigrants tap into it, there will be less left for natives. The best counter begins with the reminder that differences in labor productivity have a lot to do with the context in which someone works, rather than just his or her own characteristics. So, the impact of people moving from poor countries to rich ones isn't usually to export poverty. Successful migration from developing to developed countries takes people who are producing relatively little due to underdevelopment at home and supercharges their productivity by connecting them with more advanced institutions, technology, management practices, and so on. If their gains come mainly from increased productivity, no one has to lose at their expense.

Suspicion Among Senders

The big fear about migration in most poor countries is that brain drain of skilled professionals departing to earn higher wages in rich countries deprives the local economy of talent and steals away the expected returns on the country's scarce education investment. The evidence here is also surprisingly reassuring. While the number of skilled migrants out of poor countries has risen, the *proportion* of skilled workers leaving has not, due to rising education levels.[42] And there are intriguing findings indicating that the possibility of emigration actually contributes to more human capital formation in poor countries, at least in part offsetting the loss of skills when educated workers emigrate. The basic idea is that if educational attainment is a "ticket" to emigration, more young people may work toward that possibility, even though only some of them will actually leave the country.[43]

Set against concerns about brain drain are huge gains that those who stay behind in developing countries reap when their conationals—especially family members—go abroad. The most obvious gain is money that migrants send back to their home countries, transfers known as remittances. Remittance flows, which exceed foreign aid, have been linked to higher educational enrollment of children who remain at home as well as "household welfare, nutrition, food, health, and living conditions in places of origin."[44]

Migrants also bring skills back to developing countries, contribute to innovation, provide access to international networks, and so on. These effects are better appreciated when one considers that skilled migration isn't just a one-way flow. One recent estimate indicates that about half of skilled emigrants return to their home countries, typically after about five years.[45] Another study suggests that far lower return rates suffice to ensure positive social gains for some of the world's smallest, most vulnerable countries, the Pacific Islands, from the migration of skilled labor to Australia and New Zealand.[46] So, mobility of skilled workers is far from a pure loss or brain drain for developing countries. Rather, diasporas are a resource that countries such as India are increasingly trying to tap for developmental purposes—as I can testify from personal experience.

Toward a More Balanced World

Flows of capital and of migrants can, if unbalanced, cumulate into substantial stocks. Both suggest a need for policy intervention because of the long lags to which purely private, market-based processes for adjusting those stocks are likely to be subject. Regarding capital imbalances, the big surprise about the global financial crisis to many economists (or at least to many of those who were surprised) was not that capital markets could get out of line with fundamentals but how far out of line they could get and for how long. As far as human imbalances are concerned, governments already intervene heavily, mostly to restrict cross-border flows, and decentralized, domestic responses to demographic forecasts—what one might call the "laissez-faire l'amour" approach to population policy—would presumably take a generation to kick in, if at all.

That said, the risks and rewards involved in "holding" stocks of foreign capital and of migrants couldn't be more different. Capital eventually has to be paid back, and the only ways to get out of that obligation—default or devaluation—are highly damaging. Furthermore, big debts can turn moderate financial problems into crises. Migration, in contrast, tends to be a moderating force, with flows following a more countercyclical pattern—and ADDING value to sending and receiving countries as well as personally to the migrants in multiple ways. Furthermore, migrant stocks don't have to be returned. Naturalization is a far more benign unwinding process than default or devaluation. It is unsurprising, then, that this chapter suggested rather different approaches to dealing with imbalances in cross-border capital and labor flows.

The simple models described in the first half of this chapter indicate that while capital imbalances are not one of the standard forms of market failure recognized by economists, they *can* create significant problems. The previous chapter described how rapid unexpected outflows of capital can suck the air out of an economy. This chapter focused on how chronic capital imbalances can, even in simple models that exclude standard sources of market failure, bleed a country of its productive capacity, putting downward pressure on consumption and living standards over time.

Since most of us have grown up expecting to enjoy higher living standards than our parents (refer back to figure 1-1 for some of the reasons why), and since it is hard to ratchet down firmly held expectations, these are fearsome prospects. The good news is that they need not come to pass. Coordinated policy action *can* bring about a more gradual unwinding of capital imbalances, perhaps through a binding agreement on current account limits. But as we have seen, there are fundamental drivers such as demography involved as well as many other interlocking factors, so the process of any such unwinding is likely to be somewhat tumultuous, with particular tensions to be expected between the United States and China. Chapter 13 provides a broader perspective on the U.S.-China relationship and how it might be managed in the decades to come.

The policy recommendations regarding unbalanced cross-border flows of people are very different and far more positive: facilitate more migration, especially from developing to developed countries. But they must reckon with limits to the stock of immigrants most societies feel they can handle. Folk wisdom suggests that there is a significant increase in the salience and stickiness of immigration-related issues when the percentage of the population born overseas hits the low teens, although this estimate probably also depends on whether one is talking about a neighborhood or a large nation-state, how recently immigrant intensity has built up, and the state of the general economy (anti-immigrant sentiment tends to be countercyclical). In any case, the task of an enlightened government in this context is to make its country more receptive to the level of immigration required—and ensure that some integration as well as immigration takes place—rather than just to cave in to political pressures. Part III of this book provides additional discussion about how to pull this off.

If one still can't abide the idea of many more permanent immigrants, guest worker programs provide an alternative. Thus, Qatar and the UAE, where migrants greatly outnumber natives, essentially segregate labor markets for the two groups—although it is hard to call them models given how badly many of the migrant workers are treated. Of course, even more humane guest worker programs might offend sensibilities that see all men and women as created equal, but are such programs really much worse than restrictive visa policies?

To conclude, immigration serves as a counterpoint to financial imbalances in reminding us that managing imbalances doesn't always mean restricting flows. In that sense, the examples parallel the pairing in the previous chapter, which explained how placing some limitations on capital flows might makes us safer—but also why the reverse would be true for trade in food. This chapter has emphasized the need for governments to take coordinated action to control capital imbalances but also the huge losses imposed by preventing people from crossing borders to reach places where they can be more productive. These contrasts foreshadow the policy recommendations for World 3.0 that are developed further in chapter 12 and that call for government to serve dual functions, of integrator and regulator.

The next chapter continues where this one leaves off in considering the impact of globalization on labor. In a sense, it touches on another potential kind of imbalance that has been discussed most explicitly in the context of technological progress rather than globalization. Nearly eighty years ago, in the throes of the last really big global financial and economic crisis, Nobel Prize winner John Hicks pointed out that there was no economic reason to expect labor's share of GDP to stay constant over time. Hicks explained that labor-saving technological change could actually reduce labor's share of GDP over time, and Pigou added the even gloomier possibility of absolute labor-saving change reducing the absolute wage level.[47] Many fear that globalization may exert similar pressure on workers' earnings and job security. It is to such worries that we turn next.

Global Exploitation

Source: Khalil Bendib

MOST ECONOMISTS FOCUS on the *efficiency* of market outcomes—how to deliver the most goods and services using the fewest resources. And in fact, previous chapters looked at a number of hot-button fears relating to the breakdown of market efficiency—concentration, externalities, risks, and imbalances. But efficiency isn't everything. Most people care about fairness or equity, and many think globalization is at best unfair and at worst blatantly exploitative. So we need to consider how the benefits and costs of cross-border integration are distributed across people instead of looking at just their aggregate impact.

The cartoon that begins this chapter conveys two distinct distributional concerns. In rich countries, concerns abound that trade with poor countries threatens high wages, job security, and hence living standards. In developing countries, some people fear that globalization locks in positions of relative disadvantage, depriving countries and individuals of paths to prosperity that today's rich once traveled. Behind both arguments lies the notion that globalization has been imposed by the more powerful on the less powerful, and that in particular it benefits owners of capital over workers, since capital is mobile but labor mostly is not.

This chapter will begin by reviewing these concerns and will then turn to look at the evidence. It will first summarize economic differences among people around the world and the countries in which they live. Then it will turn to globalization's impact on workers in advanced economies, addressing concerns about rising inequality and declining pay levels and job security. And finally, it will assess globalization's effects on workers in developing countries. We'll see that globalization is *not* inherently exploitative, but that some do lose out when markets get integrated. The chapter concludes with suggestions for shaping integration so as to create a fairer as well as more prosperous world.

Inequality and Integration

Economists have a tendency to avoid distributional issues in favor of a "value-free" emphasis on efficiency. When they do engage with value-laden distributional issues, though, they usually focus on income inequality, which will also be the tack taken here. But it is useful to begin by noting two critiques of this focus on equality / inequality.

From the right, Milton Friedman has argued that a focus on equality inevitably ends up focused on the equality of outcomes instead of the equality of opportunities, to the detriment of the latter and at the expense of long-term economic growth.[1] The distinction between equalization of outcomes and of opportunities is indeed important. But the trade-off that Friedman highlights is just a possibility that is particularly likely to apply if the equalization of outcomes is pushed too far. This is not an obvious characterization of a world in which 60 percent of the variation in individuals' positions in the global income distribution has been estimated to be accounted for by the countries they are born in and another 15–25 percent by parental (within-country) income class.[2] Other measures attribute between 66 to 87 percent of income inequality among individuals around the world to differences in countries' mean incomes.[3] While we lack comparably detailed data on the distribution of wealth, which is what gets transmitted between generations, circumstances—as in country of birth and parental position—seem to account for even more of the variation along that dimension!

These data suggest that equality of opportunities as well as of outcomes lag in the real world. It is at least plausible that we are operating in a part of the policy space where equalization of opportunities and of outcomes might go hand-in-hand instead of being subject to a fundamental trade-off. And so we shouldn't simply assume that it would be futile—or worse—to work to reduce global inequality: the possibility merits attention.

From the left, noted trade economist Jagdish Bhagwati has labeled measures of global inequality as irrelevant—since there is no global polity—and a distraction from the real problem of poverty.[4] This is a forceful reminder that the conditions of the very poor are of particular concern—a point that will be followed up on in Part III as well as later in this chapter. It also hints at the difference between reducing inequality by lifting people out of poverty versus dragging down the rich: the former is clearly preferable. But that said, it still seems useful to start to take stock of where we are by looking at the rich, the poor, and everyone in between—although we might then want to focus our analysis on particular parts of the income distribution (the very poor) or particular subgroups (women, children . . .) or particular geographies.

The usefulness of taking stock is enhanced by people's tendency to underestimate the extent of global income inequality by large margins. To see this, try to get people you know to guess the levels of some of the measures of inequality presented in this chapter.

Traditionally, economists have seen some inequality and risk of job losses as necessary but undesirable by-products of the incentives required to spur economic growth. They've seen redistribution as reducing growth by lowering incentives to get rich.[5] Newer theories view inequality as *itself* hampering growth by creating political and social instability and discouraging the rich from accumulating wealth.[6] The World Bank has affirmed that "policies to improve the distribution of income and assets can have the double benefits of increasing growth and increasing the share of growth that accrues to poor people."[7] Of course, high levels of inequality don't only hurt the poor. Inequality impedes happiness among the middle classes due to pressure to "keep up with the Joneses." Some research even indicates that people will deny themselves material gains if they think accepting those gains would unfairly give even larger benefits to others. And Jeffrey Sachs also linked inequality to a number of the economic failures that lead to failed states.[8]

What is of particular interest here is the relationship between globalization and inequality. The most famous theoretical result in the literature is the so-called factor price equalization theorem, now more than fifty years old, which states that in the absence of market imperfections, frictions, and restraints, trade will lead to an equalization of factor prices—including wage rates—across countries, even without any cross-border movement of labor and capital. This predicted reduction in inequality used to be promoted as another benefit of trade, and a big one. But with rising worries in countries such as the United States about wages there coming under pressure from low wages in countries such as China, there has been some rethinking or at least shift in emphasis.[9]

Thus, in 2004, Nobel Prize winner Paul Samuelson, one of the developers of the factor price equalization theorem, published an article emphasizing that technical progress of *a particular sort* in a trading partner such as China could reduce welfare in the United States.[10] Various critiques have since been offered: the mechanism proposed by Samuelson isn't new; the losses under his mechanism reflect reduced rather than increased trade; and the dynamics assumed by the mechanism don't fit with the empirical evidence.[11] But to me, the salient point is that Samuelson, of all people, chose to emphasize what he did when he did—and that it aroused huge attention in the media where, despite his disavowals, it was mostly seen as an argument for protectionism.

More broadly, the whole controversy seems to me to be an illustration of the muddle that comes from using thought experiments associated with moving to World 2.0 to guide behavior in World 3.0. To expose the problem, let me start with an even more basic model: an image, really. Visualize a tub filled with water, with a barrier in the middle. On one side, the water level is high; on the other, it's low. Remove the barrier, and they equalize. Likewise, in a borderless world, we would expect that wages would converge or jobs would move from the high side to the low side. If this model seems outrageously simplistic to you, that's good, but don't assume everyone agrees. This is basically the "giant sucking sound" Ross Perot predicted would send U.S. jobs to Mexico under NAFTA. Pat Buchanan, author of tirades such as "Suicide by Free Trade," and Lou Dobbs might not be using much better models.

In reality, labor markets don't much resemble bathtubs. You don't just lift a barrier and go from World 1.0 to World 2.0, instantly overpowering all cultural, administrative, geographic, and economic differences. Even with complete integration along all other dimensions, we'll never see a single labor market shifting to a single new wage level. Labor is not a simple commodity; people have different skills, experiences, preferences, capabilities, and so on. Also, the informational problems described in chapter 7 abound in labor markets. Picture millions of little pools of labor with mazelike connections, some operating inefficiently, many internal to companies, most local or national, and only a few regional or global. Considering how borders actually work in semiglobalization, opening up is more like partially opening valves between pools than removing barriers wholesale.

The simplistic bathtub model of job losses also leaves out gains from trade and all other sources of growth. And it fails to incorporate the fast-growing *domestic* demand for labor in emerging markets. In rich countries, it might seem like the whole massive populations of the developing world are clamoring to sell you cheap products and services, but in reality, even a country like China sees mostly domestic development. Yes, developing countries seek increased share in export markets based on cheap labor, but don't forget, cheap labor means relative poverty, which is precisely what those countries are racing to escape as fast as they can.

Oversimplified models also overlook productivity differences. Wages have been shown repeatedly to track labor productivity very closely, a point to which I will return at the end of this chapter. As long as workers in developed countries are more productive, they'll still enjoy higher pay, and that's going to be the case as long as they use more capital equipment, have more education, enjoy better business environments, and so on.

So, we need to cast aside images like a global pool of labor, along with more sophisticated treatments like factor price equalization, that don't account for the complexities of World 3.0. More realism leads to the conclusion that integration is sometimes a win-win deal for everyone, including workers, but that in other cases, some do gain at the expense of others. When there are both winners and losers, we have to try to provide some kind of protections for the latter—but this is rarely best achieved by imposing trade protectionism.

And for those of us who would like to see more integration, it's also important to keep an eye on inequality because economic disparities can be a barrier to globalization. Data suggest that countries with higher inequality engage in less trade. Inequality also dampens public attitudes toward markets and protectionism. And such sentiments can have a real impact on policy. Jeffrey Williamson links rising inequality in the New World before World War I to a backlash against immigration (reminding us of the particular need to manage that cross-border flow) and trade that contributed to deglobalization during the interwar years.[12]

So while the Communist notion of enforced equality of outcomes is clearly a bad idea, distributional concerns cannot and should not be ignored. There are good reasons to try to provide more equality of opportunity, if not more equitable outcomes themselves. Let's start to explore them by looking at some real data on inequality—first globally and then within advanced and developing countries.

Global Inequality

The top tenth of the world's population got 57 percent of the world's income while the bottom 70 percent got only 5 percent in 2002.[13] But it is useful to look more systematically at the shape of income distributions rather than simply focusing on one or two data points, and to put present levels of inequality into historical perspective. There is no single ("value-free") way of summarizing an income distribution into a number, but the most widely used measure of inequality is the Gini index (see "The Gini Index of Inequality").

Before agriculture, in the early days of World 0.0, virtually no inequality existed, i.e., the Gini index was close to zero. Everyone was poor. What inequality there was reflected differences in the natural bounty of different locations. Keep this distinction in mind—some inequality results from differences in prosperity across places ("location inequality"), which is different from inequality caused by local or national social stratification ("class inequality").

If we fast forward to World 1.0, we find that the Gini index measuring inequality among individuals around the world was 43 in 1820 according to an estimate by Branko Milanovic,[14] about the same as the U.S. Gini in the early 1990s.[15] Furthermore, class inequality (inequality based on one's position within a country's income distribution) explained 65 percent of global inequality, with only 35 percent reflecting differences in average incomes across countries.[16] Differences in relative prosperity were more muted than today, and more of the differences occurred within rather than between countries.

The Gini Index of Inequality

The Gini index is probably the single most widely used measure of income inequality. It is best visualized in relation to the Lorenz curve, which plots the proportion of the total income of the population (y axis) that is cumulatively earned by the bottom x percent of the population (see diagram). The line at 45 degrees represents perfect equality of incomes. The Gini index can then be thought of as the ratio of the area that lies between the line of equality and the Lorenz curve (marked "A" in the diagram) over the total area under the line of equality (marked "A" and "B" in the diagram); i.e., $G = A/(A + B)$.

The Gini index can range from 0 to 1 but is usually multiplied by 100 to yield a percentage between 0 and 100. A low Gini index indicates a more equal distribution, with 0 corresponding to complete equality, while higher Gini indices indicate more unequal distribution, with 1 corresponding to complete inequality.

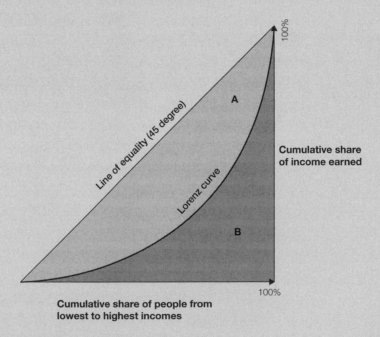

Milanovic's analysis indicates that inequality soared during the rapid economic expansion that took place in World 1.0. By 1950, the Gini index for individuals around the world had risen to 64, and location inequality had overtaken class inequality. *Differences in average incomes across countries accounted for 86 percent of the inequality among people around the world.*[17] What happened? Actually, nothing you don't already know. Some countries got rich before others. World 1.0 borders were really strong, making for some large differences in economic circumstances. A small number of rich countries rose up, and everywhere else, pretty much everyone stayed poor, as shown in figure 9-1.

As far as globalization goes, the period after 1950 holds the most interest. Given the concern about exploitation, it's surprising that all of three of Milanovic's inequality measures shown on figure 9-1 registered almost all of their growth *before* 1950, whereas exports as a proportion of GDP (i.e., globalization) really took off *after* 1960. The proportion of inequality among individuals explained by cross-country differences in average income (location inequality) also basically stopped rising after 1950.

New analysis by Maxim Pinkovskiy and Xavier Sala-i-Martin, based on a different methodology than Milanovic's, is even more encouraging. They estimate that the global Gini declined from 68 to 61 from the early 1970s to 2006, largely due to tremendous growth in East Asia, as shown in figure 9-2. Present institutional arrangements certainly haven't prevented the emergence of (some) formerly poor countries.

So recent trends give us strong reason for hope. But there's still much too much inequality and poverty. The Gini index of individual income inequality around the world lies somewhere between 60 and 70,[18] and looking at wealth rather than income, the global Gini is probably closer to 90.[19] The decline in total inequality at the individual level in recent decades masks mixed patterns for its two components: inequality *between* countries and inequality *within* countries (see figure 9-3). Inequality between countries rose after the industrial revolution because some got rich while others remained poor. The last few decades suggest,

FIGURE 9-1

Global inequality versus average income and exports as % of GDP, 1820–2002

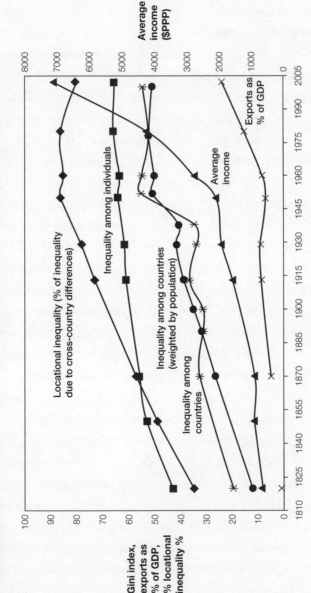

Sources: Inequality among individuals and average income: Branko Milanovic, "Global Inequality and Global Inequality Extraction Ratio: The Story of the Last Two Centuries," MPRA Paper 16535, July 31, 2009. Inequality among countries (weighted and unweighted): Branko Milanovic, "Worlds Apart: Measuring International and Global Inequality," Powerpoint presentation, Carnegie Endowment for International Peace, Washington, DC, September 28, 2005. Exports as % of GDP: Angus Maddison, World Bank Development Indicators (WDI).

FIGURE 9-2

Global income distribution by region, 1970 versus 2006

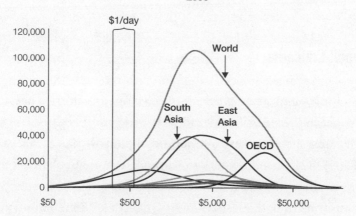

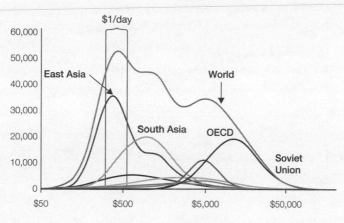

Source: Adapted from Maxim Pinkovskiy and Xavier Sala-i-Martin, "Parametric Estimations of the World Distribution of Income," NBER working paper 15433, October 2009.

however, that integration has been leveraged—especially in East Asia—to reduce inequality by bringing up the bottom end of the global income distribution. But the pattern is quite different for inequality within countries, which has increased in recent decades. To explore inequality further, the sections that follow distinguish between developed and developing countries.

FIGURE 9-3

Inequality between versus within countries, 1970–2006

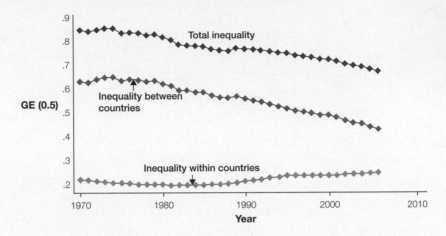

Source: Adapted from Maxim Pinkovskiy and Xavier Sala-i-Martin, "Parametric Estimations of the World Distribution of Income," NBER working paper 15433, October 2009.

Developed Concerns

Globalization's impact on workers in developed countries has aroused much concern these last few decades. Let me address three broad worries: that unskilled workers fall behind skilled workers; that workers overall lose out versus owners of capital; and that jobs become less secure. I'll start with the first. Inequality has increased in many developed countries over the last couple of decades.[20] One country where this trend runs strong is the United States, where inequality has long exceeded that in other developed countries. The U.S. Gini rose from 40 in 1980 to 47 in 2007.[21] Median inflation-adjusted earnings of adult males working full-time jobs haven't really risen since the 1970s,[22] and the proportion of wage income reported on tax returns by the top 1 percent almost doubled from 1980 to 2005.[23]

Observing the widening pay gap in the United States, economists grew worried because existing theories seemed to indicate that growing trade with poor countries might be at fault. An IMF report explained,

"With exports from emerging markets and developing countries being intensive in labor, especially unskilled labor, traditional trade theory would predict that the integration of these countries into the world labor market would exert downward pressure on wages (corrected for productivity) of workers in advanced economies."[24] News coverage of companies closing factories in the United States and opening new ones in lower-wage countries further stoked fear and spread it among the general public. But while the media might have portrayed globalization as the main suspect, economists saw it as just one of many factors. The economy was shifting from manufacturing toward services, unions were declining, labor-saving technology was advancing rapidly, changes were taking place in unemployment benefits and in tax policies, and so on.

By the late 1990s, vigorous debate had produced something of a consensus among economists: technological change was the main cause of rising inequality, not globalization. Maybe globalization caused 10–20 percent of the increase in the wage gap—and some economists still maintained it didn't factor at all. As they saw it, trade with poorer countries was just too small in proportion to the rich economies to have such a big impact. Nonetheless, as trade with developing countries and inequality both grew in the 2000s, some economists reconsidered their earlier conclusions. Paul Krugman, Ben Bernanke, and Lawrence Summers all expressed the possibility that trade might play a bigger role than previously estimated.[25]

Robert Lawrence cast doubt on globalization's role after scrutinizing changes in the U.S. income distribution. The pay gap between skilled and unskilled workers had indeed risen in the 1980s. However, in the 1990s, he reported, "wages near the top of the income distribution (90th percentile) continued to rise more rapidly than wages at the median, but wages at the bottom of the distribution kept up or actually increased faster than wages in the middle. Since 2000, with the exception of the very top, wages have generally moved in tandem."[26]

The United States became more integrated into international markets in the 1990s and 2000s, *without* widening the pay gap between skilled and unskilled workers. How can we square that with our (admittedly limited) theoretical understanding? Lawrence suggests three possible explanations for why the rest of the income distribution didn't become more unequal:

> One is that the goods that the United States imports are actually very sophisticated and produced in the United States by relatively skilled workers. While it may cause displacement and could put downward pressure on wages generally, competition from low-wage countries does not increase wage inequality. A second more benign view is that a significant amount of what America imports today is no longer produced domestically. Thus, declining import prices simply yield consumer benefits and do not exert downward pressure on US wages or cause dislocation of US workers. A third view is that while US imports may be produced using labor-intensive methods abroad, when produced in the United States, capital- and skilled-labor-intensive methods are used.

Among the more intriguing observations that Lawrence makes while discussing these explanations is that "manufactured imports overall, even those from developing countries such as China and Mexico, are concentrated in US manufacturing sectors that pay significantly higher than average US wages. This means that import displacement does not fall disproportionately on less skilled workers."[27]

Evidence indicates that, at least recently, trade hasn't increased inequality among the vast majority of American workers. However, as Lawrence suggested, American workers—skilled and unskilled—might *all* be losing out due to globalization. Is globalization letting more mobile capital claim an edge over less mobile labor? Here we can review evidence across advanced economies. The proportion of national income going to labor fell 3–4 percent in the United States and other Anglo-Saxon economies and about 10 percent in Europe and Japan from 1980 to 2006.[28] But before we get too panicked about this, we should note that in the United States, Europe, and Japan, labor's share of the pie was in part just reversing earlier gains (see top panel of figure 9-4 for the U.S. data).

FIGURE 9-4

Labor share and compensation trends in developed countries

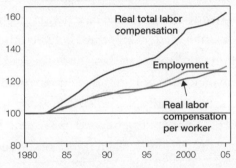

U.S. share of labor compensation in national income, 1947—2006

Advanced economies real labor compensation and employment, 1980—2005

Sources: Top panel: Robert Z. Lawrence, *Blue-Collar Blues: Is Trade to Blame for Rising US Income Inequality?* Peterson Institute for International Economics, January 2008. Bottom panel: Florence Jaumotte and Irina Tytell, "The Globalization of Labor," chapter 5 of *IMF World Economic Outlook,* April 2007.

What explains labor's declining share of national income across developed countries since the 1980s? Economists at the IMF did attempt to quantify the impacts of various factors: technology, cheaper traded goods, offshoring (trade in intermediate goods and services), immigration, and changes in labor market policies. Their results reaffirmed that technological change was again the most important factor reducing labor's share of national income. Falling prices of traded final goods, in contrast, appeared to increase the labor share across most developed countries, leading to the conclusion that "cheaper imports have increased the size of real total labor market compensation, implying that workers have participated in the benefits of the bigger economic 'pie,' although their share of it has declined."[29] Note that this is exactly what the bottom panel of figure 9-4 indicates.

The IMF study also estimated that immigration and offshoring reduced the labor share to varying degrees across countries, with immigration having a larger impact than offshoring.[30] But immigration's estimated impact on natives' wages was very small and often temporary.[31] And offshoring was estimated to contribute less than 0.1 percent annually to labor's declining share of income.[32]

Let's move to our third concern—does globalization make jobs less secure? In the United States, the Great Moderation of the last few decades did not translate into more stable incomes or enhanced job security. Household income volatility—particularly men's labor income volatility—skyrocketed. The standard deviation of changes in U.S. household income "increased by one-third between the early 1970s and early 2000s," with most of the growth prior to the mid-1990s.[33] Average job tenures and the incidence of long-term employment also declined.[34] And worries about job security weren't exclusively an American phenomenon. Much of Europe experienced persistent high unemployment. Strong labor protections curtailed job losses but also stifled job creation.

Theoretically, there are a number of ways in which globalization could make labor markets more volatile. As markets open up and comparative advantage shifts among countries, workers in industries where imports are growing face a heightened risk of job loss, which could also lead to more frictional unemployment.[35] Another proposed link between globalization and employment volatility is the concern that globalization could make it easier for employers to substitute foreign for domestic workers. In this case, workers might "have to incur greater instability in earnings and hours worked in response to shocks to labor demand or labor productivity."[36] However, econometric studies have cast doubt on the presumed increase in substitution of foreign workers for domestic ones.[37]

So much for theory—what about real jobs? Only 2–3 percent of U.S. job losses in the 1990s and early 2000s were related to competition from imports or firms relocating positions overseas.[38] And that counts only losses. It's harder to track the jobs created because of trade, but research suggests that a given amount of demand growth from exports creates more (and better-paying) jobs than a similar increase in domestic demand; and more jobs than would be lost if imports grew by the same amount.[39] Earlier studies mainly reflected the loss of manufacturing jobs, and today there's more fear about offshore services. But the phenomenon still is not big enough to affect national employment patterns.[40] Furthermore, we can take comfort in knowing that rich countries more open to trade and FDI don't systematically suffer from higher unemployment. Some of the most open countries have among the highest employment rates.[41]

While some workers in rich countries really do lose jobs to foreign competition and offshoring—and theories can explain how globalization could help lower wages—labor markets remain overwhelmingly domestic. We need to do better at assisting workers who get hurt by globalization, but if we really care about labor markets in advanced countries, we should expend most of our energy addressing factors with bigger effects than globalization.

Developing Concerns

Free trade enjoys stronger public support in poorer countries than in rich ones, yet that hasn't stopped intellectuals on the left from arguing that "neoliberal" free-trade agreements pursued during the last twenty or so years systematically exploit the poor.[42] Why so much skepticism about globalization's benefits for poorer countries when the prevailing economic theories imply that integration promotes growth *and* convergence, which are obviously good for the poor? Much of the worry about globalization that exists in the developing world reflects the real exploitation that many countries suffered under colonial rule. Recall that economists believe all *freely chosen* transactions should be mutually beneficial. Under previous episodes of globalization, poorer countries engaged in a host of transactions that were far from freely chosen: exporting mineral resources, purchasing manufactured goods from colonial masters, and so on. With that kind of history, it's no surprise that foreign ownership of major industries might be met with some suspicion.

Let's look at what actually has happened under globalization in developing countries. Most importantly, poverty has declined markedly, as shown in figure 9-5 (top panel). The number of human beings living on less than $2 a day declined from 1.6 billion in 1970 to 850 million in 2006, even though the world population almost doubled over the same period.[43] That 850 million people live on under $2 a day is a tragedy, but claims that the integration of the last few decades harmed the poor just don't fit the facts. Skeptics argue that graphics like figure 9-5 focus on gains in big countries like China and overlook smaller countries that have done poorly. Actually, many (though not all) smaller economies are also benefiting. Think of the growth of commodity producers, particularly in Africa, fueled by China's rise.

Rising inequality within many developing countries is also a concern. This trend might seem surprising based on trade theory, but scholars have tied it to shifts toward more technologically advanced exports along with domestic developments like urbanization.[44] Back in 1955, Simon Kuznets famously linked early stages of economic development to rising inequality,[45] though subsequent research has cast doubt on that relationship.[46]

Consider China's changing income distribution (bottom of figure 9-5). Before what Chinese leaders call the "period of reform and opening up" began in 1978, China had very little inequality and a lot of poverty (the vertical lines on the graph show the poverty line at only $1 per day). But as China's leader at the time, Deng Xiaoping, explained, "Some people will become prosperous first, and then others will become prosperous later."[47] China is now much less equal than thirty years ago, but the country has nearly eradicated poverty at the $1 a day level. And recent data indicate that Chinese inequality may be starting to decline with the government's emphasis on building a "harmonious society."[48]

FIGURE 9-5

World poverty rate at $1/2/3/5 per day versus exports as percent of GDP (top) and China's income distribution (1970–2006) (bottom)

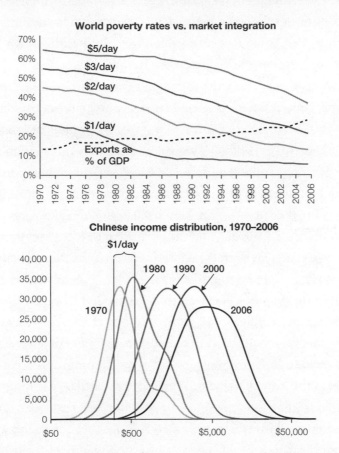

World poverty rates vs. market integration

Chinese income distribution, 1970–2006

Sources: Poverty rates and Chinese income distribution from Maxim Pinkovskiy and Xavier Sala-i-Martin, "Parametric Estimations of the World Distribution of Income," NBER working paper 15433, October 2009; exports as percent of GDP from World Bank; World Development Indicators.

How inequality is generated also influences its effects on growth: the concentration of wealth among entrepreneurs is very different from its concentration in entrenched oligarchies. Studies have shown that self-made billionaire wealth promotes faster economic growth, while high levels of heir-controlled wealth subtract as much as two percentage points a year. Entrenched wealth poses a particular challenge in some developing countries: billionaires' holdings average less than 3 percent of GDP in industrial countries but 13.3 percent in some East Asian countries.[49] Globalization can help by broadening the playing field.

While labor market globalization generally looks attractive from the perspective of developing countries, it is worth remembering that poor people can also lose jobs due to foreign competition—with consequences that can, in their cases, literally include starvation. Consider Haiti's rice farmers. Three decades ago, Haiti exported rice. During the 1990s, the United States pushed Haiti to open its rice market. Now 80 percent of rice eaten in Haiti is imported. Six pounds of U.S. rice cost only $3.80, versus $5.12 for Haitian rice, a big benefit for Haiti's poor.[50] But rice farming employed some 20 percent of the population in cultivation and many more in related sectors; cheaper American rice hardly makes up for their losses.[51] In March 2010, former U.S. President Bill Clinton apologized, saying, "It was a mistake that I was a party to . . . I have to live every day with the consequences of the lost capacity to produce a rice crop in Haiti to feed those people."[52] Despite globalization's big benefits for the poor, we need to think twice before doing anything to jeopardize the livelihoods of those who are already so vulnerable.

In summary, globalization does seem to benefit most categories of workers in developing countries. And the demographic pattern we looked at in the previous chapter, rapid growth of the working age populations in most developing countries, implies that such countries should keep pushing for more openness to fuel more job creation. Demographic windows of opportunity don't automatically translate into growth. Smart policies and effective entrepreneurship are required to convert demographic potential into real prosperity.

Toward a Fairer World

As we have seen, globalization isn't fundamentally exploitative, but some people do lose out. The strength of the antiglobalization movement—however misguided its ideas—indicates that prevailing approaches to making trade fair for all have failed to pass muster with broad segments of the public. Part of the problem is rhetorical. World 2.0 believers get so enamored with integration that they fail to acknowledge any negative consequences, and their lack of sensitivity fuels the backlash.

Public demands for government to stop the "exporting of jobs" lead predictably to World 1.0 proposals to restrict trade. It's as if policy makers are using the simplistic bathtub model and think everything will turn out fine if you plug up the leaks and keep the "domestic jobs" at home. The trouble is that these policy makers seldom seem to pay attention to the actual costs. In 2009, the United States imposed a special tariff to protect the U.S. tire industry from a surge of Chinese imports. According to a very rough estimate by economist Brad DeLong, the tariffs will cost Americans $140,000 per job saved per year, and that doesn't include the cost of retaliation by China and dented perceptions of the U.S. business climate.[53] Earlier and more systematic studies indicate it costs $170,000 to save an American job via trade protection,[54] and even more in some industries like shipping ($415,000) and sugar ($600,000).[55] Obviously the costs exceed the relevant workers' salaries.

Furthermore, if we're concerned about inequality, we should think twice about raising tariffs, since these tend to serve as a particularly regressive form of tax. In the United States, staple consumer products—especially low-priced ones—draw among the country's highest tariffs,[56] putting the cost of protectionism squarely on lower-income Americans, as well as on people in poorer countries, who produce most of these goods.[57] Tariffs on raw material inputs and intermediate goods can be even worse. The high U.S. sugar tariffs discussed in chapter 3 drove the production of Life Savers candy to Canada, costing the United States six hundred jobs.[58]

Another problematic proposal inspired by World 1.0 involves curbing the international expansion of domestic firms to make it harder for them to shift work abroad. Bad choice. German data indicate that domestic firms that expand overseas actually have a *better* track record of retaining home country jobs than those that stay at home.[59] Protecting jobs is thus a losing proposition. Downstream producers and consumers both lose. More efficient producers overseas lose. The costs far exceed the benefits.

My mantra for creating a fairer and more prosperous World 3.0 is to *promote productivity and protect people*, rather than protecting jobs. Protecting jobs is outrageously expensive. And think about the jobs your grandparents had. Do we really want to lock ourselves into the past? Given the push for prosperity, we should seize on gains from trade and other opportunities to grow the pie. But we shouldn't let ourselves forget real people's yearning for job security and the pain caused by job losses. For most of us, a job is a lot more than a source of income.[60] A recent study in Sweden showed that "overall mortality risk for men was increased by 44 percent during the first four years following job loss."[61]

So how should we go about promoting productivity while protecting people? On the protection of people, the ideas are familiar ones. Start with investment in education to make workers more flexible. And cushion the blow when job losses come: many developed countries have trade adjustment assistance programs, but most seem inadequate. And in terms of innovation, experiments with "wage insurance" show some promise.[62] Such programs supplement workers' income when they move into new jobs that pay lower wages, reversing the incentive to wait longer for a higher-paying job, which can be associated with long-term unemployment.

What tend to get underplayed are the ways of promoting productivity that help create the right kinds of jobs as well. Instead of an abstract account, let me focus on this point in the context of Spain, where the unemployment rate was nearly 20 percent at the end of 2010—the highest of any OECD economy. Much of this reflected the collapse in the real estate and construction sectors. But a contribution was also made by a high structural rate of unemployment due to labor market institutions that included a bewildering variety of labor contracts (44, according to the head of an employers' federation), a two-tier structure underlying them that coddled those with permanent contracts while forcing temporary contracts on the young and other newcomers to the workforce, and relatively high social overheads and costs of firing workers. In the aftermath of the financial crisis, the Spanish government did attempt to effect some changes in these labor market institutions, but with limited success.

But other engines of productivity and jobs growth, particularly business-related ones, still hadn't gotten as much attention as of this writing. Entry continued to be discouraged by the barriers to starting a new business: according to the World Bank, Spain ranked around 150 out of roughly 180 countries in ease of doing this. And existing firms, especially small and medium enterprises, took it in the chin: the number of firms with 10 to 500 employees fell by 20 percent between 2008 and 2010 (versus 8 percent for all other firms) and although they accounted for 46 percent of total employment in 2008, they were responsible for 66 percent of the (net) jobs shed between 2008 and 2010. Many such firms collapsed for lack of working capital—while official funds earmarked for such financing reportedly sat undisbursed.

The Spanish government seemed more focused on the country's largest enterprises. Thus, at the end of 2010, Spanish Prime Minister Zapatero invited the heads of the country's thirty-seven largest enterprises—accounting for roughly 5 percent of total employment—to a summit on refloating the Spanish economy. Subsidies and cash handouts were also primarily directed at large firms in the auto and construction sectors and seemed geared toward preserving jobs that added relatively little value on a relatively high capital base instead of facilitating changes in enterprise strategy or the creation of new jobs. The larger firms also seemed to be the primary beneficiaries of earmarks for innovation (frequently billed as "the" strategy despite its limited job creation potential in the short to medium run). The smaller firms would have done better, probably, with more of an emphasis on the diffusion of innovations, rather than just on innovation. And if all this emphasis on productivity growth seems somewhat removed from the business of job creation or preservation, remember that probably the most worrying thing about Spain is that it has experienced no growth in total factor productivity since about 2000 (maybe longer). It is hard to imagine a robust employment scenario without productivity growth picking up.

Policies to promote productivity and protect people are, as the Spanish example suggested, mainly the purview of national governments. Governments have the ability to stimulate sophisticated demand, open up access to foreign inputs, increase firm rivalry, facilitate redeployment of resources, fund education and unemployment insurance, and so on. But many people fear that globalization is robbing governments of the flexibility to respond to the citizens' concerns, and sapping their power in favor of multinational corporations. Thus it is to worries about globalization's impact on politics and policy that we turn next.

But before moving on, it is worth noting that it is hardly fair to conclude a discussion such as this one with an exclusive focus on jobs in rich countries. We can also do a lot more to make globalization more fair for developing countries. The plight of Haiti's rice farmers, alas, is far from unique. Cutting rich countries' agricultural trade protection would be a good step, since farmers suffer in many poor countries. Also, less emphasis might be put on trying to get the poor to pay for lifesaving drugs. Intellectual property deserves respect, but so does access to medicine. To make globalization fairer for the poor, we need to think about integration from their perspective. They need to be met partway instead of being made to conform to rules they had no part in writing and don't see as inherently legitimate.

And while such policies can help, what we really need is a longer-term mental shift. We have expanded our circles of sympathy and trust enormously since World 0.0, but the extent of inequality that persists is shocking. One World Bank estimate indicates that by 2050, African per capita income will be in the $2,000–$4,000 range, as compared with $100,000 in the United States. Trying to worry more about absolute rather than relative income, and approaching distant people with more understanding and compassion, would take us a long way toward building a fairer, safer, and more prosperous world. How we might move ourselves in this direction is the topic we will return to in chapter 15.

Chapter Ten

Global Oppression

Source: John Backderf

RECENT CHAPTERS HAVE focused on anxieties about potential economic dysfunctions linked to globalization and greater openness. We've seen that problems such as concentration and inequality—problems relating to the economic consequences of markets not working—can occur, but also that they are not nearly as damaging as popular perceptions suggest, and that there are ways that national governments can manage them while still pursuing greater openness. Market failures are not, therefore, an insurmountable barrier to World 3.0; on the contrary, they help define the contours of a kind of limited and sensible regulation that protects us without taking us all the way back to World 1.0.

Of course, not all fears about opening up involve market dysfunctions. The opening cartoon expresses two powerful *political* concerns related to globalization: the notions that the United States is taking over the world thanks to greater openness, and that corporate interests are also out of control, threatening the freedom of everyday people like you and me. While crudely expressed in the cartoon, such fears are to be encountered across the political spectrum, left, right, and center.

This chapter argues that these dark forebodings are wildly exaggerated, if not totally disconnected from reality. It does so by examining several fears about globalization's political impact and arguing that considerations of freedom, far from preventing us from moving toward a more open World 3.0, should probably push us in that direction. It concludes by looking at what really underlies the various political complaints about globalization—and what might be done about it.

Pax Americana?

Isn't America taking over the world? Might not "globalization" be just another name for American transnational empire and hegemony exercised in both the military and business realms? Such fears were more prevalent before the crisis, but remain widespread.

Let's begin with the military realm. After the demise of the Soviet Union, military power became more concentrated in the hands of the United States: in 2009, the United States accounted for nearly one-half of the world's total military expenditure, roughly seven times as much as China, which ranked second.[1] But it is important to realize that such military might—hard power, in Harvard political scientist Joseph Nye's terms—is limited in its ability to bring about desired foreign policy outcomes.

The most vivid examples of this point are Afghanistan and Iraq. The total cost of the wars there is estimated at more than $2 trillion—which represents ten times the GDP of those two countries—and yet the United States has had only partial success in meeting its objectives.[2] It's worth noting too that in 2008, when Russia sent tanks into Georgia, a strong American ally in Russia's backyard, the United States found itself essentially unable to act, despite its large military. Domestic politics also severely constrain the use of American force, a fact illustrated in the United States' attempt to pacify Somalia during the early 1990s. After the embarrassing 1993 ambush of a U.S. Army Rangers force at the hands of relatively unsophisticated and ill-equipped forces fielded by local warlords, the United States wound up turning away from military intervention in those third world conflicts that were judged not to bear directly on U.S. national interests.

Turning to business, we also find reason to question whether globalization really equals Americanization or American hegemony. We don't see evidence of U.S. companies being disproportionately or increasingly successful in international competition. In fact, recent decades have seen large *decreases* in the number of U.S. companies figuring among the world's largest and in their market shares across a broad spectrum of industries—decreases only partly explicable by exchange rate realignments. In 1971, fifty-nine of the (capitalist) world's one hundred largest manufacturing corporations were based in the United States and they accounted for 66 percent of the top one hundred's sales, proportions that were probably down already since the 1950s.[3] By 2010, only thirty-two of the world's one hundred largest companies were American, and they accounted for only 34 percent of total sales.[4]

In financial terms, the previous chapter already discussed the United States's negative and declining net international investment position. Other financial indicators such as share of equity market capitalization point in the same direction. And one can even make some of the same points about technology indicators such as shares of R&D, patents, PhDs granted, and foreign student enrollment. Along all these dimensions, assertions of U.S. hegemony look more dubious than they did a few decades ago.

The possibility of collective hegemony exercised by the triad of the United States, Europe, and Japan is sometimes cited as an alternative to U.S. domination. But given the growth now being posted by China, and to a lesser extent India, and the sluggishness of the triad, this seems a particularly odd time to harp on triad power. Rather, what does seem to have affected the economic fortunes of particular nations is their degree of openness. The concentration of international trade and investment flows declined over the last two decades among relatively open economies, whereas the opposite was true of relatively closed economies.[5] This is at least somewhat reassuring. It suggests that continued marginalization is more likely a product of domestic policies in relatively closed countries than an ineradicable feature of globalization.

Looking to the future, economists are forecasting faster growth in the Chinese and Indian economies, and in emerging economies in general, than in the triad. In fact, what is being predicted for 2050 is a shift from dominance by America, Europe, and Japan to a situation where China and India are two of the world's three largest economies. This will return us roughly to where we were in 1820, when China and India represented almost half of the world's economy and the G7 just a quarter.[6] And while the United States' stature as the world's lone superpower erodes, the simple arithmetic of GDP distributions suggests that neither China nor India nor anyone else will rise to take its place over the next several decades. The dominant dynamic of the next few decades, according to many observers, is likely to be one of a shift away from the much-discussed Pax Americana toward *multipolarity*.

Corporate Overlords?

Okay, so maybe no nation, not even the United States, has quite taken over the world thanks to globalization. But what about multinational companies (MNCs) as opposed to nations? Haven't the largest MNCs become larger than many countries, with far-reaching implications for national sovereignty? Note that this is an issue around *superconcentration across* industries, in terms of the share of national or world GDPs accounted for by a handful of companies, as opposed to industry-level concentration, measured in terms of shares of worldwide output in particular industries, which was discussed in chapter 5. While industry-level concentration raises issues of power in particular markets, superconcentration stirs concerns about economic, social, and political power on a broader front.

As an aid to calibration, compare global levels of superconcentration with the global concentration levels of the individual industries looked at in chapter 5, which exhibited an average five-firm concentration ratio in the range of 30 percent. In 2009, the sales of *all* MNCs' foreign affiliates, not just the largest, accounted for an estimated 54 percent of global GDP; however, correcting this to focus on value added reduced the fraction to 11 percent of global GDP.[7] And while the global sales of the world's hundred largest nonfinancial MNCs by foreign assets nominally accounted for 15 percent of global GDP,[8] adjusting revenues just to focus on value added probably reduces this to less than 5 percent. And while this measure does seem to have increased in recent years, that has to be seen in the context of an earlier decline, starting in the mid-1980s.

The value-added correction is a reminder of one of the problems of simply comparing the sales of an MNC with a country's GDP: the former has to be adjusted downward, often by more than 50 percent, whereas the latter already embodies such a correction. But there is an even more fundamental problem with comparing large businesses to governments that is exposed by considering the ways in which each of these agents influences outcomes in markets. Businesses and governments are both economic *participants*; they procure or provide goods and services, and they can also serve as venture partners/owners. But governments perform a second role that companies don't: they set the *rules* for markets, which is what tremendously expands the scope of governmental power relative to business.

More specifically, governments force businesses (and public enter-prises) to adhere to all sorts of rules as market participants, including taxes, subsidies, price/profit restrictions, disclosure requirements and other financial regulations, regulations over products and manu-facturing processes, requirements that products be made with local ingredients, trade and industrial policies, requirements that compa-nies be locally owned, policies governing competition, restrictions on company access and expansion, patent law, intellectual property right recognition, technology transfer policies, and the list goes on and on.

Governments make all these laws; companies, along with other inter-ested parties, can only influence their passage through the political process. And companies' degree of influence in this regard is typically limited, at least if confined to legal channels. My experience of business leaders such as the late Ken Lay of Enron has taught me to recognize that, when I (occasionally) hear companies bragging about being rule makers rather than rule takers, they may actually be talking about being rule breakers.

To summarize, the relative sizes of companies versus governments does not, even if corrected for value added, begin to take into account government's special function and authority as a rule maker. It also ignores the other roles that governments play in markets besides eco-nomic participant and rule maker, including adjudicating disputes about the rules, insuring market risk, overseeing public investment (on a different basis, ideally, than pure profit maximization), and even rep-resenting "their" companies' interests at multilateral organizations such as the WTO.

Openness, superimposed on a system of this sort, can boost competi-tive vitality in a broader sense by placing some constraints on the relation-ships between governments and businesses. In closed economies, more effort and money tends to be expended on lobbying politicians and gov-ernment officials to try to shape public policy to provide private bene-fits for particular industries, companies, or individuals. As noted in chapter 4, a closed economy may dissipate a significant fraction of its potential GDP in this fashion, not just a few percentage points. Also note that most sources of nonmarket power that permit this to happen reside at the national rather than the global level, particularly in one's home country (think Enron, once again), and so are typically reduced by globalization.

The Golden Straitjacket?

Fears that globalization might remove room for domestic discretion in regulatory policies really resurfaced with the collapse of the centrally planned economies or (in the case of China) their movement, in some respects, toward becoming market economies. This created false perceptions of a new consensus about economic policy that was typified by works such as Francis Fukuyama's *The End of History*. And in this context, the "Washington Consensus," a set of principles originally designed as the "standard" reform package for crisis-wracked developing countries, metastasized into a general recommendation of market fundamentalism for all countries. As my friend and former Harvard colleague Dani Rodrik wrote in 2006 in the authoritative *Journal of Economic Literature*, "'Stabilize, privatize, and liberalize' became the mantra of a generation of technocrats."[9]

Rodrik also formalized the notion that global competition might narrow the policy space available to national governments in terms of the "political trilemma of the world economy," according to which deep international economic integration either requires nation-states to accept constraints on their ability to freely choose particular policies (including regulations), which curtails mass politics, or mass politics has to operate internationally, setting aside the primacy of the nation-state.[10] In other words, Rodrik's point is that policy makers can pick any two of the three objectives—deep international economic integration, nation-states, and mass politics—but not all three.

Enter Thomas Friedman with his conviction that deep international economic integration is already (almost) here with World 2.0. Given the

unlikelihood, even to him (and especially now) of nation-states wither-
ing away in favor of a world government, he predicted the forces of
integration (and particularly the "electronic herd" moving money
around the world) would force nations to don a "Golden Straitjacket,"
restricting themselves to business-friendly policies and therefore leach-
ing mass politics at the national level of any meaningful influence on
policy choices. As he apocalyptically put it, "Once your country puts
on the Golden Straitjacket, its political choices get reduced to Pepsi or
Coke—to slight nuances of policy, slight alterations in design to account
for local traditions, some loosening here or there, but never any major
deviation from the core golden rules."[11] In other words, Friedman saw
deep integration and nation-states as givens, and so predicted that mass
politics—the third element of the trilemma—would be marginalized.

But the whole point of World 3.0 and particularly my diagnosis, in
chapter 2, of semiglobalization is that given current levels of integration, it is perfectly possible to take shelter behind national borders. In
fact, the big risk today, if the overreaction in the 1930s onward to the last
big failure of market capitalism is any guide, is of too much sheltering
of this sort. Given this backdrop, and instances of external integration
even substituting for internal regulation rather than precluding it, simply focusing on instances of tension between the two is counterproduc-
tive. The reality of semiglobalization means that there should be—now
and for the foreseeable future—ample scope for regulation *and* integration. In other words, Rodrik's policy trilemma isn't wrong; it just doesn't
seem relevant in most respects.

These conceptual intuitions are backed up by at least some empirical
evidence. First, government spending hasn't fallen as integration has
increased. Rather, government expenditure as a proportion of GDP has
generally been on an increasing trend over the last half-century. And
while there was particular fear that government social expenditure in
advanced countries would get crimped due to low cost competition,
gross governmental social expenditures in the OECD countries rose, on
average, from 16 percent of GDP in 1980 to 21 percent in 2005.[12] Even
the amount of money officially spent on lobbying the U.S. government

rose by 150 percent between 1999 and 2009.[13] This would make no sense if politicians had no sway over policy.

Finer-grained studies of potential links between globalization and government spending have focused on weighing two opposing effects that have been proposed. On one hand, many economists and political scientists assert on the basis of the risks and distributional concerns explored in chapters 7 and 9 that fears about globalization create pressure for governments to combine integration with increased welfare expenditure. (Note that such fears could drive policy even if they are not actually rooted in reality.) But on the other hand, it is argued that in order to attract or retain mobile capital, governments are forced to curb taxation (especially taxes on capital) and rein in social spending. The results of studies weighing these proposed effects have come down on both sides of this argument, reflecting differences in measures of integration and spending used, countries covered, time periods, and so on, leading one author to conclude, "Globalization has not induced a pervasive race to the bottom in welfare state regimes. Nor have governments responded to market integration by increasing their welfare efforts across the board. The reality surely lies somewhere between these two extremes."[14]

One reason that such studies don't find uniform impacts of globalization on domestic policy is that politics still matters, as targeted research confirms. One study of advanced industrial economies, for example, finds that globalization leads to higher levels of welfare spending in general but that the magnitude of this effect is conditioned by the number of players in a domestic political system with veto power and the ideological distance between them.[15] Another indicates that in Western Europe, globalization causes social expenditure to increase in countries with conservative welfare regimes and decrease in those with social-democratic welfare regimes, and has no effect in countries with liberal and southern welfare regimes.[16] And yet another study notes the impact of partisan politics, "Countries in which the balance of political power is tilted to the left continue to be more responsive to redistributive demands than those dominated by center-right parties."[17]

Mistaken intuitions about the "golden straightjacket" probably reflect underestimates of how much differences between countries matter and a resultant overestimation of how footloose economic activity actually is across countries. Note that such misperceptions have probably been reduced in recent years as national governments have undertaken a variety of highly assertive responses to the recent crisis. And if we look more closely at cases where countries do seem to have been straitjacketed (e.g., Greece), we find that the problem is not globalization and openness to capital flows per se, but rather the level of public exposure or indebtedness. Especially since financial markets seem to be subject to random fluctuations of their own, countries can gain more freedom of motion and reduce vulnerability to shifts in overseas sentiments simply by not relying too much on external debt, as discussed in chapters 7 and 8.

The Death of Democracy?

Is globalization toxic to democracy, as globalization's opponents contend? Intuition would suggest otherwise, and so does the evidence. Intuitively, opening up to the outside, particularly in the form of freeing up flows of information and ideas, should be associated with political opening up inside. In fact, writers as different as Immanuel Kant, Joseph Schumpeter, Friedrich Hayek, and Niels Bohr have identified a causal relationship between openness and democracy. In Bohr's words, "The best weapon of a dictatorship is secrecy, but the best weapon of a democracy should be the weapon of openness."[18] It's no accident that Communist China long maintained strict control over its borders in the interest of suppressing dissent, and that countries like Myanmar and North Korea continue to do so to this day.

Others attempt to go beyond arguments based on obviousness or anecdotes. Some simply point to the fact that the recent period of globalization has also seen a spread of democracy: in 1975, thirty nations of the world had popularly elected governments, but by 2010 that number had grown to 116.[19] More specifically, and in ways that attempt to get at underlying mechanisms, scholars point to the experiences of countries in central and eastern Europe and in South America as evidence of a close relationship between openness and democracy. The evidence from these regions has been read as suggesting that the suppression of democracy and confinement of political power to a ruling junta or oligarchy tend to require a closer control of borders, whereas greater openness tends to encourage democracy and the more equitable distribution of political power within a society.

The most sophisticated efforts to establish a link between globalization and democracy have focused on the effects of international trade and investment: the link between openness and information flows seems to be seen as too trivially obvious or even tautological to be worth as much attention. In addition to reviewing more than a dozen previous studies, economists Barry Eichengreen and David Leblang deploy their own sophisticated analytical approach to conclude that "positive relationships running both ways" do in fact exist "between globalization and democracy, though exceptions to this generalization appear to obtain at particular times (during the Bretton Woods period) and places (in labor-scarce countries)."[20]

How could trade and financial integration promote democracy and vice versa? As we have seen, products and services have informational content, which creates a link between trade and cross-border information flows. Gains from economic integration also support economic growth, and we know that democracy is more stable in countries where per capita income is above $3,000 to $6,000.[21] Financial integration and policy transparency are also complementary. In chapter 7, we got a taste of how capital markets react to informational problems. And even more simply, the freedom to form links across borders is probably harder to deny in a context where government protects individual liberty and answers to the general public rather than the other way around. Additionally, it seems that geographic distance conditions the spread of democracy. Thus, researchers have recently undertaken statistical examinations of the domino theory, according to which the implantation or removal of democracy in one country "infects" neighboring countries, increasing or decreasing their likelihood of being democratic. And in fact, some effects of this sort do seem to show up in the data: countries do tend—albeit to a limited extent—to track increases or decreases in the democratization of their neighbors.[22]

It's true that if a country is subject to a high level of inequality (e.g., if it has a very high Gini index), democracy may lead to a backlash against globalization as people focus on domestic redistribution; a country like Bolivia provides a recent example. But the fundamental political problems in such situations, as in many others, are rooted in the domestic context, rather than being intrinsic to globalization. Restricting globalization does nothing to resolve such problems that would offset its numerous other costs. And allowing it might even serve as a catalyst for updating political institutions to reflect societal changes, fostering more representative democracy.

Widespread Wars?

The final political concern about cross-border integration covered here is that it may also promote cross-border conflict. This concern was not without foundation in the Age of Empire: for example, it has been argued that Germany's largely unsuccessful attempts to acquire colonies were an important factor underlying World War I. But in the modern period, the influences at work seem to be quite different. Thus, the discussion in chapter 4 of the loci of all U.S. military interventions between 1990 and 2002 and their juxtaposition against countries' involvement in disputes at the WTO suggested that economic engagement and military trouble tend to be substitutes: if you don't get the one, you get the other.

Further insight into problems and opportunities is afforded by looking more closely at wars. While interstate *and* intrastate warfare have both declined dramatically since the early 1990s, intrastate or civil wars remain much more frequent, and are much more serious in their impact.[23] Very poor countries are several times as likely as rich ones to be embroiled in armed conflicts, and ethnic disputes are estimated to be responsible for the majority of deaths, with religion coming a distant second and money related to contraband such as drugs and conflict diamonds third.[24] What to do about ethnically divided and, more generally, fragmented countries is discussed further in the next section. What needs to be noted here is that ascribing their internal conflicts to globalization, when many of them are not very integrated with the world economy in the first place, seems a bit of a stretch.

That said, even when such conflicts do remain confined within a country (which can't always be counted on—think of East Africa), their effects spill over national boundaries. Thus, one study estimates that the economic cost of failed states amounts to as much as $270 billion per year, a figure that includes lost income due to nonfunctioning economies (but excludes the costs of threats such as terrorism and drug trafficking that are spawned by failure). The bulk of this cost—87 percent, to be exact—is estimated to be borne by neighboring countries, themselves usually poor, whose income is depressed by the turmoil next door.[25]

This is, of course, an example of a cross-border externality. Note that it provides yet another answer to the question of why failed/failing states shouldn't simply be left to expire. And like most such externalities, it is less than fully global: neighbors should be expected to take a particular interest in reviving failing/failed states.

Finally, amid all the chatter about globalization and conflict, it is worth remembering that much conflict is driven by nationalist sentiments rather than impulses to globalize. You might think that after two world wars and millions of deaths we'd have learned our lesson; the reality is that radical nationalism tends to flare back up in times of financial crisis and economic uncertainty. In fact, you can measure it. One study suggests that a one percentage point decline in the growth rate is associated, roughly, with one percentage point more support for extreme right-wing or nationalist parties in a country, and even more in countries where income is relatively well distributed.[26] The bad news is that such xenophobia is on the rise; the good news is that ADDING value through globalization in the ways flagged by World 3.0 may be the best way to bolster general attitudes toward globalization.

Independence and Integration

Aspirations toward the creation of new nation states, a driver of some of the internal conflicts mentioned in the previous section, have also been linked to globalization. Here, some historical context is useful. As we saw in chapter 1, there were nearly a million independent political entities in 3000 BC, averaging only a few dozen people each—but since then, their average size has increased several hundred thousand times as they have consolidated into nation-states with millions of inhabitants, sovereignty over defined territories, and extensive state apparatus.[27] Political concentration was actually at a maximum in the Age of Empire prior to World War I, when the number of independent political entities (not including sub-Saharan Africa) decreased to just over fifty. By the end of World War II, there were about seventy-five independent countries in the world, and now there are nearly two hundred—a number not seen for about two centuries. So the last century has seen a (small) reversal of a pattern of political consolidation that stretches back into prehistory.[28]

Some of this fragmentation was the "natural" consequence of decolonization. But the process seems to have proceeded beyond that point—leading some scholars to conclude that "the 'globalization' of markets goes hand in hand with separatism."[29] The idea is that in a closed world, large countries enjoy economic advantages over small ones because political boundaries determine the size of the market. But with free(r) trade, even relatively small cultural, linguistic, or ethnic groups can form smaller, more homogeneous political jurisdictions that are economically viable.

Also note that such fragmentation has been accompanied by countries ceding some authority to (international) regional and global bodies (e.g., the European Union, the United Nations, the WTO) as well as, in some instances, (intranational) regional devolution of authority. These put additional pressure on the traditional nation-state, from above as well as from below.

The Spanish region of Catalonia, whose capital, Barcelona, I call home, provides a good example. Catalan separatism from Spain is sometimes traced as far back as the (unsuccessful) proclamation of a Catalan republic in the seventeenth century. But it found its modern expression in the aftermath of Francoism. General Franco brutally suppressed Catalan language and culture as payback for the region's opposition in the Spanish civil war (memorialized by George Orwell in his *Homage to Catalonia*). With Franco's death and Spain's transition to democracy, Catalonia's political aspirations were recognized by the Spanish government in a statute of autonomy passed in 1979. In a 2006 revision, the Spanish government recognized Catalonia's "national reality as a nationality." But in 2010, Spain's highest court ruled that the only legal nation recognized by the constitution was Spain. This sparked another surge in Catalan separatism, with one large poll indicating majority support for independence.[30]

At the same time, the Catalan government has continued to try to strengthen Catalan over Spanish (which is still spoken by more people in Catalonia) with ever more insistent policies and practices. Thus, in summer 2010, it was decided that all professors who teach in Catalonia had to be able to do so in Catalan.

Underlying these political and cultural moves is the sense that the European Union has done a good enough job of integration that governance at the level of Barcelona and Brussels dispenses with the need for an intermediate level of government in Madrid. Similar sentiments can be encountered in other parts of Europe—Spain's Basque region, northern Italy, Belgium, Scotland, and so on—with one source predicting that as many as ten new countries may emerge in Europe in the course of the twenty-first century.[31]

I know (or have learned) better than to suggest to Catalans, for example, that they shouldn't pursue independence or promote Catalan above all other languages. All I can do is suggest that costs as well as benefits should be as fully accounted for as possible in making such existential decisions. To be specific, if separatists (like most people, as we saw in chapters 2 and 3) overestimate current cross-border levels of integration and underestimate residual border effects, they are likely to be too quick for their own good to approve secession.

Thus, in the Catalan case, its interregional merchandise trade with the rest of Spain is four-fifths the value of its merchandise trade with the rest of the world and—more importantly—helps convert an *international trade deficit* equal to 11 percent of Catalan GDP to an *international and interregional trade surplus* equal to 7 percent of GDP. Applying the estimate of a pure border effect reducing trade intensity by two-thirds, the decrease in Catalonia's interregional trade volumes implied by the erection of a national border between it and the rest of Spain would decrease its GDP by 12 percent, and transform its external trade balance from a 7 percent surplus to a 5 percent deficit. Note that if the border effect reduced trade by only one-third, these shifts would be halved—but would remain substantial in their effects—at a time when local politicians are trying desperately to achieve 1–2 percent annual GDP growth.

I hasten to add that this is a back-of-the-envelope calculation rather than an adequate basis for a policy recommendation. But the point is that I've never seen the issue of border effects mentioned, let alone quantified, in the debate about whether to secede or not. It is certainly possible to decide to "consume" some of the benefits afforded by greater integration at the European and global levels in the form of political independence. But before deciding to do so, it might be useful to figure out how much independence would really cost—in terms of not just reduced (interregional) trade flows but also forgone opportunities for further economic integration.

Another indicator of latent separatism is provided by geography—the degree to which national borders are straight rather than squiggly, and therefore likely to have been drawn arbitrarily without attention to the realities on the ground. The most artificial states, as in the ones that rank in the top tier in terms of both ethnolinguistic fragmentation and straightness of borders, are Chad, Ecuador, Equatorial Guinea, Eritrea, Guatemala, Jordan, Mali, Morocco, Namibia, Niger,

Pakistan, Sudan, and Zimbabwe.[32] Countries like these Troubled Thirteen are the really hard cases, where there is so little love lost among different ethnolinguistic groups that relatively little else seems likely to be lost—some have argued—by their going their separate ways. Thus, foreign policy analyst Parag Khanna has suggested that thirty to forty of the countries that currently exist are worth splitting up or otherwise restructuring.

While recognizing the enormity of the challenges facing the most "artificial" countries, I am inclined to be much more cautious. Perhaps the situation is irremediable in countries with ongoing civil wars, but only one of the Troubled Thirteen, Chad, is listed in this category by the Center for Systemic Peace (CSP).[33] Otherwise, though, I would hesitate to put countries on the operating table, for reasons that will be clarified by considering Africa, where widespread surgery of this sort is often advocated.

Africa's ethnolinguistic fragmentation and the fact that 80 percent of its borders follow latitudinal and longitudinal lines imply that African countries tend to rank quite high on artificiality/fragility: twenty-five of the thirty most fragile states, as calculated by the CSP, are on that continent.[34] To consider a specific one, focus on Nigeria, which figures in the top half of the CSP's top thirty in terms of fragility.

Nigeria's 150 million people are divided into more than 250 different tribes. Is reemphasizing tribal loyalties likely to offer a way forward? How about a division between the Muslim north and the Christian south? Actually, this was already tried on a smaller scale by Biafra—a tragedy that also reminds us of the blood that gets spilled in the course of most efforts to restructure borders. What about the continent as a whole? Since Africa is located far from and is otherwise poorly connected to other regional markets, and since it is fragmented internally into many small, poorly integrated national markets, what seems to be required is an expansion in the spatial scale of cooperation, to the supranational level, rather than a contraction to the subnational (tribal) level (that is, a reversion to World 0.0). Chapter 13 discusses the way forward for Nigeria in more detail.

More broadly, a focus on restructuring national borders betrays to me a basic World 1.0 bias: the idea that if we could only get people stowed away into the right countries, everything would be all right. This focus is subject to all the problems with World 1.0 discussed in chapter 1, including the basic gaps in coverage in a state-based partitioning of the world that are dramatized by the difficulties of dealing with failing/failed states.

Failing states loom particularly large because, as noted in the previous section, most sources of armed conflict are now internal rather than international, and of course, failed/failing states are their usual hosts. Simply trying to get around the problem by disaggregating until one ends up with homogenous polities doesn't make sense because there is, practically speaking, no end to how finely one can discriminate among people.

To make the same point a different way, ever-increasing fragmentation is not the same as ever-increasing freedom. In fact, going by historical analogies, such fragmentation seems more likely to be associated with an escalating fear of others rather than a sense of freedom or security, and runs counter to the expanding circles of cooperation witnessed over the last five millennia (see chapter 1) as well as the current imperatives of dealing with global externalities, risks, and imbalances while continuing to open up.

Toward a Freer World

In summary, this chapter has gone beyond market failures to explore and explode a number of myths related to the contention that more openness begets political oppression. The more integrated economic order of World 3.0 doesn't seem likely to lead to particular countries or companies lording it over the world, nations having to don a "golden straitjacket" and losing their freedom to act; democracy going the way of the dinosaur; or an expansion of armed conflict. In fact, opening up seems to directly improve certain kinds of political outcomes and should help indirectly by boosting growth, which historically has tended to lead to increases in social justice, democracy, liberalization, and respect for human rights (while periods of stagnation have tended to usher in more authoritarianism).[35] So political concerns of the sort reviewed in this chapter are *not*, generally speaking, reasons to slam the brakes on globalization.

The proposition that openness should increase political freedom is, in a sense, very intuitive. The real question, then, is why there is so much of a tendency to leap to conclusions—or at least to dwell on political anxieties—that are counterintuitive or contradict the kinds of information presented earlier in this chapter. Some of the other patterns on display, particularly the increase in the number of independent countries since 1900, suggest that the deep, underlying distinctions between "us and them" that we encountered in chapter 1 are still at work, fueling calls to keep "them" on the other side of the borders of our sovereign states. But as the previous section highlighted, putting up new borders does impose significant costs. So softening the conflicts that divide us and expanding circles of human concern and affection may be a better path forward. Chapter 15 offers some suggestions about how to accomplish this.

Chapter Eleven

Global Homogenization

*"It's amazing! No matter what planet you go to, it's
the same stores in every mall."*

Source: www.CartoonStock.com

CHAPTER 10 ADDED political fears about globalization to the economic preoccupations discussed in the preceding chapters—and addressed those fears. This chapter does the same for cultural fears, as exemplified in the cartoon. Critics have decried globalization as a tidal wave of homogenized American consumer culture that tears "authentic" local cultures asunder. And on the surface, they seem to be right. Fly into any large, cosmopolitan city on any planet in our solar system and you encounter restaurants like McDonald's and KFC as well as their local imitators. The American global presence goes well beyond restaurants to include films starring Tom Cruise and Angelina Jolie, music by the likes of Willie Nelson and Lady Gaga, brands like Nike and Apple, and of course, the language spoken in malls around the known universe, English. So even if globalization is no longer about Pax Americana, does it force Pop Americana on everybody?

The answer is no. National cultural barriers may have fallen to some extent in recent decades, but they are still extremely important, and they will continue to remain so. And we're not just talking here about food and entertainment, but also about deep aspects of culture that at best make home a place of comfort and belonging, and at worst harden into parochialism, ethnocentrism, and racism. These darker manifestations are visible even in countries we think of as advanced, tolerant, and stable. For example, in 2009, Switzerland passed a constitutional amendment banning the construction of new minarets. Almost 60 percent of voters approved this measure, giving voice to deep and widespread fears about Muslims that were both religious and cultural in nature.[1]

World 2.0 thinking tends to equate globalization with cultural homogenization or convergence, but the purpose of this chapter is not to push the opposite point of view—that all we have today are differences and the hardened cultural identities of World 1.0. Rather, it is to suggest that reality is far removed from both extremes, and to redirect attention to World 3.0, in which cultures don't converge but also aren't entirely uninfluenced by each other. In such a context, we have much to gain and little to fear on the cultural front from more cross-border interaction.

The cultural tableau that spreads out before us includes cultural differences or barriers that won't change anytime soon, as well as cultural differences that *will* fade, albeit to a more limited extent than one might expect, and other differences that will evolve instead of dissolving. The latter are what are responsible for the numerous cultural benefits of globalization.

Of course, there are also some hard cases where increased openness *does* pose a clear cultural threat, and these have to be taken into account. But the generalized cultural resistance to opening up seems to reflect fear of foreigners rather than reasoned analysis of the cultural costs and benefits. It is tempting to speculate that such fears may once have been adaptively useful but aren't any longer (at least not to the same extent), and thus can be worked on. The chapter concludes by describing some mechanisms for actually doing so.

Resilient Cultures

In chapter 3, we saw that the United States and Canada share a common language and cultural heritage, yet even in this case, there are enough cultural differences—maybe as a reaction to all that is shared—to sustain strong national identities on both sides.

Looking beyond North America, we can cite numerous casual examples of cultural difference. Citizens of the United States maintain a culture around owning guns that most Europeans can't fathom. The Czechs drink way more beer than people in Saudi Arabia, and even more than the Irish, who come in second.[2] Pakistanis google *sex* more often than any other national population, just slightly more than the Vietnamese and far more than the Irish and Czechs. Eritreans google *god* the most as well as figuring in the top five nationalities searching for *sex*.[3] India and China are so close geographically that they still haven't resolved their territorial disputes, but couldn't display more distinct food cultures, particularly around which animals and parts of animals should or shouldn't be eaten. Argentines see psychotherapists more often than other nationalities, and Brazilians spend a higher proportion of their income on beauty products than the citizens of any other major economy.[4]

More systematic research has revealed the surprising resilience of cultural differences. Analysis of data from the World Values Survey, a study covering sixty-five countries and 75 percent of the world's population, has found that although modernization has wrought tremendous cultural change, underlying values do remain intact. As the researchers involved noted, "A history of Orthodox or Islamic or Confucian traditions gives rise to cultural zones with distinctive value systems that persist even after controlling for the effects of economic development."[5] Traditional values can also reemerge even after modernization, globalization, and economic development have seemingly swept them away. The late Harvard political scientist Samuel P. Huntington has spoken of a "clash of civilizations" between East and West running along ancient cultural and religious fault lines, while *Economist* editors John Micklethwait and Adrian Wooldridge have noted the resurgence of religious fundamentalism in their book *God Is Back*. As we discussed in chapter 1, the late twentieth century also saw a resurgence of regional fractures and separatism in the Balkans, the Middle East, and elsewhere along traditional ethnic, religious, and tribal lines.

Critics of globalization nonetheless point to any number of villains who are supposedly destroying traditional cultures and imposing homogenization. European nationalists fear the bureaucrats in Brussels, who are allegedly pushing aside national cultures in favor of a European identity. Europeans, Islamic nationalists, and others fear hegemonic national cultures, particularly that of the United States. Many anticorporatist believers in World 1.0 fear multinationals like Coca-Cola or McDonald's, arguing that they tend to lure consumers into adopting a single superficial, unhealthy global lifestyle. And perhaps most broadly, postcolonialist theorists fear that Western concepts and mores are exercising a sort of imperialist power, pushing aside indigenous traditions under a guise of universality.

In point of fact, these villainous agents of cultural corruption and decay have proven much feebler than alleged. Europe, as we noted in the last chapter, may have grown more united in recent years, yet unification has also spawned geographically based, separatist countermovements in places like Kosovo and Catalonia. And for all their alleged power, corporate-driven consumerism, cultural imperialism, and homogenization have all proven far from overwhelming. As evidence of this last point, let's briefly consider four large consumer-focused U.S.-based multinationals frequently mentioned as agents of these trends.

Begin with McDonald's, that bogeyman of antiglobalization, and a veritable icon of homogenization, efficiency, and corporate marketing. We often tend to think of McDonald's as a relentlessly consistent purveyor of fast food around the world: a Big Mac is a Big Mac is a Big Mac. But if one has the appetite to visit the company's outlets around the world, it is obvious that it actually offers a dizzying array of local menu items, including the McArabia in Saudi Arabia, the McShawarma in Israel, and the Bulgogi Burger in South Korea (for even more examples, see table 11-1).

McDonald's has found that the most successful business strategy in our semiglobalized world is an adaptive approach that combines the standardization of certain core brand elements with localization of others. Thus, despite McDonald's diverse menus, it still requires that French fries have sugar content of exactly 21 percent, no matter where in the world they are produced, and that a pound of cheese yield thirty-two slices, no more, no less. To further complicate matters, standardization is not necessarily unidirectional. For example, McCafé, a coffee-house-style food and drink chain that was developed in Australia in an attempt to compete with the many local coffee shops, was later introduced to the United States, Japan, and other countries. This nuanced mix of localization and standardization is what has helped McDonald's generate 60 million customer visits per day.[6]

McDonald's is hardly the only Western fast-food chain to have profited by melding standardization with a respect for and affirmation of traditional cultural tastes. In China, Yum! Brands offered the same original recipe chicken in its KFC restaurants, yet supplemented it with locally oriented products such as soup, noodles, bamboo shoots, and the "Dragon Twister," a sandwich featuring chicken, Peking duck sauce, cucumbers, and scallions. The result of such a hybrid approach? KFC became the largest restaurant chain in mainland China, with more than three thousand outlets there in 2010, compared to 263 in 1998, and returns on investment substantially greater than those posted by KFC's other geographies.[7]

Turning to beverages, we find that Coca-Cola, the world's most valuable and ubiquitous brand, has likewise adopted a strategy of respecting

TABLE 11-1

Ten local menu items available at McDonald's

Menu Item	Country	Description
McArabia	United Arab Emirates, Saudi Arabia, other Middle Eastern countrles	Small grilled chicken or beef patties, served in pita with vegetable toppings and garlic mayo
Shogun Burger	Hong Kong	Teriyaki pork patty with lettuce, served on a sesame seed bun
McAloo Tikki Burger	India	Vegetarian burger made with potatoes, peas, and spices
McShawarma	Israel	Shawarma flatwich sandwich, using kosher meat
Bubur Ayam McD	Malaysia	Translates literally as "chicken porridge"
McPalta	Chile	Avocado paste and pork sandwich
Kiwiburger	New Zealand	All-beef patty, egg, tomato, lettuce, cheese, onion, cooked beetroot, sauce, and mustard on toasted bun
McNifica	Panama, Argentina, Costa Rica, and other Latin American countries	Salted beef patty with cheese, lettuce, and tomato
Wiesmac	Poland	Beef patty, onions, lettuce, one slice cheddar cheese, mustard, and horseradish sauce
Bulgogi Burger	South Korea	Pork patty in bulgogi marinade

Source: Wikipedia; Peter Gumbel, "Big Mac's Local Flavor," *Fortune*, May 5, 2008.

cultural differences while still offering some standardization. Coke serves local tastes by varying its core cola product (using cane sugar in Mexico as opposed to corn syrup in the United States) and, more importantly, by marketing local brands in different countries. Ever hear of Avra, BURN, Cappy, Fernandes, Kvass, or Real Gold, all of which are owned by Coca-Cola? You might if you lived in Greece, Poland, Croatia, the Netherlands, Russia, or Japan, respectively.[8]

Or consider a newer multinational that attempted standardization in a supposedly susceptible media industry. In the late 1980s, Bill Roedy, president of MTV Networks International, used to explain MTV's globally standardized strategy by saying, "A-lop-bop-a-doo-bop-a-lop-bam-boom means the same thing in any language!" Fifteen years later, his tune had evolved—as had the company's: "MTV India is very colorful, self-effacing, full of humor, a lot of street culture. China's is about family values, nurturing, a lot of love songs. In Indonesia, with our largest Islamic population, there's a call to prayer five times a day on the channel. Brazil is very sexy. Italy is stylish, elegant, with food shows because of the love of food there. Japan's very techie, a lot of wireless product."[9]

This proliferation is not unconnected to profits, of course. Globaloney notwithstanding, the role of language and distance effects in what music gets played where have stayed roughly constant since the 1960s—and the degree of home bias has actually increased sharply since the late 1990s![10]

Corporate-driven consumerism, cultural imperialism, and homogenization are visible to some extent with the opening up of borders. But even in our four minicases—hard cases, since they involve large, U.S.-based, consumer-oriented multinationals often cited as homogenizers of popular culture—they are not nearly as pronounced as globalization's critics think.

Cultural Gains and Losses

So far we've argued that globalization hasn't automatically swept away traditional cultures. We should also account for the important cultural *gains* that have accrued from openness, and that could be added to if we pursue additional openness under World 3.0. Scholars such as Tyler Cowen have suggested a number of ways in which cultural exchange has fostered cultural innovation, multiplying the number of cultural choices available.[11]

Inspiration is one such pathway to cultural innovation: Starbucks, for instance, originated in an attempt to recreate an Italian espresso-bar experience in the United States. *Mixture* represents another: creole languages are a good example, so much so that creolization has come to denote cultural mixtures or hybrids more broadly (e.g., in cuisines). *Transplantation plus adaptation* is arguably even more important, given the need to adjust to variations in local culture: Starbucks actually started out by copying Italian espresso bars so faithfully that it featured recorded opera music and bowtied waiters—but quickly figured out those features did not fit its U.S. clientele. And the *transnationalization* of cultures, such as the one joining the global business elite or global scientific communities, supplies yet another route to innovation—one whose importance is probably escalating because technology has made it easier to connect and mobilize across borders.

Beyond cultural innovation, a culture of openness also brings another source of gain whose importance is often overlooked: the diffusion of new technologies, knowledge, and ideas. With its us-versus-them logic, World 1.0 thinking doesn't address diffusion very much, because national societies are seen as largely self-contained and "safe" behind national boundaries. And World 2.0 takes it for granted that diffusion happens automatically and effortlessly in an unbounded world.

The truth is that diffusion doesn't happen automatically—but when it has happened at certain key moments in history, it has exposed societies to new knowledge and greatly enhanced human welfare. Many people in the West have a negative view of China today, but a thousand years ago Europeans benefited immensely from the introduction of Chinese technologies such as the compass, the wheelbarrow, and movable type. Similarly, during the Middle Ages, Arabs brought mathematics to the West from India, helping fuel the scientific revolution. As Amartya Sen has observed, "Europe would have been a lot poorer—economically, culturally, and scientifically—had it resisted the globalization of mathematics, science, and technology."[12]

In a specifically cultural context, diffusion can be fruitful in another way as well: by helping preserve what is being diffused. Consider a contemporary example of cultural diffusion, from the West to China. Interest in Western classical music has been dwindling in countries such as the United States for decades now. China, however, seems headed in the opposite direction with its 30 million piano students and 10 million violin students, prompting some to credit it with "saving" the genre.[13] And Western classical music has also led to innovations in Chinese music: according to one expert, "The whole revamped approach to traditional Chinese music is based on Western sonic ideals."[14]

Finally, even when there is cross-border displacement of a traditional culture, that may still offer some gains because not all elements of that culture may be worth preserving. The caste system in India provides an example—one that Karl Marx had in mind when he offered a curiously mixed impression of the effects of English colonization:

> *English interference ... dissolved these small semi-barbarian, semi-civilized communities, by blowing up their economical basis, and thus produced the greatest, and to speak the truth, the only social revolution ever heard of in Asia. Now, sickening as it must be to human feeling ... we must not forget that these idyllic village-communities, inoffensive though they may appear, had always been the solid foundation of Oriental despotism, that they restrained the human mind within the smallest possible compass.*[15]

Having discussed the gains that accrue from cultural exchange and openness, we also need to acknowledge that some cultural losses are possible. Openness seems to render some cultures vulnerable to extinction, especially small, economically marginal cultures that typically exist at the subnational level. But some aspects even of a threatened culture may be more robust than others. Cuisine and music, for example, have the potential to achieve niche status, contributing even on a very small scale to the variety of available options. In such cases, certain kinds of connections with the outside world—for instance, trade—can help maintain or even revitalize a traditional culture, albeit in possibly modified form. Language, on the other hand, is harder because it is subject to network externalities, so its value declines sharply as the number of speakers falls.

Let's focus on the hardest possible case, in which a traditional way of life might be sustainable if a community remains isolated, but not if it is connected. Suppose you're a member of a subsistence culture, and all of a sudden you encounter a modern welfare state that funds subsistence with generous cash handouts. In such a situation, would you want us to keep your community isolated in the interests of preserving diversity across the world? Many have argued forcefully against this, and the philosopher Kwame Anthony Appiah has gone so far as to see attempts to preserve "authentic" traditional cultures as a form of injustice and servitude levied on people who, by no choice of their own, are members of those cultures. Appiah notes that in any case, "authenticity" is illusory, since cultures are inherently in flux; judging something "authentic" reflects more what we as elite, outside observers value about a culture than what an insider values. We might try to pay homage to a traditional culture by "saving it," but really we are only making our own cultural statement on the backs of those who actually have to live in a traditional culture, and who very well may want exposure to "modernity."[16]

One way to assess such hard cases is to see them as, in effect, extreme examples of a trade-off that often exists between widening an individual's cultural options via globalization and keeping national cultures diverse. Tyler Cowen evokes this trade-off in his book *Creative Destruction* when he argues that trade tends to *increase* the diversity of choices available to individuals within countries even as it *decreases* the cultural differences across national borders. And Appiah is clear about how he would resolve this trade-off, even in hard cases: in favor of the individual.

Appiah's position draws on widespread (although by no means unanimous) agreement that development is or should be about broadening and deepening individuals' capabilities, which requires maximizing both physical and intellectual/cultural choices available to individuals. It's worth noting that liberalism in general is consistent with this view. The concept of a "marketplace of ideas," for instance, sees human progress as drawing on an intellectual market in which the best answers to a problem arise out of an articulation of and competition among the largest number of possible answers.

A further argument for cultural enrichment at the individual level goes beyond instrumentalism and even expansion of choices to encompass something that might be called *appreciation of choices*. What-ever else diversity and openness are good for, they are inherently valu-able because they enrich human experience. In Sanskrit literature we find the story of the well-frog who lived in a well and had never been outside its confines. The frog's entire worldview, in other words, con-cerned the well, and it remained suspicious of life outside. This caution-ary parable suggests that seclusion impoverishes us as human beings, and that there is something intrinsically enriching about having a broader outlook on the world. From this perspective, diversity and dif-ference are worth nourishing in their own right, quite apart from any other effects they may have on human social and material progress.

The Fear Factor

Despite all the potential gains from cultural exchange described in the previous section, the evidence from the section before that one suggests that most of what is dear to us culturally isn't about to go away because of globalization. Some of this is due to differences in values or, more simply, preferences that reflect conditioning and are therefore hard to change. As the Greek historian Herodotus wrote in the fifth century BC, "If anyone, no matter who, were given the opportunity of choosing from amongst all the nations in the world the set of beliefs which he thought best, he would inevitably, after careful considerations of their relative merits, choose that of his own country. Everyone without exception believes his own native customs, and the religion he was brought up in, to be the best."[17]

The point of this section is that such differences in values or prefer-ences don't seem to be all that come into play. The Swiss minaret contro-versy, for example, suggests something very different at work. There are only four mosques with minarets in the whole country, and they have long been prohibited from using loudspeakers to issue the traditional call to prayer due to noise pollution laws. Moreover, Switzerland has long prided itself on its ability to integrate immigrants, who comprise 20 per-cent of the population—while Muslims make up only 5 percent.[18] Clearly, the movement to ban new minarets was motivated by deep-seated insecurities rather than a rational consideration of cultural threats—and of damage to Switzerland's image and influence around the world, particularly in Muslim countries. Proponents of the ban played on these insecurities by warning of "the possible introduction of Shariah law in Switzerland" and producing provocative posters such as the one shown in figure 11-1, in which the Swiss flag bristles with black minarets.[19]

I've picked on the Swiss, but irrational insecurities in the face of exposure to foreign cultures are widespread and manifest themselves

FIGURE 11-1

Swiss poster depicting minarets as missiles

Source: Poster campaign at Zurich train station, November 2009 (© Naeem Mohaiemen/Shobak.org).

not merely as assertions of the superiority of one's own culture, but also in the form of disparagement of foreigners' cultures. Consider figure 11-2, based on survey data from around the world, which maps perceptions of cultural superiority against perceptions of the need for cultural protection.[20]

In the bottom left-hand corner of the chart, we find countries with little sense of either cultural superiority or a need for protection, and in the top right-hand corner, countries with a strong sense of cultural superiority and fear of foreigners. By these measures, Swedes appear pretty laid-back about foreigners—or were back in 2007—whereas Indians, to my dismay, are not. Overall, we find high levels of belief in cultural superiority (with two-thirds support in the median country) and in the need for cultural protection (with three-quarters support in the median country). The two are obviously related; in fact, the correlation coefficient between perception of cultural superiority and need for cultural protection is a lofty 0.68.

The correlation is a curious one: if people think that their culture really is superior, one might not expect them to clamor for cultural protection. Economic well-being (or lack thereof) seems to play a role: the four countries in the Pew sample that score highest on self-perceived

FIGURE 11-2

Cultural concerns

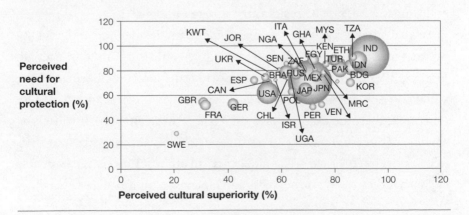

superiority are, in decreasing order, India, Indonesia, Tanzania, and Bangladesh; the ones that score lowest are, in increasing order, Sweden, Britain, France, and Germany. What we seem to be seeing here is cultural insecurity rather than aggressiveness—which is good news when it comes to the prospects for confidence-building measures of the sort discussed later in this chapter and in chapter 15.

It's hard to analyze fear of foreigners and foreign cultures directly, but we can do so indirectly by considering levels of trust. Whole books have been written about how country-level measures of trust relate to other factors.[21] Trust falls when "bads" such as the Gini index of economic inequality and corruption indices rise, and trust rises with increases in "goods" such as indices of openness of markets and of globalization, Internet usage, economic growth rates, education spending, transfer payments from rich to poor, democracy scores, and postmaterial values.[22]

For our purposes, though, it makes more sense to look at the *geography* of trust rather than at how much trust in strangers exists in one's own country. Different data are required, involving measures of trust between country pairs (bilateral measures) rather than country by country (unilateral measures).

The best data available come from Eurobarometer surveys that measure trust among citizens of different countries, mainly within Europe.[23] Surveys in sixteen West European countries asked people whether they trusted their countrymen, the citizens of the other fifteen countries, and people from some East European countries, Japan, the United States, and China "a lot."[24] The results are reported in figure 11-3.

Several interesting patterns are evident in the data underlying the figure. First, people trust their fellow citizens much more than they do foreigners. Thus, 57% of Germans reported trusting other Germans a lot, while only 26% reported trusting Swedes, the next highest country listed. Of course, there are exceptions to this rule, of which Italy is the most conspicuous example. Italians reported generally low levels of trust in their fellow citizens (19%) as well as citizens of all other countries in the sample (11%), but they did trust the Swiss and Japanese a bit more (26% each).

FIGURE 11-3

Levels of trust

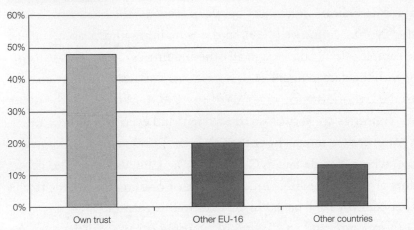

Source: Survey conducted by the European Commission among all European countries to measure trust, 1996.

At the other extreme, the data indicates that Swedes (and to a lesser extent, other Nordic countries) tend to be the most trusting overall (40%). What's especially striking is that this country, which as we've seen is the least superior/defensive about its own culture, is also the most trusting and well trusted itself. A more general pattern is evident here: for the fifteen countries (twelve European) for which all the data are available, the correlation coefficient between levels of trust earned and self-reported cultural superiority is −0.83 and between trust and the reported need for cultural protectionism is −0.85!

The case of Sweden—and other Nordic countries—also illustrates a general correlation between trust extended and trust earned; these countries tend to rank high on both dimensions. What this suggests is that people from Nordic countries may simply be less prone to unreasoning fear of the "other."[25] But that said, the election of an anti-immigrant right-wing government in Sweden in 2010 is also a reminder that Swedes aren't perfectly fearless either.

In thinking about trust, it's helpful to move beyond a dichotomy of trust in fellow citizens versus trust in foreigners. In the Swedish example, the data indicate differences between trust in fellow citizens (64%), in other Nordic countries (63%), in the remaining European countries in the sample (40%), and trust in all other countries (29%). This pattern, along with the data in figure 11-3, starts to suggest that trust is also subject to the law of distance: in terms of the CAGE framework, the other Nordic countries are very close to Sweden, and even non-Nordic European countries are much closer than the non-European countries in the sample, which include Japan, China, and the United States. The determinants of variation in how much citizens of one country trust citizens of other countries will be discussed later in this chapter.

It is also interesting to take a look at some other countries that are highly trusted—and those that are not. Switzerland, presumably benefiting from its proximity to the EU-16 as well as a general reputation for probity, ranks highest in terms of general trust earned (34%), and Japan also fares relatively well (19%). But those are the only above-average performers of the "other countries." The remaining fall below this subgroup's average trust level of 12 percent. Turkey was the least-trusted country in the sample; only 7 percent of respondents from the EU-16 countries reported trusting the Turks. Since these numbers were collected in 1996, and since mutual impressions seem to have declined since then, these data represent an early indication of the difficulties Turkey has faced in finding acceptance within the EU.

Looking at trust levels, then, affirms that cultural biases can have concrete administrative and economic implications. More broadly, differences in how much people in a given country trust people in other countries greatly affect cross-border interactions. Statistical studies suggest that moving from lower to higher levels of bilateral trust can increase trade, direct investment, portfolio investment, and venture capital investment by 100 percent or more, even after controlling for other characteristics of the two countries.[26]

I should add that most of these data are for Western Europe, a region where nationalism has been more or less held in check, and where countries have pursued formal administrative integration to an extent unparalleled in other regions. This region is also relatively well educated, which tends to raise general trust levels. Chances are, then, that in other countries, trust in foreigners is likely to be lower than in figure 11-3, and the fear factor higher.[27]

Excess Xenophobia?

We have seen that modern Europeans, enjoying peace and prosperity, still trust foreigners less than their fellow citizens, and many harbor deep-seated cultural fears. Fear of foreigners, or xenophobia, must be taken seriously, despite its more absurd manifestations such as the Swiss minaret ban.

Xenophobia may have been adaptive back in World 0.0 in the evolutionary sense of helping our ancestors survive and pass on their genes. Thus, xenophobia has been linked to disease avoidance based on the observation that outsiders were more likely to carry pathogens to which a given population lacked antibodies.[28] This fear of foreigners as carriers of disease is the basis for slurs like "Jewish vermin" and "Tutsi cockroaches" as well as for "ethnic cleansing" as a euphemism for genocide.[29] The deep roots of xenophobia are also reflected in the fact that related behaviors have been documented in a wide variety of animal populations, and that human infants as young as three months old display fear of strangers without ever having had negative contact with them. Such findings lead some to theorize that genetic factors contribute to fear and hostility toward people who are different.[30]

Game theory also provides rationalizations for xenophobia or, conversely, favoritism toward members of one's own group. Among the simplest rationales is that interactions with fellow group members are more likely to be repeated than one-off, facilitating cooperation rooted in reciprocity. In the absence of any other constraints (think World 0.0), it could make sense to take advantage of strangers (but not fellow group members), based on the assumption that you'll never meet them again. More recent research by Robert Axelrod and Ross Hammond has shown that "in-group favoritism can overcome egoism and dominate a population even in the absence of reciprocity and reputation, and even when 'cheaters' (mimics) need to be suppressed." Their model also indicates that "competition with outgroups helps promote harmony of ingroups" even without agents who have sophisticated cognitive abilities.[31]

These are all explanations of why our biases against foreigners run deep and must be taken into account. But that doesn't mean xenophobia or ethnocentrism is still generally adaptive or useful today. As UCLA anthropologist Dan Fessler explains, "We often respond to today's world with yesterday's adaptations. That's why, for instance, we're more afraid of snakes than cars, even though we're much more likely to die today as a result of an encounter with a car than a reptile."[32] Sociologist William F. Ogburn coined the term *cultural lag* to help explain such phenomena. Ogburn wrote, "A cultural lag occurs when one of two parts of culture which are correlated changes before or in greater degree than the other part does, thereby causing less adjustment between the two parts than existed previously."[33]

While it is beyond the scope of this chapter to chart the benefits and costs of wariness of foreigners, there are reasons to suspect that the benefits have declined over time and the costs have risen. With today's more integrated disease pools, vaccines, disinfectants, and so on, foreigners no longer pose much of a threat to our health. Barbarians no longer sneak in and loot our encampments during the night, and if thefts do occur we can call the police instead of rounding up a posse. Furthermore, most violent crimes occur between people who know each other, and the most intense conflicts tend to be among those who are close (who have more to fight about) rather than far apart, which casts doubt on whether it really makes sense for trust to decline monotonically with distance. And we have seen the tremendous economic gains we enjoy from international trade and investment (chapter 4), which would be very costly to reverse.

For all these reasons, it is worth trying to reduce the fear factor. The next section discusses how.

Toward a More Harmonious World

By digging deeper into patterns of how trust and fear vary among populations, we can identify drivers that may help allay fear of foreigners. The Eurobarometer survey data, described above, have been mined extensively toward this end.[34] One group of scholars has concluded that trust falls as the populations of any two countries grow more different in terms of their languages, religions, genes, body types, geographic distance, and incomes, and if they have a more extensive history of wars.[35] The fact that England and France were at war for 198 of the years since 1000 probably helps explain why the United Kingdom trusts France less than any other EU-16 country (8%), and why the French trust the United Kingdom. only marginally more (10% versus an average of 17% for the remaining EU-15).

Factors like language, religion, and body type, cannot readily be adjusted to improve trust, but others are more flexible. The more pleasant people in country *A* perceive people in country *B* to be, the more they trust people in country *B*. But more news coverage tends to *reduce* how much people in a given country trust people in another country, probably because of the negative bias in news about overseas.[36]

Research has also confirmed that several other factors have the potential to influence the prevalence of cultural chauvinism and related fears. Higher education levels in a country cause levels of nationalism and suspicion of outsiders to decrease; one study found this to be true across the board in ten countries with quite different educational systems.[37] The extent to which an individual participates in the network of global economic, social, and cultural relations and of inclusive social identification with the world community seems important as well.[38] Traveling and living abroad seem to broaden individuals' perspectives while also improving creativity.[39] Finally, scholars have found that security of property rights and the role of law serve as prerequisites for trust to emerge, rather than what they often seem—vital substitutes for trust. Scholars have also emphasized the importance of private and public-private initiatives aimed at building and sustaining public trust, or at least mitigating its absence.[40]

Based on these findings, we can identify several concrete steps for reducing the fear factor and smoothing the way toward increased openness under World 3.0. These steps include more education; monitoring of negativism in the media and in political discourse; encouraging more interpersonal contacts across cultures, and ensuring that they are as "pleasant" as possible; and building a more cosmopolitan global social identity (something chapter 15 describes). We might also try to focus on building cross-cultural understanding among countries where economic potential exists yet political and cultural relationships are strained (India-Pakistan and Israel-Palestine come to mind), prioritize support for the rule of law, and encourage the private sector to become involved in building bridges across cultures.

Of course, when all is said and done, the factor with probably the greatest influence on public perceptions about foreigners—and of cultural and political arrangements generally—is how well a country is faring economically. It's interesting that in 2010 nine out of ten Chinese reported feeling happy and optimistic about where their country was headed—a higher percentage than almost any other country, despite China's relative lack of political freedom.[41] One scholar put it this way: "As respondents became more resentful of modern life, more suspicious of consumerism and the free market, and believe that their traditional way of life is disappearing, they are consistently more likely to have negative opinions of globalization, regardless of whether we are talking about economic or cultural globalization."[42] We thus return to a point made in previous chapters: despite the short-run pressures that we are experiencing, and the inevitable questioning of free trade and the turn toward World 1.0, the best way of dealing *in the medium to long run* with the issues discussed in this chapter is to generate economic results. And the best way to do that is to focus on the steady growth of World 3.0 rather than either the stagnation of World 1.0 or the higgledy-piggledy growth of World 2.0.

To summarize, then, this chapter has focused on a final fear about globalization: that it would destroy traditional cultures and leave us with a bland, homogenized cultural experience. We began by discounting a number of the negative effects that have been attributed to cultural openness. In the process, a brighter picture emerged—that of real gains that might still be realized from more cultural contact between diverse peoples. The chapter concluded by examining a potential barrier to more globalization—negative reactions driven by irrational xenophobia—and considered some measures that might help neutralize it.

Having explored the several market failures and fears associated with more openness, we're now in a better position to focus on the problem we've been tackling all along: how we might move forward from the current unsettled state of the world. That is the topic of Part III.

Part Three

The Choices

Chapter Twelve

Toward World 3.0

SO FAR WE'VE EXPLORED the potential gains from further globalization, and we've also spent seven chapters taking an extended look at globalization's suspected or supposed problems. None of these problems turned out to be a show-stopper, and some even revealed themselves as blessings in disguise. Nevertheless, the sheer number of pages I've spent on market failures and globalization might suggest a belief on my part that the problems outweigh the potential. Nothing could be further from the truth.

One way I can stake out my position more clearly is in relation to the thought of John Maynard Keynes. Writing after the onset of the Great Depression, Keynes offered a concise, useful appraisal of globalization and cross-border exchange: "Ideas, knowledge, art, hospitality, travel—these are the things which should, of their nature, be international. But let goods be homespun whenever it is reasonably and conveniently possible; and, above all, let finance be primarily national."[1]

I would agree with two-thirds of that—the parts concerning cross-border information and capital flows. Joining many of Keynes's otherwise devoted students, I'd take a much more optimistic view of trade in goods and services, although I do worry about chronic trade deficits. And I've argued in chapter 8 for allowing more immigration into many rich countries, a point consistent with Keynes's arguments elsewhere.[2]

Beyond offering specific views on these subjects, the previous chapters have started to sketch a different way of thinking about globalization and market failures, what I've called World 3.0. We've seen in area after area that World 3.0 yields a distinctive set of recommendations about cross-border integration that account not only for market failures but also for semiglobalization, the underlying differences between countries, and the law of distance.

Resetting our worldviews to World 3.0 is urgent because we desperately need more prosperity *and* more security. The rich world faces its toughest economic recovery in decades while dealing with unprecedented demographic change. But that doesn't mean those of us fortunate enough to be in rich countries should entertain any perverse envy of our counterparts in the "developing" world. Alleviating poverty and closing the gap in living standards demand faster, more reliable economic growth even more desperately there.

Although integration across borders isn't the perfect growth tonic—Part II is all about its alleged side effects—it is almost undoubtedly the best one out there. In an environment where a 1 percent increase in GDP growth or employment is to die for in many countries, opening up further offers the potential for net gains that are much larger, as we saw in chapter 4.

So what's stopping us? It's not just the specific market failures and fears covered in the previous chapters. Rather, the representation of our policy choices as a tug-of-war between World 1.0 and World 2.0—between regulation and integration—has short-circuited discussions of how to pursue additional cross-border integration while managing any side effects. Envisioning World 3.0 requires unbundling this representation into two related but distinct domains of choice. Instead of repeating the arguments advanced in chapter 1 about the desirability of doing so, this chapter deals with the implications of shifting to a World 3.0 mind-set. It focuses, in particular, on what we can say about the management of integration *and* regulation. The chapter begins with a broad intellectual history of the debate about regulation and how it has and hasn't been globalized. It then builds on the discussions earlier in this book to articulate six core propositions about how to jointly manage the regulation of markets and their cross-border integration—that is, what to do in World 3.0.

This chapter—and the rest of Part III—then pushes further on the integration-related dimensions of World 3.0, because those are where the potential gains seem to reside, not in the realm of regulation, even though regulation is required in certain situations. This chapter concludes by supplying some broad guidelines about how to redraw our mental maps of the world to better represent the realities of World 3.0. As we shall see in the coming chapters, these guidelines are useful whether we are thinking about countries, businesses, or individuals in World 3.0.

Harvard Versus Chicago

The most direct antecedents of the worldview developed in this book are provided by academic work on market failures and their regulation—which is what I focused on thirty years ago when I was a graduate student at Harvard specializing in industrial organization (IO) economics. Because that was how Harvard defined IO. My thesis chairman, Richard Caves, served as the intellectual custodian of a scholarly tradition that, beginning with the early work of Harvard's Edward Mason and Joe Bain, had focused on the possibility that concentrated industry structures might permit firms to exercise market power, raise prices, and impair social welfare (the concern addressed in a globalization-related context in chapter 5). This tradition also devoted considerable time to investigating possible remedies, principally regulation.

An appreciation of market failures and the problems that concentration, in particular, could create had dominated discussions of public policy in the United States for decades. But by the time I got to graduate school, the Harvard School's hegemony was threatened by sustained attack from the Chicago School, which championed free market solutions. As Nobel Prize winner Milton Friedman, a leader of the Chicago School, once remarked, "'Chicago' stands for a belief in the efficacy of the free market as a means of organizing resources, for skepticism about government intervention into economic affairs."[3] In macroeconomics and financial markets, this meant that the government should set and sustain a stable rate of growth of the money supply and enforce property rights, but otherwise keep its hands off the economy. By contrast, Harvard took a more activist, Keynesian view of governmental policy options.

In the realm of microeconomics, the Chicago School was far less impressed than the Harvard School with market failures. Chicago School economists generated ingenious arguments about why the standard kinds of market failures—market power, externalities, and uncertainty, the topics of chapters 5, 6, and 7, respectively—might not matter much. In their view, competition to be the monopolist might solve even the natural monopoly problem—the most extreme manifestation of market power. Externalities didn't necessarily pose a problem either, since unrestricted bargaining among all interested parties could lead to efficient outcomes. And the price system was *the* way to transmit and coordinate information of the sort uncovered over time in uncertain environments, and therefore not to be tampered with.[4]

What the Chicago School was much more exercised about was the cost of market failures and distortions imposed by *governments*, not businesses. I've explored many of these governmental failures in the context of globalization at some length (see, in particular, the discussion in chapter 5 of the myriad ways governments help create and sustain market power). Add in a belief in the innate selfishness of regulators (like all individuals), which renders them vulnerable to "capture" by the industries they are supposed to regulate, and you arrive at the Chicago School's visceral antipathy to trying to regulate private-sector market failures, on the grounds that intervention would just make things worse.[5]

In effect if not in intent, then, the Chicago School had a *probusiness* bias compared to the Harvard School's *proconsumer* focus. Harvard was willing to contemplate governmental interventions to rein in business, particularly big business, and Chicago wasn't. The Harvard School did

TABLE 12-1

Comparison of the Harvard and Chicago Schools of economic theory

	The Harvard School	The Chicago School
Market outcomes	Market failures are common and can, in the absence of governmental intervention, persist	Market failures are rare or self-correcting, with exceptions mostly due to governmental meddling
Role of government	Room for beneficial governmental intervention in a variety of ways, ranging from regulation of private enterprise to public ownership	Should focus on money supply, enforcement of property rights, but otherwise laissez-faire
Performance orientation/ type of surplus effectively emphasized more	Consumerist/consumer surplus: e.g., ban on horizontal mergers that raise prices, regardless of whether they increase producer efficiency	Corporatist/producer surplus: conduct meant to maximize profits must, in principle, be regarded as lawful

not take any specific position on the *extent* of such intervention; it simply rejected the extreme Chicago School position of always shying away from such regulation. See table 12-1 for a more structured comparison.

Globalizing the Debate

The Harvard-Chicago debate originally had little in the way of international content. In my core subject of IO, linkages across national markets were discussed as one of several dozen elements of industry structure, conduct, and performance. It wasn't that my IO professor and thesis chairman, Richard Caves, was unaware or uninterested in international content: he happened, very unusually, to be a distinguished international as well as IO economist. But beyond evidence that import competition typically improved domestic market performance, there were few points of contact then between these two subfields of economics.[6]

Developments in international economics actually appeared to provide a more promising path forward at the time. Research in that subfield had traditionally assumed perfect competition, thus ruling out most categories of market failure. But that started to change in the 1980s, with the development of "new trade theory"—which was even described by one of its key contributors, James Brander, as the "industrial organization (IO) approach to trade theory."[7]

New trade theory mostly focused on research into *monopolistic competition*: a slightly less perfect form of competition that involves limited economies of scale and (as a result) a large but finite number of differentiated producers, each with a very limited amount of market power. Such models had first been developed in IO back in the 1930s; international economists such as Paul Krugman now began to use them to study industries marked by intraindustry trade in variety, with different varieties produced in different locations due to fixed set-up costs but then traded internationally to satisfy within-country preferences for diversity. Given the salience of intraindustry trade, work on monopolistic competition has taught us a great deal. However, as I argued in chapter 4, such models are very limiting from an IO perspective since they do not allow for concentrated industry structures featuring just a few competitors.

Other lines of work aimed at incorporating insights from IO into international economics proved less fruitful. Thus, in the early 1980s, amid heated debate over U.S. international competitiveness, there was a surge of excitement around models of "strategic trade policy" in which a governmental precommitment to particular policies (e.g., subsidies) could, in the presence of a small number of competitors, improve one country's welfare at the expense of others.[8] But the excitement faded once economists realized that small changes in assumptions could reverse this conclusion and, even more significantly, that letting multiple governments precommit rather than just one could trap countries in a prisoner's dilemma (e.g., a subsidy war), threatening to leave *all* of them worse off. By the 1990s, much of the excitement had shifted—largely thanks to pioneering work by Paul Krugman, once again—to the incorporation of geography instead of IO into trade theory, as discussed in chapter 3.[9]

IO economists' interests shifted over this period as well, toward using game theory to research small-number interactions. This reflected not only interest in looking more rigorously at strategic behavior but also fascination with applying a new kind of math to economics.[10] Considerable progress *was* made toward that substantive objective, but game-theoretic modeling also threw up a profusion of possibilities that undercut professional economists' interest in the broad Harvard-Chicago debate (as I learned from trying to publish on the topic in the late 1980s).[11]

Even more significant, however, was the shift that took place in public sentiment. During the 1980s, as the conservatism of Ronald Reagan and Margaret Thatcher took hold, a wave of deregulation swept around the world and was seen as vindication of the Chicago School and its theories. This attribution was ironic—or so it seemed to Harvard-trained IO scholars—because much of the legislative impetus for the early deregulatory efforts in the United States came from liberal politicians, notably the late Edward Kennedy. The economists advising politicians like Kennedy held views closer to Harvard's than to Chicago's; they understood that while theoretical rationales for regulation existed, these rationales required case-by-case assessment. As Alfred Kahn, who as chairman of the Civil Aeronautics Board presided over the airline industry's deregulation in the 1970s, subsequently wrote in his textbook on regulation, "Industries differ, one from the other, and the optimal mix of institutional arrangements for any one of them cannot be decided on the basis of ideology alone."[12]

Be that as it may, in the court of public opinion at least, deregulation denoted victory for Chicago's views about market failures and, more broadly, about how to manage competitive processes: as little as possible. And reinforcement was supplied by the course of the Cold War.[13] Facing a real threat from the Soviet Union, many Americans came to think of socialism as a dirty word, and advocacy of a bigger role for government as almost treasonous. The fall of the Berlin Wall and the collapse of the Soviet bloc in the early 1990s simply solidified beliefs that Chicago was right—beliefs that spread around the world.

As a result, when Milton Friedman passed away in late 2006, Lawrence Summers, the quintessential Harvard economist when not in public service in Washington, included the following in his obituary, titled "The Great Liberator":

Not so long ago, we were all Keynesians. ("I am a Keynesian," Richard Nixon famously said in 1971.) Equally, any honest Democrat will admit that we are now all Friedmanites ... While much of his academic work was directed at monetary policy, Mr. Friedman's great popular contribution lay elsewhere: in convincing people of the importance of allowing free markets to operate.[14]

Note here the association of the term *free* (not exactly a value-neutral term) with unregulated markets, the result of an impressive rhetorical push by Friedman and Hayek.[15] While capitalism does depend on the freedom to engage in mutually beneficial exchange, freedom and unregulated markets hardly go hand in hand. In fact, there are numerous strands of evidence that suggest the opposite conclusion: the fact that governments supply some of the infrastructure required for markets to work; indications that World 0.0 societies with minimal governmental infrastructure tend(ed) not to have well-developed markets; the observation that countries today can still sustain high levels of openness alongside large amounts of state intervention (e.g., Scandinavia); and a large body of evidence suggesting that markets work better when participants trust each other than when they are entirely selfish.

But it wasn't until the recent crisis, and the welter of additional evidence it presented that deregulation *can* go too far, that people started publicly reassessing Chicago's "victory," at least in public. Paul Samuelson, Summers's uncle, opined in one of his last columns, published at the end of 2009, "Gone forever, one hopes, are the idiocies of Friedman-Hayek libertarian selfishness."[16] Even more recently, Nobel Prize winner and Harvard (or, more accurately, Cambridge) economist Amartya Sen pointed out that market fundamentalists appeared to be misreading their patron saint: "Adam Smith viewed markets and capital as doing good work within their own sphere, but first, they required support from other institutions—including public services such as schools—and values other than pure profit seeking, and second, they needed restraint and correction by still other institutions—e.g., well-devised financial regulations."[17]

People who forgot all this in the course of market mania are now being forced to relearn old lessons about market failures and how to counter them. Part II of this book discussed regulatory and nonregulatory responses to a range of market failures and fears, with a focus on managing the effects of (further) cross-border integration. It not only sought to formulate specific policy recommendations but also to explore the nexus between market failures and the cross-border integration of markets. It is time to pull together the threads of that inductive effort.

Dual, Not Dueling, Choice Domains

World 3.0 is an essential construct because focusing on just World 1.0 and 2.0 conflates questions of integration and regulation into a tug-of-war along a single dimension. Before the crisis, I too had tended to associate globalization with deregulation and high barriers at national borders with regulation within them. In my case, the food crisis of 2007 (replayed in 2010) forced me to think through situations where markets hadn't worked well but where the case for additional cross-border integration continued to be strong. This case really underlined for me the point that there were two distinct dimensions of choice, integration and regulation, to be taken into account, not just one.

As figure 12-1 (reproduced from chapter 1), reminds us, distinguishing between these two types of choices opens up a third possibility, World 3.0, that is qualitatively distinct from both World 1.0 and World 2.0.[18] World 3.0 takes market failures seriously, as Harvard historically did, but explicitly accounts for cross-border interactions in formulating responses.

Of course, the 2×2 game board in figure 12-1, while a significant improvement on the traditional tug-of-war, is still grossly oversimplified. After all, this book has discussed four broad types of cross-border flows and of distance, seven types of market failures and fears, and myriad responses. Even if we unbundle integration and regulation, associating a single binary choice with each is not enough. Integration and regulation have to be treated as vectors of choices, many of which can take on more values than "on" or "off." And this combination of multiple dimensions and multiple options leads to an explosion of possibilities. For an

FIGURE 12-1

Dual, not dueling, choices

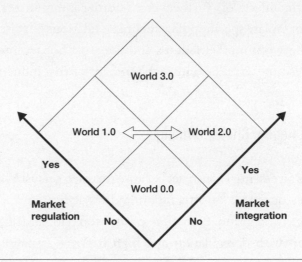

illustration, note that the traditional 3×3×3 Rubik's cube has 43 quintillion possible permutations, versus "only" 3.7 million for the simplified 2×2×2 pocket cube—that is, more than 10 trillion times as many!

Optimization across uncountable policy possibilities is obviously impractical, although that is what economic models routinely assume. What can be offered here, based on explorations in the earlier chapters, are six broad propositions about the nexus between market failures and fears and market integration—propositions about how to manage World 3.0. And if "proposition" sounds too definite to you, think of them as heuristics to help with the search for better policy solutions in a complex, multidimensional policy space.

Proposition 1: Market failures and fears need to be incorporated into analyses of integration

We have seen that the traditional market failures of concentration (chapter 5), externalities (chapter 6), and informational imperfections (chapter 7) aren't the only problems that can arise in the cross-border context. Flows sometimes build into dangerous imbalances (chapter 8).

Furthermore, the benefits of integration aren't always shared fairly, although globalization isn't the main culprit behind inequality and job insecurity (chapter 9). And even when fears are unfounded (as are most of the ones we saw in chapters 10 and 11), they can still represent real barriers to integration.

Taking market failures and fears seriously requires incorporating them into the analysis upfront, instead of as an afterthought. The European Union's envoy to the World Trade Organization, John Clarke, explains the differences in how analysts and policy makers approach trade liberalization: analysts tend to focus on the economic benefits associated with specific initiatives, while policy makers screen initiatives by looking first at the political pain they will create—and shelve ones that are deemed too painful even if the economic benefits being promised are very large. Paying attention to proposition 1 in the course of the analysis would yield findings more attuned to political realities instead of tone-deaf to them.

Fears of exploitation deserve particular attention in this context. Choices concerning integration and regulation almost always mix opportunities to grow the economic pie with potential shifts in how it gets shared. Unless we are forthright—and honest—in making the distinction strategists call for between "creating value" and "claiming value," we will at best achieve a brittle form of integration, riddled with suspicions of exploitation. And at worst, we may miss out on the major opportunities to create value to which World 3.0 directs our attention.

Proposition 2: The cross-border integration of markets often helps correct market failures instead of compounding them

Chapter 5 presented examples of situations in which allowing foreign competition alleviated the problems associated with excessive domestic market concentration. In chapters 6 and 7, we also saw how foreign technology and market access can help curb environmental damage in the face of externalities and how deepening trade in food products can reduce price levels and volatility under conditions of imperfect information. Chapter 8 indicated that managing certain kinds of imbalances, such as of labor, requires more rather than less cross-border integration. And chapters 10 and 11 highlighted the numerous political and cultural benefits of cross-border integration.

This proposition is particularly worth emphasizing because many people associate cross-border integration with deregulation, and get very worked up about globalization-related market failures as a result. Opening up can, under certain conditions, substitute for regulation and restore markets to health—benefits that should be explored by applying the ADDING value scorecard to proposed integration initiatives to get a full sense of their potential.

Proposition 3: In many other cases, integration has a negligible effect on market failures and therefore shouldn't be restricted

We have seen that macroeconomic conditions in a given country are still determined more by country-specific factors than international influences (chapter 7), that large capital borrowing needs often reflect domestic deficits as much as trade deficits (chapter 8), and that technological progress is the main driver of changes in employment and income in developed economies, not cross-border integration (chapter 9). In such cases, decisions about integration should not be held hostage to outcomes for which they aren't responsible; they should focus instead on ADDING value.

This point might seem fairly obvious. I highlight it here anyway because globaloney often leads us to assume globalization-related forces to be stronger than they actually are and, overlaid on our World 0.0/1.0 conditioning, to blame them for our plight. Further confounding matters is the fact that we face a number of problems that are global in scope, such as global warming, and turning our back on cross-border integration would do little to alleviate them. In all these cases, it is important to prevent our dissatisfaction with the general state of the postcrisis world from leading to knee-jerk, not to mention atavistic, moves to close off borders.

Proposition 4: When integration does threaten to aggravate market failures, mix-and-match policies to try to preserve some of the benefits of opening up while curbing adverse effects

We have seen that restrictions on short-term debt flows into and out of developing countries make more sense than broader restrictions on capital mobility (chapter 7), and that countries like the United Arab Emirates can welcome a large influx of foreign labor while applying distinct rules to particular classes of workers—and force foreigners to return home when their work is done (chapter 9). The general point is that if flows must be curtailed, the scope of such regulatory measures should be targeted narrowly to avoid unnecessarily giving up benefits of integration.

Additionally, it is possible to allow openness along certain dimensions while restricting it on others, as indicated by the examples of politically repressive regimes that nonetheless manage to participate actively in world trade. The mix-and-match possibilities afforded by targeting policies to specific flows can also be augmented by tailoring policies to particular foreign countries, applying them for limited time periods, imposing caps on various flows, and so on. The example of the Rubik's cube cited earlier should convey a sense of how much this expands the policy space. Of course, taking advantage of all these possibilities requires shifting from a mind-set of a "closed" world in which all possibilities are enumerated in advance, and therefore attention is focused on selecting among them, to an "open" world that is too complex to consider exhaustively and that affords room to add value by coming up with creative strategic options, not just choosing optimally from a prespecified set of possibilities.[19]

Proposition 5: Distance sensitivity is inversely related to the optimal scope of integrative and regulatory initiatives

Lower levels of distance sensitivity tend to imply larger, more far-flung "natural" markets, expanding the optimal scope of efforts to boost cross-border integration. Compare markets for airplanes with markets for haircuts, for instance. And in terms of the costs of cross-border integration, when market failures do crop up, distance sensitivity is also a useful guide for figuring out the appropriate scope of regulation. Domestic regulation can usually address (primarily) domestic problems more effectively than restrictions on cross-border flows. Thus, if inequality is a major concern, domestic regulation is a better, more targeted way of tackling it than imposing restrictions on trade flows. And even international problems don't always require global solutions. Thus, with intermediate levels of distance sensitivity that imply that the scope of the market failure is regional, as tends to be the case for acid rain (chapter 6), regional cooperation is appropriate. Only very distance-insensitive problems like global warming from greenhouse gases require global responses, and even then one-size-fits-all policies agreed by worldwide consensus are seldom the right answer.

The point about the optimal scope of regulatory initiatives, in particular, parallels Jagdish Bhagwati and V. K. Ramaswami's classic theory of domestic distortions and policy intervention: "If the market failure arises in domestic markets, then the appropriate policy intervention is the use of domestic policy directly targeted at mitigating the effects of the market failure, while free trade is maintained externally."[20] The difference is that Bhagwati and Ramaswami's analysis, like most of traditional theory, dichotomizes between home and abroad.[21] Distance sensitivity captures additional information about how far, if at all, the effects of market failures extend beyond national borders and therefore provides some insight into the optimal scope of cross-border regulatory efforts.

Proposition 6: Large integration opportunities often exist within as well as across national borders

Thus, provincial border effects, while smaller than national border effects, still remain significant, as discussed in chapter 3. And even small countries (e.g., Belgium) often exhibit large internal distances across the CAGE dimensions. So, it makes sense to apply the propositions developed in this section to internal as well as external integration. The corollary is that multiple levels of government within a country can pursue integration, although they may also need to address market failures and fears such as concerns about inequality. Table 12-2 illustrates some of the integration initiatives that might be pursued at the provincial level.

Such opportunities are worth highlighting because neither World 1.0 nor World 2.0 calls attention to them. Thus, world maps drawn from a World 1.0 or World 2.0 perspective would both shade one's own country in a single color (either the same color as the rest of the world in World 2.0 or a different color in World 1.0). What this final proposition suggests, instead, is coloring a country of special interest in several different colors on the map, rather than just one, in order to pick up on internal heterogeneity. Using maps and other devices to better envision World 3.0 is the topic of the next section.

Envisioning World 3.0

To begin improving your vision of the world, take stock of where you're coming from and what's unique about it. World 2.0 tricks us into thinking the world is the same regardless of one's vantage point, but the reality is that what is close and what is far depends on where you are and how you are looking at the world—whether at the country, company, or individual level.

More specifically, maps of the world usually employ environmental reference systems, in which locations are specified with respect to objective features of the environment. What we need more of are *rooted maps* that employ egocentric reference systems—that is, maps that depict other countries in relation to a specific focal country, or that combine environmental and egocentric elements. In the remaining chapters, we'll see several examples of such maps.

We also need to reconsider the distances between locations—and, in particular, to account for more than just miles or kilometers. While

TABLE 12-2

Policy levers for integration within countries

Cultural	Administrative	Geographic	Economic
• Exploit language bridges	• Harmonize:	• Improve regional transportation/communications infrastructure	• Improve interregional market linkages

• Encourage interregional networks/exchanges
  • students
	• foreign investment promotion to avoid races to the bottom
	  • public procurement processes
	  • health, safety, environmental standards
		• Create an efficient energy network	• employee mobility
			  • capital markets
			  • information about interregional flows

• Promotional efforts	• Simplify cross-border regulations and paperwork	• Coordinate infrastructural investment	• Exploit scale/scope
			  • business networks/events
			  • joint embassies
			  • process for upgrading cross-border clusters

	• Bilateral/multilateral summits
	  • share best practices in government operations
	  • review regional institutions
			• Collect and disseminate information about interregional flows

Source: Pankaj Ghemawat, "The House of Growth: A Tale of Two Sectors," in *Competitiveness in Catalonia*, report prepared for Foment del Treball (with X. Vives), May 2009.

there are often similarities among geographic neighbors, the CAGE framework reminds us of the need to go beyond geographic distance to an expanded conception of spatiality that also accounts for cultural, administrative, and economic differences or distances. And it is important to keep in mind both unilateral aspects of difference, such as GDP per capita (which can be measured against a common yardstick), and bilateral ones, such as linguistic differences or geographic distance (which are relational in nature). Accounting for all these aspects of distance greatly enriches mental maps of the world: ranking schemes and uniform depictions of countries in geographic space give way to networks in which countries of varying sizes are subject to different degrees of separation depending on the dimension of distance being considered.

Having emphasized the importance of stretching things out in space, I should add that the nonlinearity of many distance effects makes them hard to account for precisely. So for many purposes, it may make sense to think in terms of basic scope categories rather than specific distance calculations. One common expedient is to distinguish between local, regional, and global spatial scales and to model their effects at that discretized level instead of trying to trace out distance effects as continuous functions of distance. Nongeographic groupings based, for example, on linguistic similarities or on whether countries are part of the same regional trading bloc can also be used in the same way.

Once you have a good sense of the real distances between countries, it's important to think through how particular kinds of international linkages or flows are affected by particular kinds of distance. Take a simple example: the sensitivity to, say, a thousand miles of geographic distance is obviously much greater when traveling by car than by airplane. Distance sensitivity—best thought of at the level of particular dimensions or subdimensions of distance—has to be calibrated for different types of cross-border activity. And for purposes of public and especially business policy, the analysis usually has to drill down to the industry level to be useful.

Finally, don't forget about internal distance. The bulk of life in our semiglobalized world still takes place within national borders, and there are large gains to be achieved in many countries from increasing levels of integration between provinces, ethnic groups, language communities, and so on. In addition, faced with the same external realities, countries, companies, or individuals differ greatly in how well they engage with them. So internal distance is relevant at each of these levels, although it takes different forms.

To summarize, uncovering and taking advantage of the opportunities afforded by World 3.0 requires recognizing what is different about your situation, remapping the world from your own perspective, understanding the CAGE factors that underlie observed patterns, calibrating distance sensitivity (whether on a discrete or a continuous basis), and remembering internal as well as external distance. As these recommendations imply, World 3.0 is a complex place. But it's that diverse and messy reality that also gives rise to the enormous opportunities associated with crossing borders. You should, at this point, have a broad view of these possibilities and, I hope, a bit less irrational fear about them. Now, it's time to continue elaborating the path toward World 3.0 from the perspectives of countries, companies, and ordinary people—perspectives that will allow further customization of the broad recommendations in this section.

Chapter Thirteen

Countries in World 3.0

THE PREVIOUS CHAPTER explained that World 3.0 typically affords policy makers broad discretion in the choices they can make and the paths they can pursue toward prosperity. It also articulated six propositions to help policy makers continue to open up while addressing market failures and fears. This chapter pushes further with the part of this agenda that involves opening up or integrating across borders— and leans particularly heavily on the CAGE framework and the law of distance to do so.

While cross-border integration could be looked at from the perspective of any polity with well-defined borders, this chapter takes a country-level perspective, that is, it focuses on national borders. As discussed in chapter 3, national borders are much more of an impediment to cross-border flows than provincial borders—although the latter should not be ignored (see table 12-2). And while there is much interest in "global cities" that are supposed to be getting increasingly connected to each other and detached from everything else, the data suggest that isn't really happening: national ties, in particular, continue to matter a great deal.[1] In any case, the principles for country-level analysis developed in this chapter also apply to larger and smaller geographic units. And in actual applications, analysis at more than one level may be warranted.

Improving international integration involves businesses—which do much of the heavy lifting—and individuals as well as national governments and international institutions. As a result, the ideas presented in this chapter should also be of interest to leaders in the business and nonprofit sectors as they think through how to leverage the unique potential of particular places to further the aims of their stakeholders. And individuals will probably want to apply these ideas to the countries or country relationships of particular interest to them.

This chapter brings country analysis in World 3.0 to life by looking at three cases in some detail: the tiny, rich European principality of Andorra; the poor West African giant of Nigeria; and the pairing of the world's largest and second-largest economies, the United States and China. The diversity of these cases helps illustrate a range of possible country strategies in response to very different circumstances. At the same time, though, one broad approach can be used across them to think about country strategy and, specifically, country integration. This robust approach is summarized after the individual case studies.

Anxious in Andorra

Landlocked Andorra, surrounded by Spain and France but separated even from them by the Pyrenees, is, roughly speaking, the world's tenth smallest country—and its tenth-richest. Yet there was a great deal of anxiety in Andorra in 2010, when I did a review of the country's competitiveness for the local business association. Tourism and related business drive 80 percent of Andorra's economy, and overnight tourist arrivals had declined every year for seven years.[2] Andorra's financial services industry (16 percent of GDP) was under pressure as a result of Andorra's being forced to comply with OECD guidelines for tax havens.[3] And while unemployment was still in the single digits, it had been zero only a few years earlier, when contract labor had to be imported to meet requirements.[4]

To understand what to do about these anxieties, it is useful to begin by understanding what is distinctive about Andorra apart from its very small size. Andorra's trade to GDP ratio of roughly 100 percent is not remarkably high for a very small country. What is remarkable is that its merchandise imports are almost twenty times as large as its merchandise exports, resulting in a merchandise deficit in excess of 40 percent of GDP.[5] Merchandise is shipped into Andorra to take advantage of the country's low tax rates, which attract shoppers, particularly from Spain and to a lesser extent France, who carry the merchandise back to their home countries—with the purchases counting as service rather than merchandise exports on that last leg. As a result of such shopping tourism and, to a lesser extent, its ski resorts, Andorra attracts more than a hundred times as many international tourists annually as it has residents, which amounts to several hundred times the average intensity of international tourist arrivals around the world.[6] Furthermore, financial patterns also suggest relatively heavy cross-border integration. Andorra is widely regarded as a tax haven and offshore banking center, which increases the volume of such activity relative to the domestic economy, and which has been the locus of the most pressure from the European Union on Andorra to bring its tax and other regulations more in line with EU norms.[7]

Keeping those distinctive features of Andorra in mind, remap the world from an Andorran perspective. Figure 13-1 presents such a map in which all other countries are drawn with areas proportionate to Andorra's imports from them. As one looks at this map, one of the things that stands out is the extreme regionalization and even localization of the Andorran economy. Put quantitatively, the intensity of Andorra's merchandise trade with the EU relative to the rest of the world is twenty-nine times, with France and Spain relative to the EU it is another sixteen times, with Spain relative to France it is five times, and with Catalonia (the region of Spain that abuts and shares the Catalan language with Andorra) relative to the rest of Spain, it is another five times.[8]

A similar pattern of localization is apparent when one looks at tourist arrivals. The intensity of overnight tourists from Spain and France relative to the rest of the world is nearly fifteen hundred times. And the intensity of day-trippers from those two countries relative to the rest of

FIGURE 13-1

Andorra's imports by trade partner, 2008

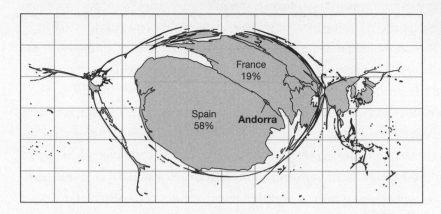

France
19%

Spain
58%

Andorra

Source: Generated based on data from Chamber of Commerce, Industry, and Services of Andorra, "Economic Report, 2008," 106–108.

the world is, of course, even greater, at nearly three thousand times.[9] It is worth noting that, once again, Spanish visitors are several times as numerous as French visitors in terms of intensities, and Catalan visitors are several times as numerous as visitors from the rest of Spain. So again, there is a pattern of extreme localization.

When one looks to explain these patterns of localization, it becomes clear that historically what Andorra has done is emphasize a few aspects of administrative difference as its basis for succeeding at international competition: differences around tax rates, banking secrecy laws, and so forth, while otherwise concentrating on regions that are very, very close to home culturally, administratively, geographically, and economically.

But that is all retrospective. Where should Andorra go from here? One important decision relates to where to compete. While the localization of Andorra's trade with France and particularly Spain is qualitatively consistent with what the CAGE framework would lead us to expect, quantitative analysis using a CAGE-based model can yield additional insight by comparing Andorra's actual trade versus what the model predicts. A rough analysis of this type suggests that Andorra's trade is overly biased toward Spain and underweighted toward France and the rest of Europe. A more rigorous analysis would be required to support a policy recommendation, but given the pressures Andorra is experiencing, it is more useful to consider a broad set of target markets rather than a narrow one.

First of all, Andorra's single largest trading partner by far is the Spanish region of Catalonia, with which it shares huge historic and linguistic commonalities as well as a land border, and whose capital, Barcelona, effectively serves as a hub for Andorra commercially and in other respects: Barcelona is where Andorrans tend to go for specialized hospital services, for example. My specific proposal to the Andorrans in this regard: instead of putting up an embassy in an additional country (they already have six), why not set up a consulate in Barcelona to help manage Catalan affairs?

The rest of Spain is Andorra's second-largest trading partner, but it appears that trading links could be deepened with a more granular approach that more explicitly recognizes the greater cultural and geographic distance to be bridged from Andorra to the rest of Spain.

Third, France seems to be underweighted in Andorra's merchandise imports and tourist arrivals. This is particularly striking in light of the "colonial link" between France and Andorra: the French president is the titular cohead of the Andorran state, along with a Spanish bishop. Of course, one can also point to geographic reasons why French-Andorran trade isn't bigger, but the fact that France *was* Andorra's largest trading partner twenty years ago suggests that these reasons may not be decisive. At any rate, it seems to make sense to figure out whether to expand links with France, and if so, how. This requires, once again, a rather different sort of outreach.

Fourth, there is the rest of the European Union, again apparently underweighted in Andorra's trade. That said, these countries generally do exhibit much larger CAGE distance from Andorra than do Spain and France, so additional care needs to be taken in figuring out how to pursue them, if at all. And then there is the rest of the world beyond the EU, to which the same points apply a fortiori, with one difference: the rest of the world is the part of the world that is expected to grow, while the

EU share of world GDP, as well as world population, is expected to fall continuously over the next few decades. Exploration of new domains makes comparatively more sense under such conditions.

In terms of how to compete rather than where to compete, recall that Andorra has historically competed on administrative arbitrage, centered on tax policy and financial regulation; however, those arbitrage advantages have been eroded by external pressure to tighten up regulation as well as liberalization of the surrounding shopping environment. Nevertheless, it seemed premature to conclude from that that Andorra should abandon arbitrage, for a variety of reasons.

First, new arbitrage opportunities often arise as old ones come under pressure. Thus, as tax rates rise in the rest of the EU, as inevitably they will given the crisis in public finances, some of the inducements to an arbitrage strategy may rise again, even as compliance efforts strain to keep those inducements within bounds.

Second, there is some untapped potential to existing arbitrage strategies. For example, given the country's focus on tourism, the fact that its minimum wage is higher than Spain's might be reconsidered. Bringing in cheaper labor might help not just with budget accommodations but with providing the kinds of high-end services that Andorra has been targeting. Andorra's beautiful scenery could also offer new bases for geographic arbitrage that are unrelated to either skiing or shopping.

Third, arbitrage isn't just an on-off choice. Luxembourg, for instance, manages to use administrative arbitrage in the financial sector to support what is reported to be the world's highest per capita income—more than twice Andorra's!—while remaining within the EU and in compliance with EU and OECD tax haven legislation. So clearly there is room to consider continuing with arbitrage strategies.

Consequently, while administrative arbitrage may continue to be an important part of the strategy for Andorra going forward, I should add that Andorra clearly also needs to do a better job of reaching out across cultural, geographic, and economic differences. Different ideas for doing this include granularity—for example, distinguishing between Catalonia, the rest of Spain, France, and the rest of the EU as key markets; the use of natural bridges such as the Catalan language in Catalonia and the euro in the euro zone; emphasis on partnerships when scale is important or distances loom large; and so on. The broader idea is that, for a variety of reasons, including growth forecasts in adjoining areas, it seems advisable to at least think of looking beyond Spain and France for certain purposes, if for no other reason than to try to shrink the supply chain from the ultimate supplier to the Andorran importer.

And finally, although this is not much talked about within Andorra, there is probably a need to reduce internal distance through internal integration as well, because Andorra is listed as the country that has the fifth-highest level of immigrants to citizens of any country in the world.[10] Foreign citizens constitute the majority of its residents, in fact.

Not Only Oil for Nigeria

Nigeria is almost the mirror image of Andorra in certain respects. Instead of being one of the richest countries in the world, it falls at about the seventy-fifth percentile in income rankings. And it is roughly two thousand times as large as Andorra in terms of both land area and population. Nigeria is actually the eighth most populous country today and is projected to rank fifth by 2050.[11]

In addition to its size, what is most remarkable about Nigeria is its dependence on natural resources, particularly oil. Estimates of oil's contribution to Nigeria's GDP range from one quarter to more than one half; it provides about 80 percent of the government's revenues and accounts for 90 percent of the country's export earnings.[12] Oil is also responsible for Nigeria's often being cited as an example of the "resource curse": the idea that countries with an abundance of nonrenewable natural resources tend to have stunted growth patterns and generally worse development outcomes than countries that lack such resources.

As one might expect, there is much discussion of the resource curse in the Nigerian context and more generally, and various approaches have been developed to help countries such as Nigeria better manage their oil revenues.[13] So in preparing for a talk to Nigerian business leaders in Lagos in late 2010, I found myself wondering if that's what would be most useful to talk about. An alternative was suggested by a contemporaneous quote from President Goodluck Jonathan: "The larger economy is the non-oil and gas and the future belongs to that."[14] So I decided that my "Nigeria in World 3.0" talk would focus on nonoil exports.

The distinction between oil and nonoil exports turns out to matter a great deal when remapping the world in proportion to Nigeria's exports to individual countries. When one looks at total exports, as mapped in the top panel of figure 13-2, what stands out is a relatively balanced map of the world with some proximity effects that tip trade toward Europe. But the bottom panel of figure 13-2 resizes countries to focus on Nigeria's nonoil exports and reveals a pattern in which Europe looks even more dominant than before, the Americas are shrunken shadows of themselves, and Africa continues to be significantly smaller than Europe.

What aspects of the CAGE framework do Nigeria's nonoil exports embody? The relatively low weight for Africa—compared to how large within-region trade would loom in most parts of the world—reflects the fact that, although Africa is much closer on geographic and other CAGE dimensions, the small size of the local market plus the unexploited potential associated with poor infrastructure, as noted earlier in this book, combine to reduce trade volumes. Nigeria's regional trade is also depressed by the fact that it is a former English colony surrounded by former French colonies who share a common currency, the CFA franc.[15]

Another attribute of Nigeria's trade that stands out in figure 13-2 is the heavy focus of Nigeria's nonoil exports on continental Europe. This is somewhat surprising because a CAGE-based estimate indicates that the United States and the United Kingdom should in fact be Nigeria's two largest trading partners. Relative geographic proximity helps explain Nigeria's trade with continental Europe, but is not sufficient to account for its weight. Rather, it seems there are other effects, most likely related to trade patterns in specific commodities that are among Nigeria's more developed nonoil exports. Leather exports to Italy and cocoa exports to the Netherlands alone accounted for 22 percent of Nigeria's nonoil exports in 2007.[16]

FIGURE 13-2

Nigeria's total exports (top) and nonoil exports (bottom), 2008

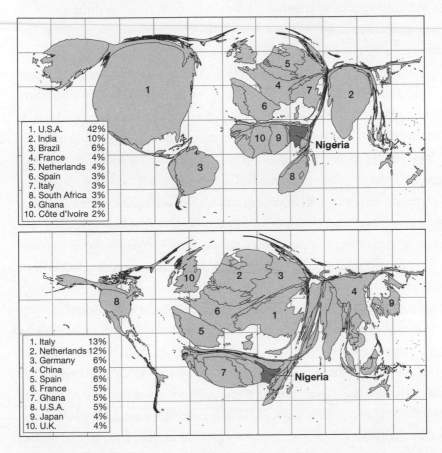

Sources: Generated based on data from United Nation Commodity Trade Database (Comtrade) (top panel) and Nigerian Export Promotion Council based on data from Cobalt International Services Returns (bottom panel).

Thinking about where else Nigeria might compete, one area of potential focus is the United States and United Kingdom, where, in addition to CAGE commonalities, there are many highly educated Nigerians.[17] A second potential focus might be large developing markets. These ultimately show up in quantitative CAGE analysis as the markets that look most attractive in terms of absolute growth potential after adjusting for the impact of CAGE differences from Nigeria's perspective.

The big wild card from the Nigerian perspective is regional trade. It is worth noting that trade with Nigeria's neighbors is underestimated because much of it is informal.[18] However, these are very poor and fragmented markets, and in some sense, Nigeria faces a choice about the extent to which it really is willing to take the lead role in fomenting further regional integration under the Economic Community of West African States (ECOWAS) or other auspices, as opposed to simply sitting back, content in the knowledge that it has the region's largest market, and therefore needs regional integration less than smaller countries do.

In terms of how to compete, it is fairly clear that most of Nigeria's nonoil exports—rubber, sesame oil, and cashew nuts along with leather and cocoa—as well as oil, of course, are traditional commodities in which international competition is driven by arbitrage. Especially given the volatility of exports from year to year, the challenges in these categories are to deepen and solidify bases of arbitrage, build longer-term relationships with buyers, and ideally migrate price bands upward. Such arbitrage strategies are often appropriate for exports to developed markets.

But regional markets offer Nigeria the opportunity—if it decides to make them a major focus—to use the scale of its domestic market as a vehicle for penetrating new markets on the basis of aggregation rather than arbitrage. Aggregation suits Nigerian companies because its smaller neighbors have less internal scale, and it offers potential for growth not just in traditional manufacturing categories but also in new categories. For instance, the market for Nollywood videos and Nigerian music in the region is potentially huge, even though its development has so far been held back by lack of distribution arrangements, piracy problems, and poor transport. Regional markets would also require some degree of adaption to requirements of other countries, consistent with the finding that among Nigerian firms, those that adapted their products and promotion strategies to foreign markets achieved better export performance.[19]

In addition to rethinking where to compete and how to compete, Nigeria faces generalized imperatives to reduce the effects of distance, particularly administrative and geographic distance since it scores poorly on indices of ease of doing business and faces particular problems relative to openness. According to a World Bank report, "Cross border procedures increase import costs for firms in Nigeria by 45 percent on average. Some enterprise managers noted that they must spend between 30–50 percent of their time on procedures alone."[20] Nigeria ranks 126th out of 139 countries in terms of "burden of customs procedures."[21] It takes 53 days to clear goods from Lagos ports, and, according to a World Economic Forum report, "it is estimated that a reduction of 'factory-to-ship' time from 41 days to 27 could increase exports from Nigeria by almost 15 percent."[22] To grow regional trade, road links and land borders also need to be improved.

Finally, it is important to remember internal as well as external distance. Nigeria, with more than 250 ethnic groups, scores in the top decile of countries in terms of ethnic and linguistic fragmentation.[23] Internal communications are poor, religious divides are pronounced, particularly between north and south, and agricultural wages in the south can be as much as 50 to 100 percent higher than in the north.[24] Regional fragmentation is also evident in the structure of Nigerian manufacturing, with many firms failing to achieve the scale economies that Nigeria's national market could at least theoretically support. So the challenge of helping Nigeria grow beyond oil is not just a matter of fitting Nigeria better into World 3.0; it also involves knitting Nigeria together.

U.S.-Chinese Uncertainties

The same broad approach that applied across the Andorran and Nigerian economies can, with some modification, be used to analyze the relationship between the United States and China. U.S.-Canadian trade is 50 percent larger than U.S.-Chinese trade but is subject to the least CAGE distance and conflict among major trading country pairs, while U.S.-Chinese trade suffers the most.

These economies were earlier seen as more complementary: "Chimerica," as described in chapter 8. Trade and investment soared, with U.S.-Chinese bilateral trade reaching nearly seven times what a gravity-based model would predict from the U.S. perspective. But surging flows brought huge trade imbalances and debt obligations, which made both sides vulnerable to the other's hostile moves. They are now anxious creditor and too-big-to-fail debtor.

The anxiety around this major creditor-debtor relationship and the difficulties of sustaining cooperation between the United States and China are compounded by deep differences and distances between them. As described in chapter 8, the two economies start with opposing superordinate goals and economic structure. China has a long time horizon; it needs to build up its capital stock rapidly and create 12–15 million new jobs annually and grow at least 8 percent per year. The United States has much more capital per person but also an apparently shorter time horizon and extensive entitlements, leading to shortfalls in savings. Connecting these two economies simply reinforces their divergent growth trajectories and unbalances trade and capital flows. A neoclassical solution would include rises in China's currency value and interest rates and in the United States' saving and taxation rates, but China sees this as capitulation while the United States sees its medicine as politically unacceptable. Both naturally value their domestic agendas over international balance, so the structural mismatch remains in place.

The noneconomic dimensions of the CAGE framework also add to the tensions between the two countries. Culturally, for instance, both countries have traditionally approached the world with exalted views of their own standing. The United States has long seen itself as an exceptional nation that, as Abraham Lincoln put it, offers humanity its "last best hope on earth."[25] China, over its much longer history, has almost equated adopting Chinese culture with being civilized itself, referring to itself as the Middle Kingdom, as in the center of the universe. The natural position of foreigners/barbarians, of course, was to pay tribute to China. And the outsiders that did conquer China adopted China's culture, not the other way around.

Administratively, of course, there is the obvious distinction between multiparty democracy and single-party rule. Chinese leaders regard this aspect of their governance as an internal matter, but that view runs up against Americans' pride in being a "beacon of democracy," which makes it difficult for them to hold any country without it in high esteem. The major disagreements around the award of the Nobel Peace Prize for 2010 to Liu Xiaobo illustrate how deep these divisions run. Additionally, the fact that China's ruling party is called Communist also conjures up unproductive cold war associations.

There are geographic tensions as well between an increasingly urban China, with massive populations concentrated in megacities, and a mainly suburban United States. This difference alone implies distinct approaches to environmental protection and energy policy as well as different patterns of competitiveness—for example, China's relative strength in urban transit and high-speed rail. Furthermore, China's higher population density and very intensive use of agricultural land fuel tension over territorial disputes.

Economically, trade and capital imbalances are far from the only source of tension between the two countries. As I write this, a *Harvard Business Review* article I wrote with Thomas Hout has just come out describing the technology squeeze to which the Chinese government appeared to be subjecting multinationals.[26] And I have at hand an issue of *The Economist* with the cover "Buying Up the World: The Coming Wave of Chinese Takeovers."[27] Given the historical record as well as the size of China's foreign exchange reserves, this seems unlikely to go entirely smoothly. And envy—on the U.S. side, of being overtaken by the Chinese economy in terms of total size and, on the Chinese side, of the U.S. continuing to be much richer per person—doesn't help.

To attach some numbers to these CAGE differences, recall that Canada ranked as the closest country to the United States along multiple dimensions, as described in chapter 3. China, in stark contrast, ranks 155th out of 163 countries analyzed in a CAGE-based model. Not only is Beijing twenty times farther from New York than Toronto, but the

United States and China don't share any of the main commonalities that made the U.S.-Canadian relationship so close: language, land border, trade bloc, colonizer, and legal origin. China and the United States are about as distant as any country pair you could select, and certainly the most distant among countries that are so deeply intertwined.

The stakes involved in getting these two countries to cooperate couldn't be higher, and the differences and tensions involved make perfect harmony an unrealistic aspiration. What can we say from a more realistic World 3.0 perspective to help improve the probability of cooperation? One basic lesson is that since distance isn't collapsing all around us, we can choose where to compete, and perhaps more importantly, where *not* to compete. Recognize spheres of influence, particularly China's reassertion of its regional position in Mongolia (sometimes referred to as "Minegolia"), Siberia, and Central Asia.[28] And more broadly, accurately size up the problem by recognizing that competition between China and the United States extends to "third" countries all around the world. China's activities in Africa have attracted the most attention, but its expanding economic relations with Latin America might serve as a reminder for the United States not to neglect its own neighbors.

Trade patterns are a seldom-noted indicator of China's rise—but an obvious one in an era when many leaders insist that foreign policy is primarily about economics. For a visualization, think of adapting the rooted maps of the previous two sections to a situation in which countries around the world have to be looked at from two perspectives rather than just one—and overlaying those perspectives. That, roughly, was the process used to generate the maps in figure 13-3, which characterize countries in terms of whether they traded more or much more (more than twice as much) with China or with the United States in 2000 (the top panel) and 2009 (the bottom panel).

To summarize, in 2000, the United States was a larger trading partner than China for roughly 90 percent of countries around the world. But by 2009, trade with the United States exceeded trade with China for only about half of the world's countries. According to a rough projection reflecting only differences in GDP growth, China's trade will exceed that of the United States with 70 to 80 percent of countries in 2030.[29] Consider, as an example, India, where the United States is seeking to strengthen relations, partly to bolster a democratic counterweight to China. In 2009, India's trade with China overtook its trade with the United States, and India could trade more than twice as much with China than the United States in 2030.[30]

The maps and projections start to raise broader issues around where to play, particularly for the United States. For example, will it consciously try to cultivate relationships with India, Southeast Asian countries, South Korea, and Japan as a way of offsetting the gravitational pull of the severalfold greater trade those countries will likely engage in with China? And if so, how will China respond? It is easy to imagine the answers to those questions being fundamental to the global balance of power in 2030.

In terms of how to play rather than where, it is worth noting that United States and Western multinationals seem to be counting on their traditional aggregation advantages, particularly in R&D and marketing, and that the Chinese challengers, traditionally arbitrageurs, are trying to leverage the explosive growth of the Chinese market into making China the origination point for the world's most advanced technologies—that is, to wrest the aggregation advantage in R&D away from established multinationals. No wonder the technology squeeze by the Chinese is such big news.

Given the small-numbers character of the U.S.-Chinese interaction, one can think further about how to play in ways that improve the likelihood of cooperation by applying the logic of game theory. Model the interactions between the United States and China as a repeated prisoner's dilemma in which each player has a choice at each decision point about whether to cooperate with the other or cheat. The two do best collectively if they both choose to cooperate, but each has an incentive to cheat on that outcome, challenging its sustainability. In the one-shot prisoner's dilemma, there is no way around the basic problem: (cheat, cheat) ends up being the equilibrium, even though it is also the worst

FIGURE 13-3

U.S. versus China trade in 2000 and 2009

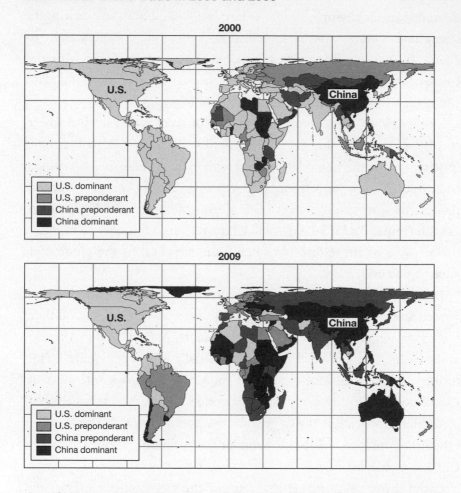

Note: U.S. dominant means that U.S. trade is more than double China's with a given country. *U.S. preponderant* means that U.S. trade with a country exceeds China's but is less than double China's. *China preponderant* and *China dominant* are based on parallel definitions.

Sources: Generated based on data from United Nation Commodity Trade Database (Comtrade) using bilateral trade values reported by U.S. and China.

possible outcome. But (cooperate, cooperate) *can* be sustained as an outcome in the repeated prisoner's dilemma, and computer tournaments between different types of strategies identify some of the attributes of strategies most likely to sustain cooperation:[31]

- *Niceness:* Don't cheat before the other player does; such attempts to capture gains up front usually backfire by provoking damaging cycles of retaliation.

- *Retaliation:* Retaliate at least some of the time if the other player cheats, or you will be exploited.

- *Forgiveness:* Avoid retaliating at least some of the time when the other player cheats (or appears to cheat) to avoid long cycles of revenge.

- *Nonenvy:* Focus on maximizing your own gains instead of worrying about whether you are gaining more or less than the other player.

To these principles for managing a repeated prisoner's dilemma productively, one might add recognition of genuine differences in perceptions and interests (rather than assuming that something makes sense for them because it makes sense for us), proportionate rather than disproportionate responses, a willingness to make trade-offs across issues instead of putting one above all else, and improvements in information flows in order to minimize miscommunication and ideally help build mutual confidence.

That last point leads, naturally, in the direction of thinking about how reducing external and internal distance might also help foster cooperation. Improving external connectivity could help in several different ways. The United States, in particular, has some catching up to do in learning about China. As Singapore foreign minister George Yeo keeps reminding Western audiences, the Chinese know much more about the West than Westerners know about China. Americans have been distracted because of the need to focus on multiple countries, while the Chinese could simply focus on the United States. Democracy also makes this task harder, because the electorate itself, or at least politicians in both major parties, need to do the learning rather than a stable set of specialists ensconced in Beijing.

The possible bridges aren't confined to simply learning more about the other side. More tourism, for example, might help both the Americans and the Chinese develop more realistic perspectives about the other. In this regard, mention must be made of restrictive U.S. visa policies that fuel resentment in China and prevent more Chinese from getting an accurate picture of the United States. And on the Chinese side, blocking access to popular U.S.-based Web sites such as Facebook, Twitter, and YouTube (all inaccessible from China as of this writing) converts another potential bridge into a barrier.

Reducing internal distance and improving national solidarity within the United States and China might be another way to help reduce the tension between them. With more internal cohesion, U.S. consumers and U.S. workers whose jobs are complements rather than substitutes for Chinese labor (like the California-based designers of the iPod) might be more amenable to the cheaper option of helping U.S. workers who are harmed by a cheap yuan, rather than supporting costly measures like tariffs. And in China, rebalancing would mean some losses in the export sector, but it also implies higher real incomes for the Chinese people who continue to put in grueling hours of labor making products for export, as well as ultimately a reorientation toward producing products for themselves and their fellow Chinese to enjoy. Reducing internal distance in this context implies addressing domestic distributional concerns to make support for integration more robust.

The U.S.-Chinese relationship, with its tensions, will be an enduring feature of World 3.0. Recognizing its broader consequences, respecting spheres of influence, avoiding unnecessary provocations, improving connectivity, and strengthening solidarity can all contribute to making it a motor of the world's progress rather than a stumbling block.

Think Differences

Looking across the three cases, perhaps what stand out the most are the differences among them. This is a useful observation in and of itself: it suggests starting out by analyzing what is particularly different or unusual, if anything, about the case being considered. This should, among other things, be a bulwark against "one size fits all" thinking. World 3.0 implies not one model but multiple possible submodels.

The rest of the recommended approach keys more specifically off differences/distances between that reference point and locations in other countries. Two additional diagnostic elements involve remapping the world to figure out what is close and what is far and understanding how CAGE factors shape cross-border flows. These provide important inputs into strategic choices about where and how to compete. In addition, there are the generalized strategic imperatives of working to reduce distance and distance sensitivity and remembering to tackle internal as well as external distance. Note that these points were all anticipated in chapter 12. The case studies now permit richer contextualizations of them.

1. Recognize what is different about your situation

Without a clear understanding of where you're starting from, you will inevitably be drawn toward one-size-fits-all models that fail to fully exploit the possibilities of World 3.0. The cases considered in this chapter highlight some of the dimensions of variation that can be important.

The case of Andorra highlights the dimensions of country size and landlockedness. While this book has tended to focus on relatively large countries, there are more than a hundred countries with fewer than 10 million people, and fifty have fewer than 1 million. Smaller countries gain more in relative terms from openness, which is why openness is a common policy agenda that many of them band together, given their strength in numbers, to try to promote. And landlocked countries face particular challenges in building up relationships with nonneighbors.

The case of Nigeria highlights yet another dimension—dependence on natural resources. Resource-rich economies face distinctive sets of challenges related to the so-called resource curse: large streams of resource rents seem to disrupt the development of the rest of the economy. And finally, the U.S.-Chinese relationship reminds us to look at bilateral as well as unilateral influences to figure out what is really distinctive about a country.

2. Remap the world from your perspective

With some sense of where you're coming from, figure out what is close and what is far and map the key relationships. The kinds of visualizations that maps permit cannot be achieved with textual material. Also, maps are particularly well suited to the visualization of spatial relationships, which makes them ideal for the present task.

The specific idea, as described in chapter 12, is to develop rooted maps that depict other countries in terms of how important they are from the perspective of a focal country. The maps of Andorran and Nigerian trade patterns included in figures 13-1 and 13-2 are examples: all foreign countries are scaled to approximate their volume of trade with the focal country but attempts are made to preserve the shapes of and rough spatial relationships across countries so as to exploit preexisting geographic templates. And the U.S.-Chinese maps can be thought of as overlaying maps drawn from a U.S. and a Chinese perspective.

Beyond such mapping efforts, it is worth calling attention to rapid advances in geographic or geospatial information systems (GIS) that involve the computer in capturing, storing, analyzing, and presenting data that are linked to locations. This merger of mapmaking, statistical analysis, and database management is leading to large improvements in our ability to discern and display interesting spatial relationships—that is, to envision World 3.0—and should therefore become even more important over time.

3. Understand CAGE effects

Having mapped what's close and what's far, or which relationships are large and which ones are small, try to understand the CAGE effects—the effects of differences versus similarities—on the relationships that are observed, and how those effects might be changing.

In the Andorran case, for instance, geographic proximity and associated cultural and administrative similarities clearly had a very large influence on imports—and an even greater impact on exports—but the key administrative differences underpinning the arbitrage model had come under pressure over time, thanks in part to integration within the European Union. In the case of Nigeria, geographic distance didn't seem to matter much for oil exports but did influence nonoil exports, given Africa's significant size as a destination and continental Europe's status as the largest such market for Nigeria, thanks to a combination of proximity and overall market size. And the U.S.-China discussion flagged several dimensions of distance between the two countries as contributing to the tensions between them.

For purposes of figuring out what to change, it is also worth looking for counterfactuals: key relationships that might be expected to appear in the data, but don't. Nigeria's nonoil exports to the United Kingdom and the United States, which are surprisingly limited given cultural and administrative links with them, are a good example. The CAGE parameter estimates can be used to systematize the analysis of predicted flows versus actual flows to figure out which ones appear to be below potential.

4. Reexamine where you compete

Comparing actual flows with potential or predicted flows is, of course, a critical element of reexamining where to compete—or, if you prefer, where to emphasize additional integration.[32] From this perspective, overweighting (e.g., of Spain in Andorran trade flows) is just as interesting as underweighting (e.g., of the United Kingdom and the United States in Nigerian nonoil exports).

Given the limitations of the CAGE-based gravity models used to form such diagnoses, however, I typically employ them to support a broader discussion of different types of countries as markets—and how to engage with them—rather than to dictate decisions to expand or shrink presence in particular countries. The discussions of opportunities for Andorra in Catalonia, the rest of Spain, France, the rest of the EU, and the rest of the world, and for Nigeria in continental Europe, the United Kingdom, and the United States, big emerging markets and the rest (particularly the west) of Africa are examples.

Note that neither World 1.0, with its emphasis on foreign countries being far away, nor World 2.0, with its assumption that all of them are really close, picks up on this kind of variation in external relationships. That is an opportunity highlighted by World 3.0, with its explicit recognition that countries vary in how close or far apart they are.

5. Reexamine how you compete

Consideration of how to compete intertwines with consideration of where to compete. As we saw in the Andorran case, the focus on destinations that were very close minimized exposure to differences and adaptation requirements beyond a few very specific administrative differences that underpinned the country's arbitrage strategies. While Andorra was extreme in this respect, such distance aversion is a general problem to which we will return under the next point.

Nigeria, in contrast, illustrates the typical approach of developing countries that try to compete in advanced markets: they start off by pursuing economic arbitrage and, over time, try to upgrade by establishing relationships and moving up price bands within the targeted categories. The caveat to this is that if Nigeria makes regional markets an important part of its strategy going forward, a different way of competing will be required, one focused more on exploiting similarities and the aggregation advantages afforded by Nigeria's large home base than on arbitraging differences.

The overlay of aggregation on arbitrage is a road the Chinese have already traveled much farther down, stepping on Western competitors' toes. Established multinationals have to reinforce their traditional strengths at aggregation with more effective adaptation and arbitrage if they are to succeed against challengers from emerging markets—particularly on the latter's home turf. The strategies of aggregation, adaptation, and arbitrage (the "AAA strategies") will be covered in more depth in the next chapter from a business perspective.[33]

6. Reduce distances and distance sensitivity

Even if a country does elect to perpetuate specific dimensions of difference, as in the Andorran case, it should generally seek to reduce distance and distance sensitivity along other dimensions.[34] This recommendation reflects the large gains from additional cross-border integration discussed in chapter 4 and the general failure of the market failures and fears scouted in Part II to outweigh them. It is also worth recalling the many worthwhile reductions in distance and distance sensitivity that can be pursued unilaterally (at least in part): administrative streamlining as well as opening up, cultural facilitation, improved physical/virtual connectivity, and so on.

Interest in unilateral improvements reflects, in part, impatience with multilateral initiatives, many of which have stalled in recent years: thus, the WTO's Doha round of trade talks is now in its second decade. While the global economic crisis hasn't helped, these problems also reflect a structural shift, from dominance by the United States (and, on occasion, the European Union) toward multipolarity, with more say for big emerging economies in particular. Yet the multilateral approach does have distinctive value and does need to be pursued: Doha would, in addition to the benefits on the table, lock in low tariffs and sustain the momentum around continuing liberalization. And if that last bit seems weak, note that according to the U.S. envoy to the WTO, Doha is important because it might be another quarter century before we see full implementation of liberalization measures agreed to under the *next* round of world trade negotiations.

Multilateralism is too broad a topic to be tackled in its entirety here, but a World 3.0 sensibility does suggest a half dozen points that I'll mention briefly. Two are directly related to the enormous heterogeneity across countries highlighted in this book. This probably requires, for one thing, more varied responsibilities than many multilateral accords envisage. Thus, while Doha has proposed special protections for "small and vulnerable economies," that idea could be taken further: forcing sub-Saharan Africa to pay high prices for life-saving drugs doesn't make a lot of sense. Second, because of variations in bargaining power, perfect fairness is probably also unrealistic: while it is reasonable to check that your country gains from a multilateral accord, insisting on the fair division of gains can end up ruling out win-win outcomes.[35]

Third, many multilateral bodies, although *not* the WTO, need to be reorganized around country size or growth potential rather than income levels, to better reflect the weight of large emerging markets. Fourth, while the WTO's one country–one vote approach has several attractions, including protecting smaller countries with little leverage of their own, having more than 150 member countries in the room does get a bit unwieldy. Is it time to consider—as suggested in the discussion of global warming—a two-track approach, with all countries being consulted as well as informed, but with negotiations concentrated among a core group? Fifth, the broader point is that World 3.0 is about multiple parallel efforts and diversity, not single-track uniformity. Appropriately constructed bilateral and regional trade agreements, for instance, can be useful complements to global trade deals. And last, while a multilateral structure such as the WTO can help marshal some support for multilateral processes such as the Doha round, there are limits to how far it can go without support from the national level—which is what seemed, as of the end of 2010, to be wanting.

7. Remember internal as well as external distance

Finally, in addition to doing the things that need to be done to connect a country more effectively with the outside world, there is also the idea of reducing internal distance. Opportunities for internal integration are, in many situations, as large as if not larger than the opportunities for external integration. For example, even for tiny and in some respects very open Andorra, intranational economic activity exceeds international economic activity. And even in that case, I inferred some integration issues associated with the foreigners living in Andorra. Nigeria presents a whole panoply of internal integration opportunities that, given the country's size and poor internal connectivity, are probably larger and more urgent than its regional integration opportunities. And even the U.S.-Chinese relationship could potentially benefit from the reduction of internal distance within those countries.

The tools for internal integration parallel those for external integration (see table 12-2 and the accompanying discussion), so I won't repeat them here. What I do emphasize is the idea that achieving such distance reductions often requires shifts in mind-sets—not just among governmental policy makers but also among business executives and even the general public. The kinds of shifts required of business executives and of individuals are elaborated in the two chapters that follow. What needs to be noted here is the role that government can and should play in helping orchestrate them.

Maximizing Country Potential

As we have seen, there's a lot of room in World 3.0 for countries to pursue strategies aimed at maximizing their potential. Invest the time required to get a clearer understanding of the internal and external distances that condition the opportunities and challenges in your own part of the world. Figure out which distances are the most important to bridge, where to compete, and how best to capture the benefits of integration. And, of course, don't forget to address the failures and fears that won't be going away any time soon.

All that is fairly workmanlike. Ideally, a pinch of vision can be added to the mix. Think about the context in which the idea of forming the European Coal and Steel Community, precursor to the EU, was proposed. The year was 1950. How would you have reacted, in the wake of World War II, to a proposal by the French foreign minister to integrate Europe so that "any war between France and Germany becomes not only unthinkable but materially impossible"?[36] My point here is not always to decide in favor of such big visions, but to give yourself the freedom to think big and to be open-minded in your evaluation. Today's European Union, all the (justified) worries about the euro zone notwithstanding, represents the triumph of a vision of integration that was preposterous when it was hatched. That kind of vision does not, for now, seem to have taken hold in West Africa, or in my native South Asia.

Chapter Fourteen

Business in World 3.0

NATIONAL GOVERNMENTS' jurisdictional and historical legacies condition them to start from the World 1.0 perspective, and only with prodding do they embrace the World 3.0 dual roles of integrator and regulator. By contrast, business leaders tend to be among the most ardent supporters of World 2.0 because of the seemingly limitless opportunities for profit that it promises. But when World 2.0's exaggerations run up against the reality of semiglobalization, the results disappoint. Companies that fail to respect the law of distance suffer performance penalties, and inflict collateral damage on society at large. Companies with a greater appreciation for differences can perform better both from a private and a public perspective.

My fundamental prescription for business is, therefore, to *think different*. Not just think differently—but think different, in the sense of becoming more sensitive to and genuinely welcoming of local differences. For most companies, thinking different entails nothing less than a fundamental restructuring of a firm's global strategy. Corporate approaches to dealing with globalization often presume that the world will continue to become much more integrated and that companies just need to keep up with rising levels of globalization. But that kind of World 2.0 thinking leads to blunders rooted in underappreciation of differences and, at the extreme, even in a lack of respect for individual countries' sovereignty. Shifting to a World 3.0 mind-set can help managers avoid such costly mistakes. Furthermore, if businesses really respect differences, they will improve their business performance in ways that also better contribute to society at large, fostering a climate of broader trust and confidence that can pave the way for further integration while dampening protectionist pressures. And in case prolonged economic malaise does lead to a resurgence of World 1.0's protectionist forces, companies that respect differences will also better position themselves to deal with the increase in cross-country distances that such an eventuality would imply.

Some might question whether corporations today really need to worry that much about globalization. Since the financial crisis, there have been moves by many companies to retrench and refocus on home markets. Scanning the annual reports of the world's one hundred largest companies, you find that the percentage of firms in developed economies that emphasized international or global business in their letters to shareholders declined from 51 percent in 2006 to 31 percent in 2008.[1] (In contrast, the percentage increased among the few companies in the group that were headquartered in emerging economies.) And use of the words *global* and *globalization*, while up significantly, mostly occurred in reference to the economic slowdown and its impact on company performance.

Becoming homebodies, however, is usually a bad idea for firms based in the developed world, particularly since the biggest growth opportunities are now in developing countries. That leaves managers with the task of crafting a globalization strategy that accounts for the business implications of persistent semiglobalization and the law of distance. This chapter summarizes these implications in terms of five broad principles for developing a cross-border strategy. For a more extended treatment, please see my 2007 book, *Redefining Global Strategy*, which is devoted entirely to this topic.[2]

Map Real Distances in Your Industry and Company

Reviewing a range of possible postcrisis futures, cross-country differences seem unlikely to disappear. The crisis may serve to decrease a few kinds of differences, but many other kinds of differences should grow more salient. First of all, the crisis has accelerated the shift of the world's economic activity and dynamism toward major emerging markets, particularly ones in Asia. This increases the diversity confronting companies that want to tap rapidly growing markets. Second, governments around the world are participating more actively in national economies. Given the diversity of political systems and of policies being enacted, the administrative distance or barriers between countries is increasing. Third, protectionism remains a major wildcard. Companies need to prepare for the possibility of new restrictions on trade, investment, migration, and potentially even information flows, while working with governments to contain such protectionism. Getting a better handle on cross-country differences and distances should therefore be a priority for business leaders.

The final section of chapter 12 articulated several principles for discerning differences and improving mental maps. For business it is particularly important to do such remapping at the industry level. Consider the two information technology (IT) services industry cartograms shown in figure 14-1 and again think about what kinds of CAGE distances are apparent.

The map on the top of the figure shows countries proportional to their total spending on IT services: writing custom software, managing and maintaining computer systems, and the like. Unsurprisingly, IT spending is closely related to economic development, and there are clear scope or threshold effects: the use of IT services falls off sharply when you move out of the richest countries, and the poorest countries disappear from the map entirely. Maps for IT versus, say, agriculture should be as different as those that look at the world from Nigeria's versus Andorra's point of view.

Now look at the map on the bottom of the figure. From Bangalore, it might seem like Indian IT is taking over the world, but here we can see

FIGURE 14-1

IT services industry cartograms: Global spending versus Indian exports

World IT services spending

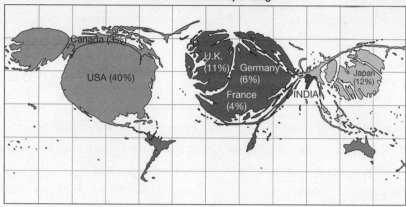

Indian IT services exports

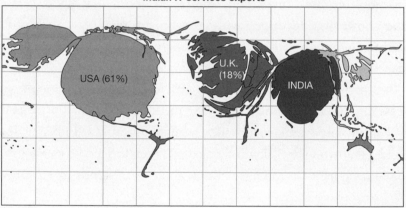

Note: On both maps, India is proportional to Indian domestic IT services market size.

Source: Generated based on data from Gartner (top panel) and Nasscom (bottom panel) for 2007, with gaps filled by author's estimates.

the overwhelming impact of cultural distance, in particular language. Nearly 80 percent of India's IT exports go to the United States and United Kingdom, whereas Japan and continental markets are much smaller than in the map on the top. And if you thought the industry that inspired Thomas Friedman to believe that the world is flat had outwitted geography, you might be surprised to know that a significant fraction of the work delivered by Indian IT companies to their foreign clients is done on-site at client locations, so geographic distance matters as well, as does administrative distance in the form of visa requirements. Of course, the reason for going to all this trouble is to arbitrage across economic distance.

Think through how different kinds of distance and difference impact your own industry using similar visualization techniques and frameworks. Consult chapter 3 for background on the CAGE framework. And refer to table 14-1 for factors that make specific industries more sensitive to particular kinds of distance than others, a topic that is elaborated at greater length in chapter 2 of *Redefining Global Strategy*.

While conducting your industry-level remapping exercise, try to incorporate some reflection of within-country diversity in parts of the world that are particularly important to your company. If you have a good mental map, you'll find that when you zoom in on key countries, their whole territory isn't painted one color. If your map of China doesn't extend past Beijing and Shanghai, you're missing the 88 percent of China's urban population that resides in cities with less than 5 million

TABLE 14-1

The distance sensitivity of industries: indicators

Cultural distance	Administrative distance	Geographic distance	Economic distance
High linguistic content	Government involved in funding, procurement, regulating standard-setting, before international bodies, etc.	Low value-to-weight or bulk	High intensity of labor, other factors prone to absolute cost differences
Strong country of origin effects (vertical distance)	Strategic industry status (votes, money, staples, state control, national champions)	Hazards in transportation	Potential for international scale/scope/experience economies
Significant differences in preferences/standards (horizontal distance)	Specialized, durable sunk capital (and holdup potential)	Perishability/time-sensitivity	High income-related increases in willingness-to-pay
Entrenched tastes/traditions	Restraints on trade/FDI (e.g., agriculture)	Need to perform key activities locally (favors FDI over trade)	Differences in customers/channels/business systems

people, where much of the country's future growth is projected to take place.[3] And China's second- and third-tier cities are very distant along multiple CAGE dimensions from Beijing or Shanghai, so adding them to your mental map will take some serious on-the-ground effort. It's also crucial to prioritize. McKinsey projects that in 2025 China will have 221 cities with more than 1 million inhabitants (including twenty-four with more than five million),[4] and the Boston Consulting Group has identified 717 emerging market cities worldwide with populations of more than half a million that it describes as the "world's largest growth opportunity."[5] You certainly won't have time to develop a detailed understanding of every place that might be of interest to your company.

Another kind of difference I find merits special emphasis when conditioning executives to cross-country distance is the diversity of corporate forms and governance around the world. When you do business across borders, the company you're negotiating with may not resemble very closely the style of company you know best. The standalone, widely held American corporation, while the most studied capitalist organizational form in management education programs around the world, is the least typical. Most market economies' corporations are not widely owned by public shareholders but instead are parts of larger interconnected sets of companies principally owned and controlled by families, business groups, or states. These varied corporate forms and governance structures have significant implications for company goals and ways of operating—as well as ability to divert money. Think through the incentives that your business associates are operating under and respond accordingly. And recognize that it is often harder to work with companies with different governance structures from your own. According to one study, the success rate for joint ventures between pyramidal groups in Brazil and standalone foreign firms was 7 percent, versus a 60 percent success rate when the Brazilian and foreign parents were both parts of pyramidal groups![6]

Similar visualization techniques and frameworks can also be applied to distances within a company. For example, map the breakup of sales revenues by country that you are targeting five years from now versus the composition of the nationalities of your executive team, or the geographic footprint of your R&D function. Then look at your reporting relationships. For most companies, organization and staffing are still stuck in World 1.0 even if their executives have their eyes firmly fixed on World 2.0. Thus, of all of the directors of U.S. S&P 500 companies in 2008 only 7 percent were foreign nationals, only 9 percent had degrees from non-U.S. institutions, and only 27 percent had any international work experience.[7] Shifting to a global rather than U.S. dataset and looking at CEOs rather than directors, the picture isn't much better. Of the 2008 *Fortune* Global 500 companies, only 14 percent had a nonnative CEO.[8] And these datasets are dominated by firms from advanced countries. The vast majority of firms, even very large ones, from emerging markets would seem to be significantly less internationalized in terms of such indicators.

Customizing mental maps at the industry level, achieving within-country granularity in key countries, and carefully addressing internal distance all take a lot of effort, as I have emphasized. To maximize the efficiency of this learning process, it is usually best to start at the global level with a few industry-level visualization exercises and an assessment of what kinds of CAGE distance matter most for your business. This provides mental scaffolding that substantially increases the efficiency of firsthand learning on subsequent visits to key countries—for which there is ultimately no substitute. In other words, such analytical work complements on-the-ground experience.

Avoid Market Imperialism

Many companies in recent years have adopted what might be called an "imperialist" approach to globalizing their business. They've blindly oriented themselves toward expansion, seeking to extend their reach into every corner of the globe by gobbling up as many foreign assets as possible. According to one survey of *Harvard Business Review* readers before the financial crisis, 88 percent reported thinking of global strategy as an act of faith rather than as an alternative to be evaluated, and 64 percent believed that "the truly global company should aim to compete everywhere."[9]

Such appetites were nourished by rising asset prices: many companies thought of globalization as one long asset accumulation play involving relatively little risk because they assumed that assets that proved surplus to requirements could be resold for more than they had cost.

If you have developed a reasonable mental map that accounts for the real diversity within and across countries, you're unlikely to regard *ubiquity*—as in competing everywhere—as a sensible goal. And apart from a handful of global giants, the reality of multinational business would conform to your revised thinking. Thus, in 2004, less than one percent of all U.S. companies had foreign operations, and of these, the largest fraction operated in just one foreign country, the median number in two, and 95 percent in fewer than two dozen.[10] Furthermore, none of these statistics had changed much in the past ten years!

With the bursting of the asset bubble, executives have received a rude reminder about the need to actually evaluate the economic performance of specific country operations. Research confirms that for many firms, a considerable portion of their global operations actually *subtract* value over time. Data that Marakon Associates analyzed at my request revealed that "half of the [large] companies we have looked at [8 out of 16] have significant geographic units that earn negative economic returns . . . [We] know from our clients that their profitability by geography has stayed fairly stable over time unless they have specifically targeted action at specific countries/regions."

As companies become more mindful of national differences and depart from a misguided "get bigger at all costs" mind-set, they take a more considered view of international expansion. Such thinking leads companies to reevaluate their current country portfolios. Downturns (and their immediate aftermath) are more obvious occasions to restructure or exit weaker markets than upturns. Nokia, for example, announced in November 2008 that it was exiting the Japanese mobile handset market (except for its high-end Vertu brand) after years of investment yielded only a meager one percent market share (versus about 40 percent globally). Exiting the world's fourth-largest market must not have been easy for Nokia, but it's a realistic decision considering

Japan's idiosyncratic, highly demanding consumers, different standards, and the dominance of local firms. Or to mention another example, Dr. Reddy's, the largest Indian-owned pharmaceutical firm, recently used the CAGE framework and the ADDING value scorecard to help scale back from 50 markets to fewer than 20. While the latter was deployed in this book mainly at the macro level, in chapter 4, I originally developed it to help companies with such assessments.[11]

Eschewing market imperialism aligns with a number of other, more nuanced strategic shifts. In an increasingly fragmented world, with growth opportunities in Western markets drying up, Western companies competing in big emerging markets like China and India can't just hope to blast in there and dominate, nor can they prosper merely by continuing the practice of addressing themselves to local, urban elites. Rather, they will need to pay serious attention to local competitors and to think about extending their presence to secondary cities. And those local competitors may talk of inheriting the earth but again, instead of assuming that they hold all the cards, they have to reckon with the advantages of established multinationals.[12]

Reining in "size-ism" in international expansion has benefits that go beyond improving financial profitability. It can also help curb protectionist tendencies and reinforce support for continued market integration. As companies acquire foreign assets with little rhyme or reason, they come across to the public as voracious and greedy, and capitalism itself seems inherently impersonal and destructive. Dispensing with market imperialism and treating foreign country markets in ways that respect their local sovereignty, uniqueness, and internal diversity can go a long way toward improving companies' reputations and, more broadly, the environment in which business as a whole has to operate.

Revamp Market Strategies

Strategies rooted in semiglobalization involve integrated consideration of both borders and distance—of the barriers and the bridges between countries. In chapters 4 to 7 of *Redefining Global Strategy*, I described three fundamental ways that companies can create value across borders in a world where differences still matter: the *AAA strategies* of *adaptation, aggregation*, and *arbitrage*. *Adaptation* strategies try to adjust to cross-country differences in order to be locally responsive. *Aggregation* strategies attempt to overcome cross-country differences to achieve scale / scope economies that extend across national borders. And *arbitrage* strategies seek to exploit differences—as in buying low in one country and selling high in another. My general prescription was for managers to select a combination of these strategies, tailored to their company's own industry, position, capabilities, and intent.

Given their focus on differences, the AAA strategies remain the relevant strategy set for companies in World 3.0—and can even help countries with their decisions about how to compete, as we saw in the previous chapter. But given the crisis and its aftermath, it may make sense in the medium term for many companies to emphasize *adaptation* more than *aggregation* or *arbitrage*—although this should ultimately depend on each firm's industry, history, and strategy.[13] It can take years for companies to execute meaningful shifts in this regard, so they need to consider longer-term plans and expectations for industry evolution in making such decisions. The rationale for strengthening *adaptation* is that becoming more responsive to local conditions increases robustness in case of protectionism, helps to address the growing role of governments, and is necessary in many cases for participating in the growth that is available in emerging markets. In addition, becoming more respectful of differences can actually help lower the likelihood of protectionism.

Adaptation encompasses a broad range of levers and sublevers that companies can use to respond to cross-country differences. *Variation* is the most obvious kind of adaptation: if local markets exhibit different preferences, offer them different products or services. It can also make sense to vary company policies, business positioning, and even metrics and targets across countries. However, variation is costly and also results in a great deal of complexity that can be hard to manage. Therefore, smart adaptation typically involves not only appropriate decisions about the amount of variation but adroit application of one or more complementary substrategies such as *focus, externalization, design,* and *innovation,* each of which can help reduce the costs of variation.

Focus involves purposefully narrowing scope so as to reduce the extent of differences encountered and the amount of adaptation required. Typical bases for focus include regions, market segments or value added steps. *Externalization* involves splitting activities across organizational boundaries to reduce the internal burden of adaptation—for example, via the use of joint ventures or franchising, or even by relying on customers to customize their own products or services. Companies have long found partnerships to be particularly attractive when dealing with large cultural and administrative distances, as partners can provide access to local knowledge and relationships that would otherwise be hard to develop. *Design* can also deliberately reduce the cost of variation—for example, via the use of platforms or modularization. And finally, *innovation* sometimes yields whole new ways around the problem of adaptation.

While adaptation seems to require increased emphasis, *aggregation*—short of complete standardization or one-size-fits-all—is still important because most multinationals try to leverage some element of scale or scope across markets to outdo local firms. This contrasts with their use of adaptation, which is mostly aimed at minimizing disadvantages vis-à-vis local firms.

Arbitrage remains important as well because of the large, continued differences between countries, along with broad pressures to reduce costs. But companies do need to recognize that arbitrage has become more politically sensitive in the present environment. The pressing need to reduce global trade imbalances from record and clearly unsustainable levels and the rise of protectionism and environmental concerns are raising issues around arbitrage plays, such as the "Chimerica" model, in which the United States imports large volumes of cheap goods and capital from China. As a result, companies that became accustomed to offshoring before the crisis need to take a second look at the practice now. It's noteworthy that the U.S. global giants that were financially healthy and confident enough to make major operations investments recently have stressed the extent to which those investments were located at home. Intel, for example, has talked a great deal about its new semiconductor plants in the United States, and GE about its new U.S. wind turbine facilities. Of course, these are just two particularly vivid examples: both companies continue to invest substantially if quietly overseas. But that holds its own lesson: if offshoring does make sense, managing the discourse around it is more important than ever.

For smaller companies, rebalancing among the AAA strategies may involve somewhat different considerations. Such enterprises usually find adaptation essential. Aggregation, while perhaps a long-term goal, is generally not something they can attempt on a global scale even if they possess the minimum efficient scale required to expand overseas. And while engaging in cross-border arbitrage by employing people or sourcing inputs from lower-cost locations may work for some born-global startups, many small companies may find that out of their reach as well. Such companies can, nonetheless, at least attempt to import ideas or best practices from abroad.

Manage Internal Distance

In the previous chapter, we looked at how national governments have more authority to shape distances and flows within their internal boundaries than across them. The same holds true for companies. Their choices concerning supply chains, organizational structure, foreign investment and cross-border innovation represent levers for internally shaping the four main types of flows we've focused on in this book—products, people, information, and capital. In making such choices, it's useful to think in terms of both reconfiguring internal distances and adjusting the ease or difficulty with which they can be traversed.

Start with production and supply chains. Unless protectionism spikes, significant offshoring will most likely continue. But many companies are taking action to make their supply chains shorter, simpler, and more robust, in effect reducing internal distance within the company's production network. Such moves reflect concerns about the environment and sensitivity to energy prices as well as the threat of protectionism. A 2009 survey of logistics providers revealed that nearly one-quarter of North American and European clients had taken steps to shorten their supply chains during the previous year.[14]

Companies also seem to be reducing internal distance in production by adjusting the levels of automation across their different factories. Traditionally, companies have tended to automate less in plants in countries with lower wage levels. But recent reports on manufacturing firms—for instance, the global components survey sponsored by the Alfred P. Sloan Foundation—reveal that many Western multinationals have actually started to import some of their less-automated processes back into plants in high-wage regions.[15] Experience in low-wage countries has shown them that less-automated plants can enhance flexibility without compromising reliability.

Selective de-automation also says something about how innovation and knowledge flows are changing and are likely to continue to do so. It reminds us, among other things, that experience may yield innovations or insights in one context that we can transfer to others and that such innovations need not originate in a firm's largest or most advanced markets. But harnessing such possibilities is likely to require disrupting the traditional home-first model that multinational companies have historically used to organize innovation.

Innovation for emerging markets also requires different business models, not just or even primarily whiz-bang technology. Whereas corporate R&D labs located in advanced markets excel at creating technology, firms seeking to develop new, locally relevant products and locally effective business systems will increasingly need the informed creativity that only boots on the ground in local markets can provide. Thus, Nokia has located more than a thousand R&D staff in India. Their product adaptations for rural and other lower-income markets, while effective, are decidedly low-tech and include such items as a basic mobile phone that doubles as a flashlight for use during power outages and a phone designed to be shared by multiple people.

While enthusiasm about such learning from emerging markets has escalated, we need to remember that the country differences that impede transplantation from developed to developing markets also apply in the reverse direction. And such difficulties are exacerbated by the fact that while consumers in emerging markets still get excited about the latest technologies from California, technologies that flow the other way carry somewhat less cachet. So, we shouldn't get too carried away about a flood of new products and processes from poor countries taking the rich world by storm.

Thinking about R&D and innovation should also be related to better alignment of people and market strategies. Technical manpower is growing rapidly in emerging markets at the same time that global supply shortfalls are forecast for many categories of engineers and other technical personnel. Thus, labor market pressures add to the case for many companies to shift R&D to emerging markets. Intel, in fact, has already designed one chip almost entirely in India: the Xeon 7400 processor, introduced in 2008.

Such developments will require us to become much smarter about the way we manage interactions among diverse, far-flung employees. Although companies have globalized their footprints, managers still communicate across geographies mostly by traveling to and fro, holding conference calls, and, to a lesser extent, exchanging e-mail. Few companies have gotten very far at exploiting the new collaborative tools of the Web, such as chat rooms and online bulletin boards, to build a stronger sense of community. Part of the problem is that the challenges of cross-border communication can be quite subtle. Language barriers, for example, pose less of a problem for those providing information than for those receiving it. It may be easy for a Chinese manager to make a comprehensible presentation in English but harder to get people listening to it to invest in comprehension: research shows that people quickly tune out on accents they have trouble understanding.

Indeed, companies could do much more to leverage technology to improve internal communication. But again, there are limits because technologically mediated interactions often just mirror the distance-driven patterns of real-world relationships. We still have no perfect substitutes for face-to-face interactions, management development programs, expatriation, and other initiatives designed to knit organizations together across long distances. And especially if they intend to become more adaptive, companies really do need to become more representative of the markets they are targeting. A pre-crisis study by the Boston Consulting Group of large multinationals and their aspirations in sixteen rapidly developing economies found a gross mismatch between the amount of growth targeted in these geographies (about 33 percent then, probably more now) and the percentage of top personnel from or located in them (less than 10 percent then and probably now as well).[16]

Shifting production, knowledge, and human resource configurations, along with their implications for capital allocation also indicate deeper shifts with respect to corporate power structures. We may even see some organizational power flow back to country managers as companies tone down their attempts to eliminate or exploit cross-border differences and instead look to adapt better to local conditions.

The bigger development, however, will be the shifting center of gravity of large multinational firms toward major emerging markets. IBM's global procurement office, for instance, is now located in Shenzhen, and Cisco set up Cisco East as a second headquarters in Bangalore. Perhaps the most dramatic example is provided by the General Motors reorganization. The company's Mexican and Canadian operations will continue reporting to the person overseeing the United States, but operations pretty much everywhere else apart from Europe will now report to the head of China, which has overtaken the United States as the automaker's largest market in terms of number of vehicles supplied. This is a basic realignment of the power structure within a hitherto U.S.-centric GM, whose China operation is now regarded by many as the most interesting part of the company. And looking forward, people are talking of multinationals with dual headquarters, one in the West and one in Asia (most likely China).

In summary, managers need to pay more attention to internal distance and to ensure that organizations and operations are configured in ways that support their companies' strategies. For many companies,

TABLE 14-2

Managing internal organizational distance

1. Hiring for adaptability
2. Formal education
3. Participation in cross-border business teams and projects
4. Utilization of diverse locations/media for team and project interactions
5. Immersion experiences in foreign cultures
6. Expatriate assignments
7. Cultivating geographic and cultural diversity at the top
8. Dispersion of business unit headquarters or centers of excellence
9. Maintaining openness to the environment
10. Defining and cultivating a set of core values throughout the corporation

organizations will have to become more diverse to support emerging market growth strategies, and that diversity will create more internal distance that will need to be bridged. Table 14-2 highlights practical tools companies can draw from to knit together increasingly diverse and far-flung organizations.

Think Beyond the Market

Given World 3.0's recognition that markets do fail, companies need to take a broader view of the implications of their actions for society at large. The crisis as well as a seemingly unending parade of corporate scandals has pushed business's reputation to an all-time low, at least in the United States. Thus, in a survey conducted in 2009 by the Pew Research Center, U.S. respondents ranked business executives at the very bottom of a list of occupations in terms of their social contributions. Only 21 percent of respondents thought business leaders contributed a great deal to society, while 23 percent thought lawyers, the second-least-favored occupation, did. (The military and teaching professions ranked the highest, with scores of 84 percent and 77 percent, respectively).[17] Attitudes look more positive in emerging markets, yet the standing of capitalism and private business there is also being challenged in fundamental ways.

Such sentiments are particularly dangerous because of the threat of protectionism that might yet move us back toward World 1.0. According to Global Trade Alert, "Since the first G20 crisis-summit in November 2008, the world's governments have together implemented 638 beggar-thy-neighbour policy measures." According to the same report, "No four-digit product line or 2-digit UN classified economic sector has emerged unscathed by crisis-era protectionism."[18] Since studies show that protectionism flourishes when trust in economic institutions is low, the restoration of trust in business takes on increased importance given the value of fostering openness.

Any exercise at improving reputation should first examine the reality of one's performance and then turn to communication. When markets operate efficiently, what's good for profits is also what's good for society, but when markets fail, interests diverge. Think twice about exploiting "opportunities" with such characteristics. Although it might take a while for regulators to catch up, reputational damage is a significant possibility—for your company and for business overall. Pretending you're operating in World 2.0 risks pushing us all back toward World 1.0 instead of forward to World 3.0.

Communication also matters a great deal, of course, and affords another arena for improvement. In particular, with the role of government on the rise, firms must pursue a well-thought-out program of corporate diplomacy. Instead of placing markets on a pedestal, they need to show more sensitivity to regulatory, legal, political, social, and cultural differences. If business leaders don't get out there and credibly lobby nonmarket players in favor of more openness, rest assured, advocates of protectionism will.

Beyond government, business also needs to address itself to the public at large. Given how poor business's image currently is, responsible corporate leaders should place a premium on responding publicly to social and environmental concerns—including those about globalization. Coca-Cola's former chairman, Neville Isdell, has emphasized that multinationals with a large stake in globalization have not tried very hard, in general, to make the case for it. Instead, they have tended to lie low and hope that their private initiatives to globalize will avoid attracting adverse attention. Unfortunately, that leaves antiglobalizers free to dominate the public debate. Whether protectionism comes to pass is not just a function of the broader social and economic landscape. Businesses need to push for openness and ensure that the public and politicians fully understand the case against protectionism.

Beyond Business

My own profession, business academia, shares some blame for the gap between the business world and the general public on views about globalization—and for managers' general tendency to have an insufficient appreciation of cross-country differences. Surveys indicate that less than 1 percent of business school deans and of strategy professors believe that globalization is basically bad or mixed in its results. Business students also tend to have positive views about globalization, though not quite as uniformly positive as their professors. And while I take a basically positive view as well, I worry that this near-unanimous support for globalization (rare in academic pursuits) has generally led schools to neglect the exploration of counterarguments to globalization in their classrooms. This leaves their graduates unprepared for the views they actually encounter when they have to manage people, sell products, and interact with governments in the real world.

I find this outcome particularly distressing because my experience teaching young MBA students has convinced me that many aspire to contribute to society in broader ways than only as managers of for-profit businesses—see the next chapter for an inspiring example. While this book does not fully elaborate the implications of World 3.0 for nonprofit or nongovernmental organizations (NGOs), many of the lessons for businesses outlined in this chapter also apply to philanthropic organizations. When you're trying to help people far away or very different from yourself, be very cognizant of the baggage that you bring to such a situation. Taking account of your origin is even more important in this context than for business, because while customers may appreciate a product's country-of-origin as part of its value proposition (e.g. French wine), in charitable work, people will seek to appraise your values themselves, and given limited contextual information will often make assumptions based on where you're coming from. Really accounting for distance also implies requirements for adaptation and focus that parallel those described in the section on revamping market strategies.

Distance sensitivity has implications for the scope of charitable work as well. Think, for example, about relief efforts after natural disasters. The science of predicting aftershocks and tsunamis following an earthquake is relatively distance insensitive, so it makes sense for the world's top experts to apply their knowledge globally. Engineering work related to rebuilding is somewhat more distance sensitive. And at the other extreme, first aid and psychological support for victims are extremely sensitive to geographic distance and cultural distance, respectively. When distance sensitivity is low, it may make sense to mount relief efforts across long distances, but when it is high, it may be better to focus just on bridging economic distance by funding local relief efforts.

Maximizing Business Potential

If governments enact helpful policies—or just refrain from protectionism—the possibility of much greater prosperity is a real prospect. The tremendous potential for GDP growth that we studied in chapter 4 isn't just macroeconomic esoterica: it's the sum of opportunities for investment returns, employment expansion, salary raises, and so on. Pretty exciting stuff. But as with any business opportunity, these benefits will not be realized until managers go out there with smart strategies and strong execution and make things happen. That's the broader responsibility of business as the visible hand of globalization: converting potential into reality and delivering World 3.0.

Most companies have a long way to go to get to World 3.0. With limited mental maps and World 2.0 rhetoric prompting managers to believe that they can get off a plane anywhere in the world and operate effectively, companies stumble far too often. Products and services don't quite hit the target with customers. Marketing messages fall flat. Offense is taken, charges of imperialism fly, and the cry goes out for more protectionism. World 2.0 sets us up for failure. But the right answer isn't to turn inward and retreat to World 1.0. World 3.0 calls, instead, for cosmopolitan corporations that genuinely appreciate the challenges and opportunities posed by diversity and distance.

What does such cosmopolitanism require? Use a structured framework like industry-level CAGE analysis to remap your business environment. Invest in the organizational glue necessary to make a company more than the sum of its parts. Consider strengthening adaptation to deal better with external distance. And pay more attention to what might be called "social alignment." Is your company contributing to broader social welfare or taking advantage of market failures to gain at society's expense? Are you actively making the case to the public and to political leaders about the benefits of integration, or are you free riding on the efforts of others? And finally, are you and your people really ready on a personal level for World 3.0?

For many companies, the greatest challenge may be fostering the human capacity to connect and cooperate across distances and differences, internally and externally. How much would your profitability increase if you could broaden circles of trust and cooperation across departments, countries, and business units so people really work together rather than against each other? What if your people could stretch their perspectives to care more deeply about customers, colleagues, and investors? Knowing what we know about distance effects, it's unrealistic to think of a big company as a family: a multinational firm can never become a World 0.0 tribe or clan. But people *can* broaden their sympathies to bring "them" a little closer to "us," with inspiring results. That's the topic of the final chapter.

Chapter Fifteen

Us and Them in World 3.0

THIS BOOK HAS FOCUSED, so far, on how to improve the world for the people in it. This chapter is about how to improve the people themselves—or rather, ourselves. Not in general, but in terms of how to rethink our own relationships with the rest of the world. The security of existing levels of integration and the possibility of additional gains from opening up ultimately depend on popular opinion supporting or at least continuing to tolerate openness. In the words of former British Prime Minister Tony Blair, "Educating people to be open to the other person—I think that's the challenge of the twenty-first century."[1]

The unfortunate truth is that we're far from open to others at present. In fact, as this chapter suggests, distance shapes our emotions and personal relationships far more than we usually think. As philosophers have long noted, we tend to interact with, trust, and care more about people who are closer to us; as distance increases, human connectedness declines. Recognizing the full extent of such distance sensitivity and reducing it is important to realizing more of the gains from World 3.0.

Psychic Distance

The notion of distance sensitivity cropped up in the domain of the human psyche *fifteen hundred years* before it emerged in the physical sciences with Newton's law of gravitation. The Stoic philosopher Hierocles was the pioneer in the human domain:

> Each one of us is as it were entirely encompassed by many circles. The first and closest circle is the one which a person has drawn as though around a centre, his own mind . . . Next, the second one further removed from the centre but enclosing the first circle; this contains parents, siblings, wife, and children. The third one has in it uncles and aunts, grandparents, nephews, nieces, and cousins. The next circle includes the other relatives, and this is followed by the circle of local residents, then the circle of fellow-tribesmen, next that of fellow citizens, and then in the same way the circle of people from neighboring towns, and the circle of fellow-countrymen. The outermost and largest circle, which encompasses all the rest, is that of the whole human race . . . Once all these have been surveyed, it is the task of a well tempered man, in his proper treatment of each group, to draw the circles together somehow toward the center.[2]

Eighteenth-century Scottish philosopher David Hume supplied a more pointed characterization of the problem that preoccupied Hierocles: "Sympathy . . . is much fainter than our concern for ourselves, and sympathy with persons remote from us much fainter than that with persons near and contiguous."[3] Other thinkers who have written about these circles and the challenge of drawing the outermost ones closer to the center include Immanuel Kant, Ralph Waldo Emerson, Mahatma Gandhi, Albert Einstein, Martha Nussbaum, and Peter Singer. Figure 15-1 provides a visual representation of this concentric circle model.

The best term to describe the distance that Hierocles wants us to reduce, the radii of the circles, is *psychic distance*, but the definition of this term has been muddied over the years. First, it refers to subjective or perceived distance—not actual objective distance—even though

FIGURE 15-1

Greek philosopher Hierocles' circles of identity—extended

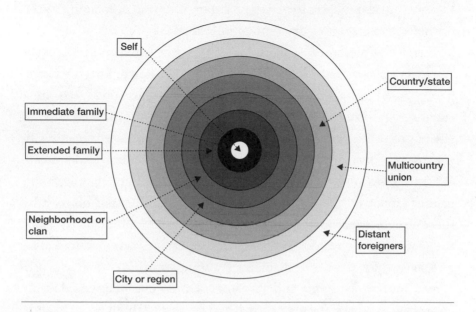

researchers have often analyzed it based on objective metrics.[4] And second, its scope, particularly in business and economics, has expanded vastly, to the point that it has come to span at least the cultural and economic dimensions of the CAGE framework, often incorporates administrative differences as well, and sometimes even adds in geographic factors.[5] Thus, the Wikipedia entry on psychical distance concludes with the statement, "The CAGE (Cultural, Administrative and Political, Geographical, and Economical) framework is commonly used to analyse psychical distance when investigating international expansion opportunities."[6] Valuable precision is lost by simply collapsing all the CAGE dimensions into one distance category. Instead, I prefer a narrowly scoped and thus more distinctive definition of psychic distance: the (subjective) degree of emotional or sympathetic detachment maintained toward a person, group, or place.[7]

Since the concentric circles and increasing detachment across them have been discussed for two millennia now, I will attempt something a bit more novel: I'll try to calibrate, very crudely and as dichotomies/trichotomies, how some indicators of engagement versus detachment—reported trust levels, news coverage and official aid—depend on distance. In other words, I'll try to attach numbers to perceived distances instead of focusing, as the previous chapters mostly did, on actual distances.

Chapter 11 presented a calibration of this sort, based on Eurobarometer data on how much citizens of EU-16 countries reported trusting people based on national origins. As we saw, 48 percent on average indicated significant trust in fellow citizens, 20 percent indicated trust in citizens of other EU-16 countries, and 13 percent indicated trust in citizens of the thirteen other, mostly East European countries included. While this is a very rough classification (focusing on just the three outermost circles in figure 15-1), it does suggest a reduction of trust by more than one-half for the "near abroad" and nearly three-quarters for the "far abroad" (which, given its East European/developed country bias, isn't really as far as it might be). By comparison, an extreme World 1.0 vision that saw home and abroad as sharply opposed would imply equal trust ratios for the near abroad and far abroad (both equal to zero, in its most xenophobic variants), and a truly integrated World 2.0 would presumably exhibit ratios of 1:1 across the board, because the distinctions between "us" and "them" would cease to exist.

Since trust is the aspect of engagement that has been studied the most, the other findings about it that were cited in chapter 11 are worth recapping. Bilateral trust decreases with geographic, linguistic, religious, genetic, and somatic distance (measured by an index of body type differences) as well as with income differences and a history of wars—findings that hit on all four dimensions of the CAGE framework but especially the cultural dimension.[8] And while variations in trust might seem too ethereal to affect much on the ground, moving from lower to higher levels of bilateral trust can increase trade, direct investment, portfolio investment, and venture capital investment by 100 percent or more, even after controlling for other characteristics of the two countries.[9]

Beyond trust, we can attempt to quantify the extent to which we possess sympathy or concern for others. News coverage of natural disasters affords clear-cut if chilling evidence: while overseen by the organiza-tions that bring us the news, it is presumably tuned to our willingness to take an interest. Compare two disasters that occurred within a year of each other, the Asian tsunami and the devastation of the U.S. city of New Orleans during Hurricane Katrina. Katrina generated more news coverage in the United States, even though nearly a hundred times as many people perished in the Asian tsunami.

More systematically, a study of more than five thousand natural disasters suggests that from the standpoint of U.S. media coverage, each dead European was "worth" three South Americans, forty-three Asians, forty-five Africans, or ninety-one Pacific Islanders.[10] The same study also confirmed the influence of factors that in an ideal world wouldn't matter at all. For each person killed by a volcano, more than forty thousand people would have had to die in a drought to receive the same expected news coverage. And even more disturbing, when the news media was occupied with nondisaster news, such as the Olympics, the number of dead had to be three times more than during a slow news period to have the same chance of receiving government relief.

That last finding is particularly disturbing because it goes beyond sug-gestions of arbitrariness and bias in media coverage to point out that it has a real effect on relief efforts. And while that study focused on the United States, an analysis of Japan also linked official disaster relief to coverage of the disaster in Japanese media and predisaster trade interac-tions.[11] In addition, Muslim-majority countries appeared much less likely to receive Japanese aid!

The suggestion of very large differences in willingness to help is borne out if we compare aid to the domestic poor versus official devel-opment assistance (ODA) to the rest of the world's poor. Based on the weighted per-person averages for fourteen developed OECD econo-mies, national governments spent 30,000 times as much helping each domestic poor person as each poor foreigner.[12] (The actual domestic-to-foreign ratios of help per person ranged from 20,000 to 100,000-plus, with Switzerland topping the list at 140,000.) So aid levels, measured by these numbers, seem to be only .003 percent—1/30,000—as high for the foreign poor as for the domestic poor. And no matter how one redoes my calculations, it is hard to avoid the conclusion that domestic-to-foreign aid ratios run into the thousands, at least.

These sympathy discounts are graphed in figure 15-2.[13] Although the data are very sparse, several important points do stand out. While a flat World 2.0 would predict a flat line—the bold one running across the top of the grid—our real-world measures of trust, concern, and aid all slope downward, decaying with distance. At the other extreme, World 1.0 might be interpreted as implying zero international engagement—see the bold vertical line in the figure—but that isn't a good representation of reality either. Psychic distance sensitivity clearly falls in between these two extremes. But it varies greatly depending on which particular measure we're talking about, which is why I had to use a logarithmic scale to make things fit. Trust actually appears to be *relatively* distance insensitive, although this may reflect self-reporting and the relatively homogeneous set of countries included in that analysis. But our sympathies are revealed to be much more distance sensitive—that is,

FIGURE 15-2

Distance decay curves for sympathy: Illustrative

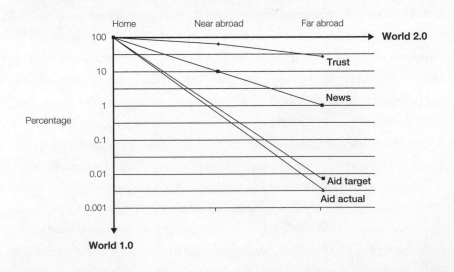

localized—when it comes to concern for others (news coverage) and, especially, aid.[14]

The high distance sensitivities underscore how detached we are from what happens overseas, but also remind us of the huge room for improvement. Thus, asking rich countries to fulfill the promises they made in 1992 at Rio de Janeiro—to give 0.7 percent of GDP as official development assistance—is *not* equivalent to asking them to target anything near a 1:1 domestic-to-foreign ratio of the sort evoked by World 2.0, but instead, to reduce that ratio from an average of about 30,000:1 to about 15,000:1! While that target may or may not be achieved, it doesn't seem nearly as impossible as a target of 1:1.

The magnitudes of these sympathy discounts surprised me when I first calculated them. Yet perhaps they shouldn't have, given how intensely localized most of our daily interactions still are. Telephone traffic still behaves like aid flows: scaled by population, the intensity of domestic phone calls is about 10,000 times greater than international calls, and international calling intensity itself is more than 40 times higher between countries whose main cities are less than 500 kilometers apart.[15]

Face-to-face contact is even more localized, of course, since it is limited by people's physical movements. One study of cell phone users in a rich country found that nearly three-quarters mainly stayed within a ten-mile radius over six months and tended to return to the same few places over and over.[16] Likewise, residential proximity still predicts best how often friends socialize.[17] And while improvements in information and communications technologies have relaxed the old rule that most collaborations happen among people working less than fifty feet apart, knowledge flows remain very significantly localized, as explained in chapters 2 and 4. The "Twitterzone" and social networks have generally been superimposed on Hierocles' circles, allowing for "eccentric" connections, but that doesn't change a basic reality: most people we are close to in cyberspace are people we are close to offline along the CAGE dimensions, and we generally continue to lack connections to people who are very far away.

Rethinking Cosmopolitanism

If you're like me, you may have found the steeper lines in figure 15-2 depressing overall, not just surprising, as indicators of how parochial our concerns still are. And if so, our attention naturally gets directed toward how to change this state of affairs. But the question of what duties and obligations we do have to people at varying distances from ourselves is not a simple one. Table 1-1 included discussion of the individual mind-sets that guide responses to such questions, associating Worlds 0.0 through 3.0 with communitarianism, nationalism, cosmopolitanism, and rooted cosmopolitanism, respectively. I'll focus here on elaborating the differences between the conventional cosmopolitanism of World 2.0, which aspires to a state in which distance doesn't matter, and the *rooted cosmopolitanism* of World 3.0, which recognizes the continued importance of distance as well as its essentially egocentric character. What's close and what's far for you depends on where and who you, at the center of the concentric circles, are.

Let's start with World 2.0. The cosmopolitan project central to ethical conceptions of World 2.0 is basically the one articulated by Hierocles: "to draw the circles together somehow toward the center." Philosopher Martha Nussbaum is a contemporary proponent: she defines a cosmopolitan as "the person whose allegiance is to the worldwide community of human beings" and explains that "whatever else we are bound by and pursue, we should recognize, at whatever personal or social cost, that each human being is human and counts as the moral equal of every other."[18] True cosmopolitans strive to sever the link between political boundaries and people's life chances, and they typically focus on alleviating conditions in the poorest countries given the extent of economic deprivation there (see chapter 9).

Philosopher Peter Singer offers one specific rationale for such cosmopolitanism with his image of the shallow pond.[19] Singer argues that if one saw a child drowning in a shallow pond and could save him or her without any risk to one's own safety, with no inconvenience other than getting one's clothes wet and dirty, one should literally leap to the rescue.

By extension, since many emergency needs of this sort still exist where our help could easily save lives (especially the lives of children), we shouldn't think of anything else until those basic needs are met—which they currently are not.

The practical problem facing many would-be do-gooders is the sense that what they are confronting is not a shallow pond but a bottomless pit. The difficulties are twofold. First, looking at the lines in figure 15-2, particularly the aid line, and remembering that the scale is logarithmic, we realize that the challenge of complete equality is very daunting indeed. And second, the invitation to focus *all* of one's social energy on helping very poor people who are mostly very far away doesn't resonate with the psychology bequeathed to us by Worlds 0.0 and 1.0, which emphasizes obligations to people close to us.

In recognition of this problem, another prominent philosopher, Kwame Anthony Appiah, stresses local obligations *in addition to* duties to those far away. Appiah contrasts how we value friends with how we value money: "You may not mind whether you have this million dollars or that million dollars; but you value your friend not as a token of the type friend but as this particular person with whom you have a highly particularized relationship. A radical egalitarian might give his money to the poor, but he can't give his friends to the friendless."[20] His own position is that we have duties to strangers by virtue of our shared humanity, and we also have *additional* obligations to particular people and communities that are close to us by virtue of our relationships with them. And of the terms Appiah has used to describe his view, I prefer *rooted cosmopolitanism* because it suggests that deep connections to particular people and places are necessary for the cultivation of an individual's capacity to live a cosmopolitan life.[21] For Appiah, this is a "composite project, a negotiation between disparate tasks."[22]

The idea of negotiating multiple deeply held commitments allows us to frame rooted cosmopolitanism in terms of shifting the whole distance decay curve—or some part of it—upward instead of focusing just close in (communitarianism) or far out (cosmopolitanism).[23] That way, we can retain some of the strivings of cosmopolitanism while redefining progress not as a focus on the unattainably distant norm of perfect sympathy for everyone everywhere, but in terms of improvements to a highly imperfect reality where sympathies are still highly localized.

The rooted cosmopolitanism of World 3.0 recognizes that the gain, or at least potential, from helping out is, by a number of measures, greatest in the very poorest countries. But it also accounts for Zipf's law, the principle that it takes more energy to connect to those far away than to those nearby. To that, one might add the reality that sometimes when we try to help people whom we don't understand well enough, we do more harm than good. Thus, most of us shouldn't drop everything, including family and friends, to help the distant poor. But we also can't allow ourselves to simply abandon fellow humans who are suffering far away.

What to do and where depends, in World 3.0, on where we're coming from and what we're interested in achieving. In addition to making it more appealing to help others, flexibility in this regard opens up the cosmopolitan project to all of us, rather than just the rarified few who can operate on a totally global scale. My daughter, Ananya, whom you'll meet later in this chapter, is a very (rooted) cosmopolitan soul with a keen yearning to help the world's neediest, but she does have to finish high school in Barcelona. So she helps out at a local center for the children of immigrants while nursing hopes of spending a summer doing social work in India.

Table 15-1 summarizes these and other contrasts between cosmopolitanism, rooted cosmopolitanism, and communitarianism/nationalism— under the acronym COSMOS. The distinction between cosmopolitanism and rooted cosmopolitanism—as conceptualized here—is much more than a nuance and the differences from the other "isms" loom even larger.

The elements of rooted cosmopolitanism summarized in the table sound energizing. But to really live them, we need to shift our own mindsets, which is a little bit like performing brain surgery on ourselves. How do we pull *that* off? The rest of this chapter recommends an approach organized in terms of what I see as the three progressive stages of relating better to others across distance: awareness, acquaintance, and altruism. The focus across all three stages is on how to engage with and ultimately increase sympathy for others, particularly distant others.

TABLE 15-1

Rethinking cosmopolitanism

	World 0.0/1.0: Communitarian/ nationalist	World 2.0: Cosmopolitan/ global citizen	World 3.0: Rooted cosmopolitan
Concern for foreigners	Zero	Equal to domestic welfare	Positive but distance-dependent
Objective function	Maxmin* (local/ national welfare)	Maxmin* (global welfare)	Reduce distance sensitivity
Self-identity	Local/national	Global	Multiple identities
Mind-set	"Realism"	Idealism and illusions	Idealism without illusions
Operational requirements	Minimal	Maximal	Variable
Spatial focus	Local/national	"Shallow ponds"/ poorest countries	May depend on origin and interests

*To take the maxmin of an argument is to maximize its minimum value. Thus, the usual cosmopolitan imperative in terms of income (or welfare) levels is to focus on increasing the lowest levels in the world.

Stage One: Awareness

To say that we should become more aware of the world around us is rather trite, so let me begin with an illustration of a basic misperception that might matter a great deal. It concerns (lack of) knowledge of one's own country's involvement abroad, which might be expected to exceed knowledge about foreign countries themselves. In 2002, the Chicago Council on Global Affairs polled Americans as to how much of the federal budget should go to foreign aid, and how much actually was devoted to that purpose. Respondents said, on average, that 31 percent of the U.S. government's budget went to foreign aid, and that 17 percent would "be more appropriate."[24] In fact, *only about 1 percent of the U.S. federal budget goes to foreign aid*. Another poll in March 1997 had asked Americans which budget area (social security, defense, Medicare, and the like) sucked up the most dollars. Almost two-thirds cited foreign aid, even though each of the other areas mentioned dwarfs it in spending.[25] Other surveys indicate that respondents were generally unaware of frameworks for aid such as the Millennium Development Goals—associated with the UN project, headed by

Jeffrey Sachs, that aims to eradicate extreme poverty—and looked more favorably on aid when acquainted with them.[26]

Misinformation is also manifest when it comes to the help the United States gives in times of crisis. During the Asian tsunami, media reports in the United States widely touted Americans' generosity. Actually, the $350 million given by the U.S. government was smaller as a percentage of GDP than donations proffered by many other developed countries. And U.S. private giving lagged as well.[27] In sum, information about foreign aid is so bad that more accurate media representations might conceivably help shift the outcomes. And, if our knowledge of foreign countries themselves is even worse, then we clearly have a lot of learning to do.

Beyond figuring out all that we need to know more about— the wishlist also includes knowledge of levels of integration, relative distances, distance sensitivity, et cetera—it seems even more useful to review *how* we might make ourselves more aware. Here I introduce a simplified version of a diagnostic tool I developed, the Global Attitude Protocol (GAP).[28] Many of us like to think of ourselves as reasonably cosmopolitan and enlightened. Take this survey if you want to assess how far your exposure to the world's peoples and cultures really goes.

Global Attitude Protocol

Please respond to each of the numbered statements below with the one of the following five responses that best fits your own behavior or beliefs: "Strongly Disagree," "Disagree," "Not Relevant," "Agree," or "Strongly Agree." If you own your copy of this book, you may want to write down SD, D, N, A, or SA next to each of the statements.

1. I speak multiple languages.

2. I have lived in countries other than my home country.

3. I enjoy traveling to and getting to know people from different parts of the world.

4. Some of my closest friends are of nationalities different from mine.

5. I think I would enjoy working in a country in which I haven't previously lived.

6. When I travel/live in another country I try to learn about the political, legal, economic, etc., institutions of that country—and how they differ from my own.

7. When I travel/live in another country, I try to learn about the cultural traditions of that country—and how they differ from my own.

8. I think I can develop an opinion about a person independent of any preconceived image of his/her national culture or religion.

9. I am comfortable working with people located in different countries.

10. I am comfortable working together with people from different cultures and backgrounds in the same location as me.

11. I understand the socioeconomic/political ramifications of world events and can evaluate how they might affect my business or investments.

12. I read newspapers and magazines with significant international content (e.g., *International Herald Tribune, Economist, Fortune*).

13. I listen to the world news on international TV channels (e.g., CNN International, BBC World Service, Al Jazeera).

14. I have used the Internet to expand my access to international news and commentary.

15. When I travel/live in another country, I make some attempt to look at local media as well.

Scoring: For each response, give yourself −2 points for Strongly Disagree, −1 point for Disagree, 0 points for Neutral/Not Relevant, 1 point for Agree, and 2 for Strongly Agree; then add up scores across questions to get your overall GAP score. 20+ implies no (serious) gap, 10–20 some gap, below 10 a significant gap, and below 0 a huge gap!

What score did you come up with? With which types of questions did you tend to disagree or strongly disagree? These might suggest areas in your life to focus on in order to become more open and improve your awareness of the world out there. Remember, accurate mental maps and an understanding of distant places don't develop automatically: they require personal action. The U.S. journalist Walter Lippman articulated the agenda more than eighty years ago, writing: "The world that we have to deal with is out of reach, out of sight, out of mind. It has to be explored, reported, and imagined. Man is no Aristotelian god contemplating all existence at one glance."[29]

Even those who tend to think of themselves as relatively urbane, global, or sophisticated often fall short of the kind of openness that Lippman had in mind. Technology can help us learn about and connect with distant people and places, but really understanding distant others often requires putting yourself out there mentally and, if possible, physically. Mere passport stamps don't count: thus, there is evidence that very short trips, treks, et cetera tend to have very short-lived effects.[30]

Stage Two: Acquaintance

Awareness is one thing; getting to the next level of acquaintance and affinity is quite another. Acquaintance requires multiple contacts and engagement over time—in other words, a true exchange. For trust to develop, let alone sympathy, repeated interactions between people must take place. A process of learning about "the other" in the abstract usually isn't enough.

As a model for such interactions, I point to what technologists have called Web 3.0, the contextuated or semantic Web. Web 1.0 allowed us to look up information; Web 2.0, the one we are currently working with, expands that functionality by allowing social networking and mass collaboration. Web 3.0 is supposed to work even better, because machine-based learning and natural language processing are supposed to provide a *context* for online requests for information and other communications.[31] In the same way, World 3.0 ideally requires not just communication across borders, but communication that is cognizant of and sensitive to what continue to be large differences in national context, that is, communication with understanding.

For an example of how far such a process of really understanding another local context might go, consider my family's move from the United States to Spain from the perspective of my fifteen-year-old daughter, Ananya. I recently asked Ananya to write down her thoughts about what the move—which she had protested bitterly as an eleven-year-old—had meant for her and particularly her self-identity. The box "Really Getting into Other Cultures" contains what she came up with, without further prompting or editing.

Really Getting into Other Cultures

Four years ago, I moved to Barcelona, Spain from Cambridge, MA. I left my primarily white, primarily Jewish private school for an international school, Benjamin Franklin, where most people spoke several languages fluently. Even though I had grown up speaking two Indian languages at home (Hindi and Bengali), I had more or less stopped actually speaking them, even though I could still understand when my parents spoke in them.

On my first day at school in Barcelona, I didn't know what to expect. I knew that everyone spoke English, and it was an international school, but I had no idea what that meant. I soon learned that at my school, no one would ask you, "Where are you from?" because no one student identifies themselves from one place.

The first time I was invited to a sleepover, all the girls called their mothers before they went to sleep—a symphony of Russian mixed in with lilting Dutch, Swedish and Afrikaans. They then hung up the phones and resumed chatting in a mixture of English and Spanish. At that moment, I realized exactly what being a global citizen meant—*it is being able to go from one culture to another while retaining parts of previous cultures, and therefore, taking something from the earlier countries, languages and customs.*

Halfway into our first year in Spain, I realized that I could no longer attempt to be *just* American, as I had been doing for as long as I could remember. I started to talk to my parents in Hindi and Bengali again and worked hard to learn Spanish. At the age of fifteen, I speak English, Spanish and Bengali fluently, I have basic skills in French and Hindi, and I am able to read and understand Catalan, the language spoken in the state of Spain that I live in.

One of the best parts for me about leaving the US was being able to see my homeland from a different point of view. In freshman year at my school, our social studies class studied "US History." In September of that year, I thought I would pass the class without having to work in the slightest, because, well, I'm American. I could not have been more wrong. In the US, learning American history meant learning which Native Americans lived in eastern Massachusetts, or what year the Townshend Acts were passed. In Spain, it wasn't about who won, or who was right, so much as how the culmination of so many events could produce such a revolution.

So where *am* I from? Everywhere, and yet no specific place. I get emotional when I land in Logan International Airport and a security guard says, "Welcome home." I will always love the smell of the soil in India after the July monsoons, and yet I also know that because Spanish law allows citizenship after seven years of residence, I will be filing for that right as soon as I turn 18. To me, at this point, Boston is my hometown, India is where my family is from, and Barcelona is my home. I don't think I will ever identify myself as being from one place, or one culture, or one type of people, and I'm glad. I wouldn't change this for the world.

—Ananya Ghemawat

Ananya expresses the power of changing contexts in cultivating rooted cosmopolitanism. As she suggests, you don't leave behind the local cultures and identities you've made your own, yet you don't identify perfectly with any one of them, either. Rather, you become more deeply acquainted with multiple cultures by understanding them in a comparative context. Relocating to a new country is particularly transformational because the overwhelming bulk of your interactions now take place with people who were formerly foreign to you, and you have to fit your own life into the flow of their lives, institutional arrangements, customs, et cetera.

Picking up and moving to a different country is, of course, a fairly extreme way of broadening your circle of acquaintances. For many, a more practical starting point is to focus on learning about one foreign country or region in detail. Learn about its geography and history and what they reveal about its links to other places. Understand its internal and external distances. Try to empathize with the problems people face there, and remember that even in places that seem idyllic from afar, real people there still have real worries that deserve respect. Then bring this context alive through interaction and travel with real people, not just once but over an extended period.

Stage Three: Altruism

Awareness and acquaintance are steps on the way toward achieving the rooted cosmopolitan ideal of helping people at some distance from oneself, but they are not, by themselves, sufficient. As the Dalai Lama has observed,

> Only a spontaneous feeling of empathy with others can really inspire us to act on their behalf. Nevertheless, compassion does not arise mechanically. Such a sincere feeling must grow gradually, cultivated within each individual, based on their own conviction of its worth. Adopting a kind

attitude thus becomes a personal matter. How each of us behaves in daily life is after all, the real test of compassion.[32]

Since I can't say much more about how to develop such empathy, let me simply share with you an example that I encountered as I was wrapping up this book. After moving to Barcelona, I joined the board of Ananya's school, and met David Risher, a Harvard MBA and former tech executive, who chaired it. When David stepped down from the board in summer 2009 to spend a year traveling with his family before returning to the United States, I was sorry to see him go—and surprised as well as pleased to see him turn up again in 2010, which is when he explained Worldreader.org to me.

Worldreader.org is a venture that seeks to make digital books available in the developing world. It was sparked by an epiphany that David had while visiting an orphanage in Ecuador. David noticed a small dusty building, all locked up, which upon inquiry, turned out to be the library. And when he expressed interest in seeing the books in there, he was told that the key had been lost long ago. The contrast with how his family had been using e-readers to keep up with the children's education while traveling was striking!

David returned to Barcelona and shared his epiphany with Colin McElwee, another MBA working as director of marketing at a local business school who, in a fit of enthusiasm, drew up a "business plan." And the two decided that if they were to pursue this opportunity, they would have to do so full time. David deferred his plans to look for paid work, Colin resigned his paid job, and the two set up WorldReader. org, initially funding the nonprofit through their own savings and David's tech contacts. They focused first on Ghana, an English-speaking country and former British colony relatively close to Barcelona, whose government seemed willing to fund broad deployment of the new technology if Worldreader.org could prove its value with a large-scale field trial.

Talking to David and Colin was interesting not just because of the story's intrinsic appeal—they've already appeared on CNN and been discussed in the *Wall Street Journal*, among other places—but because of the perspective that their case provided on the topics of cosmopolitanism and social business.

While David and Colin had focused on West Africa out of a desire to help some of the least fortunate, the notion of shallow ponds didn't resonate with them: they were more interested in making a lasting impact than providing short-term relief. They validated what they were trying to do there in terms of the theory of market failures, concluding that creating a culture of reading offered huge positive externalities that might not be internalized adequately by market forces. And their choices about what to focus on were rooted not just in perceived needs, but also in their own passions, talents, and interests. Both David and Colin had enormous faith in education's transformative powers—faith that reflected their sense of the role that education had played in their own life possibilities. Moreover, the combination of David's tech background and contacts and Colin's expertise in marketing educational programs implied some degree of fit with their capabilities as well as their interests. Such conditioning on where people are coming from is incompatible with the general cosmopolitanism of World 2.0 but integral—as a way of building engagement and effectiveness—to the rooted cosmopolitanism of World 3.0.

As I listened to David and Colin describe what they were doing, I also thought back to a conversation I had had a few weeks earlier with Muhammad Yunus, the founder of Grameen Bank and a winner of the Nobel Peace Prize, about his concept of social business. Worldreader. org fit with his sense that people should try to work toward their desired social outcomes themselves, instead of waiting around for governments. But its emphasis on raising money "to close the gap between the cost of the devices and the price local governments can pay, until the unit cost of e-readers falls below an appropriate local market price" went beyond Yunus's emphasis on self-sustaining models of social business. David and Colin were wary of applying too strict a market test to attempts to address the large market failure that they thought they had identified.

Instead, Worldreader.org actually seemed to bridge the gap between traditional businesses and traditional nongovernmental organizations. As a nonprofit, it had to articulate its goals more carefully, bound its scope more explicitly, and be clearer about its funding mechanisms, including the role of prices, in trying to recover its costs, than the typical private business, in which most of these parameters are determined by profit-maximization. But as we have already seen, David and Colin's clarity and crispness was entirely businesslike when it came to questions about what they were trying to do, why and where—not to mention whom to work with (the entire value web: donors, ministries, hardware and content suppliers, cell phone companies, teachers, students . . .), what metrics to use and how to run really rigorous field trials.

Like most nascent ventures, Worldreader.org still faces a large number of uncertainties, but I find its story wonderfully inspiring. Not all of us can go nearly so far down the path of helping those who are far away, but building awareness of and acquaintance with others can only help with the achievement of this higher objective—as well as being useful in and of themselves.

Maximizing Human Potential

Throughout most of this book, I've exhorted readers to change their personal attitudes about globalization: to shake off the myths that lead to an awful amount of misdirection, to understand its real benefits and costs, and to push for much more openness and some—but only as necessary—regulation. Building bridges across cultural, administrative, geographic, and economic distance, where markets fail to do so, as David and Colin are attempting, is perhaps the highest form of global citizenship. In support of such an assessment, who better to cite than Adam Smith, the alleged prophet of selfishness as a virtue: "To feel much for others and little for ourselves; to restrain our selfishness and exercise our benevolent affections, constitutes the perfection of human nature."[33]

The awareness-acquaintance-altruism sequence laid out in the preceding sections was meant to help us move in that direction, even if we don't get as far as David and Colin, by suggesting how to open up to the rest of the world at the individual level. Note the focus on reducing internal distance at the individual level instead of the country or business levels that were targeted in earlier chapters—a focus on the barriers that exist within one's own mind. But to ask a more basic question, why does this progression make sense? It is worth concluding by (re)summarizing the several levels at which it may help maximize human potential.

First, this progression holds several possible attractions at the individual level. In Ananya's case, I'm cheered by recent research indicating that biculturals/triculturals have the potential to serve as particularly useful connectors in organizations that cross borders and bridge distances. In addition, I think her cross-border experiences have enriched her in a way that is independent of any material benefits. And then, as the Dalai Lama has emphasized, there is a transcendental appeal to developing—as I hope she is—the capacity to do the right thing for unselfish reasons.

But ultimately, individual benefits from the kinds of engagement with the world advocated in this chapter are just the icing on the cake. The real gains accrue at the societal level. If enough of us broaden our sympathies—even just a little—it could go a long way to help in addressing obvious challenges: the threat of protectionism, surges in anti-immigrant sentiment, tensions in the U.S.-Chinese relationship, the risk that the poorest among us, particularly in Africa, may fall even farther behind, and so on.

And while particular challenges will eventually pass (one hopes), the need to promote more cross-border engagement and sympathy will persist. The darker legacies of Worlds 0.0 and 1.0—the imprint of a vast span of human history—are always with us. So I'm skeptical of optimistic arguments that circles of cooperation, having expanded over the last few millennia, will continue to do so, or that that may even be the "destiny" of life on earth.[34]

Instead, I find myself more inclined to agree with cognitive scientist Steven Pinker: "Global cooperation and moral progress will not increase toward some theoretical maximum or Teilhardesque Omega Point, but will level off at a point where the pleasures resulting from global cooperation (having more stuff than you had before) are balanced by the pleasures resulting from non-cooperation (having more stuff than your neighbors, or the warm glow of ethnic chauvinism)."[35] And since openness tends to expand (and contract) in fits and starts, we shouldn't even expect it to move smoothly toward a single equilibrium.

How far we are going to get in unlocking the full potential of World 3.0, then, depends on our mind-sets, which is why this chapter focused on how we might open them up. The really great news—about mind-sets as well as actual levels of integration—is that there is so much room to do better! When we conquer irrational fears and don't let the excesses of market failure get out of hand, we can confidently reach out and improve the possibilities for ourselves and for humanity around the world. And that vision—with openness as a source of inspiration and hope rather than fear—is the promise of World 3.0.

Notes

Chapter One

1. See Pankaj Ghemawat, *Redefining Global Strategy* (Boston: Harvard Business School Press, 2007), especially chapters 4–7 or, for an abbreviated treatment, Pankaj Ghemawat, "Managing Differences: The Central Challenge of Global Strategy," *Harvard Business Review*, March 2007, 58–68.

2. Wolf Schäfer, "Lean Globality Studies," *Globality Studies Journal*, no. 7 (2007): 1–15.

3. See Douglass C. North, John Joseph Wallis, and Barry R. Weingast, *Violence and Social Orders: A Conceptual Framework for Interpreting Recorded Human History* (New York: Cambridge University Press, 2009), 21.

4. Smithsonian Museum of Natural History, "Homo Sapiens," http://humanorigins.si.edu/evidence/human-fossils/species/homo-sapiens.

5. This is the period of the Neolithic revolution, see "The History of Cities," *Encyclopaedia Britannica*, http://www.britannica.com/EBchecked/topic/118952/city/61355/The-history-of-cities?anchor=ref232180.

6. See, for instance, Jared Diamond, "The Worst Mistake in the History of the Human Race," *Discover*, May 1987, 64–66, http://www.environnement.ens.fr/perso/claessen/agriculture/mistake_jared_diamond.pdf. Lesser inequality actually leads Diamond—but very few others—to assert the superiority of World 0.0.

7. See, for instance, Lawrence H. Keeley, *War Before Civilization* (Oxford: Oxford University Press, 1996).

8. See Elman R. Service, *Primitive Social Organization: An Evolutionary Perspective* (New York: Random House, 1971), 159; Robert L. Kelly, *The Foraging Spectrum: Diversity in Hunter-Gatherer Lifeways* (Washington, DC: Smithsonian Institution Press, 1995), 209–216; Allen W. Johnson and Timothy Earle, *The Evolution of Human Societies: From Foraging to Agrarian State* (Stanford: Stanford University Press, 1987), 246; North, Wallis, and Weingast, *Violence and Social Orders*, 1.

9. The estimated number of independent polities in 3000 BC is drawn from Rein Taagepera, "Expansion and Contraction Patterns of Large Polities," *International Studies Quarterly* 41, no. 3 (Sept. 1997): 475–504.

10. North, Wallis, and Weingast, *Violence and Social Orders*, chapter 1.

11. This is based on rough estimates in *Struggling to Survive: Children in Armed Conflict in the Democratic Republic of the Congo*, Watchlist Country Report, April 2006, http://www.watchlist.org/reports/files/dr_congo.report.20060426.php?p=0).

12. Joseph Henrich et al., "Markets, Religion, Community Size, and the Evolution of Fairness and Punishment," *Science* 327, no. 5972 (March 19, 2010): 1480.

13. In case you worry about—or are waiting for—world government, extrapolations of this long-run trend toward political consolidation suggest that the world will coalesce into one political entity after AD 3000 or even AD 4000.

14. See Taagepera, "Expansion and Contraction Patterns of Large Polities."

15. Thus, medieval Italian city-states—in which influential families lived in fortified keeps and fought street battles (think Romeo and Juliet) and violent death rates remained more than a hundred times higher in Europe than they are today—still resembled the anocracies of World 0.0.

16. Karl Marx and Friedrich Engels, *The Communist Manifesto* (London: Penguin Classics, 2002), 223.

17. See, for instance, Karl Deutsch and Alexander Eckstein, "National Industrialization and the Declining Share of the International Economic Sector 1890–1959," *World Politics* 13 (1961): 267–299.

18. Keyword search of Library of Congress Catalog, January 2010.

19. See, respectively, Paul Kennedy, *Preparing for the Twenty-First Century* (New York: Vintage, 1993); Anthony Giddens, *Runaway World: How Globalization Is Reshaping Our Lives* (London: Profile, 1999); and Joseph S. Nye and John D. Donahue, *Governance in a Globalizing World* (Washington, DC: Brookings Institution Press, 2000).

20. Benedictus XVI, Encyclical Letter *Caritas in Veritate*, June 29, 2009, permalink: http://www.zenit.org/article-26386?l=english; and Jörg Eigendorf, "Dalai Lama—'I Am a Supporter of Globalization,'" *Welt Online*, July 16, 2009, http://www.welt.de/international/article 4133061/Dalai-Lama-I-am-a-supporter-of-globalization.html.

21. Brian Sullivan, "Rupert Murdoch Interview: Economy Weak; Danger of Inflation Great," Fox Business Network, April 27, 2009, http://seekingalpha.com/article/133580-rupert-murdoch-interview-economy-weak-danger-of-inflation-great?source=commenter.

22. Matt Ridley's *The Rational Optimist* (New York: HarperCollins, 2010) is an atypically interesting example of this subgenre.

23. Karl Polanyi, *The Great Transformation: The Political and Economic Origins of Our Time* (Boston: Beacon Press, 2001), 145.

24. David Ignatius, "Populism Popular at the World Economic Forum in Davos," *Washington Post*, January 31, 2010, http://www.washingtonpost.com/wp-dyn/content/story/2010/01/29/ST2010012903888.html?sid=ST2010012903888.

25. See, for instance, Ian Bremmer, *The End of the Free Market: Who Wins the War Between States and Corporations?* (New York: Penguin, 2010).

26. "U.S. Seen as Less Important, China as More Powerful. Isolationist Sentiment Surges to Four-Decade High," Survey Report of the Pew Research Center, December 3, 2009, http://people-press.org/report/569/americas-place-in-the-world.

27. Phillip Blond, "The Rise of the Red Tories," *Prospect*, February 28, 2009, http://www.prospectmagazine.co.uk/2009/02/riseoftheredtories/.

28. Raj Patel, *The Value of Nothing: How to Reshape Market Society and Redefine Democracy* (London: Picador, 2010).

29. Matt Ridley, *The Rational Optimist: How Prosperity Evolves* (New York: HarperCollins, 2010), 34–35.

30. Loretta Radeschi, "The 100-Mile Suit," *The Crafts Report*, http://www.craftsreport.com/insight-gained/99-philadelphiasuit.html

31. See http://ecoseny.blogspot.com.

32. Even before the crisis, cross-country evidence indicated a general connection between these ideas in many people's minds: those who were suspicious of free markets were more likely to hold negative opinions of globalization. See Martin S. Edwards, "Public Opinion Regarding Economic and Cultural Globalization: Evidence from a Cross-National Survey," *Review of International Political Economy* 13, no. 4 (October 2006): 587–608.

33. The impact of trade barriers on the volatility of food prices and better ways of responding than each country striving for self-sufficiency are discussed further in chapter 7.

34. Specific data in this regard will be provided in chapters 11 and 15.

Chapter Two

1. Thomas Friedman, *The World Is Flat* (New York: Farrar, Straus and Giroux, 2005), 176.

2. Arundhati Roy, "Globalization Is Ripping Through People's Lives," speech in Lannan Foundation in Santa Fe, New Mexico, September 18, 2002, published September 27, 2002, on socialistworker.org.

3. For World 1.0, I've used various quotes, including the following precrisis quote from a former professor of mine: "Local decision-making, productivity-enhancing technological change, and the growing demand for services will be the key forces shaping our futures—not globalization, meaning the global flow of goods and capital" from Bruce C. Greenwald and Judd Kahn, *Globalization* (Hoboken, NJ: John Wiley and Sons, 2009). And since excitement about intermediate levels of integration tends to be even more muted, I looked long and hard for a prior incarnation of World 3.0 before settling on the following quote from a former CEO whom I know: "There is a balance on the spectrum between 'local' and 'global' that represents the 'sweet spot' . . . I've referred to this concept of the right balance as 'the race to the middle.' "

4. "Many U.S. Parents Outsourcing Child Care Overseas," video report, Onion News Network, http://www.theonion.com/content/video/report_many_u_s_parents.

5. For a more extended discussion of semiglobalization and common misconceptions often articulated about the extent of globalization, see chapter 1 of Pankaj Ghemawat, *Redefining Global Strategy* (Boston: Harvard Business School Press, 2007) or, for more scholarly treatments, Pankaj Ghemawat, "Semiglobalization and International Business Strategy," *Journal of International Business Studies* 34, no. 2 (March 2003): 138–152; and Edward E. Leamer, "A Flat World, a Level Playing Field, a Small World After All, or None of the Above? A Review of Thomas L. Friedman's *The World Is Flat*," *Journal of Economic Literature* 45 (March 2007): 83–126.

6. Estimates based on data from the Universal Postal Union and the International Telecommunication Union.

7. Estimate based on data from TeleGeography Research and Cisco.

8. Pankaj Ghemawat and Steven A. Altman, "The Indian IT Services Industry in 2009," pp. 2–3, unpublished draft, August 2009, available from www.ghemawat.org.

9. Len Klady, "International Box Office: Boom Times," *Screen Daily*, May 6, 2010, http://www.allbusiness.com/economy-economic-indicators/economic-conditions-recession/14397137-1.html.

10. Pew Project for Excellence in Journalism, "The State of the News Media: An Annual Report on American Journalism," March 15, 2010, http://www.stateofthemedia.org/2010/. The study includes content analysis of TV (network and cable), newspapers, online news sites, and radio.

11. MediaTenor, "Different Perspectives: Locations, Protagonists, and Topic Structures in International TV News," March–April 2006. The European figures provided are based on recent data from Switzerland, Austria, Germany, United Kingdom, and Italy.

12. Calculations by Ethan Zuckerman, as reported in "A Cyber-house Divided," *Economist*, September 4, 2010, 58.

13. See, for instance, Parag Khanna, "Remapping the World," in List of 10 Ideas for the Next 10 Years, *Time*, March 11, 2010.

14. The figures are for a 30GB fifth-generation iPod introduced in late 2005.

15. Greg Linden, Kenneth L. Kraemer, and Jason Dedrick, "Who Captures Value in a Global Innovation Network? The Case of Apple's Ipod," *Communications of the ACM* 52, no. 3 (March 2009); Greg Linden, Kenneth L. Kraemer, and Jason Dedrick, "Who Profits from Innovation in Global Value Chains? A Study of the iPod and Notebook PCs," *Industrial and Corporate Change* 19, no. 1 (2009): 81–116.

16. On the foreign content of Chinese exports, see Robert Koopman, Zhi Wang, and Shang-Jin Wei, "How Much of Chinese Exports Is Really Made in China? Assessing Domestic Value-Added When Processing Trade Is Pervasive," NBER working paper 14109, June 2008. For cross-country evidence, see Guillaume Daudin, Christine Rifflart, and Danielle Schweis-guth, "Value-Added Trade and Regionalization," OFCE Centre de Recherche en Économie de Sciences Po Paris, September 2008; and Robert C. Johnson and Guillermo Noguera, "Accounting for Intermediates: Production Sharing and Trade in Value Added," unpublished draft, June 2009.

17. One reader pointed out that one might also want to account for the fact that some products and many services simply can't be traded across borders: think of the market for haircut services or restaurants. But even if one figures that only 40% of the U.S. economy consists of tradables (see Menzie Chinn, "Does Manufacturing Matter? An Update," Econbrowser blog, August 21, 2006, http://www.econbrowser.com/archives/2006/08/does_manufactur.html), the export-to-tradables ratio is less than 30% for the U.S., and less than 50% for the global economy. And more importantly, pronouncements about World 2.0 such as Friedman's aren't qualified as applying to just the tradable sector, so it gives them too much of a free ride to allow for nontradability when they do not acknowledge its importance.

18. This complete integration benchmark is equal to 100% minus the Herfindahl concentration ratio of countries' GDPs, for reasons that the interested reader can work out. Similar calculations can be performed for complete integration benchmarks for other types of cross-border flows and typically yield values in the 80%–90% range, i.e., significantly greater than the actual integration levels laid out in this chapter.

19. These data are drawn from various issues of UNCTAD's annual *World Investment Report*.

20. Estimate based on data presented in Joshua Aizenman and Jake Kendall, "Internationalization of Venture Capital and Private Equity," NBER working paper 14344, September 2008.

21. Figure is for 2005. Calculation is a weighted average based on market capitalization for forty-two countries based on data presented in Piet Sercu and Rosanne Vanpee, "Home Bias in International Equity Portfolios: A Review," Katholieke Universiteit Leuven working paper AFI0710, August 2007.

22. Estimate of cross-border ownership of bank deposits is a weighted average of regional estimates of the proportion of bank assets held by foreign owners. Regional estimates are from the IBM Institute for Business Value's report, "No Bank Is an Island," February 2008. The proportion of bank assets from each region is from International Monetary Fund, "Global Financial Stability Report, Market Development and Issues: Statistical Appendix," September 2006, 95. Estimates were made to fill in data gaps. Estimate of cross-border ownership of public debt is based on numerator (Gross External Public Debt) from World Bank Quarterly External Debt Database and denominator (Total Public Debt) from the Economist Intelligence Unit (EIU). Forty-eight countries were covered for calculation of this metric (based on data availability).

23. Only 2% of it goes beyond U.S. borders, says the American Association of Fundraising Counsel. See Susan Kitchens, "Contrarian Charity," Forbes.com, May 10, 2004, http://www.forbes.com/forbes/2004/0510/102.html.

24. Data sources for the material in figure 2-1 are as follows: mail data (covering letter post) from Universal Postal Union Postal Statistics; telephone calls (minutes) data from International Telecommunication Union; university students data from UNESCO Global Education Digest 2009; immigrants data from UN Population Division International Migration 2009; charity (private giving) data from Geneva Global; foreign direct investment data from UNCTAD World Investment Report (various issues); patents data (for OECD countries) from OECD Science Technology and Industry Scoreboard 2009; venture capital data from Aizenman and Kendall (2008); internet traffic data from TeleGeography and Cisco; trade data (covering exports of merchandise and services, roughly adjusted for double-counting) from World Bank World Development Indicators; stock market data from Sercu and Vanpée (2007), op cit.; U.S. news data from State of the Media 2010; bank deposits data from "No Bank is an Island" (2008), IMF; government debt data from World Bank and Economist Intelligence Unit.

25. The wage rate comparison is based on Economist Intelligence Unit database (EIU).

26. Pankaj Ghemawat, "Why the World Isn't Flat," Foreign Policy, no. 159 (March/April 2007): 54–60.

27. Two such measures, ratification of international treaties and membership of international governmental organizations, didn't vary very much across the countries in the 2007 sample. And apart from Taiwan, the lowest scores in treaty ratification went to Iran, Israel, and the United States—countries with very different levels of international political connection and influence! A third measure of political engagement, contributions to UN peacekeeping forces, is simply odd. Such forces number less than 100,000 and are not considered particularly formidable. And the fact that the three leading contributors, by a large margin, are Pakistan, Bangladesh, and India suggests that contributions to them may have more to do with labor economics than political engagement or influence.

28. David Livingstone, The Last Journals of David Livingstone, in Central Africa, from 1865 to His Death (Cirencester: The Echo Library, 2005), 351.

29. John Dewey, The Public and Its Problems (New York: Holt, 1927).

30. Henry Ford, My Philosophy of Industry (London: Harrap, 1929), 44–45.

31. H. G. Wells, The Shape of Things to Come (London: Hutchinson, 1933).

32. George Orwell, "As I Please," Tribune, May 12, 1944, reprinted in CEJL 3: 173.

33. Martin Heidegger, "The Thing," in Poetry, Language, Thought (New York: Harper and Row, 1971), 165.

34. Marshall McLuhan, Understanding Media (New York: Mentor, 1964), 19.

35. See, for instance, Gregg Easterbrook, Sonic Boom: Globalization at Mach Speed (New York: Random House, 2009).

36. For a much more extended treatment of the relationship between technology and globalization and additional arguments against technotrances, see David E. Edgerton, "The Contradictions of Techno-Nationalism and Techno-Globalism," New Global Studies 1, no. 1 (2007).

37. See Tom Standage, The Victorian Internet: The Remarkable Story of the Telegraph and the Nineteenth Century's On-Line Pioneers (New York: Walker and Company, 1998); and Kevin H. O'Rourke and Jeffrey G. Williamson, Globalization and History (Boston, MA: The MIT Press, 1999).

38. "Google Breaks $100bn Brand Value Threshold," Marketing magazine, April 28, 2009, http://www.marketingmagazine.co.uk/news/901390/Google-breaks-100bn-brand-aluethreshold.

39. Valery Kodachigov and Anastasia Golitsyna, "Google Tracks Traffic in Moscow, St. Pete," *Moscow Times*, August 12, 2010, http://www.themoscowtimes.com/business/article/google-tracks-traffic-in-moscow-st-pete/412178.html.

40. Natalya Hmelik, blog post, "The Kremlin Gets Tech Savvy," August 12, 2010, http://frontpagemag.com/2010/08/12/the-kremlin-gets-tech-savvy/.

41. "Google.com Has Tweaked Its Global Strategy for India," News Relay, May 2, 2009, http://webcache.googleusercontent.com/search?q=cache:q-dX5qKuyZ8J:www.news-relay.com/latest-news/googlecom-has-tweaked-its-global-strategy-for-india/+google+globalizati on+strategy&cd=13&hl=en&ct=clnk.

42. "A Virtual Counter-Revolution," *Economist*, September 2, 2010.

43. Zuckerman, "A Cyber-house Divided."

Chapter Three

1. Note that distance, or to be more precise, *external* distance, is an attribute of two countries or locations, not one.

2. See, for instance, Mykyta Vesselovsky, Florence Jean-Jacobs, and David Boileau, "Canadian Performance in the U.S. Market, 1995–2009," analytical paper series 007, Foreign Affairs and International Trade Canada, 2010.

3. John F. Helliwell, *How Much Do National Borders Matter?* (Washington, DC: Brookings Institution Press, 1998), 38.

4. James E. Anderson and Eric van Wincoop, "Gravity with Gravitas: A Solution to the Border Puzzle," *American Economic Review* 93, no. 1 (March 2003): 170–192.

5. See, for instance, Patricia Lovett-Reid, "The Real Cost of Cross-Border Shopping," *MSN Money*, November 13, 2009, http://money.ca.msn.com/investing/patricia-lovett-reid/article.aspx?cp-documentid=22580504.

6. I prefer this approach to the one of backing out intranational trade from total production minus exports. The trouble with this latter approach is that it is hard to know what distances to associate with intranational trade—yielding wildly varying estimates. See, for instance, Matthias Helble, "Combining International Trade and Intra-national Transport Flows," working paper 13/2006, Graduate Institute of International Studies, Geneva.

7. Ibid.

8. The median value was a pretty astounding sixty-two!

9. See, for instance, Natalie Chen, "Intra-national Versus International Trade in the European Union: Why Do National Borders Matter? *Journal of International Economics* 63 (2004): 93–118.

10. Calculated on the basis of the gravity models described later in the chapter.

11. Jarko Fidrmuc and Jan Fidrmuc, "Integration, Disintegration and Trade in Europe: Evolution of Trade Relations During the 1990s," ZEI working paper B 03-2000, University of Bonn, 2000.

12. Jeffrey A. Frankel, *Regional Trading Blocs in the World Economic System* (Washington, DC: Peterson Institute for International Economics, 1997), 12.

13. Volker Nitsch and Nikolaus Wolf, "Tear Down This Wall: On the Persistence of Borders in Trade," Warwick Economic research paper 919, University of Warwick, October 2009.

14. Marie Daumal and Soledad Zignago, "Border Effects of Brazilian States," Centre d'Etudes Prospectives et d'Informations Internationales (CEPII), June 2008.

15. Sandra Poncet, "Measuring Chinese Domestic and International Integration," *China Economic Review* 14 (2003): 1–21; and Sandra Poncet, "A Fragmented China," *Review of International Economics* 13 (2005): 409–430.

16. By contrast, estimates for U.S. states and Canadian provinces suggest border effects are lower than five. See Holger C. Wolf, "Intranational Home Bias in Trade," *Review of Economics and Statistics* 82, no. 4 (2000): 555–563; John Helliwell, "National Borders, Trade and Migration," *Pacific Economic Review* 2, no. 3 (1997): 165–185.

17. In addition to the U.S., where internal trade is significantly larger than international trade, data for countries such as Japan, France, Germany, and Spain indicate internal trade comparable to if not much greater than their total international trade.

18. Edward E. Leamer, "A Flat World, a Level Playing Field, a Small World After All, or None of the Above? A Review of Thomas L. Friedman's *The World Is Flat*," *Journal of Economic Literature* 45 (March 2007): 83–126, 100.

19. UNCTAD, *World Investment Report 2010*, 18, and comparisons drawing on earlier World Investment Reports.

20. Elizabeth Thompson, "That Which We Sell as a Jelly Bean by the Same Label Would Taste as Sweet," *Montreal Gazette,* August 22, 2007.

21. David Ganong, telephone interview by author, August 20, 2008.

22. NACC, "Enhancing Competitiveness in Canada, Mexico, and the United States: Private-Sector Priorities for the Security and Prosperity Partnership of North America (SPP)," Initial Recommendations of the North American Competitiveness Council (NACC), February 2007, 19.

23. David Ganong, telephone interview by author, August 20, 2008.

24. This is a reason why official statistics overestimate the real amount of trade, as discussed in chapter 2.

25. Mark Andrew Dutz, "Harmonizing Regulatory Mechanisms: Options for Deepening Investment Integration in South Asia," World Bank working paper 36249, October 2004.

26. Bruce Campbell, "More Than Jellybeans: The SPP Regulatory Framework Agreement and Its Impact on Chemicals Regulation," Canadian Centre for Policy Alternatives, North American Deep Integration Series 1, no. 1 (September 2007): 6.

27. Thompson, "That Which We Sell as a Jelly Bean."

28. Since Ganong is privately held, its profitability is not publicly known.

29. Trade Data Online from Industry Canada, http://www.ic.gc.ca/sc_mrkti/tdst/tdo/tdo.php?headFootDir=/sc_mrkti/tdst/headfoot&naArea=9999&lang=30&searchType=CS&toFromCountry=CDN&currency=CDN&hSelectedCodes=|3113&period=5&timePeriod=5|Complete+Years&periodString=&productBreakDown=Complete+Years&reportType=TE&productType=NAICS&areaCodeStrg=9999|TOP&runReport_x=37&javaChart_x=&gifChart_x=&outputType=RPT&chartType=columnApp&grouped=GROUPED#tag.

30. At a 20% threshold—the standard one.

31. The exceptions are Quebec in Canada and Louisiana in the U.S.—former French colonies that retain, to some degree, French-style civil law, even though the French ceded political control more than two centuries ago.

32. This calculation is based on a coarse definition of legal origins; a finer-grained one would significantly reduce that percentage.

33. Samuel P. Huntington, *The Clash of Civilizations and the Remaking of World Order* (New York: Simon and Schuster, 2003); Geert Hofstede, *Culture's Consequences: Comparing Values, Behaviors, Institutions and Organizations Across Nations* (Thousand Oaks CA: Sage Publications, 2001).

34. Hofstede's original schema, probably the most widely used of its kind, focuses on four dimensions of culture: power distance, individualism, masculinity, and uncertainty avoidance. Subsequent work on East Asian cultures prompted him to add long-term orientation as a fifth dimension.

35. Randy Boswell, "Canadians Approve U.S. Goals: Poll; Identify with Southern Neighbours More Than Other Nations," *Montreal Gazette,* September 10, 2007.

36. Lydia Saad, "In U.S., Canada Places First in Image Contest; Iran Last," Gallup, February 19, 2010, http://www.gallup.com/poll/126116/Canada-Places-First-Image-Contest-Iran-Last.aspx.

37. Jefferson Morley, "World Opinion Roundup: Canada's Anti-American Impulse," *Washington Post,* January 23, 2006.

38. Amita Batra, "India's Global Trade Potential: The Gravity Model Approach," Indian Council for Research on International Economic Relations, December 2004. The ratio of India's potential to actual trade with Pakistan is estimated at 52.2 based on analysis using PPP-adjusted GNP and GNP per capita. Based on GNP and GNP per capita at current exchange rates, this ratio is 26.7. The estimate of 2%–4% is based on the general range implied by these ratios.

39. Another geographic attribute that might be treated as Canada-specific rather than as a bilateral attribute of Canada and another country is Canada's privileged location relative to world markets. Scaled by distance in the way described in the next section, Canada faces effective overall export demand nearly seven times that of Australia, a country far removed from nearly everywhere else.

40. Waldo R. Tobler, "A Computer Movie Simulating Urban Growth in the Detroit Region," *Economic Geography*, 46, 2 (1970): 234–240. For a more explicitly multidimensional discussion of distance and of whether such distance dependence deserves to be described as a law or as an observed regularity, see Waldo Tobler, "On the First Law of Geography: A Reply," *Annals of the Association of American Geographers*, 94 (2) 2004: 304–310.

41. Even here, there are exceptions having to do with cultural, administrative, and geographic arbitrage. See Pankaj Ghemawat, *Redefining Global Strategy* (Boston: Harvard Business School Press, 2007), especially chapter 6.

42. Traditional models of comparative advantage imply the former prediction; models of intraindustry trade based on monopolistic competition are more consistent with the latter.

43. Edward E. Leamer and James Levinsohn, "International Trade Theory: The Evidence," in Gene M. Grossman and Kenneth Rogoff, eds., *Handbook of International Economics* (Amsterdam: Elsevier Science, 1995), 1339–1394.

44. Many of the differences cited in table 3-1 *aren't* followed up on in the specific estimation exercise reported on in the text, for varied reasons. Religion didn't work well in past empirical studies, nor did Hofstede-style cultural values. Legal origins are highly correlated with colonial history—which is more sharply measured in terms of colony/colonizer linkages than common colonizers. Political hostility is hard to measure systematically (although prior wars are reported by one study to shrink trade by 80%!). Most countries of any size do not vary much in terms of membership in the usual set of international organizations or ratification of the standard set of international treaties (although the U.S. is an outlier). Data on internal geographic distance continue to be problematic, and systematic, comparable data across broad cross-sections of countries are simply publicly unavailable for many of the kinds of economic differences/distances listed in table 3-1.

45. Note that this distance sensitivity is an elasticity in the sense that a distance sensitivity of –x% implies that a 1% increase in geographic distance leads to a predicted x% decrease in trade. The overall effect of geographic distance on trade is proportional to distance raised to the power of that distance sensitivity. For a distance sensitivity of –1, this formula simplifies to relative trade intensity being the reciprocal of relative distance.

46. This positive effect is consistent with traditional arbitrage theories.

47. Note that this figure picks up variations in the height of border effects rather than the (average) heights discussed earlier. It thereby quantifies, in a sense, the actual degree of difference, or distance. Also note that among the many dimensions of difference or distance missing from the calculation in the text is one that plays the single biggest role in boosting U.S.-Canadian trade relative to the averages: geographic proximity.

48. These values are, once again, elasticities. See note 44.

49. Christian Daude and Marcel Fratzscher, "The Pecking Order of Cross-Border Investment," European Central Bank working paper series, no. 590, February 2006. *Journal of International Economics* 74, no. 1 (2008): 94–119.

50. Jean-Michel Guldmann, "Spatial Interaction Models of International Telecommunication Flows," Department of City and Regional Planning, Ohio State University (paper prepared for presentation at the 40th Congress of the European Regional Science Association, Barcelona, Spain, September 2000).

51. Joshua Lewer and Hendrik Van den Berg, "A Gravity Model of Immigration," *Economics Letters* 99, no. 1 (2008): 164–167.

52. World Bank, *World Development Report 2009* (Washington, DC: World Bank, 2009), 149–152.

53. Yao Li, "Borders and Distance in Knowledge Spillovers: Dying over Time or Dying with Age? Evidence from Patent Citations," CESifo working paper series 2625, 2009.

54. To calibrate the effects of such variations in distance sensitivity, consider two focal distances, 1,000 kilometers (corresponding, roughly, to interactions within continental regions) and 10,000 kilometers (the interregional level). A distance sensitivity of –1 means, as noted above, that interactions over distances ten times as long will be only one-tenth as intense. A distance sensitivity of –0.25, in contrast, implies an intensity multiple of over one-half; one of –0.5 a multiple of about a third; and one of –0.75 a multiple of about a sixth. And increasing distance sensitivity farther, to –1.25, would reduce the intensity multiple to about one-twentieth.

55. It also found that common membership in a trading bloc no longer had a significant effect. Daude and Fratzscher, "The Pecking Order of Cross-Border Investment."

56. Based on data for 2006 from the U.S. Bureau of Economic Analysis processed by Bill Mataloni at the request of the author.

57. Paul Krugman, "The New Economic Geography: Where Are We?" discussion paper presented at International Symposium "Globalization and Regional Integration from the viewpoint of Spatial Economics," IDEJETRO, 2004, http://www.ide.go.jp/English/Inter/Sympo/pdf/krug_summary.pdf.

58. Céline Carrere and Maurice Schiff, "On the Geography of Trade: Distance Is Alive and Well," *Etudes et documents*, CERDI, May 2004.

59. Anne-Célia Disdier and Keith Head, "The Puzzling Persistence of the Distance Effect on Bilateral Trade," *Review of Economics and Statistics* 90, no. 1 (2008): 37–48, figure 3.

Chapter Four

1. Recent estimates of the gains from the proposals on the table in the Doha Round include Antoine Bouët and David Laborde Debucquet, "The Potential Cost of a Failed Doha Round," IFPRI discussion paper 00886, July 2009; and Gary C. Hufbauer, Jeffrey J. Schott and Woan F. Wong, *Figuring Out the Doha Round* (Washington D.C.: Institute for International Economics, 2010). For a critique that suggests that such estimates are too high and have been shrinking over time, see Frank Ackerman, "The Shrinking Gains from Trade: A Critical Assessment of Doha Round Projections," Global Development and Environment Institute, working paper 05-01, October 2005.

2. John B. Shoven and John Whalley, *Applying General Equilibrium*, (Cambridge, UK: Cambridge University Press, 1992), 3.

3. Dominique van der Mensbrugghe, "LINKAGE Technical Reference Document," World Bank, January 2005, http://siteresources.worldbank.org/INTPROSPECTS/Resources/334934-1100792545130/LinkageTechNote.pdf.

4. The characterization that follows applies to the bulk of such models, but there *are* individual modeling efforts that allow for imbalances, imperfect competition, other kinds of barriers to trade, and other extensions, usually one at a time. And several authors, e.g., Thomas Hertel and Terrie Walmsley of Purdue University's Global Trade Analysis Project, have worked on multiple extensions to the standard modeling set-up. I rely on and cite some of the nonstandard modeling efforts later in this chapter.

5. The focus on efficient outcomes is enabled by the assumptions listed, which ensure that a decentralized market economy, with individual agents maximizing their own utilities (deciding on work, investment, consumption, and savings) based on their endowments and (common) information on prices and investment opportunities, will achieve a competitive equilibrium in which market clearing prices accurately reflect value. Note that this is Adam Smith's invisible hand as formalized by Kenneth Arrow and Gerard Debreu, "Existence of an Equilibrium for a Competitive Economy," *Econometrica* 22, no. 3 (July 1954): 265–290.

6. More precisely, one should add up all the consumer surplus and producer profits generated by the increased trade—although, since producer profits are zero in such models, all the action is on the consumer side, with price decreases increasing their surplus.

7. Yvan Decreux and Lionel Fontagné, "Economic Impact of Potential Outcome of the DDA," CEPII-CIREM, February 2009.

8. Ximena Clark, David Dollar, and Alejandro Micco, "Port Efficiency, Maritime Transport Costs, and Bilateral Trade," *Journal of Development Economics* 75 (2004): 417–450.

9. Souleymane Coulibaly and Lionel Fontagné, "South-South Trade: Geography Matters," *Journal of African Economies* 15, no. 2 (June 2006): 313–341.

10. See the World Bank's *World Development Report 2009: Reshaping Economic Geography*, (Washington, DC: World Bank), 187.

11. Nannette Christ and Michael J. Ferrantino, "Land Transport for Exports: The Effects of Cost, Time, and Uncertainty in Sub-Saharan Africa," Office of Economics working paper, U.S. International Trade Commission, October 2009.

12. Note that the fourth category of CAGE differences, economic ones, has not been addressed here. The reason is that the usual conceptions of liberalization or opening up involve reducing artificial or unnecessary administrative, cultural, and geographic barriers so as to allow economic differences fuller play in determining cross-border outcomes. Given that, it would be inappropriate to treat economic differences as affording another separate array of levers for policy interventions.

13. Pankaj Ghemawat, *Strategy and the Business Landscape*, 3rd ed. (Englewood Cliffs, NJ: Pearson Prentice Hall, 2010).

14. Paul Samuelson and William Nordhaus, *Economics* (New York: McGraw Hill, 2004).

15. W. Antweiler and D. Trefler, "Increasing Returns and All That: A View from Trade," *American Economic Review* 92, no. 1 (2002): 93–119.

16. See, for instance, John Sutton's "Quality, Trade and the Moving Window: The Globalization Process," *Economic Journal* 117, no. 524 (November 2007): F469–F498.

17. Paul Romer, "New Goods, Old Theory, and the Welfare Costs of Trade Restrictions," *Journal of Development Economics* 43 (1994): 5–38.

18. In this respect, there *is* a fundamental difference between the ADDING value scorecard from the perspective of a private company as opposed to society: the intensification of competition is typically bad news from a private perspective even though it is good from a social perspective.

19. See, for instance, Padma Swaminathan and Thomas W. Hertel, "Introducing Monopolistic Competition into the GTAP Model," Global Trade Analysis Project technical paper no. 6, 1996.

20. Interest in such situations was motivated by the observation that intraindustry trade—much of it presumably trade in different varieties of a product (or an intermediate)—accounts for a substantial fraction of international trade.

21. Eduardo Pérez Motta, presentation at the ICTSD-World Bank-WTO Workshop on Recent Analyses of the Doha Round, Geneva, November 2, 2010.

22. Jagdish Bhagwati, *Free Trade Today*, (Princeton, NJ: Princeton University Press, 2003), 41. Bhagwati extended the idea of rent-seeking to encompass directly unproductive profit-seeking activities in general. For the original discussions, see Anne O. Krueger, "The Political Economy of the Rent-Seeking Society," *The American Economic Review* 64, no. 3 (June 1974): 291–303, and

Jagdish Bhagwati, "Directly Unproductive, Profit-Seeking (DUP) Activities," *The Journal of Political Economy* 90, no. 5 (Oct. 1982): 988–1002.

23. Robert M. Solow, "A Contribution to the Theory of Economic Growth," *Quarterly Journal of Economics* 70, no. 1 (February 1956): 65–94.

24. For an exception see Ken Itakura, Thomas Hertel, and Jeff Reimer, "The Contribution of Productivity Linkages to the General Equilibrium Analysis of Free Trade Agreements," Global Trade Analysis Project working paper no. 23, 2003.

25. Bruno Cassiman and Elena Golovko, "Productivity of Catalan Firms: International Exposure and (Product) Innovation," in *Competitiveness in Catalonia*, eds. Pankaj Ghemawat and Xavier Vives, Reports of the Public-Private Sector Research Center, IESE Business School, prepared for Foment del Treball, July 2009.

26. See Wolfgang Keller, "International Trade, Foreign Direct Investment, and Technology Spillovers," in *The Handbook of the Economics of Innovation*, eds. B. Hall and N. Rosenberg, (Oxford: North-Holland, 2010), 792–829.

27. For a survey focused on this point, see E. J. Bartelsman and M. Doms, "Understanding Productivity: Lessons from Longitudinal Microdata," *Journal of Economic Literature* 38 (2000): 569–594; and, for a recent study suggesting that the contribution of churn to productivity growth may have been underestimated significantly, see Lucia Foster, John Haltiwanger, and Chad Syverson, "Reallocation, Firm Turnover, and Efficiency: Selection on Productivity or Profitability?" *American Economic Review* 98, no. 1 (March 2008): 394–425.

28. Meeting with Pascal Lamy, Chongqing China, September 9, 2010.

29. Gianni Zanini with Andreas Maurer and Aaditya Mattoo, "Services Trade, Reforms, and International Negotiations," April 20, 2010, http://www.thecommonwealth.org/files/223344/FileName/TrendsandPerformance-GZanini.pdf; and Aaditya Mattoo with Ingo Borchert and Batshur Gootiiz, "Services in Doha: What Is on the Table?" presentation at the ICTSD-World Bank-WTO Workshop on Recent Analyses of the Doha Round, Geneva, November 2, 2010.

30. Decreux and Fontagné, "Economic Impact of Potential Outcome of the DDA," 2009.

31. For a discussion of how to incorporate FDI into CGE models, see Csilla Lakatos and Terrie Walmsley, "Modeling Cross-Border Investment in CGE: Some Alternatives and Mechanisms," Global Trade Analysis Project, unpublished draft, April 2009.

32. See Bob Hamilton and John Whalley, "Efficiency and Distributional Implications of Global Restrictions on Labour Mobility: Calculations and Policy Implications," *Journal of Development Economics* 14, no. 1–2 (1984): 61–75; and Jonathon W. Moses and Bjørn Letnes, "The Economic Costs to International Labor Restrictions: Revisiting the Empirical Discussion," *World Development* 32, no. 10 (2004): 1609–1626. A more up-to-date treatment focused on current issues in U.S. immigration policy is provided by Angel H. Aguiar and Terrie L. Walmsley, "A Dynamic General Equilibrium Model of International Migration," Center for Global Trade Analysis, 2010.

33. These calculations are based on GNP per capita adjusted for terms of trade effects. See D. Turner et al., "The Macroeconomic Implications of Ageing in a Global Context," OECD Economics Department, working paper 193, 1998.

34. Keller, "International Trade, Foreign Direct Investment, and Technology Spillovers."

35. The data are drawn from Martin Grueber and Tim Studt, "2010 Global R&D Funding Forecast" for forty countries in *R&D* magazine, December 22, 2009, www.rdmag.com.

36. Adam B. Jaffe and Manuel Trajtenberg, "International Knowledge Flows: Evidence from Patent Citations," *Economics of Innovation and New Technology* 8, no. 1 (1999): 105–136.

37. Wolfgang Keller, "The Geography and Channels of Diffusion at the World's Technology Frontier," NBER working paper no. W8150, March 2001.

38. David T. Coe, Elhanan Helpman, and Alexander W. Hoffmaister, "International R&D Spillovers and Institutions," IMF working paper WP/08/104, April 2008.

39. Cited in G. Pascal Zachary, *The Global Me: New Cosmopolitans and the Competitive Edge—Picking Globalism's Winners and Losers* (New York: Public Affairs, 2000), 59.

40. Scott E. Page, *The Difference: How the Power of Diversity Creates Better Groups, Firms, Schools, and Societies* (Princeton, NJ: Princeton University Press, 2008), 131–173.

41. Tyler Cowen, *Creative Destruction: How Globalization Is Changing the World's Cultures*, (Princeton, NJ: Princeton University Press, 2002): 129.

42. Barry Eichengreen and David Leblang, "Democracy and Globalization," *Economics and Politics* 20, no. 3 (2008): 289–334.

43. See Randall Morck, David Stangeland, and Bernard Yeung, "Inherited Wealth, Corporate Control, and Economic Growth," in *Concentrated Corporate Ownership*, ed. Randall Morck (Chicago, IL: University of Chicago Press, 2000), 319–369.

44. This includes all forms of military response: combat, show of force, contingency positioning or reconnaissance, evacuation or security, and peacekeeping.

45. Quoted in Wagner James Au, "The Second Life of Thomas P. M. Barnett," *New World Notes*, October 27, 2005, http://nwn.blogs.com/nwn/2005/10/the_second_life.html.

46. Andreas Hatzigeorgiou, "Migration as Trade Facilitation: Assessing the Links Between International Migration and Trade," *B. E. Journal of Economic Analysis and Policy* 10, issue 1, article 24 (2010): 1–33.

47. For further discussion of symbolic—and other—commitments, see chapter 2 of Pankaj Ghemawat, *Commitment: The Dynamic of Strategy* (New York: Free Press, 1991).

48. Antoine Bouët and David Labourde, "Assessing the Potential Cost of a Failed Doha Round," *World Trade Review* 9, no. 2 (2010): 319–351.

Chapter Five

1. Karl Marx, *Capital* (London: Penguin Classics, 1990) , 929.

2. Bruce D. Henderson, *Henderson on Corporate Strategy* (Cambridge, MA: Abt Books, 1979).

3. Bernard Wysocki Jr., "No. 1 Can Be Runaway Even in a Tight Race, " *Wall Street Journal*, June 27, 1999, "Outlook" section.

4. This information is drawn from UNCTAD's ranking of the top nonfinancial transnational corporations based on 2007 foreign assets, http://www.unctad.org/templates/Page.asp?intItemID=2443%26lang=1.

5. World Car Market 1927, 1920-30.com, http://www.1920-30.com/automobiles/world-car-market.html.

6. For a history of Maruti Suzuki, see R. C. Bhargava with Seetha, *The Maruti Story: How a Public Sector Company Put India on Wheels* (Noida, India: Collins Busines, 2010).

7. Pankaj Ghemawat and Fariborz Ghadar, "The Dubious Logic of Global Megamergers," *Harvard Business Review* 78, no. 4 (July–August 2000): 64–72. Ghadar and I were working with a Herfindahl measure of concentration (the sum of squares of firms' market shares) that went down significantly in autos even though the simple ten-firm concentration ratio reported in figure 5-1 did not. To see why, note that figure 5-1 indicates steeper declines of the five-firm and three-firm concentration ratios (as well as of the share of the single largest firm—although it is not reported) than the ten-firm concentration ratio. This indicates a tendency toward convergence rather than divergence in size among the ten largest automakers, which depresses the Herfindahl ratio but not the simple ten-firm concentration ratio.

8. Pankaj Ghemawat and Fariborz Ghadar, "Global Integration ≠ Global Concentration," *Industrial and Corporate Change* 15 (August 2006): 595–623.

9. More specifically, the focal period was ten-plus years up to the second half of the 1990s. The data was available from a variety of different sources; as noted above, there are no standardized sources of data for concentration measures. Details on the data can be found in Ghemawat and Ghadar, "Global Integration ≠ Global Concentration."

10. This is based on comparing Herfindahl concentration ratios in 1950 compiled by Raymond Vernon and his associates at Harvard for cargo and passenger airlines, aluminum

smelting, automobiles, copper, oil production, and paper and board with our calculations of Herfindahls (based on the same data used above to calculate five-firm concentration ratios) for more recent years.

11. John Sutton, *Sunk Costs and Market Structure: Price Competition, Advertising, and the Evolution of Concentration* (London: MIT Press, 1991).

12. Also note that Euromonitor concentration data are probably biased upward by their weaker coverage of emerging markets, where most recent growth has been located. Advanced country multinationals that dominate the ranks of the top five in most categories have had trouble, so far, building their positions in emerging markets up to the share levels that they command in markets in advanced countries.

13. Steffen Lauster and Samrat Sharma, "Is Category Consolidation Inevitable? Shaping Category Dynamics to Win in CPG," Perspective, reports and white papers from Booz & Company, 2010. While the Booz study focuses on market shares in the U.S., if global concentration levels were actually increasing significantly, it would be unlikely for national concentration to exhibit such a mixed pattern in what is still, for most categories, the world's largest single market.

14. John Sutton, *Technology and Market Structure: Theory and History* (Cambridge, MA.: MIT Press, 1998) chapter 5.

15. Jeffrey Hayzlett, chief marketing officer of Kodak, speaking at a Houston Interactive Marketing Assoc. (HiMA) luncheon as cited by Savage in "Brand Strategy: Reinventing Kodak," blog post, March 8, 2010, http://blog.savagebrands.com/kodak-brand-strategy/.

16. Joseph A. Schumpeter, *Capitalism, Socialism, and Democracy* (New York: Harper, 1942), 84.

17. While other sources have suggested smaller decreases, there is general agreement that the five-firm seller concentration ratio in this industry has dropped since the mid-1980s.

18. Pankaj Ghemawat, *Redefining Global Strategy* (Boston: Harvard Business School Press, 2007), 21.

19. United Nations Conference on Trade and Development (UNCTAD), Iron Ore Market 2009–2011, Geneva, June 2010.

20. Notice on the Definition of Relevant Market for the Purposes of Community Competition Law, EC Communication 97/C 372/03, http://europa.eu/legislation_summaries/competition/firms/l26073_en.htm.

21. Susan S. DeSanti (coord.), "Competition Policy in the New High-Tech, Global Marketplace," Federal Trade Commission, May 1996, 4.

22. Joseph Farrell and Carl Shapiro, "Antitrust Evaluation of Horizontal Mergers: An Economic Alternative to Market Definition," *B. E. Journal of Theoretical Economics* 10, no. 1 (February 2010).

23. John A. Quelch, quoted in Barnaby J. Feder, "For White Goods, a World Beckons," *New York Times*, November 25, 1997.

24. This is based on comparing Herfindahl concentration ratios in 1950 and more recently for the seven industries out of our basic sample of eleven for which Raymond Vernon and his collaborators compiled 1950 data.

25. For more detail, consult my textbook, *Strategy and the Business Landscape*, 3rd ed. (Upper Saddle River, NJ: Pearson Prentice Hall, 2010), particularly chapters 2 and 4.

26. United Nations Conference on Trade and Development (UNCTAD), Iron Ore Market 2009–2011, Geneva, June 2010.

27. Keith Bradsher, "After China's Rare Earth Embargo, a New Calculus," *The New York Times*, October 29, 2010, http://www.nytimes.com/2010/10/30/business/global/30rare.html.

28. Olivia Lang, "Row Over Exotic Minerals That Make Modern Life Tick," October 21, 2010, http://www.bbc.co.uk/news/world-asia-pacific-11584229.

29. "Dirty Business: China Is Squeezing the Supply of Vital Rare Earths. But Not for Long," *The Economist*, September 30, 2010, http://www.economist.com/node/17155730?story_id=17155730.

30. Keith Bradsher, "After China's Rare Earth Embargo, a New Calculus," *The New York Times*, October 29, 2010, http://www.nytimes.com/2010/10/30/business/global/30rare.html.

31. "Rare earths supply deal between Japan and Vietnam," *BBC News*, October 31, 2010, http://www.bbc.co.uk/news/world-asia-pacific-11661330.

32. Yvan Decreux and Lionel Fontagné, "A Quantitative Assessment of the Outcome of the Doha Development Agenda," Centre d'Etudes Prospectives et d'Informations Internationales (CEPII)," working paper 2006-10.

33. To some readers, price regulation may sound like an extreme intrusion of government into market functioning, but regulating prices of natural monopolies, like the utilities that distribute water and electricity to homes, is a long-standing practice. And it does not imply a broader requirement for price regulation in other types of markets.

Chapter Six

1. S. Kahn Ribeiro et al., "2007: Transport and Its Infrastructure," in *Climate Change 2007: Mitigation. Contribution of Working Group III to the Fourth Assessment Report of the Intergovernmental Panel on Climate Change*, eds. B. Metz, O. R. Davidson, P. R. Bosch, R. Dave, and L. A. Meyer (Cambridge, UK, and New York: Cambridge University Press, 2007), 328.

2. R. K. Pachauri and A. Reisinger, eds., "Climate Change 2007: Synthesis Report," Intergovernmental Panel on Climate Change (IPCC), November 2007, 36.

3. WTO, "The Impact of Trade Opening on Climate Change," http://www.wto.org/english/tratop_e/envir_e/climate_impact_e.htm.

4. International Energy Agency, "CO2 Emissions from Fuel Combustion: Highlights," http://www.iea.org/co2highlights/CO2highlights.pdf. Calculation is based on the following: according to sectoral approach, there were 28,962.4 Mt of CO2 emissions from fuel combustion in 2007. Of these, 6,632.5 Mt were from the transport sector, and 610.4 Mt and 411.6 Mt were from international marine bunkers and international aviation bunkers, respectively.

5. WTO, "The Impact of Trade Opening on Climate Change."

6. International Maritime Organization, "Prevention of Air Pollution from Ships: Second IMO GHG Study 2009," April 2009.

7. International Maritime Organization, "IMO and the Environment, 2009," http://www5.imo.org/SharePoint/blastDataOnly.asp/data_id=26878/IMOandtheEnvironment2009.pdf.

8. Ibid.

9. Air Transport Action Group, "Emissions," http://www.atag.org/content/showissue.asp?pageid=1078&level1=3&level2=472&level3=1078.

10. Air Transport Action Group, "Environment," http://www.atag.org/content/showissue.asp?folderid=472&level1=3&level2=472&

11. Carol McAusland and Christopher Costello, "Avoiding Invasives: Trade Related Policies for Controlling Unintentional Exotic Species Introductions," *Journal of Environmental Economics and Management* 48 (2004): 954–977. There are also analyses by D. Pimentel et al. indicating ongoing direct and indirect ecological costs at more than $100 billion annually: see David Pimentel, Rodolfo Zuniga, and Doug Morrison, "Update on the Environmental and Economic Costs Associated with Alien-Invasive Species in the United States," *Ecological Economics* 52 (2005): 273–288. However, such estimates include tens of billions dollars apiece for the costs of alien species such as rats and cats and should be stacked against the ongoing benefits from all the alien species ever introduced to the U.S., which would dwarf them.

12. The analysis of trade's impacts on the environment according to scale, technique, and composition effects draws on Gene M. Grossman and Alan B. Krueger, "Environmental Effects of a North American Free Trade Agreement," in Peter M. Garber, *The U.S.–Mexico Free Trade Agreement* (Cambridge, MA: MIT Press, 1993), 13–56.

13. W. Antweiler, B. R. Copeland, and M. S. Taylor, "Is Trade Good for the Environment?" *American Economic Review* 91 (2001): 878.

14. Jeffrey Frankel, "Environmental Effects of International Trade," Kennedy School of Government, Harvard University, HKS faculty research working paper series RWP09-006, January 2009.

15. Ibid.

16. Ibid.

17. Stefan Theil, "No Country Is More 'Green by Design,'" *Newsweek*, June 28, 2008.

18. Awudu Abdulai and Linda Ramcke, "The Impact of Trade and Economic Growth on the Environment," Kiel Institute for the World Economy, working paper 1491, March 2009.

19. Roldan Muradian, Martin O'Connor, and Joan Martinez-Alier, "Embodied Pollution in Trade: Estimating the 'Environmental Load Displacement' of Industrialised Countries," Fondazione Eni Enrico Mattei, July 2001.

20. Jeffrey Frankel, "Environmental Effects of International Trade."

21. Keith Bradsher, "After China's Rare Earth Embargo, a New Calculus," *New York Times*, October 29, 2010, http://www.nytimes.com/2010/10/30/business/global/30rare.html.

22. Jeffrey Frankel, "Environmental Effects of International Trade."

23. Joseph Stiglitz, *Making Globalization Work* (New York: W. W. Norton, 2007), 164.

24. Concerns have also been raised about whether the WTO might get in the way of countries' abilities to regulate local pollutants—in the sense that countries applying high standards to domestic production might not be able to enforce the same standards on products imported into their countries. Actually, WTO rulings have supported countries' ability to enact such measures as long as they do not unnecessarily discriminate against foreign products.

25. Steven Hayward and Julie Majeres, *Index of Leading Environmental Indicators 2001* (San Francisco, CA: Pacific Research Institute for Public Policy, 2001) 18.

26. European Commission, "Protection of the Ozone Layer," http://ec.europa.eu/environment/ozone/international_action.htm.

27. United Nations Development Programme, "20 Years of the Montreal Protocol," http://www.undp.org/chemicals/20yearsmontrealprotocol/.

28. See "Shell Energy Scenarios to 2050," p. 37, http://www-static.shell.com/static/public/downloads/brochures/corporate_pkg/scenarios/shell_energy_scenarios_2050.pdf.

29. Ibid., 13.

30. Alison Benjamin, "Stern: Climate Change a 'Market Failure,'" *The Guardian*, November 29, 2009, http://www.guardian.co.uk/environment/2007/nov/29/climatechange.carbonemissions.

31. David Anthoff and Richard S. J. Tol, "On International Equity Weights and National Decision Making on Climate Change," *Journal of Environmental Economics and Management* 60, no. 1 (2010): 14–20.

32. Abdulai and Ramcke, "The Impact of Trade and Economic Growth on the Environment," 5.

Chapter Seven

1. Food and Agricultural Organization (FAO) of the United Nations, "The State of Food Insecurity in the World: Economic Crises—Impacts and Lessons Learned," 2009.

2. Ian Goldin, "Globalization and Risks for Business: Implications of an Increasingly Interconnected World," Lloyd's 360 Risk Insight In Depth Report, 2010.

3. Robin Burgess and Dave Donaldson, "Can Openness Mitigate the Effects of Weather Shocks? Evidence from India's Famine Era," *American Economic Review: Papers and Proceedings* 100 (2010): 449–453.

4. Estimates based on figure 9.7 of Bruno Solnik and Dennis McLeavey, *Global Investments*, 6th ed. (Boston: Pearson Prentice Hall, 2009), p. 400.

5. See, for instance, Vivek Bhargava, Daniel K. Konku, and D. K. Malhotra, "Does International Diversification Pay," *Financial Counseling and Planning* 15, no. 1, (2004): 53–63.

6. Joost Driessen and Luc Laeven, "International Portfolio Diversification Benefits: Cross-Country Evidence from a Local Perspective," *Journal of Banking and Finance* 31, no. 6: 1693–1712.

7. Marianne Baxter and Urban J. Jermann, "The International Diversification Puzzle Is Worse Than You Think," *American Economic Review* 87, no. 1 (March 1997): 170–180, went so far as to suggest that investors should short their home country markets to diversify their home country labor market exposure. Later studies challenged Baxter and Jermann's results and indicated that labor market exposure and correlations with domestic and foreign equity markets vary significantly by country and by industry, but the broad point is still worth noting. For a more recent treatment, see Carolina Fugazza, Maela Giofre, and Giovanna Nicodano, "International Diversification and Labor Income Risk," Center for Research on Pensions and Welfare Policies, CeRP working papers no. 67, 2007.

8. John Cassidy, *How Markets Fail: The Logic of Economic Calamities* (New York: Farrar, Straus and Giroux, 2009), 171.

9. Ibid., 177.

10. Robert J. Shiller, "Stock Prices and Social Dynamics," Brookings Papers on Economic Activity 2, 1984.

11. Joshua D. Coval and Tobias J. Moskowitz, "The Geography of Investment: Informed Trading and Asset Prices," *Journal of Political Economy* 109, no. 4 (2001).

12. Bank for International Settlements, Monetary and Economic Department, "OTC Derivatives Market Activity in the Second Half of 2009," May 2010.

13. Jonathan Spicer, "Globally, the Flash Crash Is No Flash in the Pan," Reuters, October 15, 2010.

14. Irene Aldridge, "What Is High-Frequency Trading, After All?" *Huffington Post*, July 8, 2010.

15. Spicer, "Globally, the Flash Crash Is No Flash in the Pan."

16. Karen E. Dynan, Douglas W. Elmendorf, and Daniel E. Sichel, "The Evolution of Household Income Volatility," Brookings Institution, February 2008.

17. M. Ahyan Kose, Eswar Prasad, Kenneth Rogoff, and Shang-Jin Wei, "Financial Globalization: A Reappraisal," IMF staff papers 56, no. 1 (2009): 8–62.

18. Bruno Solnik and Dennis McLeavey, *Global Investments*, 6th ed. (Boston: Pearson Prentice Hall, 2009).

19. William N.Goetzmann, Lingfeng Li, and K. Geert Rouwenhorst, "Long-Term Global Market Correlations," DNB Staff Reports, no. 09/2003.

20. Between 1997 and 2007, the French stock market had a 91% monthly correlation with a European market average, a 70% correlation with the U.S. market, and a 35% correlation with the Japanese market. Over the same period, U.S. stock market had a 76% monthly correlation with Europe and a 43% correlation with Japan. These correlations are based on monthly returns in U.S. dollars. (Source: Bruno Solnik and Dennis McLeavey, *Global Investments*, p. 394.)

21. M. Ahyan Kose, Christopher Otrok, and Eswar S. Prasad, "Global Business Cycles: Convergence or Decoupling?" NBER working paper 14292, October 2008. Note: Based on a comparison of the period 1985 to 2005 with the period 1960 to 1984.

22. Carmen M. Reinhart and Kenneth S. Rogoff, *This Time Is Different: Eight Centuries of Financial Folly* (Princeton, NJ: Princeton University Press, 2009).

23. Laura Alfaro, Sebnem Kalemi-Ozcan, and Vadym Volosovych, "Capital Flows in a Globalized World: The Role of Policies and Institutions," NBER chapters, in *Capital Controls and Capital Flows in Emerging Economies: Policies, Practices and Consequences* (2007), 19–72.

24. UNCTAD, *Trade and Development Report*, 2008.

25. See footnote 4 on page 12 of Kose et al., "Financial Globalization."

26. M. Ayhan Kose, Eswar S. Prasad, and Marco E. Terrones, "Does Financial Globalization Promote Risk Sharing?" *Journal of Development Economics* 80 (2009): 258–270.

27. Kose et al., "Financial Globalization: A Reappraisal."

28. Manuel Agosin and Franklin Huaita, "Overreaction in Capital Flows to Emerging Markets: Booms and Sudden Stops," Serie Documentos de Trabajo N. 295, April 2009.

29. Kose et al., "Financial Globalization: A Reappraisal."

30. Defined typically as holding at least a 10% share in a foreign business, implying at least some degree of control over the foreign enterprise.

31. Kose et al., "Financial Globalization," 2009, 37.

32. Gianni De Nicolo and Luciana Juvenal, "Financial Integration, Globalization, Growth, and Systemic Real Risk," Federal Reserve Bank of St. Louis working paper 2010-012D, revised October 2010.

33. Kose et al., "Financial Globalization: A Reappraisal," 38.

34. Ibid.

35. Ibid., 49.

36. Philippe Legrain, *Open World: The Truth About Globalization* (Chicago: Ivan R. Dee, 2004), 289.

37. For a compelling review of such phenomena across the centuries, see Charles P. Kindleberger and Robert Aliber, *Manias, Panics, and Crashes: A History of Financial Crises*, 5th ed. (New York: Wiley, 2005).

38. FAO, "The State of Food Insecurity in the World."

39. FAO, "Food Outlook, Global Market Analysis," June 2009.

40. FAO, "Staple Foods: What Do People Eat?" Corporate Document Repository, http://www.fao.org/docrep/u8480e/u8480e07.htm.

41. World Trade Organization, International Trade Statistics, 2000 and 2009.

42. United Nations Development Programme, *Human Development Report 2003*, 155.

43. Concepción Calpe, "International Trade in Rice, Recent Developments and Prospects," (presentation to the World Rice Research Conference, November 5–7, 2004).

44. Derek D. Headley, *Rethinking the Global Food Crisis: The Role of Trade Shocks*," International Food Policy Research Institute discussion paper 0958, March 2010.

45. Paul A. Dorosh, Simon Dradri, and Steven Haggblade, "Alternative Approaches for Moderating Food Insecurity and Price Volatility in Zambia," Food Security Collaborative Policy Briefs 54630, Michigan State University, 2007.

46. Matt Ridley, *The Rational Optimist: How Prosperity Evolves* (New York: HarperCollins, 2010), 143–149.

47. Ibid., 337–340.

48. Legrain, *Open World*, 276.

49. Boris Groendahl and Albert Schmieder, "$60 bln Greek Debt Vanish and It's Not What You Think," Reuters, April 29, 2010, http://uk.reuters.com/article/idUKLDE63R2GB20100429.

50. Joseph E. Stiglitz, "Risk and Global Economic Architecture: Why Full Financial Integration May Be Undesirable," NBER working paper 15718, February 2010.

51. Nassim Nicholas Taleb, *The Black Swan: The Impact of the Highly Improbable*, 2nd ed. (New York: Random House, 2010), 312.

Chapter Eight

1. This calculation is based on the total Chinese portion of "foreign official and private holdings of U.S. Treasury securities" of $1,036 billion at the end of 2009 as reported in the U.S. Bureau of Economic Analysis report, "The International Investment Position of the United States at Yearend 2009" by Elena L. Nguyen, July 2010. Population data are based on the United Nations Population Division's "World Population Prospects: The 2008 Revision," May 2009. Figures in text were rounded to nearest hundred dollars.

2. The multicountry analysis of net foreign asset positions produced by Lane and Milesi-Ferreti based on which figure 8-2 was generated relied on the U.S. Bureau of Economic Analysis's July 2009 report on the U.S. Net International Investment Position, which showed a deterioration from –2.087 trillion to –2.140 trillion whereas the July 2010 revision of the same dataset indicated an improvement from –2.094 trillion to –1.916 trillion.

3. Nguyen, "The International Investment Position of the United States at Yearend 2009." Percent of GDP calculation uses GDP as reported in IMF, *World Economic Outlook*, April 2010 revision.

4. Goldman Sachs, "Current Account and Demographics: The Road Ahead," Global Economics Paper 202, August 12, 2010.

5. Niall Ferguson, "The Trillion Dollar Question: China or America?" *Telegraph.co.uk*, June 1, 2009, http://www.telegraph.co.uk/comment/5424112/The-trillion-dollar-question-China-or-America.html.

6. Jahangir Aziz and Steven Dunaway, "China's Rebalancing Act," *Finance and Development*, September 2007.

7. International Social Security Association, "China's Health Care Reforms Move Toward Universal Coverage," September 23, 2009, http://www.issa.int/aiss/layout/set/print/content/view/full/68609.

8. Goldman Sachs, "China's Savings Rate and Its Long-term Outlook," Global Economics 191, October 16, 2009.

9. Lawrence B. Lindsey, "Yuan Compromise?" *Wall Street Journal*, Thursday, April 6, 2006.

10. Two is the minimum number of countries required to make the basic point, but that restriction is inessential to the fundamental conclusions. Also note that countries can differ in terms of their populations, although this point is not highlighted in the analysis in the text since it is effectively conducted in per capita terms.

11. The maximization of welfare involves maximizing the present values of streams of profits and of consumer surplus. Work in the theory of growth as well as the theory of the firm indicates that the values chosen by a firm or an economy that is maximizing growth are not necessarily the same as the values chosen by an economy that is maximizing surplus or welfare.

12. Culture guru Geert Hofstede added a fifth cultural dimension, long-term orientation, to his well-known set of four—power distance, individualism versus collectivism, masculinity, and uncertainty avoidance—largely in response to work in China suggesting that the reported difference with the U.S. on this dimension dwarfs those on the other dimensions.

13. Horst Siebert, *The World Economy* (New York: Routledge, 2002), 82.

14. For some strategic discussion of the broader U.S.-Chinese relationship, see chapter 13.

15. Wolfgang Lutz and Warren C. Sanderson, introduction to *The End of Population Growth in the 21st Century: New Challenges for Human Capital Formation and Sustainable Development*, eds. Wolfgang Lutz, Warren C. Sanderson, and Sergei Scherbov (Sterling, VA: Earthscan, 2004), 1.

16. These calculations are based on GNP per capita adjusted for terms of trade effects. See D. Turner, C. Giorno, A. De Serres, A. Vourc'h, and P. Richardson, "The Macroeconomic Implications of Ageing in a Global Context," OECD economics department working paper 193, 1998.

17. David E. Bloom and David Canning, "Global Demographic Change: Dimensions and Economic Significance," NBER working paper 10817, September 2004.

18. According to the UN, the share of migrants in the world population (excluding the former Soviet Union and Czechoslovakia for comparability because their breakups caused people to become reclassified as migrants without actual movement) grew from 2.7% to 2.8% between 1960 and 2010 (United Nations Development Programme, *Human Development Report 2009*, 30). The International Organization for Migration (IOM) reports that migrants formed 2.5% of the world population in 1960 and 3.1% in 2010 (IOM, *World Migration Report 2005*, 379, http://www.iom.int/jahia/webdav/site/myjahiasite/shared/shared/mainsite/published_docs/books/wmr_sec03.pdf ,and IOM website, Facts and Figures, http://www.iom.int/jahia/Jahia/about-migration/facts-and-figures/lang/en).

19. United Nations Development Programme, *Human Development Report 2009*, 29.

20. Eric Ng and John Whalley, "Visas and Work Permits: Possible Global Negotiating Initiatives," *Review of International Organizations* 3, no. 3 (2008): 259–285.

21. N. Foner, *From Ellis Island to JFK* (New Haven, CT: Yale University Press, 2002), as cited in United Nations Development Programme, *Human Development Report 2009*, 30.

22. Ng and Whalley, "Visas and Work Permits."

23. David McKenzie, "Passport Costs and Legal Barriers to Emigration," World Bank Policy Research working paper 3783, December 2005.

24. United Nations Development Programme, *Human Development Report 2009*, 29.

25. Ibid., 30–32.

26. See Bob Hamilton and John Whalley, "Efficiency and Distributional Implications of Global Restrictions on Labour Mobility: Calculations and Policy Implications," *Journal of Development Economics* 14, no. 1–2 (1984): 61–75; and Jonathon W. Moses and Bjørn Letnes, "The Economic Costs to International Labor Restrictions: Revisiting the Empirical Discussion," *World Development* 32, no. 10 (2004): 1609–1626.

27. World Bank, "Global Economic Prospects 2006: Economic Implications of Remittances and Migration," 2006.

28. United Nations Development Programme, *Human Development Report 2009*, 24.

29. D. van der Mensbrugghe and D. Roland-Holst, "Global Economic Prospects for Increasing Developing Country Migration into Developed Countries," Human Development research paper 50, United Nations Development Programme, October 2009, as cited in United Nations Development Programme, *Human Development Report 2009*.

30. Eduardo Porter, "Cost of Illegal Immigration May Be Less Than Meets the Eye," *New York Times*, April 16, 2006.

31. George J. Borjas, "The Labor Demand Curve Is Downward Sloping: Reexamining the Impact of Immigration on the Labor Market," NBER working paper 9755, June 2003.

32. Howard F. Chang, "The Economic Impact of International Labor Migration: Recent Estimates and Policy Implications," Scholarship at Penn Law, paper no. 132, 2007.

33. Porter, "Cost of Illegal Immigration May Be Less Than Meets the Eye."

34. Gianmarco I. P. Ottaviano and Giovanni Peri, "Immigration and National Wages: Clarifying the Theory and the Empirics," NBER working paper 14188, July 2008.

35. United Nations Development Programme, *Human Development Report 2009*, 86.

36. Philippe Legrain, "Let Them In," *Forbes*, June 28, 2010.

37. Ibid.

38. Wolfgang Lutz and Sergei Scherbov, "The Contribution of Migration to Europe's Demographic Future: Projections for the EU-25 to 2050," IIASA Interim Report IR-07-024, September 17, 2007.

39. United Nations Population Department, "Replacement Migration: Is It a Solution to Declining and Ageing Populations?" 2000, cited in L. Alan Winters, "Demographic Transition and the Temporary Mobility of Labour" (paper for G20 Workshop on Demographic Challenges and Migration, August 27–28, 2005).

40. Winters, "Demographic Transition and the Temporary Mobility of Labour."

41. United Nations Development Programme, *Human Development Report 2009*, 89–90.

42. Frederic Docquier and Hillel Rapoport, "How Does Skilled Emigration Affect Developing Countries? Facts, Theory and Policy" (paper for G20 Workshop on Demographic Challenges and Migration, August 27–28, 2005).

43. Michel Beine, Frederic Docquier, and Hillel Rapoport, "Brain Drain and Economic Growth: Theory and Evidence," *Journal of Development Economics* 64 (2001): 275–289.

44. United Nations Development Programme, *Human Development Report 2009*, 72–74.

45. Ibid., 77.

46. Terrie Walmsley, S. Amer Ahmed, and Christopher Parsons, "The Impact of Liberalizing Labour Mobility in the Pacific Region," Global Trade Analysis Project working paper no. 31, 2009 (revised).

47. See John Hicks, *The Theory of Wages* (London: Macmillan, 1932); and Arthur C. Pigou, *The Theory of Unemployment* (London: Macmillan, 1932).

Chapter Nine

1. Milton Friedman, *Free to Choose: A Personal Statement* (San Diego, CA: Harcourt, 1980), chapter 5.

2. Branko Milanovic, "Where in the World Are You? Assessing the Importance of Circumstance and Effort in a World of Different Mean Country Incomes and (almost) No Migration," World Bank Policy Research working paper 4493, January 2008.

3. Branko Milanovic, "Global Inequality and Global Inequality Extraction Ratio: The Story of the Last Two Centuries," World Bank/University of Maryland, July 30, 2009 (paper available online at http://mpra.ub.uni-muenchen.de/16535/).

4. Jadish Bhagwati, *In Defense of Globalization* (Oxford: Oxford University Press, 2004), 67.

5. Philippe Aghion, Eve Caroli, and Cecilia García-Peñalosa, "Inequality and Economic Growth: The Perspective of the New Growth Theories," *Journal of Economic Literature* 37, no. 4 (December 1999): 1615–1660.

6. Machiko Nissanke and Erik Thorbecke, "Channels and Policy Debate in the Globalization-Inequality-Poverty Nexus," United Nations University—World Institute for Development Economics research discussion paper 2005/08, June 2005.

7. World Bank, *World Development Report 2000/2001: Attacking Poverty* (New York: Oxford University Press, 2001), 56–57.

8. Jeffrey Sachs, "The Strategic Significance of Global Inequality," *Washington Quarterly* 24, no. 3 (2001): 185–198.

9. The actual empirical evidence in this regard is reviewed later in this chapter.

10. See Paul A. Samuelson, "Where Ricardo and Mill Rebut and Confirm Arguments of Mainstream Economists Supporting Globalization," *Journal of Economic Perspectives*, vol. 18, no. 3 (Summer, 2004): 135–146. The mechanism that actually lowered U.S. welfare in Samuelson's paper involved faster productivity growth in China in sectors in which it imported U.S. goods diminishing trade in those sectors—with protectionism in the United States only making things worse.

11. See, for instance, the (gentle) treatment in Jagdish Bhagwati, Arvind Panagariya, and T. N. Srinivasan, "The Muddles over Outsourcing," *Journal of Economic Perspectives* 18, no. 4 (Fall, 2004): 93–114.

12. Jeffrey G. Williamson, "Globalization, Labor Markets and Policy Backlash in the Past," *Journal of Economic Perspectives* 12, no. 4. (Autumn 1998): 51–72.

13. Branko Milanovic, "Global Inequality Recalculated: The Effect of New 2005 PPP Estimates of Global Inequality," World Bank Policy Research working paper 5061, September 2009, 13.

14. For the era of World 1.0, statistics compiled by national governments allow for more formal quantification and specifically the estimation of Gini indices. The estimation given in this

sentence is for 1820. Branko Milanovic, "Global Inequality and Global Inequality Extraction Ratio: The Story of the Last Two Centuries," MPRA paper 16535, July 31, 2009.

15. U.S. Census Bureau, Income, Table H-4, Gini Ratios for Households, by Race and Hispanic Origin of Householder: 1967 to 2007, http://www.census.gov/hhes/www/income/data/historical/household/h04.html.

16. Milanovic, "Global Inequality and Global Inequality Extraction Ratio," 13.

17. Ibid., 12.

18. Range established by studies cited above by Milanovic (upper bound) and Pinkovskiy and Sala-i-Martin (lower bound).

19. James B. Davies, Susanna Sandstrom, Anthony Shorrocks, and Edward N. Wolff, "The World Distribution of Household Wealth," United Nations University—World Institute for Development Economics research discussion paper no. 2008/03, February 2008, 7.

20. OECD, "Policy Brief: Globalisation, Jobs, and Wages," June 2007.

21. U.S. Census Bureau, Table H-4.

22. U.S. Census Bureau, Income, Table P-36, "Full-Time, Year-Round Workers by Median Income and Sex," http://www.census.gov/hhes/www/income/data/historical/people/P36AR_2009.xls.

23. Robert Z. Lawrence, Blue-Collar Blues: Is Trade to Blame for Rising U.S. Income Inequality? Policy Analyses in International Economics 85 (Washington, DC: Peterson Institute for International Economics, 2008), 3.

24. Florence Jaumotte and Irina Tytell, "The Globalization of Labor," chapter 5 in IMF, World Economic Outlook, April 2007, 166.

25. Dani Rodrik's weblog, "A New Mainstream Consensus on Trade and Wages?," June 14, 2007, http://rodrik.typepad.com/dani_rodriks_weblog/2007/06/a_new_mainstrea.html.

26. Lawrence, Blue-Collar Blues, 7.

27. Ibid., 11.

28. Jaumotte and Tytell, "The Globalization of Labor," 168.

29. Ibid., 179.

30. Immigration was estimated to have caused about a 0.1% annual contribution to labor's declining share of income. Jaumotte and Tytell, "The Globalization of Labor," 187.

31. Sébastien Jean et al., "Migration in OECD Countries: Labour Market Impact and Integration Issues," OECD Economics Department working paper no. 562, 2007.

32. Here, offshoring refers mainly to international sourcing of manufactured inputs, since offshore services still comprise a very small proportion of imports.

33. Karen E. Dynan, Douglas W. Elmendorf, and Daniel E. Sichel, "The Evolution of Household Income Volatility," Finance and Economics Discussion series 2007-61, 2007.

34. Henry S. Farber, "Job Loss and the Decline in Job Security in the United States," Princeton University Industrial Relations Section working paper 520, July 2007 (rev. September 11, 2007).

35. Lori G. Kletzer, "Globalization and Job Loss, from Manufacturing to Services," Federal Reserve Bank of Chicago, Economic Perspectives 2Q 2005, and Jagdish Bhagwati, "Trade and Wages: Choosing Among Alternative Explanations," Federal Reserve Bank of New York, Economic Policy Review, January 1995.

36. Dani Rodrik, Has Globalization Gone Too Far? (Washington, DC: Peterson Institute for International Economics, 1997), 5.

37. Giovanni S. F. Bruno, et al., "Measuring the Effect of Globalization on Labour Demand Elasticity: An Empirical Application to OECD Countries," KITeS, Centre for Knowledge, Internationalization and Technology Studies working paper 153, Universita Bocconi, Milano, Italy, February 2004.

38. The 2% estimate is from Ben Bernanke, Remarks to the Fuqua School of Business, Duke University, March 30, 2004, http://www.federalreserve.gov/boarddocs/Speeches/2004/20040330/

default.htm. The 3% estimate is based on BLS data covering layoffs of fifty or more people and is from the Council of Economic Advisers, "The History and Future of International Trade," *2006 Economic Report of the President* (Washington, DC: Government Printing Office, 2006), 161.

39. Lori G. Kletzer, *Imports, Exports, and Jobs: What Does Trade Mean for Employment and Job Loss?* (Kalamazoo, MI: W.E. Upjohn Institute for Employment Research, 2002), 103–130.

40. See Lawrence, *Blue-Collar Blues*, 69.

41. OECD, "Policy Brief: Globalisation, Jobs, and Wages."

42. Kevin Casas-Zamora, "Why the Discomfort over Free Trade," *YaleGlobal*, 12 (September 2008).

43. Maxim Pinkovskiy and Xavier Sala-i-Martin, "Parametric Estimations of the World Distribution of Income," NBER working paper 15433, October 2009.

44. Susan Chun Zhu and Daniel Trefler, "Trade and Inequality in Developing Countries: A General Equilibrium Analysis," *Journal of International Economics* 65 (2005): 21–48.

45. Simon Kuznets, "Economic Growth and Income Inequality," *American Economic Review* 45, no. 1 (March 1955): 1–28.

46. See Gary S. Fields, *Distribution and Development: A New Look at the Developing World* (New York: Russell Sage Foundation and Cambridge, MA and London: MIT Press, 2001), 35–72.

47. George J. Church, "1985: Deng Xiaoping," *Time*, January 6, 1986, http://www.time.com/time/subscriber/personoftheyear/archive/stories/1985.html.

48. OECD, "Policy Brief: Economic Survey of China 2010," February 2010, http://www.oecd.org/dataoecd/22/19/44468723.pdf.

49. Randall Morck, ed., *Concentrated Corporate Ownership* (Chicago: University of Chicago Press, 2000), 323.

50. Jonathan Katz, "With Cheap Food Imports, Haiti Can't Feed Itself," *Huffington Post*, March 20, 2010, http://www.huffingtonpost.com/2010/03/20/with-cheap-food-imports-h_n_507228.html.

51. Josiane Georges, "Trade and the Disappearance of Haitian Rice," Ted Case Studies 725, June 2004.

52. Bill Clinton, "We Made a Devil's Bargain," interview with Kim Ives, Democracy Now, April 1, 2010, http://www.democracynow.org/2010/4/1/clinton_rice.

53. Bradford DeLong, "Barack Obama Does Something Really Stupid: Tire Tariffs," Grasping Reality with Both Hands weblog, September 13, 2009, http://delong.typepad.com/sdj/2009/09/barack-obama-does-something-really-stupid-tire-tariffs.html.

54. Gary Clyde Hufbauer, "Surveying the Costs of Protection: A Partial Equilibrium Approach," in Jeffrey J. Schott, ed., *The World Trading System: Challenges Ahead* (Washington, DC: Peterson Institute for International Economics, 1996), 27–40.

55. Gary C. Hufbauer and Kimberly Ann Elliott, *Measuring the Costs of Protectionism in the United States* (Washington DC: Peterson Institute for International Economics, January 1994), cited in William J. Baumol and Alan S. Blinder, eds., *Macroeconomics: Principles and Policy* (Cincinnati, OH: South-Western College Publishing, 2007).

56. Council of Economic Advisers, "The History and Future of International Trade," 157.

57. Center for Global Development, "Global Trade, Jobs, and Labor Standards," Rich World, Poor World: A Guide to Global Development (series), June 16, 2006.

58. Chris Edwards, "The Sugar Racket," CATO Institute Tax & Budget Bulletin 46, June 2007.

59. Sascha O. Becker and Marc-Andreas Muendler, "The Effect of FDI on Job Security," *The B. E. Journal of Economic Analysis and Policy* 8, no. 1 (2008): article 8.

60. See Andrew E. Clark and Andrew J. Oswald, "Satisfaction and Comparison Income," *Journal of Public Economics* 61, no. 3 (1996): 359–381; Rafael Di Tella, R. MacCulloch, and A. Oswald, "Preferences over Inflation and Unemployment: Evidence from Surveys of Happiness," *The American Economic Review* 91, no. 1 (2001): 335–341.

61. Marcus Eliason and Donald Storrie, "Does Job Loss Shorten Life?" working papers in Economics 153, School of Business, Economics and Law, Göteborg University, Sweden, December 2004.

62. Lori Kletzer, "Trade-related Job Loss and Wage Insurance: A Synthetic Review," Santa Cruz Center for International Economics, working paper series 11300, June 1, 2003.

Chapter Ten

1. See http://www.globalissues.org/article/75/world-military-spending#WorldMilitary Spending.

2. Estimates of the costs of these wars range from a few hundred billion dollars to more than two trillion dollars. See http://www.cfr.org/publication/15404/iraq_afghanistan_and_the_us_economy.html.

3. United Nations Department of Economic and Social Affairs, "Multinational Corporations in World Development," (1973) 130–133.

4. 2010 Fortune Global 500, http://money.cnn.com/magazines/fortune/global500/2010/.

5. Patrick Low, Marcelo Olarreaga, and Javier Suarez, "Does Globalization Cause a Higher Concentration of International Trade and Investment Flows?" World Trade Organization Economic Research and Analysis Division, staff working paper ERAD-98-08, August 1998.

6. The data for 1820 are drawn from Angus Maddison, *The World Economy: Historical Statistics* (OECD, 2003), 261; the data for the current period (for 2008) are from the World Bank, World Development Indicators; the projections for 2050 are from the Goldman Sachs report "The N-11: More Than an Acronym," Global Economics Paper 153, March 28, 2007.

7. United Nations Conference on Trade and Development, *World Investment Report 2010*, 16.

8. Based on UNCTAD, "The world's top 100 non-financial TNCs, ranked by foreign assets, 2008," *World Investment Report*, 2010, sales of the largest transnational companies amounted to $8.4 trillion. World GDP in 2008 has been estimated by multiple sources at roughly $58 trillion dollars.

9. Dani Rodrik, "Goodbye Washington Consensus, Hello Washington Confusion? A Review of the World Bank's Economic Growth in the 1990s: Learning from a Decade of Reform," *Journal of Economic Literature* 44, no. 4 (December 2006), 973–987.

10. See Dani Rodrik, *One Economics, Many Recipes: Globalization, Institutions, and Economic Growth* (Princeton, NJ: Princeton University Press, 2007), chapter 7.

11. Thomas Friedman, *The Lexus and the Olive Tree* (New York: Anchor Books, 2000), 106. For a mostly laudatory review of Friedman's book, see Barry Eichengreen, "One Economy, Ready or Not: Thomas Friedman's Jaunt Through Globalization," *Foreign Affairs*, May/June 1999.

12. Willem Adema and Maxime Ladaique, "How Expensive Is the Welfare State?: Gross and Net Indicators in the OECD Social Expenditure Database (SOCX)," OECD Social, Employment and Migration working papers no. 92, November 2009.

13. Lobbying database, http://www.opensecrets.org/lobby/index.php.

14. Geoffrey Garrett and Deborah Mitchell, "Globalization, Government Spending, and Taxation in the OECD," *European Journal of Political Research* 39 (2001): 145–177.

15. Eunyoung Ha, "Globalization, Veto Players, and Welfare Spending," *Comparative Political Studies* 41, no. 6 (June 2008): 786–813.

16. Markus Leibrecht, Michael Klien, and Ozlem Onaran, "Globalization, welfare regimes and social protection expenditures in Western and Eastern European countries," Middlesex University Department of Economics and Statistics, discussion paper no. 140, April 2010.

17. Geoffrey Garrett, "Global Markets and National Politics: Collision Course or Virtuous Circle," *International Organization* 52, no. 4 (Autumn 1998): 787–824.

18. Niels Bohr personal communication to Arthur Kantrowitz, cited in Arthur Kantrowitz, "The Weapon of Openness," in B. C. Crandall and James Lewis, eds., *Nanotechnology: Research and Perspectives* (Cambridge, MA: MIT Press), 303.

19. Freedom House, http://www.freedomhouse.org/template.cfm?page=439.

20. Barry Eichengreen and David Leblang, "Democracy and Globalization," NBER working paper 12450, August 2006.

21. Adam Przeworski, "Democracy as an Equilibrium," *Public Choice* 123, no. 3-4, (2005): 253–273.

22. Peter T. Leeson and Andrea M. Dean, "The Democratic Domino Theory: An Empirical Investigation, "*American Journal Political Science* 53, no. 3 (2009): 533-551, and Daniel Brinks and Michael Coppedge, "Diffusion Is No Illusion: Neighbor Emulation in the Third Wave of Democracy," *Comparative Political Studies* 39, no. 4 (2006): 463.

23. Center for Systemic Peace, "Global Conflict Trends," September 11, 2010, http://www.systemicpeace.org/conflict.htm.

24. "Quick & Dirty Guide to Wars in the World," StrategyPage, August 14, 2005, http://www.strategypage.com/qnd/wars/articles/20050814.aspx.

25. Barret Sheridan, "Somalia Illustrates the High Cost of Failed States," *Newsweek*, August 20, 2009, and Lisa Chauvet, Paul Collier, and Anke Hoeffler, "The Cost of Failing States and the Limits to Sovereignty," United Nations University, World Institute for Development Economics Research, research paper no. 2007/30 (2007).

26. Markus Brückner and Hans Peter Grüner, "The OECD's Growth Prospects and Political Extremism," *Vox,* May 16, 2010, http://www.voxeu.org/index.php?q=node/5047.

27. Rein Taagepera, "Expansion and Contraction Patterns of Large Polities," *International Studies Quarterly* 41, no. 3 (September 1997): 475–504.

28. It is worth noting that such reversals over a century or even longer *have* been experienced in the past, mostly as a consequence of the collapse of major empires.

29. Alberto Alesina et al., "Economic Integration and Political Disintegration," *American Economic Review* 90 (December 5, 2000): 1276–1296.

30. "El fallo del TC catapulta el respaldo a la independencia, que roza el 50%," *La Vanguardia*, June 7, 2010, http://www.lavanguardia.es/politica/noticias/20100718/53967434806/el-fallo-del-tc-catapulta-el-respaldo-a-la-independencia-que-roza-el-50.html.

31. "Hotbeds of Separatism in Modern Europe," *Globalia Magazine*, August 21, 2009, http://www.globaliamagazine.com/?id=802.

32. See Alberto Alesina, Arnaud Devleeschauwer, William Easterly, Sergio Kurlat, and Romain Wacziarg, "Fractionalization," Graduate School of Business, Stanford University, research paper no. 1744, June 2002, and Alberto Alesina, William Easterly, and Janina Matuszeski, "Artificial States," Center for Global Development working paper no. 100, September 2006, 13.

33. Sudan would also qualify as being the locus of a civil war by many definitions if not the CSP's. And there are, of course, countries that are gravely troubled even though they don't make the list here, such as Somalia, Yemen, and Afghanistan.

34. The other five most fragile countries in the top thirty cluster in West/South Asia.

35. Benjamin M. Friedman, *The Moral Consequences of Economic Growth* (New York: Knopf, 2005), 3–18.

Chapter Eleven

1. BBC News, "Swiss Voters Back Ban on Minarets," November 29, 2009, http://news.bbc.co.uk/2/hi/8385069.stm.

2. Anne Nugent, "The Irish Top the Charts on Alcoholic Drinks Expenditure," Euromonitor International, October 29, 2003, http://www.euromonitor.com/The_Irish_top_the_charts_on_alcoholic_drinks_expenditure.

3. Google Insights for Search, covering the period from 2004 to December 2010, accessed November 12, 2010.

4. On Argentine mental health, see "Its GDP Is Depressed, but Argentina Leads World in Shrinks Per Capita," *Wall Street Journal*, October 19, 2009, http://online.wsj.com/article/SB125563769653488249.html. On Brazilian beauty products, see Geoffrey Jones, *Beauty Imagined. A History of the Global Beauty Industry* (Oxford and New York: Oxford University Press, 2010).

5. Ronald Inglehart and Wayne E. Baker, "Modernization, Cultural Change, and the Persistence of Traditional Values," *American Sociological Review* 65 (February 2000): 19–51.

6. "McDonald's Delivers Another Year of Strong Results in 2009," McDonald's press release, January 22, 2010, http://phx.corporate-ir.net/phoenix.zhtml?c=97876&p=irol-newsArticle&ID=1377920&highlight.

7. "Yum! Brands Inc. Raises Full Year 2010 EPS Growth Forecast to 14% from 12%," Yum! press release, October 5, 2010, http://phx.corporate-ir.net/External.File?item=UGFyZW50SUQ9NjUwNDd8Q2hpbGRJRD0tMXxUeXBlPTM=&t=1.

8. Shelley Emling, "Europe Embraces Coke Culture," *Miami Herald,* October 16, 2007. Also see my previous book, *Redefining Global Strategy* (Boston: Harvard Business School Press, 2007), 25.

9. Marc Gunther, "MTV's Passage to India," *Fortune*, August 9, 2004.

10. Fernando Ferreira and Joel Waldfogel, "Pop Internationalism: Has a Half Century of World Music Trade Displaced Local Culture?" NBER working paper 15964, May 2010.

11. Tyler Cowen, *Creative Destruction: How Globalization Is Changing the World's Cultures,* (Princeton: Princeton University Press, 2002), 1–18.

12. Amartya Sen, "How to Judge Globalism," *American Prospect*, January 1, 2002, http://www.prospect.org/cs/articles?article=how_to_judge_globalism. This paragraph draws on material in his article.

13. Joseph Kahn and Daniel J. Wakin, "Western Classical Music, Made and Loved in China," *New York Times*, Monday, April 2, 2007.

14. Andrew Druckenbrod, "China Captures Music World's Ear," *Pittsburgh Post-Gazette*, June 28, 2009.

15. Karl Marx, "The British Rule in India," *New-York Daily Tribune*, June 25, 1853 (accessed at http://www.marxists.org/archive/marx/works/1853/06/25.htm).

16. Anthony Appiah, "The Case for Contamination," *New York Times Magazine*, January 1, 2006.

17. Herodotus, *The Histories,* translated by Aubery de Selincourt, revised by John M. Marincola (New York: Penguin Books, 2003), 187.

18. Deborah Ball and Anita Greil, "Swiss Referendum Stirs Debate About Islam," *The Wall Street Journal Europe*, November 6, 2009.

19. Imogen Foulkes, "Minaret Ban Marks Start of Tough Swiss Debate on Islam," *BBC News*, November 30, 2009, http://news.bbc.co.uk/2/hi/8386456.stm.

20. The Pew Global Attitudes Project, *World Publics Welcome Trade—But Not Immigration* (Washington, DC: Pew Research Center, October 4, 2007).

21. Specifically, I'm referring to the degree of trust as self-reported in response to the World Values Survey question: "Generally speaking, would you say that most people can be trusted or that you can't be too careful in dealing with people?"

22. The most notable apparent exception is that religiosity seems to be negatively associated with social trust. Niclas Berggren and Christian Bjørnskov, "Does Religiosity Promote or Discourage Social Trust? Evidence from Cross-Country and Cross-State Comparisons," Ratio working papers 142, Ratio Institute, 2009.

23. Questions on trust have been incorporated in the Eurobarometer surveys since 1974.

24. Survey respondents were actually asked to rate the citizens of other countries as well as their own on a spectrum ranging from "no trust at all" to "a lot of trust." An academic

article based on this survey summarizes data about the percentage of citizens of each West European country surveyed who report trusting others "a lot." See Luigi Guiso, Paola Sapienza, and Luigi Zingales, "Cultural Biases in Economic Exchange?" *Quarterly Journal of Economics* 124, no. 3 (August 2009): 1095–1131. The data presented in figure 11-3—median values when it comes to trust in citizens of other countries—is actually based on a previous version of the paper downloadable at http://economics.uchicago.edu/download/cultural_biases.pdf.

25. Note that with twenty-nine countries in the full sample, the generalized trust levels are dominated by opinions of foreigners rather than domestic ones, e.g., what foreigners think of Swedes versus what Swedes think of Swedes, even though the latter *is* included in the computation.

26. On the first three flows, see Guiso, Sapienza, and Zingales, "Cultural Biases in Economic Exchange?" On venture capital investment, see Laura Bottazzi, Marco Da Rin, and Thomas Hellmann, "The Importance of Trust for Investment: Evidence from Venture Capital," discussion paper 2010-49, Tilburg University, Center for Economic Research, 2010.

27. On the decline of European nationalisms, see Mattei Dogan, "The Decline of Nationalisms Within Western Europe," *International Social Science Journal* 136 (May 1993): 177–198.

28. Carlos David Navarrete and Daniel M. T. Fessler, "Disease Avoidance and Ethnocentrism: The Effects of Disease Vulnerability and Disgust Sensitivity on Intergroup Attitudes," *Evolution and Human Behavior* 27 (2006): 270. Note that further support for this view is reflected in the finding that in-group favoritism is heightened among women in the first trimester of pregnancy, when immune responses are suppressed, as described in Carlos David Navarrete, Daniel M. T. Fessler, and Serena J. Eng, "Elevated Ethnocentrism in the First Trimester of Pregnancy," *Evolution and Human Behavior* 28 (2007): 60–65.

29. Navarrete and Fessler, "Disease Avoidance and Ethnocentrism," 271.

30. See Chad Joseph McEvoy, "A Consideration of the Sociobiological Dimensions of Human Xenophobia and Ethnocentrism, 1995, http://www.sociosite.net/topics/xenophobia.php (accessed November 23, 2010).

31. Robert Axelrod and Ross A. Hammond, "The Evolution of Ethnocentric Behavior," revised version of paper prepared for delivery at Midwest Political Science Convention, April 16, 2003.

32. University of California–Los Angeles, "Ewwwww! UCLA Anthropologist Studies Evolution's Disgusting Side," *ScienceDaily*, March 29, 2007, http://www.sciencedaily.com/releases/2007/03/070328101621.htm.

33. W. F. Ogburn, "Cultural Lag as Theory," *Sociology and Social Research*, January–February 1957, 167–174, as cited in Benoit Godin, "Innovation Without the Word: William F. Ogburn's Contribution to Technological Innovation Studies," Project on the Intellectual History of Innovation, working paper no. 5, 2010.

34. Another source of some revealed favoritism data is from the Eurovision contest.

35. Guiso, Sapienza, and Zingales, "Cultural Biases In Economic Exchange?"

36. Less direct evidence is provided by a study showing that countries characterized by high aversion to uncertainty export disproportionately less to distant countries, with which they are presumably less familiar. See Rocco R. Huang, "Distance and Trade: Disentangling Unfamiliarity Effects and Transport Cost Effects," *European Economic Review* 51, no. 1 (January 2007): 161–181.

37. Mikael Hjerm, "Education, Xenophobia and Nationalism: A Comparative Analysis," *Journal of Ethnic and Migration Studies* 27, no. 1 (January 2001): 37–60.

38. Nancy R. Buchan, Gianluca Grimalda, Rick Wilson, Marilynn Brewer, Enrique Fatas, and Margaret Foddy, "Globalization and Human Cooperation," *Proceedings of the National Academy of Sciences* 106, no. 11 (March 17, 2009): 4138–4142; and Nancy R. Buchan, Marilynn Brewer, Gianluca Grimalda, Rick Wilson, Enrique Fatas, and Margaret Foddy, "The Role of

Social Identity in Global Cooperation," in press, http://mooreschool.sc.edu/UserFiles/Faculty/155/Buchan%20vita%201-10%20(2).pdf.

39. W. W. Maddux and A. D. Galinsky, "Cultural Borders and Mental Barriers: The Relationship Between Living Abroad and Creativity," *Journal of Personality and Social Psychology* 96, no. 5 (2009): 1047–1061.

40. Niclas Berggren and Henrik Jordahl, "Free to Trust? Economic Freedom and Social Capital," *Kyklos* 59, no. 2 (2006): 141–169, and Richard M. Locke, "Building Trust," unpublished manuscript, Massachusetts Institute of Technology, 2002.

41. "China and Overseas Migration," *Asia Sentinel*, July 16, 2010.

42. Martin S. Edwards, "Public Opinion Regarding Economic and Cultural Globalization: Evidence from a Cross-national Survey," *Review of International Political Economy* 13, no. 4 (October 2006): 587–608.

Chapter Twelve

1. John Maynard Keynes, "National Self-Sufficiency," *The Yale Review* 22, no. 4 (June 1933): 755–769.

2. In John M. Keynes, "Some Economic Consequences of a Declining Population," *Eugenics Review* 29 (1937): 13–17, the author writes: "A change-over from an increasing to a declining population may be very disastrous."

3. Warren J. Samuels, *The Chicago School of Political Economy* (New Brunswick, NJ: Transaction Publishers, 1993), 8.

4. These arguments are associated, respectively, with Harold Demsetz and Nobel Prize winners Ronald Coase and Friedrich Hayek (the latter an economist of the Austrian school who taught at the University of Chicago but never joined its Economics Department).

5. Chicago Nobel Prize winner George Stigler is particularly famous for his work on the topic of regulatory capture.

6. Richard E. Caves, "International Trade and Industrial Organization: Introduction," *Journal of Industrial Economics* 29, no. 2 (December 1980): 113–114.

7. James Brander quoted in Richard E. Baldwin, "Are Economists' Traditional Trade Policy Views Still Valid?" *Journal of Economic Literature* 30 (June 1992): 804.

8. See, for instance, James A. Brander and Barbara J. Spencer, "International R&D Rivalry and Industrial Strategy," *Review of Economic Studies* 50 (1983): 707–722. Brander and Spencer actually worked—as is traditional in trade theory—with just two countries.

9. For an informal recent account, see Paul R. Krugman, "New Trade Theory and New Economic Geography," October 16, 2008, http://economistsview.typepad.com/economistsview/2008/10/new-trade-theor.html; and for an academic assessment of new trade theory from the late 1980s, see Paul Krugman, "Industrial Organization and International Trade," chapter 20 in *Handook of Industrial Organization*, volume 2, eds. R. Schmalensee and R. D. Willig (Amsterdam: Elsevier Science Publishers B.V., 1989), 1179–1223.

10. Thus, by the mid-1980s, 50%-60% of the articles on industrial organization published in the top economics journals used game-theoretic methodologies, compared to 20% or less in the mid-1970s. See Pankaj Ghemawat, *Games Businesses Play* (Cambridge, MA: MIT Press, 1997): 1–28.

11. My article "The Snowball Effect," which revisited the Harvard-Chicago debate from a game-theoretic perspective, finally appeared—as the lead article—in the *International Journal of Industrial Organization* in 1990.

12. Alfred E. Kahn, *The Economics of Regulation: Principles and Institutions*, volume 1 (Cambridge, MA: MIT Press, 1988), xxxvii.

13. Hayek himself was more ardent in his excoriation of central planning than in his enthusiasm for free markets: as he wrote, "Probably nothing has done so much harm to the liberal cause as the wooden insistence of some liberals on certain rules of thumb, above all the principle

of laissez-faire capitalism." See Friedrich A. Hayek, *Constitution of Liberty* (Chicago, IL: University of Chicago Press, 1960), 502–503. But Friedman continued to insist on that "rule of thumb."

14. Lawrence H. Summers, "The Great Liberator," *New York Times*, November 19, 2006, http://www.nytimes.com/2006/11/19/opinion/19summers.html?_r=1.

15. See Hayek's 1944 book, *The Road to Serfdom* (Chicago, IL: University of Chicago Press, 1944) and Friedman's 1980 TV series, *Free to Choose*, which popularized the ideas of both.

16. Paul A. Samuelson, "Heed the Hopeful Science," *New York Times*, October 23, 2009, http://www.nytimes.com/2009/10/24/opinion/24iht-edsamuelson.html.

17. Amartya Sen, "Capitalism Beyond the Crisis," *New York Review of Books*, March 26, 2009, http://www.nybooks.com/articles/archives/2009/mar/26/capitalism-beyond-the-crisis/.

18. There is also, as discussed in chapter 1, a fourth possibility, World 0.0, which characterized our feudal past and is visible today in failed states and ones controlled by robber barons—categories with significant overlap.

19. Expedients for accomplishing this objective include external scanning, focusing on changes, analogizing, altering mental models, and gestalt switching. For further discussion, see chapter 4 of Pankaj Ghemawat, *Strategy and the Business Landscape* (Englewood Cliffs, NJ: Pearson Prentice Hall, 2009).

20. See Jagdish Bhagwati and V. K. Ramaswami, "Domestic Distortions, Tariffs, and the Theory of Optimal Subsidy," *Journal of Political Economy* 71 (1963): 44–50.

21. In addition, the Bhagwati-Ramaswami analysis is predicated on a model that ignores some of the sources of market failures and fears focused on in this book, which takes an inductive rather than theoretical look at the nexus between those failures/fears and cross-border integration of markets.

Chapter Thirteen

1. For evidence on flows of air passengers, Internet traffic, and other service sector connections, see respectively, R. Guimera, S. Mossa, A. Turtschi, and L. A. N. Amaral, "The Worldwide Air Transportation Network: Anomalous Centrality, Community Structure, and Cities' Global Roles," *Proceedings of the National Academy of Sciences* 102, no. 22 (May 31, 2005): 7794–7799; Anthony M. Townsend, "Network Cities and the Global Structure of the Internet," *American Behavioral Scientist*, special issue, "Mapping the Global Web," February 2001; and Peter J. Taylor and Robert E. Lang, "U.S. Cities in the 'World City Network,'" Metropolitan Policy Program, *Brookings Institution Survey Series*, February 2005, 1–17.

2. Chamber of Commerce, Industry, and Services of Andorra, "Economic Report, 2008," 35.

3. Associacio de Bancs Andorrans, "Andorra and Its Financial System 2009," 58.

4. Figures in this paragraph, unless otherwise stated, are drawn from the CIA World Factbook and U.S. State Department Web site. See https://www.cia.gov/library/publications/the-world-factbook/geos/an.html and http://www.state.gov/r/pa/ei/bgn/3164.htm (both accessed November 19, 2010)

5. Chamber of Commerce, Industry, and Services of Andorra, "Economic Report, 2008," and Associacio de Bancs Andorrans, "Andorra and Its Financial System 2009."

6. Andorra tourist arrivals and population data from Chamber of Commerce, Industry, and Services of Andorra, "Economic Report, 2008" and Associacio de Bancs Andorrans, "Andorra and Its Financial System 2009"; global international tourist arrivals from World Travel and Tourism Council, http://www.wttc.org/eng/Tourism_Research/Economic_Data_Search_Tool/index.php (accessed November 27, 2010). Note: This calculation includes both day-trippers and overnight tourists in Andorra's international tourist arrivals.

7. See Raphael Minder, "Andorra, a Tiny Tax Haven, Tries Openness," *New York Times* August 27, 2010, http://www.nytimes.com/2010/08/28/business/global/28andorra.html?_r=2.

8. Trade intensity calculations are calibrated by GDP.

9. Calculated from data from the Statistics Department of the Government of Andorra, http://www.estadistica.ad/serveiestudis/web/index.asp.Tourism intensity calculations are calibrated by population.

10. United Nations Population Division, "International Migration 2009," http://www.un.org/esa/population/publications/2009Migration_Chart/2009IttMig_chart.htm.

11. United Nations, Department of Economic and Social Affairs, Population Division, *World Population Prospects: The 2008 Revision* (2009), CD-ROM edition.

12. Nina Budina and Sweer van Wijnbergen, "Managing Oil Revenue Volatility in Nigeria: The Role of Fiscal Policy," in Delfin S. Go and John Page, eds., *Africa at a Turning Point? Growth, Aid, and External Shocks* (Washington, DC: World Bank, 2008): 427–460; and U.S. Department of State profile of Nigeria, http://www.state.gov/r/pa/ei/bgn/2836.htm, accessed on November 16, 2010.

13. Refer to Paul Collier, Frederick van der Ploeg, and Anthony J. Venables, "Managing Resource Revenues in Developing Economies," Oxford Centre for the Analysis of Resource Rich Economies, January 2009, as well as others at http://www.oxcarre.ox.ac.uk/index.php/Research-Papers/research-papers1.html.

14. Henry Umoru, "Nigeria's Future Depends on Manufacturing, Non-oil sector—Jonathan," Vanguard Online Edition, November 1, 2010, http://www.vanguardngr.com/2010/11/nigeria%e2%80%99s-future-depends-on-manufacturing-non-oil-sector-jonathan/.

15. French is an official language in all of the countries that are adjacent to Nigeria; among them only Cameroon also recognizes English as an official language.

16. Nigerian Export Promotion Council, Annual Statistics, http://www.nepc.gov.ng/download.htm, accessed November 26, 2010.

17. For a review of the history of Nigerian international migration, see Adejumoke A. Afolayan, Godwin O. Ikwuyatum, and Olumuyiwa Abejide, "Dynamics of International Migration in Nigeria (A Review of Literature)," paper prepared as part of the African Perspectives on Human Mobility Programme, 2008.

18. Estimates suggest that 50 to 60 percent of trade between Nigeria and Niger and 75 to 80 percent of Nigerian imports from Benin occur outside of official channels, as noted in World Bank, "Nigeria: Competitiveness and Growth," Report No. 36483, May 30, 2007, 125.

19. Oyeniyi, Omotayo, "Effect of Marketing Strategy on Export Performance: Evidence from Nigerian Export Companies," Annals of University of Bucharest, Economic and Administrative Series No. 3 (2009): 249–261

20. World Bank, "Nigeria: Competitiveness and Growth," 81–83.

21. World Economic Forum, "Global Competitiveness Report 2010," http://gcr.weforum.org/gcr2010/.

22. World Bank, "Nigeria: Competitiveness and Growth," 81–83.

23. See Alberto Alesina et al., "Fractionalization," *Journal of Economic Growth* 8, no. 2 (2003): 155–194.

24. World Bank, "Nigeria: Competitiveness and Growth," 23.

25. Abraham Lincoln, Annual Message to Congress (Dec. 1, 1862), in *Abraham Lincoln's Speeches and Letters 1832–1865*, ed. Paul M. Angle (London: Dent, 1957): 216, 225.

26. Thomas M. Hout and Pankaj Ghemawat, "China vs. the World: Whose Technology Is It?" *Harvard Business Review*, December 2010, 94–103.

27. *The Economist*, November 13, 2010.

28. Parag Khanna, *The Second World: Empires and Influence in the New Global Order* (New York: Random House, 2008): 257–320.

29. This analysis is based on historical trade reported by U.S. and China with third countries according to data from the United Nations Commodity Trade Database. Projections of differential real GDP growth rates through 2030 are according to the Economist Intelligence

Unit (EIU) as of December 2010. Where data were unavailable in primary sources or for target years, data for closest available years were used based on available sources.

30. See http://www.financialexpress.com/news/china-replaces-us-as-indias-largest-trade-partner/494785/.

31. See Robert Axelrod, *The Evolution of Cooperation* (New York: Basic Books, 1984).

32. Doing so assumes that at least some of the divergence between a country's predicted pattern of international engagement based on cross-country estimates and its actual pattern—which presumably reflects path dependence and, more broadly, a variety of idiosyncratic influences—can and should be remedied.

33. See also Pankaj Ghemawat, *Redefining Global Strategy* (Boston, MA: Harvard Business School Press, 2007), chapters 4–7 for a much more detailed description of the AAA strategies.

34. As elsewhere in this book, this conclusion is focused on cultural, administrative, and geographic differences. Many of the economic elements of the CAGE framework are better thought of as outcomes that should, ideally, reflect the results of cross-border openness and competition instead of as targets for direct manipulation.

35. In game-theoretic terms, imposing the auxiliary criterion of fairness can empty the core of cooperative games.

36. See the full text of the Schuman Declaration of May 9, 1950 at http://www.schuman.info/.

Chapter Fourteen

1. These figures are based on a rough content analysis of the annual reports of the world's 100 largest companies conducted under my supervision. The companies covered in the analysis were selected based on revenues during the period 2004 to 2008 as reported in the 2004 to 2008 editions of the *Fortune* Global 500 rankings.

2. Pankaj Ghemawat, *Redefining Global Strategy* (Boston, MA: Harvard Business School Press, 2007).

3. David Jin, et. al., "Winning in Emerging-Market Cities: A Guide to the World's Largest Growth Opportunity," Boston Consulting Group, September, 2010.

4. McKinsey Global Institute, "Preparing for China's Urban Billion," March 2009.

5. David Jin, et. al., "Winning in Emerging-Market Cities."

6. Susan Perkins, Randall Morck, and Bernard Yeung, "Innocents Abroad: The Hazards of International Joint Ventures with Pyramidal Group Firms," NBER working papers 13914, 2008.

7. Egon Zehnder International, Global Board Index 2008.

8. Herman Vantrappen and Petter Kilefors, "Grooming CEO Talent at the Truly Global Firm of the Future," Arthur D. Little *Prism*, February 2009, 90–105.

9. Online survey of *Harvard Business Review* readers conducted at my request in 2007.

10. Computations are based on Bureau of Economic Analysis data kindly carried out at my request by Raymond J. Mataloni, fall 2007.

11. To learn more about how to use the ADDING value scorecard for company-level analysis, refer to chapter 3 of *Redefining Global Strategy*.

12. For further discussion of the interactions between established and emerging multinational companies, see Pankaj Ghemawat and Thomas Hout, "Tomorrow's Global Giants? Not the Usual Suspects," *Harvard Business Review* 86 (November 2008): 80–88.

13. For further discussion of the post-crisis imperatives for companies' global strategies, see Pankaj Ghemawat, "Finding Your Strategy in the New Landscape," *Harvard Business Review* 88 (March 2010): 54–60.

14. Robert C. Lieb and Kristin J. Lieb, "Executive Summary and Regional Comparisons 2009 3PL CEO Surveys," http://www.gopenske.com/newsroom/2009_9_21_executive_summary.html.

15. Gary Herrigel, "Interim Substantive Report on Global Components Project," memo to Gail Pesyna, University of Chicago Department of Political Science, October 16, 2007. For more information, see http://www.globalcomponents.org/.

16. Arindam Bhattacharya, et. al., "Organizing for Global Advantage in China, India, and Other Rapidly Developing Economies," The Boston Consulting Group, March 2006.

17. The Pew Research Center, "Public Praises Science; Scientists Fault Public, Media," July 9, 2009, http://people-press.org/report/528/.

18. Global Trade Alert, "Managed Exports and the Recovery of World Trade: The 7th GTA Report," September 16, 2010, http://www.globaltradealert.org/managed-exports-7th-gta-report.

Chapter Fifteen

1. David Gura, "Tony Blair on War, Globalization and 'My Political Life,'" The Two-Way, NPR's News Blog, September 2, 2010, reporting on Steve Inskeep's interview with Tony Blair about his new book, *My Journey*, http://www.npr.org/blogs/thetwo-way/2010/09/01/129580726/tony-blair-a-journey-my-political-life-interview-morning-edition-memoir.

2. Hierocles (Stobaeus, *Eclogae Physicae et Ethicae*, 4.671, 7.673, p. 11), reproduced in Long and Sedley, *The Hellenistic Philosophers*, 2 vols. (Cambridge, UK: Cambridge University Press, 1987), fragment 57G.

3. David Hume, *A Treatise of Human Nature* (Lawrence, KS: Digireads.com Publishing, 2010), 329.

4. Thus, Lars Håkanson and Björn Ambos note that, "In the extant literature, 'psychic distance' is usually conceived of as a perceptual, subjective phenomenon, but it is typically operationalized as an objective, collective construct—an inconsistency that has been perpetuated over time." Håkanson and Ambos, "The Antecedents of Psychic Distance," *Journal of International Management* 16 (2010):197.

5. For the original paper focused on psychic distance in business research, which defines psychic distance in a way that excludes geographic factors and arbitrarily privileges informational flows over other kinds of cross-border flows, see J. Johanson, and F. Wiedersheim-Paul, "The Internationalization of the Firm—Four Swedish Cases," *Journal of Management Studies* 12, no. 1 (1975): 305–322 and J. Johanson and J.-E. Vahlne, "The Internationalization Process of the Firm—A Model of Knowledge Development and Increasing Foreign Market Commitments," *Journal of International Business Studies* 8, no. 1 (1977): 23–32.

6. See http://en.wikipedia.org/wiki/Psychical_distance, and, for an analogous definition from business academia, Lars Håkanson and Björn Ambos, "The Antecedents of Psychic Distance," *Journal of International Management* 16 (2010): 195–210, which defines psychic distance in its survey instrument as the "sum of factors (cultural or language differences, geographical distance, etc.) that affects the flow and interpretation of information to and from a foreign country."

7. This definition is consistent with dictionary.com's: "The degree of emotional detachment maintained toward a person, a group of people or an event" see (http://dictionary.reference.com/browse/psychic+distance), but adds back the subjective/perceptual element emphasized in earlier definitions.

8. For what it is worth—note the caveats already described about expanded conceptions of psychic distance—such trust measures are strongly and negatively correlated with the "psychic" (or actually, total information-related) distances reported by Håkanson and Ambos, op cit., based on their survey of managers in 25 countries. For the 10 countries that overlapped across the the two samples, the median correlation between reported trust in people from particular countries and psychic distance from them was –0.7.

9. On the first three flows, see Luigi Guiso, Paola Sapienza, and Luigi Zingales, "Cultural Biases in Economic Exchange?" *Quarterly Journal of Economics* 124, no. 3 (August 2009), 1095-1131. On venture capital investment, see Laura Bottazzi, Marco Da Rin, and Thomas Hellmann, "The Importance of Trust for Investment: Evidence from Venture Capital," discussion paper 2010-49, Tilburg University, Center for Economic Research, 2010 (first draft, February 2006).

10. Thomas Eisensee and David Stromberg, "New Droughts, New Floods and U.S Disaster Relief," *Quarterly Journal of Economics* 122, no. 2 (2007): 693–728.

11. David Potter and Douglas Van Belle, "News Coverage and Japanese Foreign Disaster Aid: A Comparative Example of Bureaucratic Responsiveness to the News Media," *International Relations of the Asia-Pacific* 9, no. 2 (2009): 295–315.

12. These calculations are based on the approach outlined in Branko Milanovic, "Ethical and Economic Feasibility of Global Transfers," MPRA paper 2587, University Library of Munich, 2007. Expenditures incurred to relieve domestic poverty are calculated by multiplying total social expenditure for OECD countries by the percentage allotted to means-tested transfers. The idea is to calculate purely redistributive transfers in a domestic context whose logic parallels that of Official Development Assistance (ODA) in an international context. Dividing these values by, respectively, the number of poor people in rich countries (assumed to be around 1% of national populations) and emerging countries (based on World Bank data) gives us the quantities required to compute per capita aid to the domestic poor (in rich countries) as a multiple of per capita aid to the poor in poor countries.

13. I assume a 90% us-to-them discount in terms of news coverage for the near abroad and a 99% discount for the far abroad, which is probably too conservative in light of the figures cited earlier in the text.

14. In particular, even if one assumes a hundredfold increase in distance across the horizontal axis in figure 15-2, the drop in the aid line corresponds to a distance sensitivity in excess of –2: greater than the impact of physical distance in Newton's law of gravitation, and greater than any other social sensitivity of which I am aware.

15. This analysis is based on data for domestic and international calling minutes for a sample of 63 countries between 1995 and 1999. Domestic calling minutes are drawn from International Telecommunications Union (ITU) World Telecommunication/ICT Indicators 2009 database. International calling minutes are from International Telecommunications Union, "Direction of Traffic, 1999: Trading Telecom Minutes," 1999. Population data is from World Development Indicators and data on the distance between main cities is from CEPII.

16. Marta C. Gonzalez, Cesar A. Hidalgo, and Albert-Laszlo Barabasi, "Understanding Individual Human Mobility Patterns," *Nature* 453 (June 5, 2008): 779–782.

17. Miller McPherson, Lynn Smith-Lovin, and James M. Cook, "Birds of a Feather: Homophily in Social Networks," *Annual Review of Sociology* 27 (2001): 415–444.

18. Martha C. Nussbaum, *For Love of Country?* (Boston: Beacon Press, 2002), 133. My thinking about the concept of cosmopolitanism in a business context has been stimulated by the remarks of my copanelist, Jose de la Torre, at the opening plenary of the 2010 annual meeting of the Academy of International Business in Rio de Janeiro.

19. Peter Singer, "Famine, Affluence, and Morality," *Philosophy and Public Affairs*, 1972: 229–243.

20. K. Anthony Appiah, *Ethics of Identity* (Princeton, NJ: Princeton University Press, 2005), 227.

21. Appiah was not the first writer to use the term "rooted cosmopolitanism." He was preceded in this respect by Mitchell Cohen and Bruce Ackerman.

22. Appiah, *Ethics of Identity*, 232.

23. The objective, more specifically, is to minimize the total area between the distance decay curve and the norm—which has two components, as illustrated in figure 15-2. Also note

the continuity, monontonicity, and unidimensionality assumptions built into the figure, all of which might be relaxed but which do help get the point across.

24. Chicago Council on Foreign Relations and German Marshall Fund of the United States, "Worldviews: American Public Opinion and Foreign Policy," conducted June 2002, released October 2002.

25. Eric Pianin and Mario Brossard, "Americans Oppose Cutting Entitlements to Fix Budget," *Washington Post,* March 29, 1997, http://www.washingtonpost.com/wp-srv/politics/special/budget/stories/032997.htm.

26. Council on Foreign Relations, "U.S. Opinion on Development and Humanitarian Aid," November 19, 2009, http://www.cfr.org/publication/20138/us_opinion_on_development_and_humanitarian_aid.html#p1.

27. Ben Somberg, "The World's Most Generous Misers: Tsunami Reporting Misrepresented U.S. Giving," *Fair,* September/October 2005, http://www.fair.org/index.php?page=2676.

28. This survey was validated by my IESE colleagues, Yih-teen Lee and Pablo Cardona, on the basis of administering it as well as their much more elaborate survey instrument on cross-cultural intelligence and competence to the same group of more than 200 MBA students.

29. Walter Lippman, *Public Opinion* (New York: Harcourt, Brace and Company, 1922), 29.

30. For evidence that creativity is stimulated by living abroad but not by traveling abroad, see W. W. Maddux and A. D. Galinsky, "Cultural Borders and Mental Barriers: The Relationship Between Living Abroad and Creativity," *Journal of Personality and Social Psychology* 96, no. 5 (2009): 1047–1061.

31. Tassilo Pellegrini, "Nova Spivack: Web 3.0 Will Combine the Semantic Web with Social Media," Semantic Web Company, http://www.semantic-web.at/1.36.resource.175.nova-spivack-x22-web-3-0-will-combine-the-semantic-web-with-social-media-enabling-a-new-ge.htm.

32. Dalai Lama, "The Medicine of Altruism," http://www.dalailama.com/messages/world-peace/the-medicine-of-altruism

33. Adam Smith, *The Theory of Moral Sentiments, Glasgow Edition* (Indianapolis, IN: Liberty Classics, 1982), 25.

34. Robert Wright, *Non-Zero: The Logic of Human Destiny* (New York: Pantheon, 2000).

35. Steven Pinker, "Is Evolution Goal-Oriented?" *Slate,* February 1, 2000, http://www.slate.com/id/2000143/entry/1004510. The excerpt is from Pinker's review of the book by Robert Wright cited in the previous paragraph.

Index

awareness stage of relating better to others, 325–328

Axelrod, Robert, 243

Bain, Joe, 253

Barnett, Thomas, 81

barriers to cross-border integration. *See also* CAGE framework; distance impact on cross-border flows
administrative, 66–67
analysis via gravity models, 57
country dimensions that should facilitate trade, 50–52, 53
cultural, 52, 66–67
analysis via CAGE framework, 54, 55t, 56
geographic, 59, 67–68
impact of erecting and removing borders, 44–50
law of distance, 57–60
probability that any two countries match on CAGE dimensions match, 51–52
relevance of borders and distances to trade, 60–62
sensitivity of cross-border flows to distances and differences, 57–60
U.S.-Canada border example (*see* U.S.-Canada border and trade)

benefits of increasing integration. *See also* ADDING value scorecard
barriers not included in CGE models, 66–68
barriers that can be reduced summary, 83–84
commitment's role in reducing trade barriers, 83
complementarities' role in openness, 82–83
connections between openness and democracy
estimated gains from liberalizing trade, 63–64
faster productivity growth rate benefits, 73–74
limits to estimates, 64–65
models used to estimate gains, 65–66
openness' link to international political harmony, 80–81

Bernanke, Ben, 195

Bhagwati, Jagdish, 78, 185, 264

Bharat Forge, 122

Bhargava, R.C., 94

BlackBerry, 39

Black Swan, The (Taleb), 153

Blair, Tony, 19, 315

Blond, Phillip, 14

Boeing, 104–105

Bohr, Niels, 216

borders and trade integration. *See* cross-border integration

Borjas, George, 176

brain drain, 179

Brander, James, 256

Brazil, 45, 107, 141

breakers used to reduce risk, 151–153

BRIC (Brazil, Russia, India, and China), 39, 45

business as the visible hand of trade, 46

business in World 3.0
adaptation versus aggregation or arbitrage, 304–306
analysis approach for mapping distances, 301
avoiding market imperialism, 301–303
business academia's positive views about globalization, 312
climate change role, 129–130
communication and organizational implications, 308–309
corporate forms and governance diversity consideration, 300
distances within a company, 300–301
global companies' respecting of cultural differences, 231–233
prescription to think different, 295–296
production and supply chains, 306–308
recommendations for maximizing business potential, 313–314
remapping at the industry level, 297–299
shift in corporate power structures, 309
social standing of corporate businesses, 310–311
strategies for improving a corporate reputation, 311–312
tools for managing internal distance, 310
within-country diversity consideration, 299–300

CAGE distance framework
in the Andorra trade analysis, 272, 273
described, 42, 54, 55t, 56, 57
dimensions of distance and, 100, 299–300, 318

industry level distance sensitivity, 299t
in the Nigeria trade analysis, 276–277
probability that any two countries match on CAGE dimensions, 51–52
psychic distance analysis and, 317
sensitivity of cross-border flows to distances and differences, 57–60
trust and, 242
in the U.S.-China trade analysis, 279–282
usefulness of, 68, 288–289
Canada. *See* U.S.-Canada border and trade
capital markets
  ADDING value scorecard applied to, 75–76
  arguments against open flows, 144
  arguments in favor of opening up, 143
  benefits and risks involved with specific flows, 144–145
  benefits of diversification in, 149
  cross-border imbalances and, 165, 180–182
  current account balance and, 157–160
  limits that should be in place, 145–146
  models accounting for market-based processes (*see* models based on market-based processes)
  risk reduction measures, 151–153
  volatility of food markets compared to, 148–150
carbonated soft drinks, 95–97, 99, 100
carbon dioxide emissions, 120, 121, 123, 126–127
Catalonia, 221–222
Caves, Richard, 253, 255
Center for Systemic Peace (CSP), 223
CGE (computational general equilibrium models), 65–68, 84
Chicago view of markets, 253–255
China
  conflict with Google, 38
  current account balance, 161, 162t
  game theory applied to trade relations, 283–285
  home bias for trade, 45
  poverty reduction and inequality, 200–201
  rare earth production, 106, 122
  trade with India, 283
  trade with U.S. (*see* U.S.-China trade relations)
  U.S. debt obligation to China, per capita, 156
  within-country diversity consideration, 299–300

Cisco, 309
Clarke, John, 261
class inequality, 189, 191
Clean Air Act (U.S., 1990), 125
climate change
  forecasts for greenhouse gases, 126–127
  need to account for cross-country differences, 128–129
  role of business, 129–130
  role of domestic activism and politics, 129–130
  scope of the problem, 127
  UNFCCC's proposed actions, 127–128
  usefulness of parallel efforts and diversity, 129
cloud computing, 39
Cobb, Kelly, 15
Coca-Cola, 231–232
cognitive diversity, 79
colonization impact on cross-border trade, 58
composition effect, 118
computational general equilibrium (CGE) models, 65–68, 84
computerized trading, 138
concentration of industries. *See* global concentration
contagion (macroeconomic), 139–142
cosmopolitanism, 325t
  defined, 322
  psychology involved in helping people who are far away, 323
  rooted cosmopolitanism described, 323–324, 325t
country strategy in World. 3.0
  Andorra analysis (*see* Andorra)
  internal distance consideration, 292–293
  maximizing country potential, 293–294
  multilateral accords and the WTO, 291–292
  Nigeria analysis (*see* Nigeria)
  reducing distances and distance sensitivity, 291–292
  reexamining how you compete, 290–291
  reexamining where you compete, 289–290
  remapping the world from your perspective, 288
  understanding CAGE effects, 288–289
  understanding your dimensions of variation, 287–288
  U.S.-China analysis (*see* U.S.-China trade relations)

Cowen, Tyler, 79, 233, 236
Creative Destruction (Cowen), 236
cross-border externalities
    cultural dilution fears (*see* cultural concerns about globalization)
    economic and labor fears (*see* cross-border imbalances; cross-border integration; labor concerns about globalization)
    environmental fears (*see* environmental externalities)
    political fears (*see* political concerns about globalization)
cross-border imbalances
    current account balances, 157–160
    current account balances of China and the U.S., 160–164
    disagreement over need for policy intervention, 156
    forecasted worldwide demographic shifts, 169–170, 171f
    link between demographics and economics, 170, 172f
    migration and (*see* migration and cross-border imbalances)
    models accounting for market-based processes between countries (*see* models based on market-based processes)
    risks from capital imbalances, 180–181, 182
    U.S. debt obligation to China, per capita, 156
cross-border integration
    analysis of the gains from opening up (*see* benefits of increasing integration)
    barriers to (*see* barriers to cross-border integration)
    culture and (*see* culture and cross-border integration)
    effects of state/provincial borders within countries, 45
    evidence on levels of, 26–31
    home-bias multiple, 43–45
    during the hunter-gatherer period of human history, 7
    managing (*see* integration and regulation management)
    U.S. and Canada (*see* U.S.-Canada border and trade)
    U.S. and China (*see* U.S.-China trade relations)

CSP (Center for Systemic Peace), 223
cultural, administrative, geographic, and economic distances (CAGE). *See* CAGE distance framework
cultural concerns about globalization
    arguments for cultural enrichment at the individual level, 236–237
    benign cultural differences examples, 229
    blaming of globalization for corrupting cultures, 230
    connection between response to foreigners and economic prosperity, 246
    correlation between trust extended and trust earned, 241
    cultural gains from openness, 233–235
    cultural losses from openness, 235–236
    distance sensitivity of trust, 240–243, 318
    economic implications of cultural biases, 242
    factors influencing cultural chauvinism, 245
    global companies' respecting of cultural differences, 231–233
    perceptions of cultural superiority versus perceptions of need for cultural protection, 239–240
    resilience of cultural differences, 229–230
    status of current national cultural barriers, 228
    steps for reducing cultural fears, 246
    Swiss minaret controversy, 237–238
    trust's relation to the law of distance, 242
    xenophobia as an impediment to integration, 243–244
culture and cross-border integration
    in the CAGE model (*see* CAGE distance framework)
    cross-border trade and, 52
    cultural barriers as limits to trade, 66–67
    cultural differences that inhibit global concentration, 102–103
    cultural gains from openness, 78–79
    cultural lag, 244
    cultural similarities between United States and Canada, 52
    distance sensitivity and, 59–60
    fears about globalization's impact on culture (*see* cultural concerns about globalization)
    fears about migration, 177–178

currency
  cross-border trade and, 58
  role in risk reduction, 153
  trade sensitivity to common
    currency, 58
  U.S. trade with China issues, 160–164, 167,
    189, 280
current account balance, 157–160
cushions used to reduce risk, 151–153
Czech Republic, 44

Daft, Douglas, 99
Dalai Lama, 331–332
DeLong, Brad, 203
democracy
  country-level measures of trust and, 240
  globalization's impact on, 79, 216–218
  political impacts of globalization (see
    political concerns about globalization)
  pollution management and, 124
  as a source of non-economic tension
    between countries U.S.-China
    relationship and, 281
Deng Xiaoping, 200
derivative contracts, 138
design in an adaptation strategy, 305
developed countries and labor inequality
  employment insecurity and
    globalization, 198–199
  globalization and declines in labor's
    share of income, 196–198
  pay gap between unskilled and skilled
    workers, 194–198
  promotion of productivity while
    protecting people, 204
  technological change as main cause of
    inequality, 195, 197
developing countries and labor inequality
  decline in poverty versus rise in
    integration, 200, 201f
  economic detriment of heir-controlled
    wealth, 80, 201–202
  vulnerability of the poor to foreign
    competition employment insecurity
    and globalization, 202
  promotion of productivity while
    protecting people, 204
  rising inequality, 200
  skepticism about globalization's
    benefits, 199–200
  summary, 202

Dewey, John, 36
digital photography, 97–98
distance impact on cross-border flows
  administrative distance, 59–60
  analysis via CAGE framework, 54, 55t, 56
  analysis via gravity models, 57
  Andorra and, 271–272
  border effects and views of economic
    geograph, 60–62
  businesses' managing of internal
    distance, 306–310
  businesses' mapping of real distances,
    297–301
  in the CAGE model (see CAGE distance
    framework)
  cultural and administrative distance,
    59–60
  distance sensitivity in integration and
    regulation management, 263–264
  distance sensitivity of systemic risk,
    140–141
  distance sensitivity of trade between
    countries, 57–58
  evaluating possible trading partners and,
    267–268
  geographic distance, 59
  global concentration levels, 100–101, 104
  informational imperfections and, 137–138
  law of distance, 57–60
  Nigeria and, 278–279
  pollution and, 123–126
  psychic distance (see psychic distance)
  reducing distances and distance
    sensitivity, 291–293
  trust's relation to the law of distance, 242
  U.S.-Canada border example, 53, 57–58
Doha round, 63, 64, 65, 83, 291
Dr. Reddy's, 303

Economic Community of West African
  States (ECOWAS), 278
economic fears from globalization. See
  cross-border imbalances; cross-border
  integration; labor concerns about
  globalization
Economist, 39
ecoseny, 15–16
Electrolux, 102
employment. See labor
End of History, The (Fukuyama), 213
energy markets, 149–150

Kahn, Alfred, 257
Katz, Lawrence, 176
Keynes, John Maynard, 137, 251
Khanna, Parag, 223
King, William Mackenzie, 53
Knight, Frank, 149
knowledge flows, 59, 77–78. *See also* information
Krueger, Anne, 72
Krugman, Paul, 60, 145, 195, 256
Kuznets, Simon, 200
Kyoto Protocol, 120

labor
  ADDING value scorecard applied to, 75–76
  economic fears from globalization (*see* labor concerns about globalization)
  forecasted worldwide demographic shifts, 169–170, 171f
  link between demographics and economics, 170, 172f
  migration and (*see* migration and cross-border imbalances)
labor concerns about globalization
  costs of curbing international expansion of domestic firms, 203–204
  costs of trade protectionism, 203–204
  country example of workforce policies that hurt productivity, 204–206
  critiques of the focus on equality/inequality, 184–185
  distributional concerns about labor, 184
  economic disparities seen as a barrier to globalization, 188–189
  economists' view of inequality, 186
  employment insecurity and globalization, 198–199
  factor price equalization theory and labor market integration, 186–187
  fallacy of oversimplifying labor market integration, 187–188
  Gini index, 189–191
  historic income distribution trends, 189–191, 192f, 193f
  inequality among individuals, 189–191, 192–194f
  inequality and integration, 184–187
  inequality between versus within countries, 191, 193, 194f

  inequality concerns in developed countries (*see* developed countries and labor inequality)
  inequality concerns in developing countries (*see* developing countries and labor inequality)
  making globalization fairer for the poor, 206
  promotion of productivity while protecting people, 204
Lamy, Pascal, 28, 69, 74
land borders and cross-border trade, 58
language and cross-border trade, 51, 58
law of distance
  basis of models, 57
  cultural and administrative distances' importance, 59–60
  geographic distance's importance, 59
  sensitivity of trade to distances between countries, 57–58
Lawrence, Robert, 195, 196
Leamer, Edward, 46
legal systems and cross-border trade, 51
Lindsey, Larry, 163
LINKAGE model, 65
Lippman, Walter, 326–327
Liu Xiaobo, 281
Livingstone, David, 36
Lloyd's, 134
location inequality, 189, 191
Lorenz Curve, 190
Lucas, Robert, 136
Lucas paradox, 143
Luce, Clare Booth, 34–35
Lutz, Wolfgang, 169

mapping, 265, 267–268, 288, 297–301
market failures
  cross-border imbalances and (*see* cross-border imbalances)
  externalities (*see* environmental externalities)
  Harvard versus Chicago schools and, 253–255
  informational imperfections (*see* risk concerns about globalization)
  market concentration, (*see* global concentration)
  managing (*see* integration and regulation management)

Patel, Raj, 15, 18
patents, 77, 108
people and World 3.0
  acquaintance stage of relating better to
    others, 328–331
  altruism stage of relating better to
    others, 331–334
  awareness stage of relating better to
    others, 325–328
  cosmopolitanism, 322–324, 325t
  private charitable giving and, 29, 312–313
  psychic distance (*see* psychic distance)
  vision of World 3.0, 334–336
Peri, Giovanni, 176
phone traffic and cross-border integration,
  26, 59
Pigou, Arthur, 182
Pinker, Steven, 335–336
Pinkovskiy, Maxim, 191
Polanyi, Karl, 12
political concerns about globalization
  artificial states based on ethnolinguistic
    fragmentation and straight borders,
    222–223
  Catalonia's desire for independence
    example, 221–222
  fear of promotion of cross-border
    conflicts, 218–220
  fear that America is taking over the
    world, 208–210
  fear that governments' policy discretion
    will be eroded, 213–216
  fear that multinational companies are
    taking over the world, 210–212
  fragmentation's contradiction with
    economic improvement, 223–224
  global integration's relation to a world
    government, 213–214
  globalization of markets' facilitation of
    separatism, 220
  globalization's impact on democracy,
    216–218
  governments' rule-making power as a
    check against companies, 211–212
  links between globalization and
    government spending, 214–215
  openness's ability to boost competitive
    vitality, 212–213
  pattern of political consolidation
    through history, 220
  summary, 224–225

pollution and global externalities
  air transportation as a cause, 116–117
  cross-border agreements and, 124,
    125–126
  distance sensitivity of pollutants,
    123–124, 125f
  evidence that trade can be neutral or
    positive for environment, 118–120
  evidence of trade having negative impact
    on environment, 120
  land transportation as a cause, 115
  little evidence that poor countries are
    pollution havens, 121–122
  maritime transportation as a cause, 116
  regional pollutants, 124–126
  types of, 118
prisoner's dilemma, 283–285
production and supply chains barrier
  reduction. *See* merchandise trade
  growth benefits
propositions on managing nexus of market
  failure and market integration. *See*
  integration and regulation
  management
protectionism, 28, 72, 83, 107, 146, 188, 304
psychic distance
  cross-border component of private
    charitable giving, 29
  defined, 316–317
  distance sensitivity of trust, 240–243, 318
  emotional response based on others'
    distance from self, 316, 317f
  localization of daily interactions and, 321
  news coverage of disasters and, 319
  trusting people based on national
    origins, 318
  willingness to help and, 319–321

R&D, 77–78, 97, 283, 307–308
Ramaswami, V.K., 264
Rambler, 38
rare earth production, 106–107
Realpolitik, 13–14
Reduced Emissions from Deforestation and
  Forest Degradation (REDD), 130
regulation and World 3.0
  current shift back towards a belief in
    regulation, 258–259
  deregulation wave in 1980s, 257–258
  evidence that freedom and unregulated
    markets don't go together, 258

About the Author

Pankaj Ghemawat is the Anselmo Rubiralta Professor of Global Strategy at IESE Business School. Between 1983 and 2008, he served on the faculty at Harvard Business School where, in 1991, he became the youngest person in the school's history to be appointed a full professor. Ghemawat was also the youngest "guru" included in the *Economist's* guide to the greatest management thinkers of all time, published in 2008.

Ghemawat's previous books include *Commitment, Games Businesses Play, Strategy and the Business Landscape*, and the award-winning *Redefining Global Strategy*, which the *New York Times* called "a nicely revised picture of globalization." He is also the author of more than one hundred research articles and case studies, ranks as one of the world's bestselling authors of teaching cases, and has been elected a fellow of the Academy of International Business and of the Strategic Management Society. Other recent honors include the McKinsey Award for the best article published in *Harvard Business Review* and the Irwin Award for the Educator of the Year from the Business Policy and Strategy division of the Academy of Management.

Ghemawat works with companies, governments, multilateral institutions, and business schools on international opportunities and challenges. He consults on strategy and leadership development around the world and is a regular speaker on globalization-related topics. He also served on the taskforce appointed by the AACSB, the U.S.-based accreditation body for business schools, on the globalization of management education, and authored the report's recommendations concerning what to teach about globalization, and how.

For more information, visit www.ghemawat.org.